BECOMING FILM LITERATE

BECOMING FILM LITERATE

The Art and Craft of Motion Pictures

□ ◆ □ ◆ □ ◆ □ ◆ □ ◆ □

Vincent LoBrutto

Foreword by Jan Harlan

Westport, Connecticut
London

Library of Congress Cataloging-in-Publication Data

LoBrutto, Vincent.
Becoming film literate : the art and craft of motion pictures / Vincent LoBrutto ; foreword by Jan Harlan.
p. cm.
Includes bibliographical references and index.
ISBN 0–275–98144–4 (alk. paper)
1. Motion pictures. 2. Cinematography. I. Title.
PN1994.L595 2005
791.43—dc22 2004028099

British Library Cataloguing in Publication Data is available.

Library of Congress Catalog Card Number: 2004028099
ISBN: 0–275–98144–4

First published in 2005

Praeger Publishers, 88 Post Road West, Westport, CT 06881
An imprint of Greenwood Publishing Group, Inc.
www.praeger.com

Printed in the United States of America

The paper used in this book complies with the Permanent Paper Standard issued by the National Information Standards Organization (Z39.48–1984).

10 9 8 7 6 5 4 3 2 1

To three mentors—
Everett Aison, Gary Carey, and Gene Stavis—
who taught me that the more you learn, the more you
understand how much more there is still to learn.

CONTENTS

FOREWORD

LoBrutto's book reminds me of a big party; somehow the topic of films comes up and leads to the question: "What is your favorite film?" This is like poking into an ants' nest. Suddenly the room is abuzz with titles and arguments: *The Sound of Music, Gone with the Wind, Casablanca, Citizen Kane, Dr. Strangelove, Some Like It Hot, Rashomon, Psycho, Star Wars, The Blue Angel, E.T., The Seventh Seal, Annie Hall, Les Enfants du Paradis, Fahrenheit 9/11, Manhattan, Fanny and Alexander, My Fair Lady*. . . . One skinny intellectual whispers wistfully, while extracting the last puff from his cigarette, "If I can have only one I'll have to have these three: *Hiroshima Mon Amour, Orphée,* and *Last Year at Marienbad*." What a bunch. That's who we are. All this represents us.

Look back into history: Once the great inventions and wars and all the terrible deeds of mankind have been put away into history books, what's left? What is the first entry into the past? The arts: the pyramids in Egypt, the great cathedrals, the monuments of Babylon (Iraq today), paintings, sculptures, plays and operas, symphonies, and all sorts of compositions and books. It is the arts that give us the first insight. The writers and painters, the architects and composers allow us a glimpse into prior centuries more than anything else. Since the early 1900s, filmmakers have been added to this noble group, and I have no doubt that future generations will look at the twentieth century and our different cultures on this shrinking globe through the eyes of artists like Orson Welles, Ingmar Bergman, Woody Allen, Stanley Kubrick, Carlos Saura, Edgar Reitz,

Steven Spielberg, Charles Chaplin, or Sergei Eisenstein—to mention just a few.

The answer to "What's your favorite film?" is quite significant, because the choices range from the trivial to the sublime. The greatest films, like the greatest paintings, will last for as long as the late Beethoven string quartets will last—at least as long as civilization and culture exist (which may not be for all that much longer, so we certainly must not take art for granted).

A book about "the movies" must be entertaining. LoBrutto's book certainly is, full of facts and valuable information accompanied by wonderfully subjective observations and opinions; it is a great read. He has selected fifty films from around the world and put them in alphabetical order, thereby avoiding any sort of qualitative order at all. This is perfect, this is "the movies"—each film stands alone and is unconnected to the next. (But don't be fooled: Before you know it, a flurry of titles will come to mind and you'll find yourself thinking of all the most wonderful films you've ever seen.)

So here we go on a journey from *Blade Runner* to *Blue Velvet* and from *The Seventh Seal* to *Star Wars*—via *Shock Corridor*. LoBrutto brings the films you know to life and compels you to put those you don't know on your must-see list. There are films I have never seen or heard of! Shock and horror, I am only a semi-film-literate and need to catch up! I will. Thanks, Vincent, for reminding me.

Jan Harlan, executive producer of Barry Lyndon, The Shining, Full Metal Jacket, Eyes Wide Shut, *and* A. I. Artificial Intelligence, *as well as the producer and director of* Stanley Kubrick: A Life in Pictures.

ACKNOWLEDGMENTS

A conversation with my erudite editor, Eric Levy, at Greenwood gave birth to this project. I had been thinking about creating a film canon, one that interested and devoted filmgoers could follow to become film literate. In his wisdom Eric saved me from cinematic canonization, a thankless concept that could be mired in arguments and personal opinion rather than serve as a tool to enlighten the viewer with insights about the lexicon, art, and craft of the motion picture medium. Eric also had the good judgment to steer me away from the appearance of a 100 best list philosophy. We both agreed fifty was a good number—fifty films/fifty essays on how to become film literate. My sincere thanks to Eric for this, his past and present support, his enthusiasm, and commitment to excellence—this author is all the better for it.

Also at Praeger, my sincere appreciation to editorial assistant Brien McDonald, developmental editor Lisa Pierce, assistant editor Elizabeth Potenza and production coordinator Michael O'Connor. Production editor Andrew Hudak and copyeditor Julie Palmer-Hoffman of Westchester Book Services gave the kind of love and care to the final stages of the production process that an author dreams of.

All my love and respect to my late parents, Rose and Anthony LoBrutto, for their support, bringing me to the movies as a child, putting me through film school, and for being my "first producers" in the fullest definition of that notion. My son, Alexander Morrison, has engaged in a lifelong seminar about the movies. Rebecca Morrison, my daughter, has taught me about tenacity and commitment to study. My wife, Harriet Morrison, is the best movie-going companion a guy could ever ask for. As always she was the first reader of this manuscript and is a true life partner: my love and respect for her grows with each breath.

When I was about to write this book I had an encounter with black ice that left me with one broken arm in a cast and the other badly sprained but just mobile enough to write one-fifth of the first draft with one hand, this righty's left. For expert orthopedic care my respect and thanks go to Dr. Robert Small, who put my writer's hand back together.

As I advance through my fifth decade as a perpetual student of film, it would seem appropriate to acknowledge my gratitude to those who helped me become film literate: Everett Aison for over thirty years of steadfast encouragement and inspiration; Gary Carey for lessons about the art of film criticism, the dramaturgy of the theater, and for being my thesis advisor when I wrote my critical pieces and a full-length study of Sam Peckinpah, which remains unpublished but planted a seed that did grow. William K. Everson introduced me to the masterpieces of film history. Charles Reynolds presented *Paths of Glory* to a twenty-year-old who just couldn't stop thinking about Stanley Kubrick. Jud Yalkut, the fine experimental filmmaker, gave Zen lessons on the art of Stan Brahkage, Kenneth Anger, and Michael Snow, and introduced our film class to Carolee Schneemann, who screened her legendary *Fuses* on a memorable day in the early 1970s. My appreciation goes to Gene Stavis, for his cinema salon and patient private tutoring in the history of film, and to Roy Frumkes, for his unconditional support and for sharing of much information that is left out of the official history of film. Kudos to Blackhawk Films for making cinema classics available for study on 8mm film and for providing material for personal and early editing experiments conducted in the basement of our family home. David Weber was my high school film teacher and was there at the beginning when it most matters. I am indebted to all of the editors, production designers, sound creators, cinematographers, and directors I have interviewed over the years—they have truly provided master classes in the art and craft of the cinema.

My appreciation for what I have learned from watching films extends to each and every experience, but especially to a select group of filmmakers who were my greatest teachers. They include Michelangelo Antonioni, Stan Brakhage, Robert Bresson, John Cassavetes, Werner Rainer Fassbinder, Jean-Luc Godard, Alfred Hitchcock, Stanley Kubrick, Martin Scorsese, King Vidor, and Orson Welles. PBS has provided a lifetime of archival treasures as well as many important special programs celebrating the cinema. Million Dollar Movie allowed me to see Hollywood classics like my beloved *King Kong* (1933) in many encore broadcasts in a week's time reinforcing that a good film not only holds up but continues to reveal its jewels with each viewing. Charles Champlin's television cinema series in the 1970s solidified my belief that film was truly an art. Richard Schickel's *The Men Who Made the Movies* series began my lifelong love affair with the films of King Vidor and contributed to my knowledge of Ford, Hitchcock, Capra, and others. Jonas Mekas personally sold me my copy of Brakhage's *Metaphors on Vision*, and his dedication to the art of film has motivated my passion for experimental film. In the two classes he taught that I attended before he was fired by the loud voices of the ignorant, Jack Smith taught me that conflict between music and image is a valuable cinematic lesson. During my salad days there were revival theaters that furthered my understanding. They include the Regency, the Thalia, and Elgin theaters. Dan Talbot's New Yorker Theater was a university in New Wave and revolutionary films of the 1960s and 1970s. The film program at the Museum of Modern Art was my second home during my film school years. The Whitney Museum and Anthology Film Archives broadened my perspective of film history. The New York Cultural Center educated me to the Bs of Don Siegel and XXXs of Russ Meyer. The New York Film Festival provided an ongoing exposure to cutting-edge world cinema and the honor of seeing many of the filmmakers speak about their work in person.

Film Forum continues to be a home for the gourmet delicacies of filmmaking. Three film critics who have had the greatest influence on my thinking about film are Manny Farber, Stanley Kauffmann, and Jonathan Rosenbaum. My heartfelt appreciation to American Cinema Editors (ACE) for making me a special member of their fine and vital organization and bestowing on me the honor of associate editor of their magazine *CinemaEditor*. This role allows my master classes to continue with every interview and encounter I have with filmmakers. So many film publications nurtured my insatiable thirst for film knowledge. The most influential in my early years were *Filmmaker's Newsletter, Film Culture, American Cinematographer,* and *Take One*. Before Borders and Barnes and Noble, Cinemabilia, the Gotham Book Mart, the 8th Street, Strand, and St. Mark's Bookshops were havens for readers and collectors of film literature. Joe Franklin was an inspiration by spreading his infectious unconditional love of the cinema on his daily television show and on specials in which he presented motion picture greats. Editor–director Arthur Ginsberg provided "graduate studies" during on-the-job training in the five stimulating years I worked with him. I also extend my appreciation to Jack Lorenzo Schwartz for being my youngest student during a "shot by shot" analysis of *Babe* when he was six months old.

As always and especially for a book about film education, my respect and eternal thanks go to the founder and chairman of the board of the School of Visual Arts, Silas Rhodes, President David Rhodes, and Vice President Anthony Rhodes; Reeves Lehmann, chairman of the Department of Film, Video, and Animation at SVA, for his unconditional support of my work and for providing me with the bully pulpit to teach the art and craft of filmmaking; Sal Petrosino, for his friendship and for his passion about the preservation and growth of film education; Ed Bowes, for countless stimulating exchanges on the ever-changing medium of motion pictures; Joan Brooker, who has taught me more about cinematic narratives than any living being and for me has defined the true meaning of deconstruction; Richard Pepperman, now colleague and friend, for being my first editing teacher and a man who understands that you edit with your heart and mind even before a splice is made or a button is pushed. My colleagues at SVA over the years have broadened my perspective on the artistic discipline we all adore. Most important, I thank all my students past and present, who have taught me more than they can ever imagine.

My thanks and admiration to everyone at Film/Video Arts for creating a vital and enduring institution for the study of independent film. The Mount Vernon Public Library continues to be an invaluable archive for my research. My respect and thanks to the entire staff of this wonderful archival sanctuary of learning.

Last, my gratitude to all those who write on the subject of the cinema and continue to feed my insatiable curiosity, for fueling my spirit and keeping me informed, film literate, and on a steady course to spread the word.

INTRODUCTION

The purpose of this book is to educate filmgoers about the art, craft, and lexicon of motion pictures.

A well-read or literate reader is familiar with the rules and aesthetics of language as well as with authors, movements, genres, conventions, and narrative strategies. Academics and scholars have dedicated serious thought to the development of a literary canon, an organized reading list taught in educational institutions to identify the great books of the centuries. The canon changes periodically—books and authors fall in and out of favor and fashion—but it remains a systematic learning tool that allows individuals to study and to acquire knowledge concerning literature. Likewise, the well-established mediums of music, theater, and the fine art of painting all have recognizable canons to orient students and enthusiasts to the unique characteristics of their disciplines.

Film as a discipline is taught in many venues. There are texts that are overviews of film's brief history of little more than 100 years, other more comprehensive volumes are dedicated to the films of specific countries, and there are works that chronicle a genre, style, or categories such as documentary or animation. There are anthologies of film criticism, and movies are discussed in specialty magazines and in film societies. The American Film Institute compiled a list of the 100 Greatest Movies of all time, which continues to be hotly debated. There are certainly films most would agree are necessary to acquire a knowledge of the cinema—for example, *Citizen Kane* and *The Battleship Potemkin* (both included in *Becoming Film Literate*)—

but there is no official canon of cinema for a systematic study of the particular proprieties of cinematic aesthetics, concepts, and methods. In studying this nascent medium, the tendency has been to examine film through other disciplines, especially through the prism of literature and theater as well as social, political, gender, racial, psychological, and semiotic perspectives.

In the twenty-first century, children watch educational and entertainment videotapes and spend many hours in front of the television, computer, and movie screens. Through total immersion young people have acquired a sophisticated sensibility for visual storytelling, although they rarely consciously comprehend the grammar and properties of the medium. The average adult has seen hundreds, if not thousands, of films, yet many fundamentals of the cinema remain a mystery to the movie-going public.

To become film literate you must see films that demonstrate and embody the principles of cinema. Where to begin? That's where *Becoming Film Literate* comes in. The objective of this book is twofold. The fifty essays that follow, organized in alphabetical order by film title, explore specific cinematic lessons and serve as introductions to motion pictures that might be worthy of inclusion in a definitive canon of cinema if such a monumental task could ever be undertaken. The focus of each essay is an in-depth investigation of how moving pictures work. Each chapter heading includes the film title and the major topic that will contribute to your film literacy. Within the essays are many observations concerning the inner workings of cinematic technology and the application of its visual and aural language. To enhance the breadth of your knowledge, the choice of films represents a necessarily wide range.

This is not a "best" list. The titles are destinations to further journeys; there are many directors, genres, and cinematic worlds to visit on your way to becoming film literate. At the conclusion of each essay are suggestions for further screening and reading to use as a road map.

As a teacher of the art and craft of motion pictures, I have learned that all of us inherently know more about the cinema than we can articulate. It is a codified language that is familiar to us on the surface, but each element has expressive capabilities concerning the complexity of this powerful human communication medium.

Becoming film literate involves understanding, insight, and engagement with the moving images we sit in front of. The process can be fun, inspirational, challenging, and even spiritual—enjoy the trip and get ready for a lifetime of enlightened cinematic experiences.

Note: Words that appear in **boldface type** can be found in the glossary along with other useful terms that apply to the art and craft of motion pictures.

1

Nonlinear Storytelling

Amores Perros

Throughout film history the narrative or storyline has been of supreme importance to moviemakers, but a cinematic story is substantially different from a literary or theatrical model. The prose in a screenplay will be translated into environments, atmosphere, and action through the visuals. Screenwriters create stories that rely on images as well as dialogue to convey behavior, situations, and interactions. A screen adaptation reworks the elements of a novel or play. A play can be opened up in terms of the scope of locations, and a novel can be compressed. Scenes, acts, or chapters are dropped or combined, characters amalgamated through the cinematic process. An original screenplay is written with an understanding of the narrative properties of screen acting, cinematography, editing, art direction, sound, and music.

The earliest films did not tell stories; they documented an event: a train coming into a station, a couple kissing. As the Hollywood studio system began to operate and prosper, moguls hired the best playwrights and novelists to develop stories. In the traditional three-act structure, the narrative unfolded in a compressed but largely sequential timeframe, with the exception of an occasional flashback to provide **backstory** and **exposition**. **Genre** controlled the nature of a movie story. Films were Westerns or historical dramas, crime stories, comedies, or musicals. Genres have rules that determine the themes, conventions, character types, and plot structure. The star system made an impact on screen stories. Writers wrote for stars—John Wayne, Bette Davis, Katharine Hepburn, Cary

Emilio Echevarria as El Chivo, a homeless man with a past, shown here with one of his beloved dogs, are two significant characters that link three seemingly disparate stories that dramatically connect over the course of the nonlinear narrative of *Amores Perros*. Courtesy *Photofest*.

Grant, and a bevy of actors who had distinctive personalities, qualities, personal and iconic images, and attitudes that determined film stories.

The linear story, one in which events unfold a step at a time in sequential real-time order, was preferable because the studios were convinced audiences would then be able to process the plot and subplots and follow the beginning, middle, and end. The limitations of this narrative structure are best summarized by director Jean-Luc Godard's quip that all films should have a beginning, middle, and end, but not necessarily in that order.

A significant landmark in the evolution of **nonlinear storytelling** in the cinema is *The Killing*, directed by Stanley Kubrick and released in 1956. The story concerns a racetrack robbery. A group of men with various specific skills and functions all contribute to the execution of a heist. When the plan goes into effect, the crime is presented so the viewer can see the specifics of each action set forth by each member of the team and what they encounter during the heist process. An omnipresent narrator (see **narration** in glossary) informs the viewer as to where and when each scene takes place during the timeframe of the robbery as the story shifts back and forth in time. Each scene provides specific insights about some of the same moments in time. **Intercutting** the various scenes to simulate a real-time experience would have achieved a traditional cinematic **compression** of continuous time. By shifting the same time period forward and back and repeating moments in time from the point of view of various characters, Kubrick created a nonlinear narrative—it is no longer sequential storytelling. The result is an existential presentation of an event that was doomed to fail because of human error, frailty, and the nature of greed, fear, and mistrust.

The paradigm for contemporary nonlinear storytelling is exemplified in Quentin Tarrantino's *Pulp Fiction*, which led the way for other 1990s and early twenty-first-century filmmakers. Examples include *The Usual Suspects* and *Memento*, which unfold in a backward chronology driven by the mental state of the main character. Tarrantino arrived at the structure of *Pulp Fiction* by weaving together characters and story lines he had created working in the tradition of Mario Bava's *Black Sabbath* and literary icon J. D. Salinger's handling of the Glass family in his stories and novels. The original manuscript for the *Pulp Fiction* screenplay ran 500 pages as Tarrantino incessantly comingled characters and their stories as new narrative inventions inspired him during the process. Tarrantino evolved a circular narrative structure that brought characters back to a central episode.

Amores Perros (2000), a Mexican film written by Guillermo Arriga Jordán and directed by Alexjandro González Iñárritu, benefits from the cinematic narrative experiments that came before it, but this film goes even further in constructing complex interrelationships between three seemingly separate stories that unfold during the 153-minute running time.

A full synopsis of *Amores Perros* is a daunting task that would reveal little of this daring adventure through time and space. *Amores Perros* needs to be experienced through several screenings, each revealing links, connections, and references that may be impossible to fully comprehend in their subtlety in a single viewing.

The three stories concern Octavio (Gael Garcia Bernal), a young man who is involved with competitive dog fighting, and his sexual obsession with Susana (Vanessa Bauche), the wife of his brother Ramiro (Marco

Pérez); Valeria (Goya Toledo), a fashion model, and Daniel (Alvaro Guerrero), who leaves his wife and family to live with her; and El Chivo (Emilio Echevarria), a homeless man who searches for a daughter he abandoned long ago.

Jordán and Iñárritu entered into three years of discussions that resulted in thirty-six separate story treatments. During the writing of the script, they explored a multitude of ways to connect the stories and characters into a narrative that would go beyond an episodic structure into a cohesive story employing movement both forward and back in time to reveal the impact, consequences, and destiny of the major characters in the three stories.

By manipulating time, moving forward and back, and allowing shifts of point of view and narrative logistics, *Amores Perros* brings character and plot information from one story and places it in the context of another. This becomes a narrative puzzle for the viewer. The challenge pays off because *Amores Perros* demonstrates that the order in which facts and plot points are received makes a significant impression on the viewer's perception of the story. Taken philosophically, *Amores Perros* demonstrates that although life is lived in a linear fashion, we acquire knowledge and experience action, emotions, and feelings in a chaotic order outside our control. The mind's ability to flash back and speculate into the future is the human experiential equivalent of what Jordán and Iñárritu have achieved with their experiments in rejuvenating the film narrative.

It is a violent car crash that brings the characters of the three stories together. *Amores Perros* begins with the accident from Octavio's perspective. This is the first scene in the film, but not the beginning—or the whole—story. Information concerning this event is revealed in story points throughout the film, but the entirety of that single moment is crystallized only at the conclusion of the film.

Octavio's car crashes into Valeria's car. Later it is revealed El Chivo was a witness standing on one of the corners. To begin with this information would be no more than establishing a story in which strangers are brought together because of an event or action. There is nothing experimental about that approach. *Amores Perros* is about how lives often intersect without the participants knowing it. The commonalities and contrasts of their lives provide many venues for cinematic storytelling.

There is no central protagonist in *Amores Perros*, but several thematic elements run through the stories that reflect the emotional drives of all the characters. Everyone is in love. Octavio is trapped in a forbidden love. Daniel and Valeria try to find happiness in an adulterous relationship. El Chivo loves his daughter, but they are estranged due to his behavior in the past.

The concept according to Iñárritu is that only those who love intensely and fully can survive the intensity of existence. This is reflected in every story. Octavio risks everything for Susana by challenging the destructive powers-that-be in the violent and brutal world of dog fighting. The accident threatens Valeria's professional life as a supermodel and her passionate affair and commitment to Daniel. El Chivo is a homeless man who survives by committing contract killings because of his earlier life as a political radical.

As the title suggests, dogs play a significant role in the lives of the characters in *Amores Perros*. A literal translation of *Amores Perros* is "Dog Love" but the double meaning of "Love's a Bitch" is more revealing. Octavio's dog is a champion fighter who earns him money but also puts him in danger when Octavio is duped into a con that results in a violent confrontation culminating in the tragic crash. Valeria's precious dog Ritchie falls into an open hole in the wooden floor of their apartment. This turns her life and relationship with Daniel into turmoil. El Chivo lives with a pack of dogs. When he comes into possession of Octavio's dog and nurses the wounded canine back to good health, the dog's killer instincts motivate the animal to kill all of El Chivo's loving canine companions.

Audiences have been conditioned to understand and anticipate traditional genre storylines and the familiar patterns of three-act narrative structures. In *The Thirty-Six Dramatic Situations* by Georges Polti, first published in 1921, the author establishes that all narrative plots throughout the history of literature, the stage, and cinema can be traced to just thirty-six dramatic situations. This understood, there are no new stories; but cinematic structure can lead filmmakers to new solutions to visual storytelling. Nonlinear storytelling provides the filmmaker with new story structures and an alternate means to traditional situations. The audience is challenged and active participation is achieved. A nonlinear story requires the imagination of the creator and audience to live up to the myriad narrative choices the medium of motion pictures has the potential to express.

Of Further Interest

Screen

The Killing
Memento
Mishima
Mystery Train
Pulp Fiction

Read

The Art of Dramatic Writing by Lajos Egri
The Screenwriter's Workbook by Syd Field
Story: Substance, Structure, Style, and the Principles of Screenwriting by Robert McKee
The Thirty-six Dramatic Situations by Georges Polti

2

Transformation of the American Comedy

□ ◆ □ ◆ □ ◆ □

Annie Hall

The American film comedy has a rich legacy: Charlie Chaplin, Buster Keaton, Harold Lloyd, the Marx Brothers, W. C. Fields, Bob Hope, Jerry Lewis, and, of course, the slapstick and screwball genres. By and large the humor emerged out of story and situation. The films were often crafted for the skills of the performer, but plot was the narrative engine.

The prehistory of the comedy film renaissance that took place during the 1980s and 1990s is traceable to the work of Mel Brooks and Woody Allen in the 1960s and 1970s. The humor in their films was not powered by story construction but instead extrapolated concepts, ideas, and ethnic points of view from the art of stand-up and sketch comedy.

Before *Annie Hall* revolutionized the romantic comedy form in 1977 and transformed film director Woody Allen into an internationally respected auteur (see **auteur theory** in glossary), he was a hysterically funny and very bright young topical comic. Woody Allen's roots as a television and short story comedy writer along with his distinctive work as a stand-up comic inform much that he has accomplished as a prolific and innovative film director.

From these beginnings Allen created his screen persona as a neurotic, New York anti-intellectual intellectual obsessed with sex and death. Woody Allen is the nebbish as ladies' man, a walking encyclopedia of one-liners filled with a dim, depressed life-view, who dispatches endless highbrow references to express his fears and hostilities. The Allen hero is lovable because he has such an inflated but harmless sense of his mas-

Diane Keaton as Annie Hall and Woody Allen as Alvy Singer, dressed in their iconic outfits and standing on an iconic Manhattan sidewalk during the late 1970s in *Annie Hall*, a film that both defined the Me Decade and reinvented the romantic comedy. Courtesy *Photofest*.

culinity and, like the **antihero** who emerged during the 1960s and 1970s, is sexy and cool, and has an ego too larger-than-life for his own good.

Annie Hall marks a clear delineation between the wordsmith comic who directed *Take the Money and Run*, *Bananas*, *Everything You Always Wanted to Know about Sex but Were Afraid to Ask*, *Sleeper*, and *Love and Death* and the cinematic artist who was established with this Oscar-winning landmark.

The early films were very funny, based around a premise and comprising sketches. What they lacked in craft and directorial vision they made up for in personality and originality. *Annie Hall* set out as an experiment in personal, semiautobiographical cinema. *Anhedonia* was its first title, a term describing an individual who cannot experience pleasure. The screenplay cowritten by Allen and Marshall Brickman (*Simon, The Manhattan Project, For the Boys*) was produced and put into a two-hour-and-twenty-minute first cut. The final ninety-three-minute release version is not only shorter but a radically restructured work. During Allen's collaboration with film editor Ralph Rosenblum (*The Pawnbroker, The Producers, Interiors*), the film's focus shifted. As written, the story followed the life and times of Alvy Singer (Woody Allen), a neurotic Jewish comedian, as he floated forward and back through his life in a manic demonstration of social satire. As Rosenblum and Allen searched for the film within the funny but undisciplined ramble, it centered on the romance between Alvy and Annie Hall (Diane Keaton). The result defined the essence of relationships in what writer Tom Wolfe coined as the *Me Decade*.

Two significant creative collaborations began on *Annie Hall* and both contributed to Allen's mature visual style and created a remarkably successful director–director of photography–production designer trinity. Director of photography Gordon Willis had just shot *All the President's Men* and was acclaimed for his brilliant work on *The Godfather* and *The Godfather Part II*. Willis would photograph seven more films for Allen, defining the director's **mise-en-scène**. In *Annie Hall* entire scenes are captured in one shot. When there is **interscene editing**, the **coverage** is bare minimum. Compositions in the wide-screen **aspect ratio** are visually structured in full shots that are most often directly in front of the subject and environment. The lighting appears to be natural and also frontal. At times Willis's romantic realism is achieved with low light levels that paint Allen's beloved New York City in a rich glow of color.

Production designer Mel Bourne (*Manhunter, Fatal Attraction, The Fisher King*) had often worked with Gordon Willis on commercials produced in New York. *Annie Hall* was Bourne's first feature after many years in the city's advertising and theater worlds. He would go on to design six more Allen productions. Alvy was raised in Brooklyn, as was Allen. The script identified his father as a cab driver, and the Singer family lived in Flatbush. Bourne scouted a house in Allen's old neighborhood that the director accepted as a location, but he was not enthusiastic. Bourne pressed on. In Coney Island he discovered a seventy-three-year-old woman and her 300-pound son living in an apartment built into the Cyclone roller coaster. Allen was so inspired that he rewrote the script so Alvy's father would work at the bumper car ride in the famed amusement park and the Singers would live inside the Cyclone. For the studio interior, Bourne built a scale facsimile of the coaster so it could be seen outside the window. It was the perfect comic metaphor for Alvy. The apartment shook violently with every pass of the coaster. His turbulent family life was like living in the eye of a natural disaster.

Alvy is constantly confronted with conflict. He loves the streets of Manhattan but is perpetually agitated. Even the temples of intellectual comfort, the art movie theaters, aggravate Alvy. A fan invades his privacy seeking an autograph and shouts out his celebrity spotting. An Ingmar Bergman film has just started when Annie is a late arrival. He cannot enter a film once it has begun and suggests they have coffee for two hours. When Annie refuses they go to see Marcel Ophüls's *The Sorrow and the Pity*, a four-and-half-hour documentary about Nazi-occupied France they have both seen. On yet another pilgrimage to the cinema, Alvy becomes frustrated with a pontificating man on line who claims to know everything about communications theorist Marshall McLuhan. Alvy puts the nuisance in his place by pulling the author of *The Medium Is the Massage*, out from behind a lobby display. Alvy is self-persecuted by anti-Semitism. In a signature shot suggested by Gordon Willis, Alvy and Rob (Tony Roberts) take a long walk. They start at infinity (the furthest distance the camera can "see") as the malcontent Singer recounts one of many perceived verbal attacks. He is convinced he has heard the phrase "Jew eat," not "Did you eat?" as the two men come closer and closer to the camera lens. At dinner with Annie's Waspy family Alvy is so self-conscious he imagines that Grammy Hall (Helen Ludlam) imagines him in full Hasidic garb. The East Coast/West Coast culture wars are graphically depicted by a scene of Christmas in L.A. and a Hollywood party filled with shallow types typified by a young Jeff Goldblum on the phone in distress because he has forgotten his mantra.

Annie Hall is jammed with as many cultural references as a Jean-Luc Godard film. They include *Beowulf*, Kafka, Uri Geller, Jack (Nicholson) and Anjelica (Huston), Sylvia Plath, Norman Rockwell, Adlai Stevenson, Leopold and Loeb, *Death in Venice*, Truman Capote, Groucho Marx, Masters and Johnson, the Manson Family, Henry Kissinger, Fire Island, and *The Denial of Death* by Ernest Becker. Allen arms Alvy's world with ammunition to define the characters, fuel the nonstop pungent one-liners, and layer the film with the director's deep-seated and well-observed view of the reality he finds himself embracing.

Annie Hall is a romantic comedy in which Annie and Alvy must conduct the rise and fall of a relationship as they deal with their past in a present where cocaine snorting is trendy, therapy and personal transformation is required, and the roles of the traditional boy- and girlfriend have been radicalized in the aftermath of the 1960s liberation revolutions.

Alvy directly addresses the camera in the tradition of Brecht, Godard, and Woody Allen's patron saint Ingmar Bergman in order to tell us who he is. The neurosis of the morose, depressed, and sarcastic comic is a familiar one, especially to those audience members who, like Alvy, turned forty during the 1970s. Alvy travels in time to his childhood classroom, where he points out the genesis of his oversexed obsessions and presents the future of his young mates. This constellation of 1970s stereotypes, including a white middle-class methadone addict, a blue-collar business owner, a suited Brooks Brother, a leather fetishist, and a rabbinical supplier, are added to the mix to jab at the generation's spiritual quest. The latter is ridiculed throughout *Annie Hall* as Alvy skewers cults, the human potential movement, and New Age gurus.

Allen takes Annie through her past darkly as she tries to come of age from what he calls her Norman Rockwell existence to a cosmopolitan woman who reads well, studies acting, and takes action on her dream to become a cabaret singer. Annie is Alvy's light—her beauty, energy, and zest for living is better than Valium for his jangled psyche.

At first the opposites attract. He wears Ralph Lauren and black spectacles; she wears oversized man-tailored shirts, pants, tie, vest, and hat (an ensemble that started an actual fashion trend). Allen created his characters from his former real-life romance with Keaton. They are the soul of Alvy and Annie with just enough poetic license to encourage Allen's inventive sense of comic exaggeration. In a scene often misidentified as a **split-screen** shot accomplished in the laboratory, Alvy and Annie are shown in their respective therapy sessions. He is in a dark wood-paneled Freudian environment and she in a comfortable, airy, and light space talking to an off-screen female therapist. This scene was actually shot and performed live on an ingenious set designed by Mel Bourne that allowed for the funny contrasts to flow naturally from Allen and Keaton without optical interference.

Alvy nurtures Annie's cultural development. He is supportive and encouraging to a point. Annie gets Alvy to go to the country, and in her presence he experiences the most fun his depressive nature will allow. They are immediately attracted to each other, and the awkward insecurities of the dating game are materialized by a rooftop chat of getting-to-know-you small talk as their self-doubting inner thoughts show up in subtitles.

The majority of their time together and of the film's running length is the romance, enjoying the city, wrestling with lobsters and spiders, making love, talking endlessly about their lives, and pursuing careers.

Annie Hall is a love story of its time. Annie and Alvy separate. He is too possessive and anal and most happy when he is miserable. She has found the person she wants to be and no longer yearns to be in a New York state of mind. The end comes at an outdoor café in L.A. The joys of their relationship are reprised in a **montage**. They are both better off for having had each other in their lives. Back in the Apple, Alvy is outside the Lincoln Center complex. A voiceover joke about a man who tells his psychiatrist that the man's brother thinks he's a chicken sums up Alvy's wistful observation on the need for companionship. The doctor asks why the man continues the relationship with the delusional brother and he replies, "But I need the eggs."

What influenced the transformation of Woody Allen from comic filmmaker to an-important auteur with the release of *Annie Hall*? The creative teams and members of the ever-growing acting ensemble have made lasting contributions to the films of Woody Allen. After the editing room restructuring, and, it is fair to say, editorial rewriting of *Annie Hall*, Allen began a process that involved writing, shooting, editing, rewriting, reshooting, and completion in postproduction. The budget and schedule were adjusted to accommodate this unconventional system. Rosenblum, Willis, and Bourne were followed by other significant craft members. Allen often still appears as a performer in his films supported by a *Who's who* of fine, well-trained actors. Through a directorial apprenticeship in which he searched for his voice, Woody Allen was a writer and performer. Many hailed him as an artistic genius with the arrival of *Annie Hall*. That term *artist* can be subjective. One thing is certain: On *Annie Hall* Woody Allen came of age as a film director.

Of Further Interest

Screen

Chasing Amy
High Anxiety
Manhattan
The Producers
There's Something about Mary

Read

Woody Allen: A Biography by Eric Lax
The Unruly Life of Woody Allen: A Biography by Marion Meade

When the Shooting Stops . . . the Cutting Begins: A Film Editor's Story by Ralph Rosenblum and Robert Karen
Woody Allen: A Life in Film by Richard Schickel
Method in Madness: The Comic Art of Mel Brooks by Maurice Yacowar

3

Tableau Narrative Structure and Sound Design

□ ◆ □ ◆ □ ◆ □

Apocalypse Now

Apocalypse Now (1979) takes place at the apex of U.S. involvement in the Vietnam War. Captain Willard (Martin Sheen), a man conflicted by duty and virtue, is assigned a confidential mission to hunt down and terminate with extreme prejudice Colonel Walter Kurtz (Marlon Brando), a former rising military star operating outside the purview of the military-industrial complex.

The central metaphor of *Apocalypse Now* resonates in its title: the confrontation of good and evil, the quest for a spiritual path and an inquiry into eternal truths. These themes address war, morality, and, for director Francis Ford Coppola, the very foundations of moviemaking as they existed. He set out to create a film about America's military participation in Vietnam that would travel through what Joseph Conrad called the *Heart of Darkness* to examine and question the ethical code of the United States by employing an emerging cinematic language that rebelled against the notion of the "well-made" studio film.

Apocalypse Now was a culmination of directorial expression and excess during a new golden age known as the American New Wave during the 1970s when the film director was superstar. A new generation of filmmakers took over Hollywood and transformed what had largely been entertainment into personal statements with lofty narratives and aesthetic goals.

The screenplay was written by John Milius (screenwriter of *Magnum Force, The Life and Times of Judge Roy Bean*; director of *Conan the Barbarian,*

"The horror, the horror" of war. The provocative and evocative images of Francis Ford Coppola's *Apocalypse Now*, as well as the narrative's application of Joseph Conrad's *Heart of Darkness*, were the armature for dreamlike narrative tableaus and a sound design that propels the viewer into the hell of the Vietnam War as seen through a filter of drugs, operatic emotionality, and madness. Courtesy *Photofest*.

Red Dawn) in 1969 and loosely based on Conrad's reflections on colonial infamy. George Lucas was the first director attached and at one point considered shooting the project in 16mm.

After taking on organized crime to meditate on the corruption of American political and corporate values in *The Godfather* and *The Godfather Part II*, and the invasion of privacy resulting in the destruction of self in *The Conversation*, Coppola amassed the power and artistic hubris to tackle the nature of evil as personified by the country's aggressive engagement in the affairs of Vietnam.

From the outset the project infected everyone in its path with megalomaniacal fervor. Milius raved about actually shooting the film in Vietnam as the war continued to rage in Southeast Asia. On location in the Philippines, Coppola lost touch with reality and began to fantasize that he was

Willard and that the out-of-control production was his own private trip into the belly of the beast. In reality the director was actually behaving more like Kurtz operating out on his own, risking his sanity, career, possessions, and even his family.

Apocalypse Now is a series of narrative tableaus positioned in sequential order. We are introduced to Willard as he begins to unravel mentally in a hotel room; the officer is given his orders, a boat and crew are at his disposal, and he is escorted to his point of departure. Willard then embarks on a journey upriver to the Kurtz compound deep in the jungles of Cambodia. Each scene block of the odyssey is a saga unto itself. The crew progresses into an increasingly surreal set of circumstances until Willard reaches what Jim Morrison of the Doors quantified as "The End." The structure is linear without **parallel storytelling**, **flashbacks**, or **flashforwards**. Like Dante's *Inferno*, it is a descent into hell. Coppola doesn't drive the story downward but horizontally—it is a cinematic trip upriver to Hades.

Cinematographer Vittorio Storaro (*The Conformist, Last Tango in Paris, Dick Tracy*) utilizes light, color, composition, and movement to illustrate the story and visualize motifs and the emotional actuality of the characters—their time and place. Storaro's cinematography reproduces reality of the moment and space through diaphanous layers of light.

The images of Vietnam are illuminated with a sense of empirical truth. Storaro photographed *Apocalypse Now* in the **anamorphic widescreen format** to capture the horizontal axis of the sky, the jungle, and the river that is the conduit of this road movie traveling by boat. TechnoVision in Italy had just developed lenses with the optical properties to duplicate the high level of definition seen by the human eye. This registers in the brain's storage bank and is filed along with selective memories of a given period. The light in *Apocalypse Now* produces glare, contrast, and saturated colors, which embody the immediacy of the tumultuous 1960s.

Lateral **tracking shots** evoke the film's central metaphor. Throughout *Apocalypse Now* the camera often follows a character—most notably Colonel Bill Kilgore (Robert Duvall) as he briskly leads his men and Willard to his helicopter in a prelude to an air attack. Framed in a full shot in a straight-on profile, the camera tracks right to left locked into the speed of Kilgore's confident stride. The trajectory of the camera movement not only defines the powerful charisma of the character, but the tabular direction is a gesture that continues to evoke a visual representation of the theme defining Willard's pilgrimage toward a confrontation with the other half of his psyche mirrored in Kurtz—his destiny is cinematically constant and inevitable.

Psychedelic drugs such as LSD transformed the consciousness of many young Americans during the late 1960s. *Apocalypse Now* takes place in 1969. Experiments with mind-altering substances that produced hallucinatory psychoactive states in the brain were spreading at home and at war. For the men fighting in Vietnam, the experience of leaving boyhood for the terrors of the jungle and facing an enemy they didn't fully comprehend was a surreal and horrifying transition into manhood. For them, psychedelic drugs were both a rite of passage and a way to transcend the unimaginable existence they confronted.

In *Apocalypse Now* some of the members of Willard's crew are under the influence of hallucinogens. Storaro's use of color sparks these psychic visions in the viewer's retina. Orange and green smoke fills the air with bright, gauzy fog. Lance (Sam Bottoms), the zonked-out California surfer and part of Willard's crew, fires a canister of purple smoke he calls "Purple Haze," a reference to the seminal Jimi Hendrix song. Hendrix, who provided the sonic soundtrack for drugheads during the era, named the tune after a variety of acids chemically concocted for the experimental electric musician by Augustus Owsley Stanley III, engineer of countless sensory excursions taken by baby boomers.

Cinematography is an art of chiaroscuro—the attention to light and dark in a pictorial work. As Willard and the crew float into Kurtz's heart of darkness through the atrocities of war, Storaro's photography emphasizes conflict with tonal contrast. The environmental serenity of green foliage, blue sky, and water is counterposed to the presence of warriors with dark camouflaged faces and black metal weapons, and the burning yellow and orange of explosions that ravage the land expressed in a surreal display of deadly fireworks. The Kurtz compound is heavy with brush. The colonel dwells in a cave where light is not absent but represents the other side of brightness. The stark pools of light and the gloom of its reflected rays unify to expose that light and dark—good and evil—are a configuration of each other.

The sound design by Walter Murch (*The Conversation, American Graffiti, The English Patient*) creates an aural environment that supports and enhances the thematic achievements of the visual narrative. *Apocalypse Now* is a sonic landmark, which heralded a new era in the application of film sound analogous to the accomplishments in production design attained by William Cameron Menzies on *Gone with the Wind*.

Sound effects and music interpenetrate to produce overlays of realistic, expressive, associative, and symbolic pertinence. The whirl of helicopter blades is a signature sound in *Apocalypse Now* that defines the authentic and sensory nature of the Vietnam War experience. In the opening of the film, Willard imagines the sound of a turning hotel ceiling fan into a synthesized blade *thwarp* that distinguishes his dream-state. This is then blown out of his consciousness by the audio of an actual helicopter that flies over the building, thereby returning the psychically burned-out officer to the material world of Saigon.

Throughout the film, **narration** puts us inside Willard's thoughts as he tries to reason the purpose of his journey. This inner voice is up close and resonates as if it were emanating from inside his head. It allows the viewer to experience Willard's twisted cognitive condition.

During the helicopter battle Kilgore plays a tape of Wagner's *Ride of the Valkyries*, which blares out of speakers mounted on the helicopter. The triumphant horn melody and the heavenly choral voices signify power and victory and bring associations of Nazi invasions and the superiority of a master race. The perspective of source and **score** interchange and interact with sounds of gunfire, helicopters, explosions, radio transmissions, and shouting voices of the combatants, which constantly shift to produce a hyperdramatic, cine-operatic encounter between sound and image.

To create the exterior ambiance of Kurtz's compound, Murch blended realistic Southeast Asian jungle sounds that had been recorded for the motion picture *Lord Jim*, music and singing of the Mung people of Cambodia taken from ethno-musical records, Vietnamese dialogue spoken from various depths in a hidden valley, and a track recorded at the San Francisco Zoo bird room.

The interior of Kurtz's lair is depicted as a dank, wet ruin. There are the sounds of seeping water and echoed drips from various parts of the dark location that acoustically outline the space. Jungle inhabitants are represented by cricket sounds and the suction-cupped fingers of a Philippine lizard known as a gecko.

Coppola and his team of film editors—supervising editor Richard Marks (*Broadcast News, Dick Tracy, As Good as it Gets*), Jerry Greenberg (*The French Connection, Kramer vs. Kramer, Scarface*), Walter Murch, and Lisa Fruchtman (*Children of a Lesser God, My Best Friend's Wedding, Dance with Me*)—struggled incessantly to find a fitting conclusion for *Apocalypse Now*. After trying every available possibility inherent in the raw footage, they arrived at the concept that after Willard's ritualistic killing of Kurtz, he reads the man's typewritten diary and finds the message "Drop the bomb—exterminate them all!" written in scrawl. The Doors' song "The End" is heard at the beginning and end of the film. As sung by the Dionysian rocker Jim Morrison, the modal, tribal ode is an oedipal drama that deliberates patricide. Its presence establishes a preordained affinity between Willard and Kurtz. Willard then emerges from the cave carrying the diary, throws down the murderous knife, and is acknowledged by the tribe as their new leader. Willard rejects this and leads Lance, the only survivor of his crew, back to the boat. They turn the vessel around to travel the river once again. They receive radio contact asking for confirmation but Willard shuts it off. We hear Kurtz repeat Conrad's prophetic words, "The horror, the horror." The fruitless search for a logical ending to a film about the Vietnam War is the consummate metaphor of *Apocalypse Now.* The war and the film can never truly be resolved and must lie within a conflicted American heart.

Of Further Interest

Screen

Burden of Dreams
The Deer Hunter
Fitzcarraldo
Full Metal Jacket
Hearts of Darkness: A Filmmaker's Apocalypse

Read

Novels into Film: The Metamorphosis of Fiction into Cinema by George Bluestone
Audio-Vision: Sound On Screen by Michel Chion
Notes by Eleanor Coppola
The Apocalypse Now Book by Peter Cowie
The Conversations: Walter Murch and the Art of Editing Film by Michael Ondaatje

4

The Body as Cinematic Landscape

□ ◆ □ ◆ □ ◆ □

L'Avventura

L'Avventura (Italy, 1960), directed by Michelangelo Antonioni, is a physical, emotional, and spiritual journey into the impossibility of relationships, the conflict between the ancient and modern worlds, the ennui of the rich, the culture of Italy, and the emotional pain of total alienation. The black-and-white long-form film is paced out of the boredom and inertia inbred in the characters. These upper-class Italians have little passion or emotive instinct, thereby making *L'Avventura* an arduous trip for less-than-adventurous cinema-goers. To join Antonioni on this excursion into isolation, profound loneliness, and angst with no relief is a revelation. The viewer begins the journey as an observer but after entering the scarred psyches of the characters leaves feeling emotionally devastated. The lost souls of *L'Avventura* cannot be saved by love because they don't truly believe in it unconditionally, and their riches can only prolong the pain as they travel distances without ever leaving their desperation behind.

The story of *L'Avventura* is deceptively simple. A group of wealthy acquaintances go on a yachting cruise. Sandro (Gabriele Ferzetti) and Anna (Lea Massari) are dealing with unresolved issues in their relationship. Claudia (Monica Vitti), Anna's friend, has been invited along with other members of the Italian upper class. While swimming, Anna cries out that she sees a shark. Later she confesses to Claudia that she has lied. When the boat docks on a mountainous island, it is discovered that Anna is missing. She does not turn up after a long search aided by the police.

The figures of Gabriele Ferzetti as Sandro and Lea Massari as Anna become part of the architecture and landscape in Michelangelo Antonioni's *L'Avventura*. Courtesy *Photofest*.

Struggling to stay apart from each other, Sandro and Claudia become emotionally entangled while they search for Anna in various towns and receive rumors and leads that never result in finding Anna. When Claudia eventually submits to her feelings toward Sandro, he becomes disinterested and Claudia catches him sleeping with another woman. The conclusion finds Sandro emotionally broken. Claudia stands behind him and puts her hand on his head signifying a commitment to him out of the pain they share and endure. Anna is all but forgotten by the time *L'Avventura* ends. Claudia has traded places with Anna, a metaphysical process that has evolved throughout the course of the film.

Many of the themes expressed in *L'Avventura* recur throughout Antonioni's body of work. The individual is alienated from the environment and is unable to experience pure intimacy. There is conflict between the ancient and modern worlds. The body is part of the physical landscape. Emotions are contained within a human figure whose texture and architecture is flesh and bone, part of the universe of sky, earth, water, animal, vegetable, and mineral. There is an eternal conflict between the intelligence, beauty, and emotional complexities of females and the stoic, sexually starving male, unwilling to shed centuries of macho posturing. In most black and white films, the reality of color before the lens is translated to the tones of the gray scale. In *L'Avventura* they are interpreted as organic textures—all part of a troubled universe.

L'Avventura is a total cinematic experience. Antonioni developed a rigorous language by utilizing camera, staging, and internal and external rhythms that goes beyond the illustration of the themes and elusive narrative to embody his worldview of a privileged Italian man in an existential search for relevance.

Control of the compositional frame is exacting. The characters are often viewed full figure, in a direct, sharp-focused relationship to their environment. Female characters, especially Claudia, physically adhere to interior and exterior walls. This positioning is sensual and alluring while symbolically representing a sense of confinement. Throughout *L'Avventura,* Monica Vitti, who was engaged in a long romantic relationship with the director, is poised either facing forward, backward, or in front of a wall, or is choreographed to move toward the structure that defines her space. Aesthetically, Antonioni is contrasting textures of stone, metal, wood, and weathered, aged materials with Vitti's mane of white-blonde hair. The elegant contour of her outline is referenced with the sculptural, natural, and created architecture surrounding her. This gesture also represents Claudia's alienation and is a way to physically distance her from her own conflicts and pervasive ambivalence to the life that envelops her.

The emotional state of alienation is visually achieved by the physical distance between two characters and by having one or more with their back to the others or to the viewer via the camera lens. The people in *L'Avventura* are bored, passionless, jaded, and unable to feel. The directorial pace reflects their inertia. Time moves slowly. Antonioni creates a dynamic tension between the characters, the environment, and the situations, so the narrative unfolds slowly. The depth of attention to the behavior, actions, and motivation of the characters is true and honest to the milieu. From the opening sequence viewers know they are in the assured artistic hands of a film director with intimate knowledge of his subject.

Antonioni, along with Fritz Lang and King Vidor, has been associated with a dynamic use of architecture. Sandro is a designer who respects traditional craft and ridicules the contemporary. The churches and buildings represent Italy's past and present, history and depth. They are at one with the European landscape. The contemporary buildings represent change and modernist thought. They relate to the natural environment in a less-than-organic manner. In his dialogue with Claudia on the subject, Sandro is the spokesman for the argument that architecture must serve a use. Design should relate to purpose. The ancient world in *L'Avventura* is both solid and stable or in a state of disintegration. Class structure is a prevalent theme. The main characters are elitists in lifestyle and attitude. When the search for Anna moves from the sea to the city, Antonioni explores the dichotomy between rich and poor. Sandro moves through this environment like the privileged individual he is. The lower classes move through the streets, their businesses and houses integrated with churches, an elaborate villa now a police station and roads unchanged for centuries.

In **backstory** we are told that Sandro once designed work out of his creativity as an artist, but meddling by clients diminished his ability to create for posterity and to build structures that served the land with purpose. When Sandro was asked to consult on projects, a lucrative endeavor, he gave up his ambition to create. This bitterness is always within Sandro as he agonizes about the changing landscape and is tormented by the great Italian architecture that constantly reminds him of what he could have been and what he has become.

Antonioni is that rare male film director with sensitivity and insight into his female characters. Anna is clearly dissatisfied with her relationship with Sandro. She has taken time away from him, and it has not resolved her ambivalent feelings about a commitment. Anna's father (Renzo Ricci) is concerned about her future. She has an unconditional friendship with Claudia. In a scene taking place in the ship's cabin, there is intimacy between the two women as they talk about their lives. They undress to change out of wet bathing suits. There is a moment of highly charged eroticism that is not acted on physically. Claudia is encouraged to wear one of Anna's blouses. The women represent duality throughout the film. Anna is brunette, Claudia blonde. Later in the story after Anna disappears, Claudia puts on a dark wig to change her appearance to look like Anna. Sandro is attracted to both women. When he is with Anna, the attraction toward Claudia is from afar. When he is convinced Anna is gone and he makes his intentions clear but Claudia refuses his advances, he follows in the search for Anna mainly to be with Claudia. Claudia is a replacement because she was Anna's best friend, and to Sandro a woman is a woman, and he must always have a woman in his life so he can maintain his macho exterior.

Antonioni makes many strong and visually expressive statements about how Italian men treat women as sex objects. The most dramatic and daring example is a scene when Sandro enters a building as Claudia waits outside on the piazza. At first she appears to be alone but the camera moves to reveal men on large stone steps staring at her. Claudia walks away and a tilt-up reveals men above her glaring down. Swarms of men on the ground surround her. The men are of all ages and physical appearances. No matter, they all ogle Claudia in a chauvinistic and threatening manner. There is a sense of danger as Claudia becomes the vortex of the mob's attention. As Sandro comes out of the building, Claudia escapes and runs away from all the men, including Sandro. She finds haven in a shop where she orders paint. Sandro follows and the two reunite to continue what began as a search for Anna, then became a search for companionship and love.

Sandro is all for the hunt. He does everything in his power to have a relationship with Claudia. She is in pain over the disappearance of her friend. Although she is attracted to Sandro, Claudia finds it morally wrong to be with him. Eventually there is no more talk about Anna and Claudia falls in love with Sandro. When this occurs, Sandro loses interest. He is an angry and damaged soul, full of perversity. When he sees an artist's pen-and-ink drawing of an architectural detail, Sandro knocks the bottle over and ruins the sketch. The act is not committed directly but perversely by swinging his long key chain over the ink until the keys eventually make contact with the bottle. The young artist is furious. Sandro says it was an accident but when the boy's friend breaks up a fight between the two, Sandro brags about how many fights he had as a young man. As he maintains his superiority a long procession of boys in black religious garb files by, reminding Sandro of the confining religious monarchy that presides over his world. When Sandro leaves Claudia in a hotel room to rest, he again brags about his youth and his stamina. Now that he has Claudia, Sandro is restless and free to roam. Prowling the party below, while Claudia lies fitfully in bed, Sandro gets involved with another woman. In the remaining minutes of *L'Avventura*, Claudia, worried about Sandro, finds him on the couch with the woman. The final scene, in which the jilted Claudia walks over to Sandro seated on a bench, his psyche broken, and places her hand on his head, concludes with the only true human contact in the film. The ending is ambiguous. Claudia and Sandro are destined to be together, joined by Anna, but what the future holds for them is unexplained. The viewer is left with emotional devastation and a final image, a long shot of the two engulfed within the landscape.

Antonioni, like Hitchcock with *Psycho* (see chapter 34), which was also released in 1960, takes his lead actress out of the movie early in the story. *L'Avventura* also appears to be a mystery, but Hitchcock shifts his film to darker narrative depths while Antonioni reveals that *L'Avventura* is not about Anna. He makes us care for her, and then, like the characters in the film, the audience is presented with a serous exploration of the modernist life, the empty existence of the rich and the irrelevance of their world.

The cinematography of Aldo Scavarda (*From a Roman Balcony, The Police Commissioner, Before the Revolution*), appears to be static and pristine. The precision of the framing is supported by subtle camera movements that emphasize distance, lack of human connection, and the environmental confinement of the characters. The eye is directed to discover many layers of meaning in each shot. Backgrounds are more than just visual support for the foreground. The staging, pacing, and careful **mise-en-scène** allow the viewer to look past the characters into the distance or into the space around and in front of the people. The ocean, sky, landscape, and architecture of *L'Avventura* are a key element in the totality of the image as a reminder that we can never escape our nature or environment.

Of Further Interest

Screen

American Gigolo
L'Eclisse (Eclipse)
Landscape in the Mist
La Notte (The Night)
The Sacrifice
Two Lane Blacktop

Read

The Architecture of Vision: Writings and Interviews on Cinema by Michelangelo Antonioni, Marga Conttino-Jones, G. Tinazzi, C. Di Carlo, editors.
That Bowling Alley on the Tiber: Tales of a Director by Michelangelo Antonioni
Antonioni: The Poet of Images by William Arrowsmith, Ted Perry, editor.
Antonioni or, The Surface of the World by Seymour Chatman
Passion and Defiance: Film in Italy from 1942 to the Present by Mira Liehm

5

Editing—Russian Montage

□ ◆ □ ◆ □ ◆ □

The Battleship Potemkin

The cinematic term **montage** is erroneously generalized and used all too freely to indicate rapid-paced editing, or it is tossed around encased in the more nebulous phrase "MTV editing." The most significant definition of montage concerns the theories and practice of early Russian filmmakers including Sergei Eisenstein (1898–1948; *The General Line, Alexander Nevsky, Ivan the Terrible*), Vsevolod Pudovkin (*Mother, The End of St. Petersburg, Storm Over Asia*), Alexander Dovzhenko (*Arsenal, Earth, Aerogard*), and Lev Kuleshov (*The Extraordinary Adventures of Mr. West in the Land of the Bolsheviks, The Death Ray, Dura Lex/By the Law*).

Films at the dawn of the cinema were composed of a single shot. The pioneering Lumière brothers set up their camera and recorded an event such as workers leaving a factory or the arrival of a train at a station. Eventually, filmmakers began to experiment with shot-by-shot visual storytelling. Among those responsible for this development are Edwin S. Porter with *The Great Train Robbery* and D. W. Griffith, whose work led to the creation of a cinematic language that utilized angles, shot size, composition, and a number of other elements to forge a story during the editorial process. Working with these principles, the Russians created a powerful visual grammar that employed the graphic dynamics of each shot which they edited into montages.

Sergei Eisenstein was the most consequential filmmaker of this movement. His achievements on *The Battleship Potemkin, October,* and *Strike,* along with dense intellectual writings on his theory of montage published

One shot—one montage unit—from the Odessa Steps sequence in *The Battleship Potemkin*. Sergei Eisenstein's theory of collision transformed powerful images into more than their sum worth. Courtesy *Photofest*.

as the books *Film Form* and *Film Sense*, created the basis for Russian montage. The subject as practiced by Eisenstein is complex. The presiding concept was the result of a collision effect between shots, each designed for their graphic, narrative, social, and optimum political purpose. Classical Hollywood editing was based on continuity and the matching of shots to link images seamlessly.

The Battleship Potemkin (1925) is the central work for understanding the power and aesthetic methods of the Russian school of montage. The dramatic structure is partitioned into five parts. *Part One*, "The Men and the Maggots," deals with a revolt by the sailors of the battleship Potemkin against the brutal captain and his officers. When the men are forced to eat meat rotten with maggots, a breakdown in social order occurs. Crashing waves on the shore poetically signal turbulence on the ship. A sailor wakes up the sleeping crew and begins to rouse them with passions of revolt. The sailors lying in hammocks are lit in a lazy but oppressive light. As the man speaks, a flurry of reaction shots signal the building anger.

Eisenstein used the conflict of the physical and emotional to create action. Performers and characterizations are not traditionally developed but quickly rendered with physical types and a synthesized reaction that rapidly travels to the kinetic emotive issues of the story.

The next morning, hanging meat crawling with bugs is the impetus for a calamitous confrontation within the class structure of the ship. The doctor and captain are clearly cruel disciplinarians who take a hard line against the men. Eating the food they serve becomes a question of loyalty. In a series of images Eisenstein develops several themes. Multiple angles of the ship's long guns being cleaned represent power and order. The soup with the diseased meat boils furiously in pots. The sailors eat canned goods to sustain themselves. The dining room is set up with tables hung from long rods that force them to swing back and forth. This movement creates tension and is a hanging metaphor for those who would eat the deadly meal. The men peer down from the deck. The texture of light is altered by metal grids, providing a sense of doom and the urgency for the action they must take. The montage accelerates as the men refuse to eat; the soup boils, dishes are washed, the faces of the kitchen crew grow angrier, a plate inscription, "Give us this day our daily bread" culminates in rage—the plate is smashed.

The next act, "Drama in the Harbor," is in reaction to the events and strong sentiments of the first act. Angles on a bugler set the scene. The officers and sailors assemble in formation. A repeated high-angle **master shot** is the core of the montage here. It orients the viewer and graphically presents the formality of the procedure and the consequences of the men's refusal to eat. Close-ups isolate key characters and quickly define their attitude. For Eisenstein, officers with mustaches and glasses have an arrogant air of bureaucracy and dominance over the men they govern. The movement of the men is presented with carefully composed shots that emphasize the graphic patterns of the developing discord. **Intercutting** sets up the multiaction that stems from the confrontation. Shots of men spreading the word to assemble by the gun turret are montaged with the forceful orders of the angry captain supported by his officers. An old man with long flowing hair and beard, wearing biblical dress, and wielding an oversized metal cross, stands at the top of a staircase looking down at the tense proceedings. He is not identified but appears to be a religious figure overseeing spiritual matters. Later during the rebellion he tries to bring peace but his cross is knocked to the ground by the mutineers and becomes a symbol of a hatchet. As the rebellious sailors who are to be executed are covered with a tarp, a group of marksmen file out, forming an angle that creates dynamic visual tension. As the order to shoot is given, a chaotic fight breaks out. Eisenstein choreographs this in detail not unlike a contemporary action film. In a rapid montage, guns are pulled out of a rack, there are shots of feet going down steps, and officers are thrown overboard. The men dance and rejoice in their victory over the tyrants. This is intercut with the leader of the rebellion shot and hung on a rope. The men learn what has happened and pull him up. The action progresses quickly. The fallen leader is carried by the crew and they put him in a small boat, and black and white smoke fills the air. On his body is a candle and sign that reads "Killed for a plate of soup." As the funeral vessel travels to the harbor the pace slows down.

Throughout *The Battleship Potemkin* the montage pace modulates according to the emotional content of the action, an important principle often ignored by current practitioners of the style. This is not fast editing purely for the sake of quick pace to keep the drama moving, but is carefully designed visual storytelling orchestrated to unfold a narrative in a kinetic, didactic, and ultimately visceral manner.

Part Three is "A Dead Man Calls for Justice." The narrative tone and editorial rhythm change dramatically. A montage sets the mood. A ship is on a misty sea. The sun reflects off the ocean, old ships are in the water, and birds rest on a buoy, reflecting a peaceful image not transformed into a melancholy mood until it is in the context of the watery funeral cortege in progress. On land the body of the dead hero is laid out in a tent with a black ribbon. Ships are in the port. One by one, people come to honor him. Grief and righteous anger build. There are intercuts to the dead man. In context with shots of the mourners, the emotional intensity builds. The image of the senseless murder of a man who sacrificed himself for a nascent movement is rousing to the gathering throngs. Each cut advances the call to action. The viewer experiences these feelings though the relationships created by the montage, which intensifies in breadth of shared emotions as the stirring crowd grows. The shot of the deceased man is from the **point of view** of someone sitting just outside the tent looking in. To embody the temper of the grieving, there is a shot taken from inside the tent on the mourners outside. This is held for a long duration to establish the intense grief they experience. Here Eisenstein used the outpouring from the swelling crowd and the graphic power of the staging, not montage, as an opportunity to absorb emotions and to ready for the action that will result from this communion with their martyr. An iris shot widens to reveal a long flight of stone steps, then masses of people filing toward the body appear on the steps. A procession pays respects. These images clearly influenced the conclusion of *On the Waterfront* (see chapter 32) when dock workers file in a pattern to watch Terry Malloy confront racketeer Johnny Friendly. Eisenstein staged great tableaus of human movement forming visual patterns, a structure of strength. Individuals deliver impassioned speeches to the masses. Men sing to the glory of those who died in the revolution. A group of wealthy men smirk at the proceedings. Eyelines match during cuts of groups of people looking down at their fallen leader. Shots of fists, angry faces, and arms thrust in the air are intercut with members of the crowd in **eyeline-match** with a rousing female speaker. The elite with expensive hats and groomed mustaches continue to ridicule the scene. One man says "Kill the Jews!" A rapid montage presents the violence used to put the man down. The masses march. Men from ships unite. The *Potemkin* approaches as intercuts of a huge crowd of the proletariat wave.

In over 100 years of the cinema, the most celebrated example of great editing—with the only competition being the chase sequence from *The French Connection* created forty-five years later—is contained in Part Four, "The Odessa Staircase." Known as the *Odessa Steps sequence*, it begins as boats head out to meet the ship; sailboats are on the water and sailors wave. With the skill of editorial **compression**, ships meet and people board with fresh food and fowl. The crowd continues to cheer; they are represented by a wide range of humanity: a woman in a white dress with a white parasol, a paraplegic, a mother and child, a brother and sister. The action that follows deals with a flank of soldiers quelling the unification between the masses and the sailors. The kinetic movement within shots concerns the troops with guns pointed steadily, moving down, and the people fleeing down the steps in panic and chaos. Side-angle tracking shots are used to establish the pace, spatial relationships are established through editing, and dramatic tension is inherent in the political conflict. Violence can shatter peace and joy in a heartbeat. The sequence takes an immediate terrifying turn with the horror-struck look on the face of the woman in white. Holding the parasol directly in front of her, she moves forward until the frame is obliterated in white. What follows is the relentless pursuit of the proletariat by the soldiers. The montage is detailed with intercuts of the major movement of the two groups as well as shots of individuals trying desperately to get out of harm's way. When a woman sees that her young son has been shot, she cradles the boy in her arms, turns around, changes direction, and begins to steadily walk up the steps toward the soldiers. Now the movement is on course for further confrontation. The soldiers continue downward, the woman carrying the boy forward toward them, and the masses run straight down with an even greater sense of fear. A group is inspired to speak out, determined to stand against the military and will them to stop. The woman with the boy is shot. At the foot of the steps the Cossacks arrive on horseback, creating a flank to meet the crowd chaotically racing towards them. Through choreography of the crowd and soldiers, Eisenstein has created a deadly trap ready to snap.

As all of this action is driven by the montage, there is a shot of a young woman in black high up on the steps with a baby carriage containing her infant child. The epic dramatic sweep of action now turns specific. While the other lines of action continue, Eisenstein introduces a human tragedy. The woman is shot. The montage details her state as she hangs on to life and the wheels of the carriage rock perilously back and forth on the steps. Finally, the mother dies and releases the carriage. As the baby in the carriage rumbles down the steps, it is shown in several different views. A wide shot reveals its relationship to the scene as it races down the steps. A close shot on the baby helplessly crying is presented from a downward movement of the camera, assigning the viewer with a point of view running just behind the carriage but not able to stop the inevitable. For American viewers conditioned on classical Hollywood cinema, there must be a last-minute resolution—this baby cannot die. In Brian De Palma's homage to the Odessa Steps sequence in *The Untouchables*, edited by Jerry Greenberg (*The French Connection, Scarface, The Accused*), a last-minute rescue of a child in a baby carriage also involved the good guys killing the bad. Eisenstein was defying the Hollywood convention. As the scene in *The Battleship Potemkin* culminates, an old woman with glasses is horrified at the scene. A brutal soldier approaches the camera with a sword. The carriage is about to tip over. The woman's glasses are now shattered. The soldier slashes the sword at the camera. The last shot of the sequence is of the old woman screaming. Eisenstein does not explicitly show the murder of the child but the eyeline direction—the editorial relationship between the tipping carriage to the sword-wielding man—and the constant gun shots merge in the viewer's mind's eye where one imagines seeing the woman shot in the face and the baby hacked to death with the sword. The fade-to-black leaves the viewer with the face of terror of a woman who has witnessed the unthinkable. The audience experiences the trauma of witnesses as a result of the succession of images, which demonstrates how the collision of shots elicits meaning and emotion. What you see leads to what you don't see on the screen, but it is seared into the viewer's inner vision.

Part Four ends with the ship's gun turret turning. The massive barrels reply to the massacre. The Odessa opera house is hit and explodes. A rapid montage of stone lions followed by a series of explosions signals a symbolic and actual attack on political power.

Part Five is titled "The Meeting with the Squadron." A confrontation forms at sea, with ships getting into battle position. The montage builds and maintains tension by intercutting the movement of the ships with the men getting ready for an attack. Here Eisenstein stages the action at night, producing dramatic silhouettes against a slowly dawning sky. Every image and dramatic convention signals an attack is about to begin. At the last moment before engagement, there is a happy ending but one loyal to Russia during that period in its history. Guns go down. There is solidarity among all the sailors. Men wave from deck to deck; hats fly into the air. The *Potemkin* passes through the squadron flags of freedom. As the camera lowers below the ship and men throw their hats into the air, the center of the image wipes out to black on the right and left.

The Battleship Potemkin remains a twentieth-century canonical work because it contains and demonstrates the properties of shot design and shot-by-shot storytelling driven by the editing process. It is the prehistory of much of what we call cinema. Eisenstein's daring experiment invented the very building blocks of cinematic grammar and defined editing, the medium's one original art and craft, as the key to dynamic visual storytelling.

Of Further Interest

Screen

Earth
The End of St. Petersburg
Natural Born Killers
October
Straw Dogs
The Strike

Read

Montage Eisenstein by Jacques Aumont
Sergei Eisenstein: A Life in Conflict by Ronald Bergan
Film Form: Essays in Film Theory by Sergei Eisenstein
The Film Sense by Sergei Eisenstein
Nonindifferent Nature: Film and the Structure of Things by Sergei Eisensten
Eisenstein at Work by Jay Leyda and Zina Voynow

6

Italian Neorealism

□ ◆ □ ◆ □ ◆ □

The Bicycle Thief

The Bicycle Thief, directed by Vittorio De Sica (1902–1974), is one of the most celebrated examples of Italian neorealism, a post-World War II film movement active in Italy from 1944 through 1953. The principal creators of the style were screenwriter Cesare Zavattini and directors Roberto Rossellini, Luchino Visconti, and De Sica. The influence of neorealism spread to the work of Federico Fellini, Michelangelo Antonioni, and Alberto Lattuda.

After decades of literary influence on Italian cinema, Rosellini, De Sica, and Visconti made a deep moral and stylistic commitment to realism. Just as **film noir** style grew out of fear and paranoia at the beginning of the cold war, Italian neorealism was a response to the impact of World War II, when Italy was allied with Germany. Italians experienced a collective sense of tragedy that grew from living under a system of the oppressor and the oppressed from the days of the padrone system to the fascist regime under Benito Mussolini.

Unlike film noir, which created an unofficial aesthetic and narrative rulebook, Italian neorealism had different interpretations that were based on the director's point of view. Rossellini had a personal and spiritual sensibility toward realism. Visconti was drawn to history and Italian culture and worked in a stylized theatrical reality. De Sica was a humanist interested in the cultural and political climate of postwar Italy.

There are misconceptions concerning Italian neorealism. The most common is that the films were generally low-budget productions largely im-

The relationship between the characters and their environment was a key element of Italian neorealism. The reality of seeing the honest faces of nonactors and professional performers stripped of artifice was heightened by a carefully planned cinematic design in which the frame enclosed what appeared to be the real life of wartime and post–World War II Italy. Courtesy *Photofest*.

provised and shot in semidocumentary style on the fly on the streets of Italy.

On the contrary, *The Bicycle Thief* was a costly production. It was photographed on location in Rome, but a lot of preparation was necessary to get a natural yet poetic result on film. Over forty street vendors were hired for the market sequence that appears to be shot in a **guerilla filmmaking** style right off the street. For a rain sequence, the production unit didn't wait for actual rain but engaged the Roman Fire Brigade. Six cameras were employed to shoot the essential sequence in which the bike is stolen. The film is carefully directed. De Sica choreographed the street crowds and gave specific direction to the nonactors who made up the cast.

To Vittorio De Sica the faces and gestures of the performers were the essence of his cinema. Locating the funding for *The Bicycle Thief* was difficult. Producer David O. Selznick[1] offered to finance the project if Cary Grant was cast in the lead role. De Sica refused. What made Italian neorealism an exciting new approach to dramatic filmmaking was that nonactors were often cast in the roles for stories concerning the poor and working-class.

Cesare Zavattini's (*Shoe-Shine, Yesterday, Today and Tomorrow, A Brief Vacation*) exacting screenplay was based on a 1947 novella by Luigi Bertolini. The story is deceptively simple for such an emotionally, politically, and socially complex film. Antonio Ricci (Lamberto Maggiorani) is assigned a job putting up street posters. When his bicycle is stolen, his livelihood is threatened. Antonio and his son Bruno (Enzo Staiola) search for the bike. Although they have many encounters, they never find the bicycle.

The streets of Rome are the principal locations of *The Bicycle Thief*. Out-of-work men gather outside the office of a bureaucrat to find there are no opportunities for them. The bike is stolen on a street. The search goes through a labyrinth of neighborhoods. Antonio is so driven with emotion and desperation that he and Bruno move into side streets, neighborhoods, and large avenues with little regard for anything other than finding the bicycle. The city overwhelms them. The Kafkaesque journey is a meticulously planned metaphor in which the architecture of a city swallows up a simple, working-class man. Antonio is comfortable in his place on the few blocks that make up his turf. His determination and righteous anger toward the thief do not help him to deal with the cosmopolitan city and its ruling forces.

De Sica's social and political concerns impact the narrative, confronting Antonio at every turn. He gets the job from a bureaucrat, which leads to a pawn center where poor Italians bring their belongings for cash to survive. At a police station, a detective is indifferent to Antonio's plea for help. A care center for the poor and a church are the settings where Antonio finds an old man he believes knows the thief's whereabouts. The tradition and power of the church are both a haven for the poor and a roadblock for Antonio. When he disrupts the sanctity of the church with his loud and relentless pursuit, officials stop him just as he is able to get the old man to cooperate. A restaurant is the locale for Antonio to show his attention and love to Bruno after treating the boy insensitively. The pleasure of drinking wine and chewing on mozzarella in *carrozza* (mozzarella cheese fried in bread) turns into a negative reminder of their social status. Antonio wanted to buy Bruno a pizza, but the waiter quickly advises that the restaurant is not a pizzeria for the lower class. Diners at an adjoining table are an example of people living the good life. Bruno is constantly looking over at a well-dressed, well-mannered boy eating a proper meal. Bruno can't use the knife and fork as required, so he eats with his fingers. Antonio introduced the experience as a treat, but after he has Bruno total up figures for what he would earn with the lost bike, he again becomes obsessed with finding it as the only way for his family to be happy. The great plaza surrounding a soccer stadium becomes a moral challenge to Antonio. The stadium represents the national sport and is filled with people from Rome's society. Antonio is on the outside as bike riders race by him. Hundreds of parked bikes are a temptation for him to cross the line and become a thief himself.

The directorial approach to this film is as conceptual and controlled as any dramatic fiction film. *The Bicycle Thief* is not an example of a **documentary** style applied to fiction such as is brilliantly realized in *The Battle of Algiers* (Gillo Pontecorvo, 1965). The distinction between *The Bicycle Thief* and traditional drama lies in the use of nonactors and in the devotion to a narrative that reflects and embraces unvarnished realism. The entire cast is completely believable. Casting was a painstaking process. De Sica's performers were from the working class being portrayed on the screen. They not only had the look of authenticity, but were able to take direction, repeat actions, and transmit their internal truths to the camera. Whereas trained actors will use technique to indicate the emotions, feelings, and action of characters they are playing, nonactors have life experience and a physicality that is their own—not an artistic creation.

The visualization of *The Bicycle Thief* includes camera placement and **coverage** that emphasizes the growing distance between Antonio and Bruno. The boy is constantly trailing behind his father, unable to keep up because Antonio is so determined that he is unaware of the presence of his son. Later this becomes even more dramatic when Antonio slaps his son in the face. The shot dynamics and blocking reveal Bruno's deep hurt. The boy has been so loyal, and now he is emotionally upset to be rejected by his father. Bruno walks as far away from Antonio as is physically possible within the frame. The graphics and perspective lines of these shots support the guilt of Antonio and the indignant Bruno.

When Antonio first gets his bike out of hock, he leaves it on the street and asks a small group of boys to watch it as he goes up to a fortuneteller his wife wants to repay for their good luck. The composition gives the impression that the bike may be stolen. Tension is achieved and we are relieved when the bike is still there upon Antonio's return. There are false alarms when Antonio thinks that he has found the bike, but his eyes have deceived him; they are expressed by way of the camera and editing. People and circumstance get in Antonio's way to prolong the suspense.

To visually project the determination with which Antonio tracks down the old man he believes knows who stole his bike, De Sica has the father and son follow the old man into a facility dedicated to tending for the poor. As a barber shaves the old and scruffy man, Antonio and Bruno sidle up next to him in a full shot and also in a two-shot that is intercut with the man's reaction. The camera and character choreography of the sequences in which Antonio and Bruno hunt down the thief and the old man are planned, blocked, and visualized to simulate or create the illusion of realism.

De Sica uses dramatic technique no differently than a director like Alfred Hitchcock or John Ford, and dramatic techniques are employed in the unfolding of the narrative. The establishment of Antonio's dismissive attitude toward the fortune-teller at the beginning of the film, before the bike is stolen, pays off at the end when Antonio and Bruno return to her for help as a last hopeless measure. The woman's advice—if you don't find it today, you will never find it—builds up the audience's expectation and highlights the tragedy when the day ends without success.

De Sica employs the visual power and simplicity of silent cinema. When Antonio's wife, Maria (Lianella Carell), hocks her marriage bed sheets tucked in a bag, as the clerk takes them a tilt-up reveals shelves to the ceiling of hundreds of the same. This one shot poetically communicates the dire situation of the Italian working class. The intercutting between Bruno, who has been ordered by his father to go home by bus, and Antonio, who has decided he will steal a lone bike propped up against a wall, is pure visual storytelling. As soon as Antonio makes the fateful grab, the owner appears. After a chase Antonio is harassed and beaten by locals. The man has pity when he looks at the humiliation Antonio has suffered and the shame on Bruno's face. This masterfully directed sequence ends with a shot that defines the difference between American and international cinema. Both father and son walk off and are lost in the crowd as the sun falls. They continue to walk away from the camera. There is no next shot, no last minute twist—this is life as it is. In reality happy endings are rare. The bike is lost forever, but Bruno and Antonio have come together. The family is strong—the struggle for work and survival goes on.

Italian neorealism was a powerful statement to attest that the language of cinematic storytelling could be used for realistic drama beyond literary, theatrical, or Hollywood cinema. The ramifications and legacy of Italian neorealism have been wide-ranging. Elia Kazan and Sidney Lumet were influenced by the movement, as were John Cassavetes, Martin Scorsese, and Nick Gomez. *The Panic in Needle Park, Midnight Cowboy, Mean Streets,* and many other films would not have existed without Italian neorealism.

The Bicycle Thief is a reminder that drama is embedded in the streets and in the lives of the lower classes, who fight against poverty, bureaucracy, and systems both political and financial that use entertainment to cover up social problems so they can maintain status quo. Neorealism is also a testament that artistry can reproduce life in ways that nonfiction cannot. Emotion is the tool. The open, honest actor can encapsulate and deliver dramatic reality that filmmakers must face if not to be relegated to a future of tinsel-town fantasies.

Notes

1. David O. Selznick (1902–1965) was an independent Hollywood producer who administered total control over the films he produced for his company, Selznick International. Famous for his endlessly detailed memos and as the man who brought Alfred Hitchcock from England to America, Selznick is best known for his epic production of Margaret Mitchell's novel, *Gone with the Wind*.

Of Further Interest

Screen

Boy
Miracle in Milan
Umberto D
When Father Was Away on Business
The White Balloon

Read

Vittorio De Sica: Director, Actor, Screenwriter by Bert Cardullo
Miracle in Milan by Vittorio De Sica
Popular Film Culture in Fascist Italy: The Passing of the Rex by James Hay
Italian Film by Marcia Landy
Zavattini: Sequences from a Cinematic Life by Cesare Zavattini

7

Production Design

□ ◆ □ ◆ □ ◆ □

Blade Runner

Blade Runner, directed by Ridley Scott, is adapted from the novel *Do Androids Dream of Electric Sheep?* by Philip K. Dick (author of *Man in the High Castle, Time Out of Joint*, and *Valis*). The title is derived from one of William S. Burroughs's lesser-known literary works, *Blade Runner: A Movie*. The production later learned of another book titled *Blade Runner*, by Alan E. Nourse. Both titles were acquired so the film could legally use the phrase and apply it to the story.

In the film a blade runner is a hunter contracted by law enforcement to track down and kill genetically created replicants considered to be criminals because they pose as human. The story takes place in Los Angeles during November 2019. Rick Deckard (Harrison Ford), a former member of the L.A.P.D. Blade Runner unit, is ordered by Captain Bryant (M. Emmet Walsh) to locate and terminate with extreme prejudice four escaped replicants: Zhora (Joanna Cassidy), a snake-charming exotic dancer; Leon Kowalski (Brion James), a ground-floor worker at the genetic engineering company Tyrell Corporation; Pris (Daryl Hannah), a pleasure model; and Roy Batty (Rutger Hauer), a top-of-his-class combat model. During a meeting with Eldon Tyrell (Joe Turkel), Deckard meets Rachel (Sean Young), a replicant who is unaware of her status. As he hunts down his prey, Deckard falls in love with Rachel. At story's end Deckard has completed his assignment and learns that the state of being human is far more complex than the black and white, right-and-wrong existence he had been living.

Harrison Ford, as Rick Deckard, hunts down replicants in *Blade Runner*. The Ridley Scott film, production designed by Lawrence G. Paull, combines elements of film-noir, retro-fitted, and ancient architecture to render a cinematic environment that is a universe in and of itself. Courtesy *Photofest*.

Although the screenplay by Hampton Fancher (*The Mighty Quinn, The Minus Man*) and David Webb Peoples (*Hero, Unforgiven, Twelve Monkeys*) departs from *Do Androids Dream of Electric Sheep?*, *Blade Runner* is loyal to the mindset and inner voice of Philip K. Dick, a man who was Dewey-decimaled into a science fiction ghetto but was a prolific major twentieth-century philosopher and writer, who used the sci-fi venue to explore his distinctive vision of reality and human existence. Philip K. Dick died on March 2, 1982, at age fifty-three as a result of too many actual, imagined, artificial, and shifting realities that he both lived and pharmaceutically induced. Philip K. Dick was delighted and impressed with footage from *Blade Runner* that was screened for him, but he died before the film was completed. His writing has had a formidable impact on the cinematic narratives of many films, including *Total Recall*, directed by Paul Verhoeven, and Steven Spielberg's *Minority Report*. The writer, obsessed with posing the questions "What is reality?" and "What is human?", was a man for our times in the real and imagined twenty-first century.

Ridley Scott, who had achieved great success with *Alien*, conceived and planned *Blade Runner* as mass audience entertainment. He insisted on an uncomplicated narrative to create a platform for the Dickian theme of challenging the nature of what it is to be human. The replicants who are aware of their creation express programmed emotions but seem to be human in their reactions and behavior. They are criminals who seem to think and act on their feelings. Rachel does not have knowledge of her creation and appears to have the capacity to love. The perfect application of another woman's memories through cloning makes her not just a copy, but someone with the capacity to act out of present experience. She challenges Deckard to compare his detachment and limited emotional range with replicants and questions his humanity. Ultimately, *Blade Runner* defines a human by thought, deed, action, and compassion, not birthright.

Blade Runner is a **neonoir**. It takes place in 2019 but is very rooted in 1940s culture, style, and social interaction. Deckard is crafted in the mold of the hard-boiled detective; Rachel is a femme fatale. The film takes place at night, and the world of *Blade Runner* is doom-laden. Film noir (see chapter 18) was a critical term assigned to postwar films with these and other fingerprints. They were all photographed in black and white. Creating a color noir in the 1980s changed the convention. This new movement was coined neonoir and is defined by its relationship to that historical period in film, but in the neonoir the content and aesthetics of film noir are applied to a narrative taking place in the present or, in the case of *Blade Runner*, in the future. The neonoir story has an emotional basis in the cultural past, but the visualization reflects recent aesthetic trends. *Blade Runner* has also been called a future noir, a category it established by placing the film's time frame in the twenty-first century while still embracing the noir and neonoir credo.

The content of a narrative is most often expressed by the plot and characters of a film. Ridley Scott is a **visualist**, a director who communicates through images and sound to tell a motion picture story. He kept to his promise of an accessible narrative that could be understood by a general audience, but he used the armature of the detective yarn to tell a multifaceted story. To read the film, the viewer must understand the visual language Ridley Scott employs. Every shot in *Blade Runner* is filled with elements that contribute, comment, and expand on the story. To fully experience *Blade Runner*, the audience must comprehend not just dialogue and plot, but the meaning imparted by the camera, light, sound, and, most acutely, the intricate and densely complex production design.

The fusion of the layered art direction and complex presence of shifting bands of illumination create a fully realized world. The reality of many places, time periods, and geographical influences are omnipresent. This visual diversity creates a city with its own character, history, and purpose. We see an environment in which catastrophe has altered the Earth. The population has left Earth for other worlds. Los Angeles is dark, decayed, and burning. Those who are left are the underbelly of society. Asian culture dominates. This is a third-world city.

Blade Runner takes place at night. The city is illuminated by twinkling lights, fires that spout out between buildings throughout the dense skyline, and countless large electric signs that advertise high-tech companies such as Atari and TDK from giant displays. The streets are under constant police surveillance; beams of light search everywhere. Some of the grids of the city are overcrowded; many others are empty. The light pattern, color, and texture are captured through a constant presence of rain, and a permanent choking smog that shrouds the city.

To execute the visualization of *Blade Runner*, Ridley Scott used a technique he calls *layering*. For Scott, design is more than sets; the process includes hair, makeup, costumes, visual effects, lighting, props, architecture, color, and texture. These elements contribute to the overall atmosphere and have their specific purpose in transmitting information and in eliciting an emotional and psychological impulse.

The design team for *Blade Runner* was far more extensive than on the traditional motion picture. In addition to his background as a director in feature films and advertising, Ridley Scott was an experienced art director in commercials. The production designer Lawrence G. Paull (*Back to the Future* trilogy, *Romancing the Stone, Escape from L.A.*) was a trained architect and city planner who followed his dreams to design movies by landing a position in the 20th Century-Fox art department. Visual futurist Syd Mead was a corporate designer for Ford Motor Company and later ran his own firm before contributing to the design of many films, including *Star Trek: The Motion Picture, Tron, 2010, Aliens, Short Circuit*, and *Strange Days*. Special photographic effects supervisor Douglas Trumbull (*2001: A Space Odyssey, The Andromeda Strain, Close Encounters of the Third Kind*), costume designer Charles Knode (*Never Say Never Again, 1492: Conquest of Paradise, Braveheart*), makeup artist Marvin G. Westmore (*Breaking Away, Project X, Deuces Wild*), and hair stylist Shirley Padgett (*The Driver, Romantic Comedy, The Osterman Weekend*) were all contributors to the layers of visual detail that produced the look of *Blade Runner*.

The mission was to create a total environment—a city built on a sound stage and back lot. Scott and Paull began by conceptualizing and then planning in detail every aspect of the Los Angeles of 2019, even those beyond the scope of the screenplay. Only then could they design and construct what was specifically needed to accomplish this on film and to supervise, delegate, and collaborate with the entire design team.

Paull had just returned from his first trip to Milan, Italy. The designer was struck by the fascist influence of the city built by Benito Mussolini with the support of Adolf Hitler, whose chief architect was Albert Speer. Paull observed that buildings in Milan were built right up to the curb. Narrow streets were covered with large arcades. The streets on the studio back lot were also narrow—not constructed to full size. Paull applied the lessons of Milan to the *Blade Runner* text. In the story, the middle class has left Earth for off-world colonies. The population of the city of Los Angeles is composed of the dregs that remain. The working class supplies the revenue for the unemployed and homeless. The city is dilapidated. When systems break down, they are discarded. Buildings are **retrofitted**. The city is dark, overpopulated, and poisoned with acid rain; the minority population is transient, uneducated, and speaks as if in the story of the tower of Babel.

The early work of French cartoonist Jean Giraud, known as Moebius, was a major influence on the city design of *Blade Runner*. Scott and Paull found the concept of video street monitors that broadcast public information and traffic signals in one of his drawings. Giraud created his own comic strip in 1956 at age eighteen, the result of growing up immersed in a world of comics, science fiction, and fantasy. In 1963 he appeared as Moebius in *Hari Kiri*, an underground satirical magazine, and later became one of the founding members of the magazine *Metal Hurlant*, which became *Heavy Metal* in America. Scott was intrigued with the sexually charged, dangerous futuristic world of Moebius, which became another layer in the visual universe of *Blade Runner*.

Frank Lloyd Wright, the dominant American architect who believed buildings should reflect their environment, was another major influence on *Blade Runner*. Deckard's apartment was based on Wright House on Doheny Drive in Los Angeles. Paull did not design the set on the layout or look of the Wright House but extracted the concept of that home as a cave. Paull envisioned Deckard's apartment as a womb. The rooms are laid out in a linear order. Walls are bracketed out in a series of vaults. There is a sixteen-by-sixteen poured concrete block with design work from Wright's designs in the early 1920s. Gothic vaults in a high-rise building reveal broken surfaces that jut out. Recessed lights projecting down complete the cave metaphor.

The Bradbury building was used for the residence of J. F. Sebastian

(William Sanderson), a designer of replicant parts, along with sets designed by Paull and substitutions from other buildings. The Bradbury was constructed in 1893. This unique office building was commissioned by real estate and mining entrepreneur Louis L. Bradbury. The assignment was given to George Wyman, a junior draftsman who was inspired by Edward Bellamy's novel *Looking Backward*, written in 1887. Bellamy described a utopian civilization in the year 2000. The point of connection for Wyman was Bellamy's reference to a "vast hall of light received not alone by the windows, but from a dome overhead." The Bradbury features projecting stairs and lift towers. Glazed hydraulic elevators provide access to office floors. Wyman's design allows light to filter through landings and the elevator interiors. The contrasting exterior is traditional for its era, constructed of sandstone and decorative brickwork.

The production design of *Blade Runner* reflects the eclectic mix of elements that form this dying city. The hybrid of architectural designs includes Victorian, streamline, and movements spanning from 1915 through the 1950s. Paull's design for the interior of Sebastian's apartment gives it a presidential-like suite done in turn-of-the-twentieth-century style with elaborate moldings on the walls. The glamour is contrasted with peeling paint and decay everywhere.

Syd Mead designed all of the futurist vehicles to coordinate with the total design. Charles Knode laundered the costumes in black coffee to tie the colors into the overall palette. Everything in *Blade Runner* had to be specially designed, including telephones, glasses, videophones, graphics, and newspaper headlines.

The look of every film is a collaboration among the trinity of the director, production designer, and the director of photography. Cinematographer Jordan Cronenweth (*Altered States, Peggy Sue Got Married, State of Grace*) was a meticulous craftsman who was a master of chiaroscuro—painting with light.

The studio suits were disappointed with Ridley Scott's version of *Blade Runner.* Taking the film into their own hands, changes were made to "clarify" the narrative. The devastating decision to add a film noir **voice-over** reluctantly spoken by Harrison Ford sunk *Blade Runner*'s chances at the box office. The result was a dumbed-down detective story set in the future, with enough exposition to spoil the experiential atmosphere labored over by the director and his creative team. Ten years later in 1992, Scott's director's cut was finally released to great critical and popular acclaim.

Blade Runner was a film ahead of its time when it was originally released in 1982. *Blade Runner* resonates in a twenty-first century in which human cloning is a possibility; ecological, financial, social, and political forces have eroded; and the nature of being human has been complicated by media and computer overload, New Age religions, a break with traditional lifestyles, aberrant behavior, extreme makeovers, and the widespread use of recreational and psychotropic medication.

Of Futher Interest

Screen

Alien
The Matrix
Minority Report
Star Wars
2001: A Space Odyssey

Read

Ridley Scott by James Clarke
Do Androids Dream of Electric Sheep? by Philip K. Dick
Retrofitting Blade Runner: Issues in Ridley Scott's "Blade Runner" and Philip K. Dick's "Do Androids Dream of Electric Sheep?" by Judith B. Kerman
Future Noir: The Making of Blade Runner by Paul M. Sammon
Divine Invasions: A Life of Philip K. Dick by Lawrence Sutin

8

Dream State

Blue Velvet

Dennis Hopper, a respected art collector and authority as well as the actor who plays the villainous Frank Booth in *Blue Velvet* (1986), classified director David Lynch as an American surrealist. Surrealism is an art and literature movement that began in 1924 when writer André Breton published a manifesto defining it as a "super-reality" forged by combining reality with the dream state. Surrealism embraces thoughts, ideas, and perceptions considered strange, illogical, and irreconcilable. A surrealist work springs not so much from imagination or life experience, although it may appear to, but from the deep well of the subconscious mind. Freud's theory that dreams were a manifestation of submerged thoughts and feelings served as inspiration for many of the founding practitioners of surrealism. After flourishing for two decades as a dominant aesthetic, the classical period of surrealism ended when the majority of the Europeans who created and practiced this art-of-the-irrational emmigrated to the United States. The Communist doctrine and social upheaval of the European continent was reflected in surrealism but seemed ill-suited to America as a young country where democracy was based on sound rational principles. All that changed during the Vietnam era of the 1960s, when the American Dream experienced nightmares of its own. David Lynch is a reporter from the front lines, but his sources are not fact-based—they come from the dark side of his eagle scout persona.

As a boy, David Lynch was encouraged to draw and paint by his mother, who refused to buy him coloring books, and by his father, a gov-

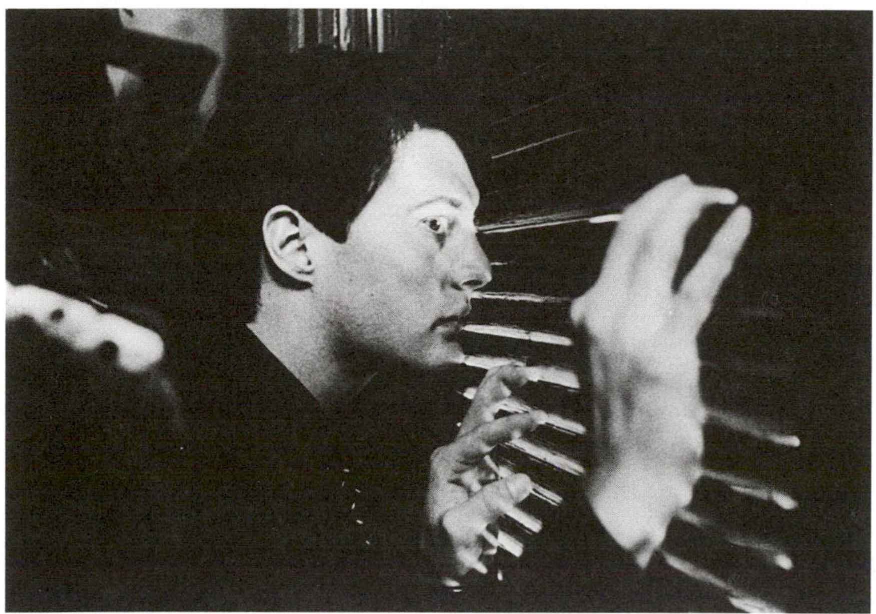

Voyeurism and the nightmare underworld hidden from civilized society is the stuff of a cinematic dream state created in David Lynch's *Blue Velvet*. Here Kyle MacLachlan as Jeffrey Beaumont, peers through the slatted door of a closet as he witnesses the horror and deviant behavior human beings are capable of. Courtesy *Photofest*.

ernment worker who brought home reams of blank paper. David drew images that represented a post-World War II world: ammunition, airplanes and Browning Automatic water-cooled submachine guns. The education of David Lynch was extensive. After attending art schools in Washington, D.C., and Boston, he went on to the Pennsylvania Academy of Fine Arts and was a fellow at the American Film Institute, where his work as a painter led him to express his emotional life through the cinema.

It is through his work as a fine artist that David Lynch can best be understood. Although he was blessed with an idyllic childhood in a small town in Montana, Lynch has always taken an extremely close look at the perfect world in which he lived. He saw black pitch oozing out of a beautiful cherry tree and millions of crawling red ants. The titles of Lynch's paintings from the 1980s and 1990s, a time in which he created the distinctive cinematic visions of *Eraserhead, Blue Velvet, Twin Peaks, Wild at Heart*, and *Lost Highway*, are entrée into a disturbing world; *Suddenly My House Became a Tree of Sores, Shadow of a Twisted Hand across My House* and *Mom's Home and She's Really Mad* are canvases in which torment and memories of fear, tedium, and dread depict images that exist below the surface of reality.

On the surface *Blue Velvet* appears to be a mystery film in which the protagonists follow the kid detective tradition of the Hardy Boys and Nancy Drew, but this story is far from the juvenilia concocted by Franklin W. Dixon and Carolyn Keene. Jeffrey Beaumont (Kyle MacLachlan) finds a severed ear in a field near his suburban home. When he brings his grisly find to Detective Williams (George Dickerson), Jeffrey develops a relationship with Detective Williams's daughter Sandy (Laura Dern). Starting as amateur sleuths, they discover a dangerous subterranean milieu, and in the depths of the darkness they fall in love. The mystery leads them to Dorothy Vallens (Isabella Rossellini), a sexually abused nightclub singer, and Frank Booth (Dennis Hopper), an evil gangster who has kidnapped Dorothy's son. Jeffrey and Sandy are pulled into a vortex of drugs, deviant sex, torture, and murder that is a hellish nightmare from which only the light of love can save them.

Blue Velvet is decipherable as a dream based on a subconscious interpretation of life in small-town America. Many films have a seminal image that encapsulates them. For *Blue Velvet* it is a shot of a bright, saturated blue sky, a freshly painted white picket fence, lush green grass, and deep red roses. It is a familiar image seen in traditional Hollywood movies and commercials—an idealized American symbol of home, family, and tranquility. This particular shot is far from traditional. It is hyper-real, as if painted by a photorealist. The intensity of the color and brightness transforms what we recognize as typical into a surreal setting that looks real but is not—an experience similar to the way we receive our nocturnal dreams.

A traditional film narrative succeeds in communicating its story because the audience has been dramatically conditioned by conventions inherent in the movies they have seen. In *Blue Velvet* the structure and logic of a mystery film are interpreted through a dream state. The inner logic of a dream reflects the emotional, psychological, and actual experience of the dreamer. A clever screenwriter can achieve this by engaging conventions or clichés universally associated with dreams. But in *Blue Velvet* David Lynch heads straight to the source of his own subconscious mind as a stimulus to penetrate the veneer of contentment in the perfect world of his childhood and happy life as an adult.

Sleep is the conduit to dreams. The rapid eye movement consciousness known as REM sleep expresses, in Freud's view, repressed desires of forbidden impulses. The dark room of a movie theater and projected images that appear constant because of our **persistence of vision** can simulate the dream experience. The flicker principle behind movies combines with these factors so that the viewer is ready to receive an altered reality. While watching *Blue Velvet* we are already asleep. The film is not about a nightmare, although there are instances when Jeffrey is dreaming. Shots of Jeffrey in bed or opening his eyes while resting in a lawn chair could be construed as a basis for the strangeness he has experienced. But Lynch does not blatantly use the well worn "It was only a dream" convention utilized in many science fiction, fantasy, and horror films. *Blue Velvet* is not about a dream—it is a dream.

Bobby Vinton's 1963 hit record "Blue Velvet" was an inspiration to David Lynch. The luxurious texture of blue velvet fabric fills the screen during the opening and closing credits of the film. Dorothy Vallens sings the song in a nightclub and acts out the first line, "She wore blue velvet," to satisfy one of Frank's sexual fetishes. The lament of the song's first-person narrator brings Frank to tears, and the fabric itself drives him wild with aberrant desire as he cuts it off of Dorothy with a pair of scissors, rubs its soft pile, and puts it in his mouth to feed an oral fixation.

The detached ear is a hidden horror guarded by swarming bugs and giant blades of grass. Instead of racing by, a fire truck floats through the frame as one of the riders addresses the camera. The town is associated with wood—this is Lumberton U.S.A. A truck of felled and cut trees twice gains our attention. On Jeffrey's wall is a split log with the letters spelling out his town, hand-cut from the inner core. A radio show begins with the sound of a tree falling in the woods, bringing to mind the Zen puzzle concerning this event and whether it still makes a sound if no one is there—we are not there, but we hear it fall. A man we later learn is Jeffrey's father waters his lawn, but the comfort of the scene is interrupted by terror when suddenly he appears to be violently attacked from within his central nervous system. In the boy's living room, family-hour television seems to be part of the mystery. The image of an oversized handgun and, later, feet walking up a flight of stairs on the small screen, may be occurring in the house—is this some sort of closed-circuit television? Sandy's entrance is every American boy's fantasy. A beautiful blonde girl-next-door in a pink dress wafts out of the blackness of the night as if the wind is beneath her feet. Sandy and Jeffrey walk the home-lined neighborhood streets, evoking déjà vu of teenage memories both real and cinematic. As they stroll and begin a falling-in-love cycle, we can't help feeling we've seen this before. Maybe it was in our hometown U.S.A., or during *It's a Wonderful Life*, with Jimmy Stewart and Donna Reed portraying the classic evening ritual, or in the perilous night air of *Rebel Without a Cause* (see chapter 37) as Natalie Wood and James Dean wander into oblivion.

A long sequence that takes place inside Dorothy's apartment is a dreadful situation in which Jeffrey is confronted with the demons associated with coming-of-age anxieties. It is night. He enters to search for clues. He cannot hear the prearranged signal of Sandy's honking horn because he has drunk too much Heineken and is listening to a long, loud toilet flush at that moment. When Dorothy enters, Jeffrey is trapped physically and psychologically. He hides in the closet. The apartment is dark, the walls a deep red–coral color with black molding. The kitchen is done in light beige and black. Wall fixtures cast a dull murky light. The rug is a red–purple color. No apartment looks like this—a representation of the young man's fear and desire. Jeffrey watches from inside a closet through the slatted doors as Dorothy undresses. **Point of view** shots put the observer in the position of voyeur and third-person angles on Jeffrey capture his conflicting emotions. Alfred Hitchcock has explored this terrain many times, most notably in *Rear Window*; Michael Powell entered the mind of a psychotic killer who murdered while filming his victims in *Peeping Tom*; those examples were filmed with a degree of expressive realism. Lynch defies narrative logic with incongruous events and a setting not rooted in reality. Dorothy hears Jeffrey and forces him out of the closet at knife point. She tortures and teases him sexually. When Frank arrives Jeffrey is back in his peeping station, as Frank, fueled by a maskful of amyl nitrite he inhaled, rapes and abuses Dorothy. During the scene Jeffrey is intimate with Dorothy, who forces the boy to accept manhood. The long and intense set piece is not engineered for a single emotional response. Depending on point of view, the audience experiences terror, titillation, absurdity, disorder, and revulsion. The interpretation of this dream world is as varied as the observer. Do not look to David Lynch for the meaning of *Blue Velvet*. He refuses to interpret or explain his films. His job is to put them on the screen.

Whose dream is *Blue Velvet*? Robert Altman dreamed the story of *3 Women*, and that film is a record of a specific dream he was conscious of when he awoke. *Blue Velvet* is not a recreation of a recalled sleep event, but a film that examines the dark recesses of America that coexist with the Rockwellian world that has been decaying since the 1960s. David Lynch still says "Golly gee," eats meals at Bob's Big Boy, and lives a happy, genteel life, but he also has the gift to see the dark side of the rainbow. In *Blue Velvet* Kyle MacLachlan is a stand-in for David Lynch in the way Harvey Keitel served that purpose for Martin Scorsese in *Mean Streets*. MacLachlan has similar physical characteristics to Lynch, but there is an uncanny sense that this good-looking, well-groomed young man appears as if he is an alien from another planet. Throughout his life, people in and out of the film industry have questioned whether Lynch is just visiting from another planet, possibly Mars. Strangeness is impossible to define in a human being, but we know it when we see it. David Lynch is weird and when he met MacLachlan while casting his production of Frank Herbert's *Dune*, he knew he found a leading man in his own image.

Sound is fifty percent of the cinematic experience. David Lynch has a full command over the atmospheric and psychological impact sound design can bring to a film. Working with Alan Splet (*Eraserhead, The Black Stallion, Henry and June*), Lynch created an aural environment to support the altered reality of the visuals. Hyper-realistic exterior sound effects, like the crickets heard while Sandy makes her magical entrance, heighten the surreal nature of *Blue Velvet*. Dorothy's apartment building has a buzzing electric sign and a low wind that can be heard through the walls. The hissing of the sexual stimulant gas Frank inhales transforms him from a bad man to a manic state of evil beyond human control.

Music is a transcendent force in *Blue Velvet*. When Ben (Dean Stockwell) lip-synchs to the Roy Orbison song "In Dreams" and is lit by the harsh light of a hand-held work lamp, the degenerate party of large-sized women with dyed hair and Frank and his gang become the demented cast of an American musical staged in hell. The love Frank experiences is not pure; it is motivated by violent sex and power over his sick domain. The focus transitions to how Jeffrey and Sandy fall in love during these evil proceedings. Jeffrey begins as a boy and grows up when infatuated by the unbalanced desires of an older woman in emotional pain. At a teenage house party, a surfing instrumental quickly fades away. Jeffrey takes Sandy to a slow dance. A song begins. Although the other kids dance in the background, it plays only for Sandy and Jeffrey. They kiss and pledge their love. The song, "Mysteries of Love," with lyrics by David Lynch, music written by Angelo Baldamenti (*Parents, The City of Lost Children, Mulholland Dr.*), and sung by Julee Cruise, is a spiritual revelation. Cruise has an ethereal voice, healing *Blue Velvet* with the sounds of an angel. The mystery becomes one of falling in love as the wind blows and a couple kisses forever. After Frank and the conspiracy of his criminal world are defeated, another ear appears. It is attached to Jeffrey. He is home with his family and his Sandy. The song continues. Dorothy is reunited with her true love—that of a mother for her son. Sandy repeats the line that encapsulates *Blue Velvet*: "It's a strange world." A mechanical bird eats a bug. The camera pans up to the blue sky, which becomes the texture of blue velvet. The film has come full circle.

This dream called *Blue Velvet* has many dimensions. The power of love and the light of love that comes out of the darkness is the overarching theme. It lifts the ending above the netherworld doom inhabited by Frank Booth and his malicious coterie. The lament of the title song repeats. This has not been a dream. *Blue Velvet* is the reality within the reality of life—and that is a true mystery.

Of Futher Interest

Screen

Eraserhead
Eyes Wide Shut
Meshes of the Afternoon
Mulholland Dr.
Twin Peaks (television series)

Read

David Lynch by Michel Chion
Blue Velvet by Charles Drazin
The Interpretation of Dreams by Sigmund Freud
The Complete Lynch by David Hughes, Jim Smith, and James Clarke
Memories, Dreams, Reflections by Carl Gustav Jung
The Passion of David Lynch: Wild at Heart in Hollywood by Martha P. Nochimson

9

The Period Film as Mirror for the Present

□ ◆ □ ◆ □ ◆ □

Bonnie and Clyde

When *Bonnie and Clyde* was released in 1967, it incited a dual controversy. The film was graphically violent, bloody, and employed slow-motion photography to further heighten the explicit damage done when criminals and cops shoot each other. What really inflamed critics and moviegoers was *Bonnie and Clyde*'s portrayal of the couple who led the Barrow gang. As portrayed by Faye Dunaway and Warren Beatty, Bonnie and Clyde were celebrities. The male **antihero** had been born over the course of the decade as exemplified by Paul Newman in *The Hustler* and *Hud*, but Bonnie and Clyde were superstars. As the ad copy for the film pronounced, "They're young, they're in love, they kill people." Bonnie and Clyde were sexy. They were heroes to the common folk—and they were also cold-blooded killers. This was a love story for a new generation in a country where the assassination of the young, vital president Kennedy was the beginning of a long descent into a late twentieth-century national nightmare.

In retrospect, *Bonnie and Clyde* marks a turning point in American filmmaking. Throughout the 1960s the studio system was collapsing. Warner Brothers, the studio best known for its gangster cycle in the 1930s and 1940s featuring James Cagney, Humphrey Bogart, and Edward G. Robinson, was in the process of being sold off when it distributed *Bonnie and Clyde*. Mogul Jack Warner, distracted by the coming end of his reign, left the film in the hands of producer Warren Beatty and director Arthur Penn.

Warren Beatty and Faye Dunaway portray the infamous depression era bank robbers Clyde Barrow and Bonnie Parker. The Arthur Penn film placed the action in the story's authentic time period while making a socio-political comment on a changing, rebellious, and ever-violent America in the late 1960s. Courtesy *Photofest*.

From *Psycho* (see chapter 34), which began the decade, through films such as *The Apartment, The Misfits, The Manchurian Candidate* (see chapter 27), *Dr. Strangelove, Seconds, Cool Hand Luke,* and *The Graduate,* American movies were breaking away from the aesthetic conventions that had governed them for decades. Their mission was not foremost to entertain, but to reflect the social and political climate of their times. The audience demographics had changed. Movies had largely been created for families and mature adults to escape the drudgery of their everyday lives. By 1967 a new under-thirty generation demanded to be heard in every aspect of American life—the movies would become a platform for that coming revolution. *Easy Rider*, released two years later in 1969, is often credited as the beginning of the American New Wave. When studied in the manner of an archeologist carefully examining the contents of a dig from an ancient time, *Bonnie and Clyde* is a motion picture by which many serious American movies can be understood. *Bonnie and Clyde* is the Rosetta Stone of baby boomer cinema.

In art, context is everything. *Bonnie and Clyde* is based on the true story of Clyde Barrow and Bonnie Parker, who were bank robbers during the 1930s. The intent of screenwriters Robert Benton and David Newman (*There Was A Crooked Man, What's Up Doc?, Superman*), producer–star Warren Beatty, and director Arthur Penn was to make a film that mirrored American life in 1967, not a depression-era gangster movie.

Bonnie and Clyde are antiestablishment figures. They despise the government, the financial establishment, and law enforcement—the military–industrial complex of their time. Like hippies and many young people of the 1960s, Bonnie and Clyde were rebels. They rebelled against all bureaucracies. Bonnie and Clyde only trusted people of their own age. Elders in power, like Sheriff Frank Hamer (Denver Pyle), were to be defied, ridiculed, and brought down by a revolution that returned power to the people. The banks were rich—the people were poor. Peace was not the way. Only violent action could change the world. After the revolution they could live their lives, but first Bonnie and Clyde had to destroy everything that was wicked.

They began their revolution with brazen action, stating their demands backed with the authority of the gun. Clyde is principled; he will attain his goal through force of personality and ideals. When their driver C. W. Moss (Michael J. Pollard) turns a getaway into a comedy of errors, Clyde kills a man. Just as peaceful hippies became radical activists, Bonnie and Clyde, like the Students for a Democratic Society (SDS) and the Weather Underground, rediscover themselves through a violent act.

Bonnie and Clyde are dimensional characters. Psychological impulses are on the surface and drive their ambitions and behavior. Clyde craves respect and attention. He is a Robin Hood out to liberate the oppressed masses. Clyde is sexually aroused by fame and the will to be known—he thrives on notoriety. He is physically repulsed by intimacy with a woman and announces that he is not a lover boy, but he is attracted to Bonnie because she is the other half of his legend. For Clyde, sexual energy is channeled into his rebellion against authority. Release comes with the blasts of his guns. In a central shootout between the gang and the law, Clyde expresses his manhood firing two guns that blaze and thrust forward.

Bonnie is a small-town waitress. She is an ambitious woman, bursting to spring from the monotony of her imprisoned life. Bonnie needs a catalyst to liberate herself and to become the careerist she longs to be. Fate intervenes as she trashes around her room, naked and emotionally starved. Clyde Barrow is outside the window stealing a family car. Bonnie sees Clyde as a way out of small-town U.S.A. The thrill of crime arouses her aggressive sexual impulses to a fever pitch. When she is physically rejected by Clyde, who is unable to consummate their union, Bonnie confronts her destiny. Bonnie Parker chooses celebrity over returning home to live a common existence. Bonnie becomes Clyde's partner and his voice. When she writes the ballad of Bonnie and Clyde and it is published in a newspaper, she has achieved immortality as half of Bonnie and Clyde.

Before the Manson Family, John Gotti, O. J. Simpson, and *Natural Born Killers*, there was *Bonnie and Clyde*. In the film the media is represented by the printed page of the newspaper. False so-called eye witness and police reports expand the legend of Bonnie and Clyde. To the nation these were criminals of mythic proportion, robbing countless banks, traveling an impossible itinerary, amassing a fortune in stolen loot. To the masses of poor hillbillies, Bonnie and Clyde were one of their own fighting the system.

On the lam, Bonnie and Clyde hole up at an abandoned house foreclosed by the bank. The owner drives by to visit his former home one last time. To show his solidarity Clyde defiantly fires his gun at the bank's property ownership sign. As his family looks on from their car, Clyde hands his weapon to the man and encourages him to rebel against the powers that oppress him. Clyde watches the symbolic act against (in sixties parlance) "the man" with satisfaction. A black man who worked the property with the owner is also empowered with a strike against the bank that has taken America away from the people. As *Bonnie and Clyde* played on movie screens around the country, America's youth were in the streets chanting "Power to the people." Clyde Barrow became their hero.

Bonnie and Clyde is a **road movie**. They steal cars to move around the country and keep ahead of the law. Many scenes take place in cars, dealing with dreams, aspirations, and the reality Bonnie and Clyde find themselves in. When the heat is on and they are running out of supplies, they stop at a roadside community of displaced people. This little tent village is made up of homeless Americans living on the barest of necessities. When Clyde drives up and asks for help, they feed the gang and encircle the car to gaze at the legends in person. In 1967 young people were living on communes all over the United States. If Jimi Hendrix, Jim Morrison, or Janis Joplin had stopped off at a commune for some brown rice, wine, apple juice, or a toke off a joint, this is what it would have looked like.

During the late 1960s the traditional family was endangered. Many young people left home to find themselves. Communes, cults, rock bands, Haight-Ashbury, Greenwich Village, and concerts were examples of the new society. In *Bonnie and Clyde* the Barrow gang is made up of Bonnie and Clyde, who were not married, Clyde's older brother Buck (Gene Hackman), Buck's wife Blanche (Estelle Parsons), and the young C. W. Moss, who was brought into the fold because he craved adventure and was captivated with antiestablishment fervor. The brothers are close, explosive, and constantly physically engaged, like the Kennedy brothers Jack, Bobby, and Ted playing football on the White House lawn. The women are worlds apart. Blanche, who comes from a religious background, is incessantly shrieking with fear. Bonnie is tough and aggressive; she sees Blanche as a liability. It has been suggested by many critics that C. W. and Clyde share homoerotic feelings. The wayward boy certainly idolizes Clyde but is not strong enough to be his own man. This family is as dysfunctional as the ones they left. Buck is irrational and doomed to die young, and the same fate goes to the star-crossed lovers Bonnie and Clyde. Blanche and C. W. both sell out the family by naming names, she to the sheriff, he to his father.

Thematically, *Bonnie and Clyde* created a new paradigm for the American film. Stylistically, it broke away from traditional Hollywood conventions by creating a visual style that would lead to a new aesthetic model for young filmmakers. Director of photography Burnett Guffey (*The Harder They Fall, All the King's Men, Birdman of Alcatraz*) was sixty-two years old when *Bonnie and Clyde* was released. He had been working in Hollywood since 1924, when he had contributed additional photography to John Ford's silent film *The Iron Horse*. Over the years Arthur Penn has commented on the difficulties he had in working with the seasoned pro, whom he felt was slow and set in his ways. This may not have been an ideal collaboration on a personal basis, but artistically Guffey imbued *Bonnie and Clyde* with the perfect visual environment and atmosphere to parallel what was taking place in America at the time. Social and political change came first in the 1960s. When the youth revolution began, the old world still existed. Guffey's photography echoes turn-of-the-century and early twentieth-century American painters. There are references to the art of Andrew Wyeth and the depression-era still photography of Dorothea Lange, Walker Evans, Margaret Bourke-White, and Arthur Rothstein. This lonely, crumbling America, with the etched faces of the abandoned, was the ideal environment for Bonnie and Clyde, two young kids who were out to change the world but were doomed from the start. The contrast of these two forces of nature against a great nation in ruins is poetic and daring. It places Bonnie and Clyde in their own time but as two people who dared to be different like their hippie, yippie, pot-smoking, war-protesting sixties counterparts.

Production designer Dean Tavoularis (*The Godfather; Apocalypse Now;*

Tucker: The Man and His Dream) read the script and, as he said in an interview in *Production Design and Art Direction* by Peter Hedgui, he immediately conceptualized the story as one about "two renegades rebelling against the world they lived in." He also proceeded in a realistic fashion by recreating the era from architecture to details of peeling paint and the elements of aging and time. When photographed by Guffey, the look of *Bonnie and Clyde* attained a lyrical realism.

Instead of a dramatic underscore, *Bonnie and Clyde* features the authentic bluegrass guitar and banjo music of Lester Flatt and Earl Scruggs. Their "Foggy Mountain Breakdown" captured time and place while also sonically supporting the manic energy of the rebellious couple in action.

The costumes by Theodora Van Runkle (*The Godfather, Part II, New York, New York, Peggy Sue Got Married*) appear to be period accurate but are exaggerated to create stars out of Bonnie and Clyde. Their clothing is a statement against the norm at the time. While America rebelled against suits and ties, and long puffy dresses, the fashion of *Bonnie and Clyde* started a commercial trend of its own and was featured in department stores as the film took hold across America.

The truly subversive aspect of *Bonnie and Clyde* is the audacious editing of Dede Allen (*Slaughterhouse Five, Dog Day Afternoon, Henry and June*). Penn and Allen moved away from traditional scene structure to give *Bonnie and Clyde* the frenetic energy of the inner life of the characters and their living-for-the-moment lifestyle. Penn did not shoot conventional coverage—**master shot**, two-shots, close-ups, and so forth—and Allen edited the film to capture two objectives: story and character. No entrances, no exits (what Allen, in an interview for my book *Selected Takes: Film Editors on Editing*, called "gezuntis and gezatus"). *Bonnie and Clyde* is supercharged with what came to be known as the "energy cut"—where the emotion and action is distilled to its very essence. The current editorial term for this approach is called **compression**. For Dede Allen, editing is not an intellectual exercise—she cuts to move a film forward and breaks many rules about matching action by creating continuity out of the soul of each moment in a film. Instead of fading a scene out and then fading the next scene in, Allen either cuts to black and then fades the next scene in, or **fades out** to black and then cuts to the next scene. Penn's direction to Allen was to propel the film as driven by the lives of Bonnie and Clyde. Allen went through the film repeatedly, accelerating the pace each time. As stated in *Selected Takes*, during this process she broke what she considered to be "her own rigid cutting rules about story, character, and how a scene plays." The result was an innovation in feature film editing.

Bonnie and Clyde established that the American film could reflect the lives of the audience regardless of genre, period, story, or the genesis of the characters. It was a violent film for violent times, graphically portraying both the physical and emotional results of the current milieu. Arthur Penn directed a film that started a revolution. Inspired by the history of film and theater and plugged into the zeitgeist, Penn, Warren Beatty, and the entire cast and crew of *Bonnie and Clyde* rewrote the Hollywood playbook. America was never the same after the sixties. American film stepped up to the challenges presented by a new generation—the medium has not been the same since.

Of Further Interest

Screen

Badlands
Natural Born Killers
Thelma & Louise
They Live by Night
Thieves Like Us

Read

The Sexiest Man Alive: A Biography of Warren Beatty by Ellis Amburn
Medium Cool: The Movies of the 1960s by Ethan Mordden
The Strange History of Bonnie and Clyde by John E. Treherne
The Bonnie and Clyde Book, compiled and edited by Sandra Wake and Nicola Hayden
Arthur Penn by Robin Wood

10

Expressionism in Cinema

□ ◆ □ ◆ □ ◆ □

The Cabinet of Dr. Caligari

Few films throughout motion picture history have had more influence on the **avant-garde**, art, and student cinema than did the German silent film *The Cabinet of Dr. Caligari*, directed by Robert Wiene (1880–1938) and first shown in 1919. This seventy-five-minute black-and-white film is a primer of expressive cinema and remains a source of fascination concerning the abstract, emotional, and psychological possibilities of the medium.

The Cabinet of Dr. Caligari is an archetypical example of German expressionism, a film movement that evolved from the expressionist art movement in painting. Expressionism grew out of the use of a vivid nonnaturalistic color palette that characterized the Fauvism movement.[1] Expressionism was more openly neurotic and morbid in its approach to subject and theme. The French practiced expressionism, but the German expressionist movement lasted longer and was a dominant art form from around 1905 to 1930. The Germans were more spontaneous and reached daring degrees of emotional extremes.

In expressionism traditional notions of realism are tossed aside for the exploration of distortion and exaggeration in shape and form, as opposed to figurative representation. Expressionism is abstract in nature, grotesque in its depiction of social and political power, and urgent in its authority to express the fervent emotions experienced by the artist.

German Expressionism began before World War I when a group of bohemian artists who all shared a sense of imminent disaster formed *Die Brüke* (The Bridge) in Munich. Led by Ludwig Kirchner, they were in-

Hand painted sets, distorted perspective, and a highly stylized acting style are the principal components of cinematic expressionism in *The Cabinet of Dr. Caligari*. Courtesy *Photofest*.

spired to revive German art by reaching back to the early primitives. To achieve a contemporary approach to art, they were deliberately clumsy in their draftsmanship, which was dominated by bold black lines rather than the naturalistic modeling practiced by figurative artists. The paintings were brooding with forbidding elements of violence and sexual tension. German Expressionism was the fashion of the avant-garde and was despised by Adolph Hitler's Nazi party that suppressed it in 1933 as degenerate art.

In the cinema, several forces created the artistic climate for German expressionism. Germany after World War I was in political and social turmoil. The theater of Max Reinhardt and the art style of Die Brüke influenced Robert Wiene's *The Cabinet of Dr. Caligari*.[2] Other German filmmakers followed with *Destiny* and *Dr. Mabuse the Gambler*, directed by Fritz Lang, and F. W. Murnau's *Nosferatu*.

The Cabinet of Dr. Caligari is structured in six acts defined by title cards that announce the beginning and end of each act. A scene in which two men sit on a bench anchors the nightmarish narrative. As a woman in a trance glides by, the younger man tells his companion that she is his fiancée. As he talks about the strange events that have occurred, the story shifts to a **flashback**.

A diabolical looking man sporting a black stovepipe hat and black rimmed spectacles (Werner Krauss) exhibits Cesare the Somnambulist (Conrad Veidt) at a fair. The twenty-three-year-old gaunt man dressed in black has been in a dream state for his entire life. Brutal knife murders begin to occur. It is learned that this evil and cunning man is the director of a mental institution. After gaining access to his library research, it is revealed he has studied the history of Dr. Caligari, who had a somnambulist under his spell who was ordered to commit murder. As the men are in the director's office and read this information in a book, the scene is still a flashback being told by the man on the bench from the opening scene. From investigation of the book there is another flashback showing how the man known as the director became Dr. Caligari and placed Cesare under his control. This sequence is a flashback within a flashback, a narrative device used by Stanley Kubrick in *Killer's Kiss* and by Oliver Stone in *JFK*. In *The Cabinet of Dr. Caligari*, the tiers of storytelling from present to flashback to a second generation of flashback plunge the viewer into a deeper nightmare level of time and space.

After a return to the recognition of the director's evil plan, the missing Cesare is found, and the director, now Caligari, is straightjacketed and shut in a cell. The story then returns to present day. Cesare is still alive and sleepwalking. Jane (Lil Dagover), the young man's fiancée, is also in a trance. The director appears, the lover is held down, screaming that he is not crazy and that the director is Caligari. The man is put in a straightjacket. The director dons his glasses and is again Caligari, who states the man is delusional for thinking that he is the mystical Caligari. The film ends with Caligari's proclamation that he knows how to cure the man.

The narrative logic of *The Cabinet of Dr. Caligari* is distorted as if it were a nightmare. It can be seen as a parable portraying a world in which evil is a constant presence winning over the struggle for rationality. The expressionist style is prevalent throughout *The Cabinet of Dr. Caligari*, including the opening scene. If the story were just a nightmare, there would be a stylistic separation between scenes of the real world and the dream world, and the narrative would be resolved when the sleeper awoke. Weine, like the German expressionist painters, was reflecting his emotional reaction to the world around him, which draws the viewer into a trance state from which there is no awakening through the duration of the film. In many ways *The Cabinet of Dr. Caligari* is a horror film with the mad scientist figure, a monster, murder, and an atmosphere of relentless fear. A social or political read of the film reveals an analogy to the moral and physical breakdown of Germany at the time, with a madman on the loose reeking havoc on a distorted and off-balanced society, a metaphor for a country in chaos.

The direct link to the German expressionist art movement is evident in the sets by Walter Reinmann (*Algol, Adventures of a Ten Mark Note, Eternal Love*), Walter Röhrig (*The Last Laugh, Faust, Rembrandt*), and Hermann Warm (*The Phantom, The Passion of Joan of Arc, The Runaway Princess*), and are largely painted in that style. *The Cabinet of Dr. Caligari* was designed in a series of tableaus, including the fair outside town, streets, the director/Caligari's office, a police station, and interiors where the characters reside. With the exception of a prop or key element of furniture, which are also expressionistic in nature, these scenes are painted onto backdrops and architectural elements are defined by studio constructions.

The painted backdrop was prominent in international art direction in early cinema. Hollywood continued the practice for decades. In *The Cabinet of Dr. Caligari*, the production designers moved beyond traditional use. These are not primarily backgrounds but total environments. The traditional background painting was either rendered in a realistic or impressionist style within the confines of figurative reality. Reinmann, Röhrig, and Warm created an environment that was physically distorted in perspective, form, dimension, scale, and representation. The images depicting locations of, and within, the town are presented in straight, curved, and angled strokes of bold, black paint. Gray and white are employed not to create the illusion of a color palette but to envision confined and hard-edged dimensions and shadows. Light and shadow, traditionally applied by the chiaroscuro of the cinematographer's art of lighting, is achieved by the art of the brush and paint. The lines create a vortex of danger. The inner logic of the design is not related to realism but is an emotional response to the terror Caligari and Cesare represent to this society. There are numbers written onto walls implying a metaphysical communication and sharp angles that defy architectural purity and order.

This extreme visualization immediately comes to life as the film opens. As a totality, *The Cabinet of Dr. Caligari* is a complete world realized in a manner that unifies theme, plot, characterization, production design, and cinematography. The plot is a story of malevolent deceit in which a madman achieves the power to control another to commit murder. The themes concern the spiritual and moral tampering with man's will. The sleepwalking Cesare can be seen as a metaphor for those without a mind of their own and follow the path of others. The psychology of the film examines the potential evil powers of the mind, the nature of sanity, and the thin-line relationship between stability and chaos. Wiene and his designers understood that realistic locations and conventional design concepts could never visually express the living, paranoid, nightmare world of the narrative.

Every element in the film addresses these issues. The costumes are stark and are as distorted as the environment in silhouette and contour, and in their relationship to the body. The makeup design is highly exaggerated, garish, and grotesque. Hair is essential as a design element, especially Cesare's jet-black, spiky, jagged locks. *The Cabinet of Dr. Caligari* is about the unreality of reality in tumultuous times. It is grounded by the engrossing story. The viewer yearns to know the story of the man on the bench. As it unfolds, the plot envelops the viewer and the expressionist sets come to life to create the environment of the film.

The acting style is as emotionally over the top as the narrative and visual style of *The Cabinet of Dr. Caligari*. The behavior of the characters represents the actors' emotional responses to the expressionistic environment and the situations in which they find themselves. Staging and movement of the actors responds to the hysteria of Caligari's machinations and to the fun-house labyrinth that appears to be the reflection of a crazy mirror, not an orderly village. The characters exist in and respond to the twisted streets, rooms with radically offset windows, doors that are not squared, and chairs that are too tall. Buildings are clustered and interconnected by a cubist take on architecture in the city where they reside, which has been transformed by evil.

From a directorial standpoint, *The Cabinet of Dr. Caligari* is more theatrical than cinematic. There is very little **interscene editing**. With little exception one scene follows another without **intercutting**. A sequence such as the fair is accomplished in two shots. One is a painted set of the street fair and the city in the background. Then a cut to another angle, deep into the fair, reveals Caligari standing in front of a painted tent that displays Cesare. There are some close-ups and isolation shots within a scene, but by and large everything is photographed from a straight-on angle. So the result is like watching a play on a proscenium stage. Camera angles were not employed to change the perspective, move the story editorially, or simulate verisimilitude. All of the temporal dynamics are designed and painted onto and into the set.

By extrapolating from painting and theater, *The Cabinet of Dr. Caligari* brought a pure form of art to the cinema. Robert Wiene's avant-garde experiment became more than a social–political statement or a genre trend.

It has endured because of its attitude. Before the Beats, hippies, punks, heavy metal, industrial music, and cyberpunk, *The Cabinet of Dr. Caligari* was an affront to the classical cinema, a personal film furious with feelings, screaming for recognition. Ultimately, the lessons of *The Cabinet of Dr. Caligari* lay in the notion that film is an expressive art form not only in existence for entertainment or to simulate life as we know it. It is a testament to the artist that fiendish thoughts, dreams, and delusions can reveal another side of human truth.

Notes

1. Fauvism was a European avant-garde painting style developed from the turn of the twentieth century until World War I. It is characterized by an arbitrary use of vivid, non-naturalistic colors utilized for an emotional and decorous impact. The most significant artist of the Fauvist school was Henri Matisse, who employed vivid contrasting colors from 1899 and broke away the traditional descriptive use of color in 1904. Fauvism was influenced by neoimpressionism and inspired the creation of German Expressionism.

2. Max Reinhardt was an innovative German theater director known for his bold use of scenic design, lighting, and visual effects. He became a sensation in 1905 with an imaginative staging of Shakespeare's *A Midsummer Night's Dream*. Reinhart was one of the prime architects of the German expressionist style in theater and film. During the 1920s and early 1930s, he trained many great German directors and actors, including F. W. Murnau, Paul Leni, Ernst Lubitsch, William Dieterle, Otto Preminger, Conrad Veidt, Emil Jannings, Louise Rainer, and Marlene Dietrich. Max Reinhardt immigrated to the United States in 1933 and is considered to be a major influence on twentieth-century drama for his contributions, which expanded the creative influence of the director.

Of Further Interest

Screen

Dr. Mabuse the Gambler
The Golem
The Hands of Orlac
Nosferatu
Waxworks

Read

Expressionism by Wolf Dieter Dube
Haunted Screen: German Expressionism in the German Cinema by Lotte Eisner

From Caligari to Hitler: A Psychological History of the German Film by Siegfried Kracauer
The UFA Story: A History of Germany's Greatest Film Company 1918–1945 by Klaus Kreinmeier
Beyond Caligari: The Films of Robert Wiene by Uli Jung, Walter Schatzberg

11

Classical Hollywood Film Style

□ ◆ □ ◆ □ ◆ □

Casablanca

Hollywood will always be associated with the motion picture. Throughout the twentieth century, the cinema was comprised of many diverse components. Movies have been produced from every spot on the globe. Independent cinema has existed as long as the medium itself. Experimentalists have created works of film art that are shown at museums, lofts, and specialized venues, rather than in local theaters that display commercial fare. To the majority, Hollywood still exists (even though it is largely in name only) in the belief that movies are entertainment for the masses. To the historian, and in fact, Hollywood movies come from a specific period in time. What is now known as the classical Hollywood cinema were movies produced by a studio system that existed from the teens to the early 1960s. Universal, MGM, Paramount, Warner Brothers, and Columbia were self-contained movie factories with production facilities, staff directors, producers, craft departments, and a stable of actors.

In the later half of the 1980s, almost twenty years after the era of the studio system, two landmark books set out to define the cinematic language, rules, conventions, and methods of the films produced by the moguls who invented Hollywood. *The Classical Hollywood Cinema: Film Style & Mode of Production to 1960* by David Bordwell, Janet Staiger, and Kristin Thompson studied a random sample of 100 films from 1916 to 1960, which were analyzed in an objective scientific manner to understand the tendencies of the studio film. *The Genius of the System: Hollywood Filmmaking in the Studio Era* by Thomas Schatz is a detailed factual his-

Left to right: Humphrey Bogart (Rick), Claude Rains (Captain Louis Renault), Paul Henreid (Victor Laszlo), and Ingrid Bergman (Ilsa) in the quintessential Hollywood Studio movie, *Casablanca*. Every shot of the film follows the conventions of the invisible continuity system created and largely sustained by the major Hollywood studios. Courtesy *Photofest*.

tory of how the studios created their productions, and it emphasizes the system itself rather than film directors. Film thought had been dominated by the auteurists (see **auteur theory** in glossary) from the *Cahiers du Cinéma* group that became the French New Wave and their American cousin Andrew Sarris, whose landmark work *The American Cinema: Directors and Directions 1929–1968* prevailed for years with its notion that the director was the author of a film. Bordwell, Staiger, Thompson, and Schatz finally broke that romantic myth. The Hollywood studio film was manufactured and governed by a system that was bigger than any individual, however extraordinary many directors from the era were. The studio system operated from a strict paradigm to manufacture the cinema product. Cereal, soup, and other consumer products are produced through a series of standards and a mode of production set by the leaders of the industries. The films of the classical Hollywood era became art and culture, but they were also a business, and in a business it is the system and control over the product that dictates the end result.

Casablanca (1942), directed by Michael Curtiz (1888–1962), is a beloved movie, enjoyed and worshiped by millions. In polls, it is always ranked very near the top of the greatest films of all time. It is a fine American film but no better than hundreds of others. The mystique of its star, Humphrey Bogart, the luminous beauty of Ingrid Bergman, the stellar supporting cast, the romance of the characters and of the place and time continue to charm and seduce generations of moviegoers. *Casablanca* is not a great American film in the way that *Citizen Kane* (see chapter 13) represents the pinnacle of film art, but it is a pristine, perfect example of the studio film model.

Casablanca begins with the Warner Brothers shield logo and theme music. This was on every film distributed by the studio. The system identified the company that put out the product so the consumer would know what to expect. Each studio had a particular look and story philosophy. *Casablanca,* like the majority of studio films, was photographed in black and white, which allowed the viewer to enter the dream world on the screen. The system believed that black and white was a medium that could pull in the audience without distraction—it was a universe of the tonal scale from black to white, with shades of gray in between.

During the opening titles of *Casablanca,* Max Steiner's (*King Kong* [1933], *The Life of Emile Zola, Bringing Up Baby*) musical **score** sets the tone for exotic intrigue; right on cue, as his credit appears, the music proudly plays "La Marseillaise" to celebrate the glory of the French World War II resistance movement, which will prevail by the conclusion of the film. The system relied heavily on almost wall-to-wall music to indicate setting, mood, and emotion.

At times an unidentified narrator (see **narration** in glossary) sets the scene. In *Casablanca* a deep-throated male voice, one that could have been heard on the radio during the 1940s, explains that during the start of World War II, people traveled to Casablanca in French Morocco in hopes of flying to the freedom of democracy in the United States.

Images set the time and place: a map of Africa under the opening credits, then a slowly turning globe. Don Siegel (editor in the Warner Brothers **montage** department, later the director of *Invasion of the Body Snatchers* [1966], *Dirty Harry*) and editor James Leicester (montages for *Destination Tokyo, Rhapsody in Blue, The Voice of the Turtle*) created a montage to illustrate the historical perspective presented by the narrator. The Hollywood montage, forged by Slavko Vorkapich (montages for *The Good Earth, Mr. Smith Goes to Washington*), Robert Florey (*The Life and Death of 9413—A Hollywood Extra, Sky Scraper Symphony*), and Siegel's work in the Warner Brothers' montage department, helped to create and adapt the highly political aesthetic of Russian cinema to quickly cover the passage of time of a specific event in Hollywood entertainment. Here, immigrants flee their countries as the Nazi machine expands its domination. Superimposed (see **superimposition** in glossary) over an animated map, their journey is traced to Casablanca, as newsreel shots of the masses leaving home in search of freedom unfold. The montage ends with a wide shot of Casablanca. An art-directed building and sky are in the background as the camera pans down to reveal a teeming street of vendors and people from all walks of life. The packed narrow street is designed to look make-believe—the way it is imagined by someone who will never actually go there. Everything in the full frame was put there by the system: costumes, props, architecture, hair, and makeup. The exotic is made palatable for entertainment.

Atmosphere and plot work hand in hand. A French officer gives orders over a phone establishing Casablanca as a place swarming with underground figures arranging illegal transport out of the country. This is transmitted in a single shot followed by a quick-cut action sequence of suspects—a term that gets repeated with variation throughout the film—being rounded up. It ends with a resistance member shot and captured. As he is brought into headquarters, the dramatic music reprises "La Marseillaise."

Gunplay in *Casablanca* is bloodless. People are shot in the tradition of the American Western—there is a loud gunshot and a body responds that it has been hit, but the pain and gravity of gun violence is romanticized.

Casablanca is filled with a large cast of character actors, extras, and specific types. A stodgy, rich couple are pickpocketed by a petty thief who lifts the man's wallet while providing more exposition about what the Nazis are doing in cahoots with French officials. Extras are dressed as various character types from many countries. They play their emotions broadly to communicate that they are desperate to flee the country.

Rick's Café Americain is first established when a plane flies above it and then lands. The crowd in the street watches the plane with anxiety. What is a piece of action also sets up the main location of the film. At the airport there is a huge stone archway that looks like a cutout of the Taj Mahal dome. This motif is used throughout *Casablanca* to establish the exotic locale to American audiences.

Captain Louis Renault (Claude Rains) escorts Nazi chief Major Heinrich Strasser (Conrad Veidt) from the airport. As the contingent marches forward, the scene is structured in several shots to keep it moving editorially. In a European film, this would be one continuous shot as they walk and discuss ridding Casablanca of infiltrators.

Characters are defined by their actions. Throughout the film, Renault is a bad good guy; he is on whatever side the wind blows and like many Hollywood characters he has a tough exterior, a glib mouth, and a good heart. Rick (Humphrey Bogart) appears to be a hard-bitten tough guy but later rescues a young couple and secures their passage to America. Renault tells him he's an old sentimentalist. There is even one two-shot that includes good and bad by framing Ilsa (Ingrid Bergman) on one side and Major Strasser (Conrad Veidt) on the other.

Ingrid Bergman is the source of romance and lost love in *Casablanca*. Her beauty is captivating and is further enhanced by delicate glamour lighting that highlights her hair and eyes. There is a softness to her close-ups that allows the audience to fall in love with her.

The nightclub is a staple of studio musicals, comedies, dramas, and crime films. It is always a place for fun, frivolity, shady business, sexual escapes, and a means of transporting the average Joe and Jane from their humdrum nine-to-five existence to the nightlife. In *Casablanca* Rick's place is all that and is also the hub of intrigue, the meeting place to escape the Nazis. It is filled with colorful characters, heartbreak, the law, the occupying presence, and above all, it is the platform for one of cinema's greatest love stories.

There is a backroom in the club. Hollywood loved the allure of the secret gambling palace; only those who dare can be admitted—those who live by the night and are willing to risk everything. The door is guarded at all times and only Rick allows passage, another one of *Casablanca*'s metaphors for escape to paradise.

Sam (Dooley Wilson) is an African American entertainer who sings popular songs and accompanies himself on the piano. Music intercut (see **intercutting** in glossary) to entertain and as a background to the developing story is a tried-and-true Hollywood convention. As Sam performs, distinct character types at various tables make deals for phony visas. The character actors were well known to audiences by face, and by name to film buffs. The ethnic stereotypes, Sacha (Leonid Kinskey), a Russian bartender, and Carl (S. Z. Sakall), a German waiter, were easily identifiable to the public. And because these stock characters were under contract, they often played the same or similar parts from film to film.

Rick's is filled with glamorous and exotic patrons. In dialogue scenes, the **walla**—background voices to indicate the club's atmosphere—supports the vibrant extras, creating the illusion that this is a real functioning nightclub full of life, where anything can happen.

The introduction of the star is an important moment. A check is handed to Rick but we only see him seated from the neck down. Next, there is an **insert** of his hand signing the check. These inserts were often photographed in an insert or montage department using the hands of another, not the star. Then there is an angle change—the hand gives the employee back the check now signed. A cigarette is picked up and the camera pans to reveal Bogart as Rick. This special treatment is worthy of a star.

When Rick and Ugarte (Peter Lorre) talk at a table, the shifty Ugarte is framed by another variation of the Taj Mahal arch to link him with the region. Rick is an American who secretly, and at times reluctantly, fights for the resistance. There are dark shadow patterns on the wall behind Rick to imply that the mystery of his past trails him. The club is filled with smoke—a rule-book element for a sexy, adventurous environment.

Shots of the club's exterior complete the illusion that the interior is a real place in the viewer's reality. In the background stands a tall building, and on top is a moving wide-beam searchlight—this signifies that Rick and his club are under constant surveillance.

Rick's is a studio set. The lighting does not strictly adhere to the theory of source lighting, in which light is established by the direction of the sun, or practical lamps on the set. The light and shadow patterns are created to shape mood and emotion. Back-, side-, and low-angle lighting result in illumination and shadow patterns that project allure and mystique—not realism. Shadows are part of the visual texture. When Rick takes money out of his safe, we see this action in shadow-play on the wall. The blades of a palm tree dance on the walls in shadows, implying there are plants and trees nearby. Shadows also wrap around characters seen in close-ups and other tightly composed shots in the atmosphere of the environment. An overhead fan in Renault's office casts a web of shadows. Signor Ferrari (Sydney Greenstreet) owns the Blue Parrot and eventually buys the Café Americain when Rick decides he must return to the cause. A black-and-white moving shadow of a parrot on a perch depicts the blue parrot and adds intrigue to the large person (also known as the Fat Man when he played a key role in John Huston's *The Maltese Falcon*, which also starred Bogart). When Rick and Ilsa discuss their past in a dark room, they are covered with slashing lines of light and shadow; they are imprisoned by the fascists and by their ill-fated love. As she tells him what really happened at the train station, they both confront the past and present. They kiss and then there is a cut to the Nazi beacon seeking out and hunting down all traitors.

When two people engage in a conversation, it is covered by the camera in a **shot–reverse shot**. This can be done in single shots of each character or in a form of two-shot called the over-the-shoulder shot, in which the back of the other character is off to the appropriate side when we see the person speaking or reacting. Other angles are employed to keep the flow moving, but the shot–reverse shot principle was the reigning rule for dialogue scenes throughout the studio era. This technique removed the presence of the camera for the audience and implied a total cinematic space where the two characters were actually standing in front of each other.

The studios wanted their movies to be entertainment, so while the plot and subplots are developing, there are moments of comedy. While the camera is following one line of action, it stops to eavesdrop on a comic exchange between a French and a Italian officer. The relationship between Rick and Captain Louis Renault (Claude Rains) is layered with quips that reveal the cynicism of these two men who deep down are very loyal to the cause against the Nazis. For an especially good line there will be a cut to a close-up to highlight the moment.

Before we ever meet Victor Laszlo (Paul Henreid), the famed resistance hero, and his wife, Ilsa Lund, the mysterious beauty who was once going to give her heart to Rick, we have a vivid word picture of them as several characters speak about them. When they finally make their entrance into Rick's, it is a moment of high drama. A series of close-ups of key characters link their reactions to the appearance of these legends.

The screenwriting technique of **backstory**, in which we learn what has happened before the film started, was a popular narrative device during the studio era. Renault tells Rick he knows his past life as a brave resistance fighter. By telling Rick about himself, Rick understands that Renault knows he isn't just a callous nightclub owner who takes advantage of others and uses his place for deals. The viewer is also let in on information not known to everyone. A selected few know when a resistance member is about to be arrested by the Nazis. We hear privileged conversations that give the audience superiority over the majority of those in the club, who are shocked when the arrest occurs minutes after we know it is about to take place.

During the war years, the studios presented a strong antifascist philosophy in their films. Although *Casablanca* is primarily a romantic entertainment, it is filled with characters and subplots concerning the fight against the Nazis during World War II. Victor Laszlo is the voice of democracy. He reignites the flame in Rick, a decent man depressed by loss of love who has become a cynic watching evil take over.

The musical score by Max Steiner is a classic of the era. The music underlines and often indicates the emotional state the audience should be in. There are two categories of film music. As labeled by film and film sound theorists, diegetic sound is sound that organically occurs within the frame. Sam's piano playing and singing, as well as other musical performances in *Casablanca,* is classified as diegetic sound. Nondiegetic sound is not produced within the screen image. This applies to the musical underscore in *Casablanca.* The combination of diegetic and nondiegetic music in the film produces a powerful emotional state that speaks to the romance, memory sense, and patriotic fervor of *Casablanca.* Sam playing the piano and singing in the club is diegetic but often the score later accompanies him. We do not see these musicians, so the effect is a result of combining diegetic and nondiegetic music. "As Time Goes By" is a song that signifies the past romance of Rick and Ilsa, so Steiner constantly refrains this theme. Sometimes the melody is obvious; other times it is almost subconsciously woven into a dramatic underscore. "La Marseillaise" is treated in the same manner. It is played in the opening, it ends the film to signal the triumph of the resistance, and it moves in and out of other musical figures at strategic times in the text. The most dramatic use of the French anthem is when Laszlo rushes to conduct the orchestra as all the French patrons sing their loyalty to drown out the German officers bellowing an ode to their homeland. Music transmits deep-seated feelings about country as the Germans are musically defeated by the proud French voices. The music is responsible for the shifting moods from romance to action to drama. Steiner's score constantly anticipates and influences the slightest variation in emotion as it appears in the narrative.

Casablanca is about memory. The song "As Time Goes By" represents an earlier life in Paris between the lovers Rick and Ilsa. Those memories drive and influence the motivations of both characters. The audience is also allowed to engage in their own memories of life before the threat of World War II. Sam is in charge of this memory device. When he is asked to play the song, he has the power to transport Rick and Ilsa back in time. Once when Sam sings the song, it almost sounds like a recording traveling directly from the soundtrack into our ears; there is only the lightest of background ambience of the club. For Ilsa the memories are tender; for Rick, they bring him great anger, the loneliness of a love lost.

Night brings despair. Rick sits alone in the club, drinking himself into submission. The surveillance beam from across the street pierces the darkness. Sam tries to lighten his boss's mood, but only enduring the pain of the song will do. A **flashback** ensues. We see the happy lovers and learn the backstory of their romance. Life in Paris is depicted with sharper images; the song, now an instrumental theme, plays; newsreel footage of the occupation brings stark reality. We learn how "As Time Goes By" became their song. At a Paris club the two lovers plan to meet and take a train to freedom; Sam is at the piano and plays the tune. When they kiss, the sound of German guns explode. As they embrace they knock over a glass of champagne, a visual symbol for what is to come. It is raining at the train station, another tried-and-true convention for Hollywood drama. Rick waits but Ilsa doesn't arrive. A letter from her is read. The insert shows her handwritten apology in pen. The rain makes the ink run. To the audience this is a representation of Ilsa's tears. A fade to black ends the scene and the pain of Rick's memory of desertion.

The famous last scene takes place at the airport. It is night and there is a dense fog, giving the illusion that we are seeing more than is really there. Rick becomes the hero and gives up the girl so that she can go on to America with her husband, a true hero. In turn, for the first time Rick becomes whole, also a true hero. He is welcomed back to the fight by the tricky Renault. What will happen to these men? A Nazi officer was murdered. Somehow they will both survive. It is the beginning of a beautiful friendship, a metaphor so rich with meaning it could only be in a film made by the Hollywood dream factory, in which a film reinvents itself in meaning to each passing generation and with each viewing, as time goes by.

Of Further Interest

Screen

Bringing Up Baby
Dinner at Eight
The Maltese Falcon
Stagecoach (1939)
Yankee Doodle Dandy

Read

The Classical Hollywood Cinema: Film Style & Mode of Production to 1960 by David Bordwell, Janet Staiger, and Kristin Thompson

The Making of Casablanca: Bogart, Bergman, and World War II by Aljean Harmetz
The Casablanca Companion: The Movie Classic and Its Place in History by Richard E. Osborne
The Casablanca Man: The Cinema of Michael Curtiz by James C. Robinson
The Genius of the System: Hollywood Filmmaking in the Studio Era by Thomas Schatz

12

Surrealism in Cinema

□ ◆ □ ◆ □ ◆ □

Un Chien Andalou

Since the birth of cinema, one form or another of dramatic realism has dominated the content of motion pictures. The traditional principle of visual storytelling is a narrative that unfolds one shot at a time, relating one image to the next in a manner that is considered logical to the audience.

Un Chien Andalou (*An Andalusian Dog*), a sixteen-minute black and white film created in 1928 by Salvador Dali and Luis Buñuel, struck out in a daring, different direction.[1] Dali and Buñuel were deeply involved in the surrealist movement and applied the tenets practiced by painters and writers to *Un Chien Andalou*. Their intention was to shock the audience. They designed a series of images out of their dreams and fantasies that had no specific or cogent meaning to them or to the viewer.

Artists and adventurous cinema-goers were astounded by the medium's ability to adapt to a non-narrative form. Dali and Buñuel interrelated movement to surrealist imagery and experimented with shot-by-shot relationships as well as with scene-by-scene connections that were elusive but, upon multiple viewing, appeared to have an internal, antirepresentational logic.

The images, action, and behavior that comprise *Un Chien Andalou* were developed during a three-day discussion between Dali and Buñuel. The film has recurring images: live ants crawling on the palm of a human hand, graphic black-and-white stripes, and religious garb. Sexual impulses, the repression of religion, the symbolic transference of people and objects through an action, and the viewer as an active witness to the rap-

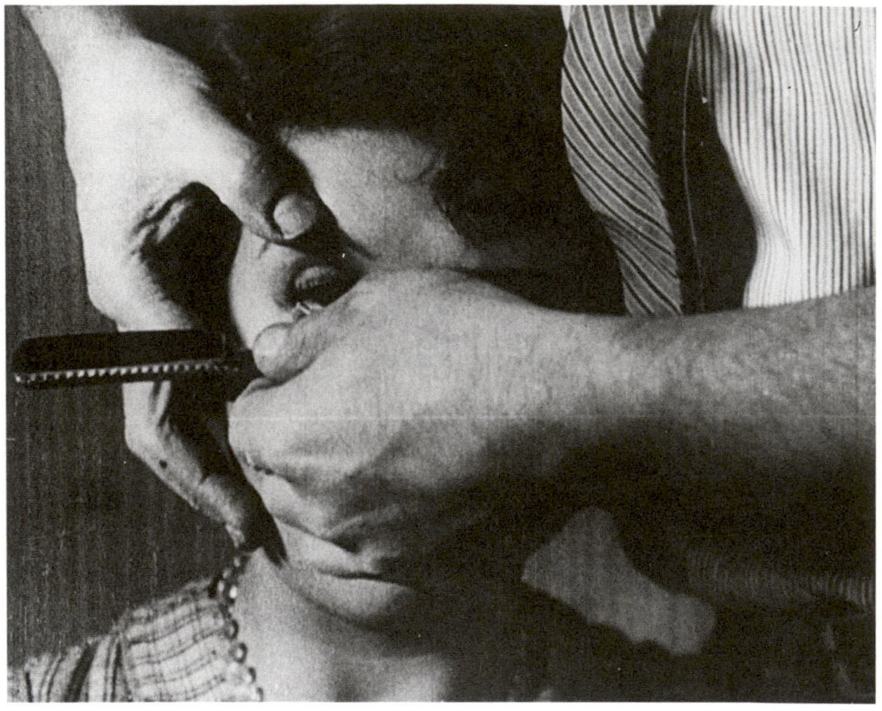

Arguably the most disturbing moment in cinema history. A man slices open the eye of a woman in the Luis Buñuel/Salvador Dali surrealist classic, *Un Chien Andalou*. Courtesy *Photofest*.

idly unfolding events are themes that form the structure of *Un Chien Andalou*. No single image in the film is totally abstract in nature. Each shot contains a recognizable object, human action, place, or thing. Most narratives concern tangible ideas. A traditional narrative presents visual images that illustrate and relate to the content of the text. The quantitative result is a plot that can be discerned by the audience. The intent of the filmmaker has a clear and specific purpose. Plot becomes the means to follow and understand a story. The surrealists had an entirely different agenda. The images in a surrealist painting are identifiable but the context is in opposition to reality.

Luis Buñuel is the first character in *Un Chien Andalou*. He sharpens a straight razor, an ordinary act in itself. It is night, identified by the image of a full moon and a linear-shaped cloud to the right. During these first moments of the film, the shocking signature image appears in extreme close-up. The razor blade slices through a human eye. Life fluid oozes out. Blatant violent acts towards a female victim became commonplace in slasher horror films of the 1970s, but this visual assault continues to scandalize audiences over seventy years since it first appeared on the screen. In the context of the scene, Buñuel goes out onto a veranda after testing the sharpness of the blade and observes the cloud moving toward the moon. Then the act of cruelty occurs and is visually related to the cloud slicing the moon. The shapes relate. Did the man get the idea from the sky, or did his action influence the stellar occurrence? The female victim played by Simone Mareuil appears throughout the film, and there is no further reference or evidence of this specific violence toward her, nor is there conclusive information that what we have seen is a **flashforward** in this film where a sense of time is elusive.

In the next scene a man is wearing the headpiece and habit of a nun (performed by Pierre Batcheff) and rides a bicycle through the streets. Around his neck is a small rectangular handbag with black-and-white vertical stripes. While riding through the street, his **point of view** is **intercut** with views of him riding the bike. A long-held **superimposition** contains the image of him riding as seen from behind. The resultant image enmeshes him in his environment, and from this juxtaposition we can see a shirt over his pants. So he is wearing clothing of both genders and represents a secular and nonsecular being at the same time. A shot of him riding toward the camera **dissolves** into a close-up of the striped pattern from the bag.

The woman reads in her apartment. Her dress sports a black-and-white pattern. She senses the rider, throws down the book, and rushes to the window. The watcher is intercut with the rider and then becomes a witness as he falls in the street. She rushes down to him. Poetic touches are everywhere. The man lies still but the upturned bicycle wheel continues to turn gently. The woman kisses him passionately, and we do not know if he was coming to see her or if he collapsed at her window for a purpose. Again, the stripes of the bag fill the screen and are used as a transition into the woman's apartment, where she is now laying out the man's apparel on the bed as if it were a body. She sits in a chair over it either grieving or waiting for recovery. A collar attached to a broadly striped necktie pops into the shot of the laid-out "remains."

The woman then turns as if sensing a presence outside the door. What appears to be in front of the door in the hall is a man staring at his hand, which is crawling with ants. The woman turns and gets up and it is revealed that the man is not outside but, in fact, is inside the room. The sequence of shots creates this illusion. They are both transfixed on the ants. He looks to her briefly, then back to the stark and shocking image. There is a dissolve to a man's underarm, then a tight shot of a furry texture, then a transition to a man probing a detached hand in the street with a stick. This turns out to be an **iris shot**, and the black area widens to reveal a crowd around him. As a policeman clears the crowd, we realize it is an androgynous-looking woman poking the hand. This theme of what you see is not what you see is the key to Buñuel's strategy. Buñuel's **mise-en-scène** follows the pattern of presenting a recognizable image and then revealing that the context is not what the viewer believed it was. This is a hallmark of the surrealist approach. After several dramatic low-angle shots of the crowd looking down at the hand, there is a shot of the woman and the man at the terrace windows looking down. Buñuel follows traditional principles of **eye-line match** and screen direction. His interscene editing appears to follow Hollywood rules, but the order of shots disorient the viewer and there is little conventional logic in actions and the sequence of events. A police officer picks up the striped bag and gives it to the woman as the two look on from above. In a high-angle **point of view**, the policeman clears the crowd and only the woman remains. Logically there would be a cut to the window to connect the point of view with the character whose view was shown, but Buñuel cuts to another angle of the woman in the street and then to the man staring down. The woman clutches the bag as if it has import to her. Cars speed by her. The man witnesses her being run down by a car; she is left in the street with the bag next to her. The sequence is created in detail with points of view of the rushing car, the woman's face in fear, and the reaction of the witness in the window. A small crowd begins to form around her.

Inside the apartment the man and woman react. Suddenly, the man becomes sexually aroused and stalks her around the room as a tango plays on the soundtrack. They move up and down against a wall. He grabs her breasts and fondles them. She fights him off and then submits. His hands on her clothed breasts dissolve to his hands fondling her naked breasts. A low-angle close-up shows him in a hyperecstatic state and a bloody drool leaks out of his mouth. As he continues to fondle her naked breasts, they dissolve into her naked buttocks. She finally gets away from him and they chase through the room, which is crowded with furniture structured by box shapes. She threatens him with an axe. After a sequence of intercutting their reactions, two ropes hauling two grand pianos with a dead animal head on top of them weigh him down. Two priests attached to the ropes are also part of this burden. The man pulls this bizarre rig to get closer to the woman, who can be seen in the corner of the room. This sequence is the most outrageous in *Un Chien Andalou* because the pianos, priests, and dead animal are totally incongruous. The woman escapes and traps the man's hand in the door. Again ants crawl all over it. A significant meaning appears to be implied here, but Buñuel and Dali do not provide any answers, only symbols that are not intended to render meaning. Now the man in the nun outfit is lying on the bed as if laid out for death. He is alive and the woman's attention shifts to him. Another man comes to the door and rings the bell. The man in bed turns and reacts, but the shot in between is of two arms coming through holes in a panel and shaking a cocktail shaker. The image is not part of a montage logically connected to the scene; rather, it is an abstract representation of a sound that should occur in this situation. Did the pressing of the bell coincide with the shaker but we never see what this is connected to? Again, Buñuel is the devilish surrealist interpositioning images to create surprise and a delirious chain of events. The woman answers the bell and the well-dressed hatted man charges up to the bed, assaults the man, strips him of the religious garb, and throws the articles out of the window piece by piece. His checkered suit is graphically related to many of the other design elements, including a nearby chair made of a frame shaped liked boxes. The man from the bed is forced up against a wall where a tennis racket hangs. The other man, who may be the same actor, walks in slow motion via a change in the camera speed, to a desk. He takes a handwritten journal, hands it to his captor, then continually shakes his head in displeasure and walks away as the camera again records slow motion. The two books in the captive's hands vanish and two pistols appear instead. He shoots the man, in effect killing himself. The victim falls in the apartment but lands in a field on the naked body of the woman, now seated in the foliage. His body is motionless and she disappears from the shot. As in an earlier sequence, people come out and surround the body. Two men walking by are stopped for help but are indifferent and continue their stroll. As the group takes care of the body, the two men walk in and stand away from the group as it carries off the man who has been shot. In a large expanse of the woods, the group is part of a procession led and backed by the two men as the corpse is carried. Fade to black.

The tango music is back. The woman walks into the apartment and sees a small butterfly on the wall. Through intercutting and dissolves, it grows larger and the view becomes a tight detail. The man appears in the room and wipes his mouth off his face. The woman applies lipstick and her underarm hair appears below his mouth as a beard. She sticks out her tongue at him in anger and leaves the apartment. As she stands in the hall in front of the closed door, wind blows her hair. A cut to her point of view reveals another man standing on a beach. She runs from the hall shot into the beach shot. He shows her his watch. They kiss and walk off down the beach in what seems to be a classic Hollywood happy-ending shot, but the camera then picks them up from a reverse angle as they continue to walk as lovers. They find the articles of clothing from the early nun/man scenes. They kiss and walk off again as if now this will be the happy-ending shot. A black card appears that reads "In Spring." The final shot of *Un Chien Andalou* reveals the man and woman lifeless, buried to their waists in sand.

It would be all too simple to impose meaning on the symbols and recurring themes of *Un Chien Andalou.* The filmmakers present death and reincarnation, or reappearance, as an ongoing theme. Gender bending is represented by the man dressed as a nun, the man who is revealed to be a woman, and the transference of the woman's underarm hair to the man's beard. The crowds who gather after each occurrence indicate a fascination with accidents and death. *Un Chien Andalou* also breaks down environmental boundaries. Transitions are eliminated so the characters can be outside and then inside within a cut. The communication between **shot–reverse shot** is devoid of traditional logic. Buñuel restructures this cinematic principle to refashion reality. Viewers expect one shot to lead to a next, but their sense of logic is controlled by the surrealist code to defy rational explanations.

Un Chien Andalou is a landmark of alternate cinema. Dreams and fantasies become the content. It was the beginning of Buñuel's long and brilliant career. With Surrealism as his method, the director savaged sexual mores, organized religion, and social codes. *Un Chien Andalou* has been inspiring film students since the 1960s. What Dali and Buñuel achieved is reflected in the careers of David Lynch, Tim Burton, and David Cronenberg. *Un Chien Andalou* is more than just a provocative film short to be programmed before the main event. It is a significant work of art, perfect in the shadow world it creates and magical in its use of cinematic grammar, which was never quite the same after its appearance.

Notes

1. Salvador Dali (1904–1989) was a Spanish painter whose flamboyant personal style and gift for self-promotion made him the most famous and recognized artist in the surrealist movement. His work employed a meticulous classical technique to create images in a dreamlike, hallucinatory manner. Among his most celebrated works are sexual subjects featuring his muse—his wife Gala. After collaborating

with Buñuel on *Un Chien Andalou,* the two men created *L'Âge d'or* (1930). Dali also contributed a dream sequence to the Alfred Hitchcock production of *Spellbound.*

Of Further Interest

Screen

L'Âge d'or
Ballet mécanique
The Blood of a Poet
Brazil
Wild at Heart

Read

Luis Buñuel: A Critical Biography by Francisco Aranda
What is Surrealism? by André Breton
My Last Sigh: The Autobiography of Luis Buñuel by Luis Buñuel
An Unspeakable Betrayal: Selected Writings of Luis Buñuel by Luis Buñuel
Dada and Surrealist Film by Rudolf E. Kuenzli

The Authorial Voice

□ ◆ □ ◆ □ ◆ □

Citizen Kane

Citizen Kane (1941) might just be the great American movie of the twentieth century. This ambitious and innovative allegory, directed by Orson Welles (1915–1985) when he was only twenty-six years old, forged a bold, new cinematic language to atomize the life of Charles Foster Kane, a man who had, and then lost, everything because he could only offer or receive love on his own terms.

Citizen Kane opens with the final moments in the life of Charles Foster Kane (Orson Welles) and provides a clue to the mystery of why his flamboyant and extravagant life ended in loneliness. Through a series of **dissolves** the camera climbs up a number of fences that seclude a castlelike mansion set back on a lofty hill. As images of the massive estate slowly continue to **fade in** and **fade out** of one another, a private zoo, canal, bridge, and golf course are revealed. In the night fog, one gothic window is illuminated. The changing views get ever closer; then suddenly the light is extinguished. Now inside a bedroom, snowflakes pass through the air, a glass globe depicting a winter home setting is dropped out of a dying hand. The man's lips fill the screen as he utters his final words—"Rosebud."

"News on the March," a self-contained sequence, meticulously follows the form and style of a "March of Time" newsreel segment.[1] The movie news obituary of Charles Foster Kane traces the creation and grandeur of his Xanadu manor, the global impact of his passing, his rise as a newspaper tycoon, the empire he built, the origin of his fortune and political

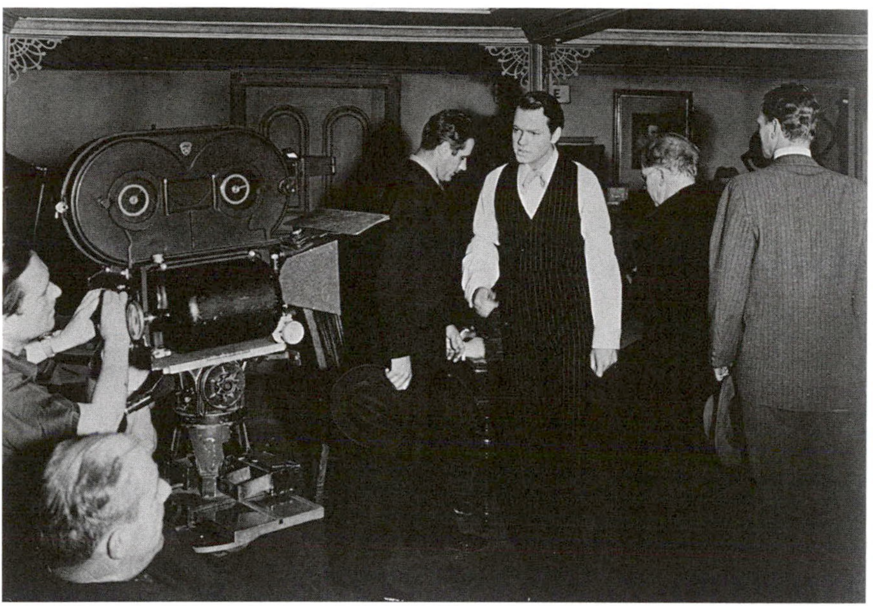

Orson Welles addresses his cinematographer Gregg Toland (directly behind camera) on the set of *Citizen Kane*. Although from the theater and radio productions, the young Welles understood the potential of the camera and the artistry of the cinematographer as the two men innovated the American cinema with Welles' motion picture directorial debut. Courtesy *Photofest*.

sway, his personal and private life, a failed run for governor, the decline during the Great Depression, old age, and, finally, isolation without intimacy. A resonant announcer narrates (see **narration** in glossary) with flowery prose, fashioning Kane as larger than life. Shots are quickly wiped off (see **wipe** in glossary), replaced by the next. The dissolve, iris (see **iris shot** in glossary), fade-in and out of black transitions—all structure and maintain the sequence at a brisk pace. Title cards and animated maps display information, multiplying the scope of Kane's influence. Footage is over- and underexposed and scratched to achieve archival authenticity.

The sound of the closing musical fanfare grinds to a halt. A group of media men in a private screening room have been watching an incomplete version of an enigmatic life. Bright beams of light stream in from the projection room portals and paint the men in degrees of shadow and silhouette. The boss wants to know what made Kane tick. Their voices blare and overlap in the confined space. He assigns Thompson (William Alland), one of his reporters, to learn the significance of Kane's last words.

The inquiry begins at a nightclub owned by Susan Alexander (Dorothy Comingore), the second Mrs. Kane. During a lightning storm, the camera travels over a roof, then looks down through a rain-drenched skylight at the inebriated and despondent young woman. She refuses to talk to Thompson, who throughout the film is photographically and metaphorically in the dark about the key to Kane's psyche.

The memorial library of Kane's guardian, Walter P. Thatcher (George Coulouris), features large vaulting chambers emphasized by cinematographer Gregg Toland's (*Wuthering Heights* [1939], *The Grapes of Wrath, The Long Voyage Home*) masterly use of **deep-focus photography**.[2] This technique is applied all through *Citizen Kane* to sharply situate Kane and his minions in relationship to his grand environment. After the stern curator's voice booms through the air, Thompson reads Thatcher's diary, as a heavenly shaft of light illuminates the pages. As the lens dances across Thatcher's prose remembrance of when he first met Kane as a boy, there is a dissolve to Charles playing with his sled in the snow in 1871.

The scene in which Thatcher arrives at Mrs. Kane's boarding house in Colorado is choreographed in three distinctive takes. Charles continues to frolic in the snow. The camera pulls back to reveal the mother (Agnes Moorehead), and Thatcher arguing with the father (Harry Shannon) about sending the boy off for a better life now that Mrs. Kane has inherited a large fortune. After signing the papers at the opposite end of the room, the camera follows her back to the window, which she opens. There is a cut to Mrs. Kane's face as she looks out at her son. As the adults leave the building to explain the situation to the boy, the camera glides back as they talk out in the snow. Charles takes an immediate dislike to Thatcher. He is disobedient, knocking him to the ground with his sleigh. The father swings at the boy to administer corporeal punishment, but the child is protected by his mother. The final shot pans down from a close-up of Mrs. Kane to the defiant child. She has justified her decision.

During a succession of short one-take scenes from Thatcher's perspective, Charles grows up and rejects his blue chip holdings to run a muckraking newspaper that attacks the now exguardian's interests. Thatcher's power over Charles is exaggerated by first an extreme low, then later a high angle. In a closing long take, the adult Kane stands to rise over Thatcher, signifying an exchange of authority.

The Thatcher memories end in 1929. From a fixed, deep-focus camera angle, Kane is told that his newspaper company is bust due to the stock market crash. As they are positioned on opposite sides of the frame, Charles tells the old man that he always wanted to be everything the banker hated.

Next Thompson visits Mr. Bernstein (Everett Sloan), Kane's loyal general manager, who sits behind his desk in a high-back chair. On the wall a large portrait of Kane hangs above a blazing fireplace. Memory and reflection are significant themes in *Citizen Kane*. The camera pushes in on Bernstein as he recalls seeing a girl in a white dress carrying a white parasol back in 1896, a memory that has never left his mind. As he takes himself back in time, his face is reflected in the shiny top of his desk.

Bernstein tells Thompson about the early days at the *Inquirer*. This flashback covers how Kane took over as publisher and turned the staid office into the nexus of exposé journalism. Perry Ferguson's (*The Best Years of Our Lives, The Stranger* [1946], *The Secret Life of Walter Mitty*) art direction for this set included a full ceiling that added to the verisimilitude while providing another dimension of spatial delineation. As the first issue is put to bed, Kane swears to "A Declaration of Principles," which he personally signs for the front page, proclaiming his commitment to stand up against all special interests for the right of every decent citizen to read an honest newspaper.

The growth of the *Inquirer* is visualized by a shot of Kane admiring a framed group photograph of the world's greatest newspaper staff, who work for his competition the *Examiner*. The camera pushes in tight until only the men can be seen. Kane then walks past them. It is now six years later and they work for the *Inquirer*. A new portrait is snapped, the men come to life, and a celebration begins.

The reporter interviews Jedediah Leland (Joseph Cotten), a former old friend and associate of Kane now living in a hospital. His first **flashback** depicts the dissolution of Kane's marriage to Emily Monroe Norton (Ruth Warrick), the niece of the president of the United States. In just six brief vignettes at the breakfast table, they progress from newlywed lovebirds to two people who no longer speak to each other. They begin seated close together, but by the last installment they are on opposite ends of the long table. Their talk concerns Charles spending too much time at the *Inquirer* and his political attacks on Emily's uncle. At first nothing comes between them, but with each change of scene, flowers, table settings, and finally the newspaper itself block off communication as both read silently—he the *Inquirer*, she the *Chronicle*.

The film returns back to the hospital, and Leland introduces the flashback of how Kane met Susan Alexander through her throbbing toothache. After he literally charms the pain out of existence, Kane is captured by her vocal serenade.

Kane runs for governor against party boss Jim Gettys (Ray Collins). During a political rally, Kane gives a fiery oratory against his opponent as he stands at a podium in a giant hall filled with people. Behind him is a massive poster portrait with KANE written on top. The dynamic proportionality and thunderous properties of his voice reverberating in the space demonstrate Kane's limitless ambition, which is shattered by a scandal that finishes his marriage and gubernatorial desires.

Kane marries Susan, builds an opera house, and puts all of his energy into making her a singing star. The first of two versions of her debut is shown from the front, looking at her on stage. As she croons weakly, the view rises straight up above the stage, her sour voice gradually evaporating. We travel high into the rafters where two stagehands watch and listen in disdain. Silently one turns to the other and holds his nose to indicate his opinion—she stinks.[3]

Leland, now the drama critic of the Chicago office, has fallen asleep over his typewriter, where he has begun to write a devastatingly bad notice of Susan's performance. Charles and Leland have not spoken in years. To prove his integrity, Kane finishes the review as Leland intended, signified by a micro-close-up of him typing the word "weak" a letter at a time, the metal typeface banging the message with each stroke. The incident terminates Leland's job and his relationship with Kane. Welles, with his editor Robert Wise (*The Hunchback of Notre Dame* [1939], *The Devil and Daniel Webster, The Magnificent Ambersons* [1942]), who went on to become a notable director on his own, then returns to the hospital. On the right wall Kane continues to type Leland's critical attack on Susan; left of the frame the elderly Leland concludes his story to Thompson. The memory image fades into a dark blank wall returning to present time.

Thompson returns to Susan's club where she consents to an interview. Her flashback portrays Kane's persistence in turning Susan into a singing success at any cost. The opening night performance is presented for the second time, now from Susan's perspective on stage looking directly out to the audience. Here we see how Kane takes her failings personally. He is humiliated at the negative reception. Standing in the dark he applauds wildly to generate praise to no avail. As the lights come up, he is mortified to be the only one still clapping.

When Susan asserts herself against continuing a singing career, Kane stands over her, seated on the floor. An extreme high-angle shot looking down at Susan in fear finds her cast in his long, dark shadow. A Hollywood studio-style **montage** in the Slavko Vorkapich tradition records the strain on Susan as she is forced to perform.[4] The recurring image of a stage light bulb and the multilayering of her thin voice indicate a breakdown, as the light and singing go out as if turned off by a switch.

In the next scene a spoon in a glass and an open bottle of medicine are in sharp focus in the foreground. Midrange, Susan lies in bed disheveled and breathing heavily in soft focus. In the background is a locked door that Kane and a servant ultimately break open to find her overdosed in a suicide attempt; this is in deep focus. The dynamics of this shot mystified viewers for years until it was revealed that the foreground was photographed separately and then printed along with the shot of Susan and Kane. This image presents information, a psychological state, and action concurrently.

Susan recovers and retires from opera to sit in Xanadu's majestic main room passing time assembling one giant jigsaw puzzle after another. This indicates the slow passage of time and serves as a metaphor for the many pieces of Kane's life that Thompson and the viewer try to put together to learn the intent of his existence.

On a systematically planned outdoor excursion, Susan bitterly complains to Kane that he only loves himself. As he slaps her face, the party outside their tent ends abruptly with the sound of a woman screaming in terror. In the next scene Susan leaves Kane, walking out of his castle as he stands helplessly alone. Back in the club, morning has broken.

Finally Thompson talks to Raymond (Paul Stewart), Kane's cynical butler. This flashback begins with a startling close-up image of a cockatoo. The bird shrieks its cry as in the background Susan walks out on Kane. Raymond looks on as she resolutely leaves the nest.

Back in Susan's room, the elderly Kane is in a fury. He trudges from wall to wall, destroying everything in his path until he comes upon the glass ball novelty with the snowy homestead scene he held with his last breath in the opening scene. Kane is reduced to tears and utters "Rosebud." He walks past Raymond and the staff, and alone he slowly moves through a rococo hall where his reflection is repeated to infinity in a huge mirror. This last image of Kane reminds us that he was many men to many people but absolutely known only to himself.

Thompson and his staff complete the catalog of the mountains of statues and keepsakes from Kane's life. At the end of his search, Thompson says he has learned very little about Kane, surmising that "Rosebud" may have been something that the man who owned everything lost. He concludes that no one word can sum up a man's life.

A crane shot travels over Kane's material possessions and slowly moves in on the sled he had as a boy. As it is burns in a furnace, we see the name Rosebud. Charles Foster Kane lost his childhood and the constant presence of his mother's love. The last clue burns up in smoke—we are again outside the gates of Xanadu looking at the memorial to a man who never really had anything because he lost the gift of unconditional maternal love.

Orson Welles had many other significant collaborators on *Citizen Kane*, including screenwriter Herman J. Mankiewicz (*Dinner at Eight, The Pride of the Yankees, The Enchanted Cottage*), sound designer James Stewart (*The Curse of the Cat People, Back to Bataan, Duel in the Sun*), and composer Bernard Herrmann (*Vertigo, Psycho, Taxi Driver*); but this great film is the vision of one man.[5] *Citizen Kane* is a testament to what a director can accomplish with complete artistic control and the necessary resources. *Citizen Kane* defines the role of the film director as a force of nature who can harness the talents of others, the crafts, a narrative, and the machinery necessary for the medium, and come out the other end with a work larger than the mere sum of its parts.

Notes

1. Created by producer–director Louis de Rochemont and Roy E. Larsen of Time, Inc., *The March of Time* was a newsreel unit that utilized documentary and cinematic recreation techniques to present news and entertainment items to movie audiences. Each edition, delivered to theaters once a month from 1935 to 1951, employed bravado showmanship as a deep-voiced narrator led the viewer quickly through the news, illustrated with maps, diagrams, and text. This influential cinema series shaped political views editorializing on impacting events such as the Great Depression and controversial figures of World War II such as Adolf Hitler, Benito Mussolini, and Japan's Tojo.

2. Deep-focus photography produces images with a depth of field that allows the foreground, middleground, and background in sharp focus. This style of cinematography requires a smaller aperture and greater amounts of light than in traditional shallow focus shots. The aesthetic results of deep-focus photography are a realistic relationship between the scene and the viewer that allows the eye to participate in exploring the planes of design and action within the shot. There is less reliance on editing and more emphasis on composition, staging, and movement within the frame.

3. This was long believed to be a single continuous shot that began on the opera stage and then craned upward above the stage into the rafters and eventually to a catwalk where the two workmen were standing. Scholarship by Robert L. Carringer in *The Making of Citizen Kane* and by others revealed this was a visual effects shot. An optical printer was employed to join shots made on separate sets to create the illusion of a single continuous upward camera movement.

4. Slavko Vorkapich was an editor, producer, screenwriter, art director, special effects creator, cinematographer, theorist, and educator born in Yugoslavia who became a noted expert in montage. He worked for MGM, Columbia, RKO, and Paramount studios, where he created specific montage sequences for films that include *Viva Villa!*, *The Good Earth*, *Maytime*, *Boys Town*, *Mr. Smith Goes to Washington*, and *Meet John Doe*.

5. In a controversial essay first published in *The New Yorker* and later in *The Citizen Kane Book*, film critic Pauline Kael stated that much of the credit for the story, characters, and structure of *Citizen Kane* belonged not to Orson Welles but to Herman J. Mankiewicz, whom she felt, after examining the original material, created many of the film's innovative narrative elements in the screenplay.

Of Further Interest

Screen

Blood Simple
Dr. Strangelove or: How I Learned to Stop Worrying and Love the Bomb
The Magnificent Ambersons
Nixon
Velvet Goldmine

Read

Citizen Welles: A Biography of Orson Welles by Frank Brady
The Making of Citizen Kane by Robert L. Carringer
The Citizen Kane Book: Raising Kane by Pauline Kael
Orson Welles: A Biography by Barbara Leaming
Citizen Kane: The Fiftieth Anniversary Album by Harlan Lebo

Shot Structure

□ ◆ □ ◆ □ ◆ □

The Crowd

Why is the black-and-white silent film *The Crowd* still as relevant and vital today as it was at its original release in 1928? Inspired by early German expressionist films (see chapter 10) and the reality of a competitive America ripe with opportunity, King Vidor (1894–1982) set out to tell a story of a couple dealing with love, the responsibilities of marriage, and finding a place in the world. The cycle of life never changes. Audiences may want to be entertained, but longevity lies in the cinematic ability to portray the human condition with honesty and compassion, and without pretense.

John (James Murray) and Mary (Eleanor Boardman) meet, fall in love at first sight, marry, and have two children. Mary transforms from a flapper to wife and mother. John remains a happy-go-lucky dreamer who likes to play his ukulele and think up catchy ad slogans. At his job, and in the bustling streets of New York City, John is just one in a crowd, but idealism nurtures his spirit. After entering a jingle contest, John wins a cash prize. As the ecstatic couple share their joy, tragedy befalls them when a truck fatally strikes down their little girl (Alice Mildred Puter) as she runs across the street toward them. Depressed, John quits his job and eventually loses Mary's confidence. John sets out to jump into the path of an oncoming train, but the love and faith of his son (Freddie Burke Frederick) renew his drive. He gets a job and returns to Mary, who is in the process of leaving him. Their love match is rekindled and their little

Director King Vidor creates a visual metaphor that reflects the major theme of *The Crowd*. His hero John Sims is just-one-of-the-crowd swept up in the anonymity of the New York City experience. Courtesy *Photofest*.

family goes to the theater, where they laugh and again become part of the crowd.

King Vidor was a master of visual storytelling. He understood that cinema may go beyond the narrative accumulation of sequential images. An individual shot unit can contain an inner structure that communicates the themes and objectives of the story. Drawing on a craft honed throughout the silent film era, Vidor relied on images, cinematic poetry, and the force of emotion to communicate the veritable and compassionate narrative of *The Crowd*. Shooting on location, often with hidden cameras that allowed the actual multitudes of New York to people the background action, Vidor captured the vitality of the city.

A production design technique called **forced perspective** places John in environments that emphasize the vulnerability of an individual struggling to find his way in a vast modern world. As a boy, John climbs a long, steep stairway as he learns of the untimely death of his father, who had promised to protect and nurture him so he could have every advantage toward success. The image is a metaphor concerning the mountains John will have to climb during his life.

Following dramatic low and **canted angles** of the skyscraper where John spends his menial workday, the camera makes a slow and mighty climb up the massive structure until it reaches a high series of windows. A **dissolve** continues the search for John's place in the towering city as the camera now moves down from an extreme high view above neat rows of desks that reach beyond the frame until we reach desk number 137, where he writes in a large ledger book. We are again reminded that he is just one in a crowd.

Later on the floor of a hospital where his first child, a son, is about to be born, John stands in front of two long hallways that angle back from the right and left of a center wall with a large door. This design pinpoints John on the long crossroad to the next stage of his life, fatherhood. He is led through the door into the maternity ward as the camera slowly dollies behind him. The room is immense with a nurse's desk and a long row of white beds with new mothers. The dramatic camera movement through this wide and deep space symbolizes the enormity of John's new and awesome responsibility.

In contrast to John as an infinitesimal being in a controlling metropolis, Mary keeps a small but cozy home in the young family's apartment. The interior is gray and plain but comfortable. The scale of this personal space gives John his proper place, where he, Mary, and his children are centered. An elevated subway train travels outside their window to remind the viewer of the down-market monetary value of the Sims's station in city life, but their love and Mary's faith in John's daydream of a future keeps them content.

When hard times fall, the environment around John and Mary's home becomes meager and dilapidated, a symbol of John's unemployment and Mary's lost assurance in her husband. After she walks out on him, John's broken figure is positioned on the side of the frame; thus the negative space of the empty room represents his feelings of separation.

The text of *The Crowd* is realistic. The story doesn't have a basis in actual events, but it draws on the verisimilitude of urban existence of its time. In the film's first act, Vidor establishes the vaulting architecture of New York City and the brisk, populous character of the inhabitants by placing his camera, character, and story within verifiable locations. This is not a Hollywood fantasy or melodrama set in a New York created on an L.A. soundstage. *The Crowd* is as authentic as a **nonfiction film** in depicting the physical milieu; Vidor is a technician and an artist. The expressionistic treatment is applied when the director wants the viewer to see John and Mary in a poetic context that utilizes artistic exaggeration and visual metaphor for philosophic purpose. For King Vidor, *The Crowd* is not a slice of life—it is life as he sees it. The people who embody the crowd are individuals who struggle to make a life in which they are happy, self-productive, and loved. To achieve his vision, Vidor married the populist and expressionist styles that would later inspire the postwar style of **Italian neorealism**, depicted in Vittorio De Sica's *The Bicycle Thief* (see chapter 6), and movies that took a candid look at American life like Billy Wilder's *The Apartment*.

A naturalistic methodology was exercised in casting *The Crowd* and for the performance style and manner in which the actors were directed. Vidor knew instinctively that a recognizable movie star would shatter the sense of realism set up in the story and the visualization approach he was creating. For the role of John Sims, Vidor searched for a common man who reflected the carefree naiveté of his character. He eventually ran into James Murray, an extra, who the director immediately knew was right for the part. After Murray was convinced that Vidor was serious about putting an unknown actor in the lead role, Murray didn't so much act the part as be who audiences would identify as one of their own. His remarkable performance sustains John's childlike innocence and relies on expression and gesture to communicate the character's sincerity.[1]

For Mary, John's loving and supportive wife, Vidor cast his then spouse, the beautiful movie actress Eleanor Boardman. To transform into Mary, Boardman abandoned the glamour image and melodrama acting style of the time. Vidor was aware that the actress had a tendency to walk through a part if she wasn't engaged in the character, but Boardman developed Mary into an emotionally real woman that reflected the reality of the situation with which she was confronted.

Design, composition, and **montage** create the external mood of *The Crowd*. Vidor brought all his cinematic powers to dramatically present the environmental powers that surround and engulf John and Mary. But he concentrated on the honesty of his actors to transmit the humanity necessary to engage the audience in a story that was devoid of the dramatic artifice they expected when they visited the picture show.

The relationship of John and Mary as they react to each other and their circumstances are captured on film in a direct manner. Photographed in close shots without overtly dramatic lighting, angles, or camera movement, Vidor allows Murray and Boardman to create and project honest emotions that communicate straight to the audience without undue cinematic interference. The editing emphasizes how the personality and behavior of John and Mary influence each other by establishing patterns of **shot–reverse shot** that capture the nuances of their development from first date to their lives as husband and wife. The most effective emotional moments are achieved by holding the camera on the actors as they react to events that have great impact on their lives. As John and Mary go from elation to anguish when they call from out of a window to their children with the good news of the contest prize, which then results in their daughter's fatal accident, the emphasis is not on what they see but on how it affects their emotional state. When Mary deals with John storming out of the house after an argument, a long take allows the viewer to watch as she goes through a series of specific emotions before running to him to resolve the issue. When John is about to jump to his death out of despair, it is the gut-wrenching look on his face that moves the audience more than simply the juxtaposition of this shot with an angle of the oncoming train. The **intercutting** heightens the drama, but it is the honesty of Murray's performance that emphasizes John's dire situation.

Vidor takes great advantage in visualizing the metaphor of the constant presence of the crowd that reminds John of the daunting competition he must contend with and ultimately accept to become a complete and gratified person. The crowd is there when his father dies, at work, when he courts Mary, as he carries the lifeless body of his daughter, when he is unemployed, and finally as he joins them in laughter at the theater as the camera pulls back in the final shot, signifying that John now accepts his lot in life.

The ironies presented by the crowd humble John. To impress Mary on their first date, he ridicules a man in a clown costume earning a living as a walking advertisement. When he can not get in the long employment lines, he vigorously pursues that very job. The image of John in the same role as the one he once mocked is ironic, sad, and ultimately rewarding because it propels him to accept the realities that frustrate his quest for happiness.

At the beginning of a century that transformed America into a melting pot, *The Crowd* is a populist story fueled by the spirit of the immigrant. John was born in America, but Vidor stages two scenes on a boat to relate his character to those who came to the country from other lands to stake their claim for democracy. The first shows John traveling by ferry to Manhattan as a passenger tells him of the challenges the city holds for the everyman. The second is on a company excursion, when John must tell Mary he has quit his job. The passengers waving from portholes bring to mind the jubilation of freedom in immigrant faces. Mary's unconditional faith in John reminds us of the determination expressed by those committed to a new life in a new world. *The Crowd* is a film empowered by the timeless themes that represent the American dream.

Notes

1. After *The Crowd,* James Murray appeared in a few films, but because of chronic alcoholism, he experienced a sharp decline in his acting career. He died in 1936 at the age of thirty-five, when he either jumped or fell into the Hudson River.

Of Further Interest

Screen

The Big Parade
M (1931)
Modern Times
Our Daily Bread
Sunrise

Read

King Vidor, American by Raymond Durgnat and Scott Simmon
King Vidor: A Director's Guild of America Oral History, interview by Nancy Dowd and David Shepard
On Film Making by King Vidor
A Tree is a Tree: An Autobiography by King Vidor
The Visual Story: Seeing the Structure of Film, TV, and New Media by Bruce Block

Thematic Unity

□ ◆ □ ◆ □ ◆ □

The Decalogue

Polish film director Krzysztof Kieślowski (1941–1996) created these ten films, each running between fifty-three and fifty-eight minutes, for television. Taken literally, this cinematic masterwork documents the Bible's Ten Commandments translated to contemporary settings. Each film deals in order with sin delivered as a commandment to Moses by God on a stone tablet. The commandments are presented in a context that is far from obvious or simplistic. Kieślowski's reading of the commandments is less representative of the church's scholarly perspective and is more the view of a moralist who truly understands that ethical quandaries test human character and an individual's commitment to maintaining a spiritual state.

The varied circumstances that confront the characters in *The Decalogue* are so compelling, it is often difficult to recognize which commandment is being examined. And that is Kieślowski's point—a rule is meaningless unless it intersects with life in progress. The complications and suffering these sins can generate is illuminated through the narrative and is revealed in a contemporary perspective. Like a bad seed, these moral dilemmas start small and germinate into a plethora of consequences.

The consistency with which Kieślowski has conceived and executed this massive work is remarkable. The story structure consists of an immediate hard cut from black. Each episode has commonalities: some form of a prologue, a set of characters, a sense of place, and an enigma. The films begin slowly and reveal a little information at a time. Often a situ-

Dorota (Krystyna) plays violin in an orchestra recital in *Decalogue II*, Krzysztof Kieślowski's cinematic interpretation of the commandment "Thou shalt not take the name of the lord thy God in Vain." Dorota, the wife of a critically ill man, faces a moral dilemma in not knowing if her husband will live or die. Dorota is pregnant with another man's child. If the husband will live, she will get an abortion. If he is to die, she will give birth and move forward to a new life with the other man. Courtesy *Photofest*.

ation is set up, but the exact interrelationship of the characters is not immediately evident. This allows for a focus on the ethical issues, rather than textual ideas. The majority of the characters seem to live in the same housing complex. There are many shots taken from the **point of view** of someone standing at a window looking out to the grounds and beyond. This aesthetic choice functions on many levels. It is a practical view that allows the camera to see what is outside a protagonist's window and the events that occur in the street. It both establishes a point of view of the characters and pinpoints their location in the high rise. Exterior shots link with this spot when another character is looking up to their windows. Characters are photographed at a window, and at times the camera becomes their eyes looking out at their world.

Each *Decalogue* episode builds in complexity on the basis of an action that leads to reactions and a multitude of responses that culminate in a moral issue with no easy answers and an abundance of irony. Each story is a progression. There is no turning back or Hollywood happy ending. None of these films end when the viewer assumes they have concluded. Breaking a commandent sets many emotions and feelings in play. To come to a conclusion, Kieślowski goes down all paths after **intercutting** several strands of narrative interactions. Each film ends with a fade to black, almost always on a face.

The color schemes of the films are cool, desaturated (see **desaturation** in glossary), and contain a limited tonal **color palette**. Close-ups that capture deeply felt emotions are abundant as are full shots with clarity and detail that relate the character to the environment. Kieślowski is economical—his camera is always where it needs to be for the story. **Interscene editing** is dictated by the characters and their actions. The music by Zbigniew Preisner (*To Kill a Priest, The Double Life of Veronique, Damage*) underscores emotion, not action. This is emotional and psychological, not thematic, music.

Other consistencies in *The Decalogue* are areas of cultural significance. All of the films are based in Poland. Knowledge of the country's social and political history enhances an understanding of the work, but the human desires, strengths, and frailties are universal. There are many rituals that define the European sensibility behind the stories. Preparing water for tea or coffee is an act that appears in the majority of the films. It often begins a day or marks the return to the home. Drinking coffee has a pure significance in this culture. It is a beverage drunk over casual or serious conversation, almost always served in a glass, so we can see the brown liquid is rich with tradition. Cigarettes are constantly lit and smoked but do not infer sexiness as in American films. They are ingrained in the lifestyle. Often they have a symbolic meaning, as when a man about to be executed for murder in *Decalogue V* is given his last smoke. He draws the smoke deep into his lungs as if it was his last breath of life. Cigarettes are smoked during times of crisis, intimacy, and loneliness.

Decalogue I covers the first commandment: "I am the Lord God; thou shalt not have other gods before me." The god here is in the form of a computer that sends messages on its own. Symbolically, it suggests that science has replaced the protagonist's belief in a spiritual being. Krzysztof (Henryk Baranowski), a professor, and his young son, Pawel (Wojciech Klata), deal with the absence of their wife/mother. The father and son love and cherish each other but the relationship lacks spirituality. When a bottle of black ink mysteriously breaks and floods the professor's notes, he takes it as a symbol of dire trouble. The boy has gone ice skating with the instruction to stay in the area the father scientifically deemed safe. Throughout the episode a homeless man sits at the snow-covered shore in front of a frozen lake. Intercutting implies a connection between the father, son, and indigent man. As in much of *The Decalogue*—and as in life—not everything is explained. Tragedy comes at the conclusion. The boy has fallen through the ice and has drowned. The homeless man is gone. Was science defied because the boy went beyond the safety zone to help the man or did the man go to the boy on his skates? The professor who believes in absolute science has had his belief system betrayed.

Poetic images set and enhance the psychological atmosphere concerning death. In the text the boy asks his father about the nature and meaning of death. It is visualized by a dead dog, sour milk poured into a glass of coffee, a frozen video image of the boy on a television monitor, a bottle of frozen water, and an image of the Virgin mother splashed with candle wax until it appears she is crying.

Decalogue II is "Thou shalt not take the name of the Lord thy God in vain." Dorota (Krystyna Janda), the wife of Andrzej (Olgierd Lukaszewicz), a critically ill man, is persistent in trying to convince a doctor (Aleksander Bardini) to tell her whether her husband will live or die. The moral dilemma facing them is that she is pregnant with another man's child. If the husband can live, she will get an abortion. If he is to die, she will have the baby and move onto another life. The doctor, who we learn lost his family in a tragic accident, is put in the position of playing god to decide life or death. The irony lies in the fact that Andrzej lives, the other relationship ends, and Andrzej awakens to the news that he is to be a father. As the episode concludes, Andrzej is talking to the doctor about the importance of a child—this from a man who will never learn he is not the biological father of his child, to a man who knows he can only be a false god because his child was taken away from him by what is commonly called an act of God.

Dorota and the doctor have a combative relationship. She, we are told, once ran over his dog with her car. We learn about the doctor's past in scenes taking place in his kitchen over coffee with his housekeeper. So only the viewer learns the reason for the doctor's seemingly detached behavior—he is protecting himself emotionally. Dorota smokes; he does not. At one emotional point, she has to ash her cigarette and uses the match box. The matches instantly ignite. The flare of fire visually defines her volatile state, signals a reaction from the doctor, and underlines the charge between them. An answering machine in Dorota's apartment is a dramatic device to communicate her relationship to the lover and the call from the doctor that she keeps expecting. The scene in which the husband comes out of his sleep state is masterly cinematic in its structure and presentation. Dorota is at her window at night. The camera tracks down into darkness and settles on the doctor's face. Then it pans right along the building, which now becomes her husband's hospital room. His eyes open and look up. There is a cut to a bug struggling to hang onto a spoon in a glass of tea or coffee. After a long ordeal it makes it to the rim of the glass, a poetic metaphor for the man's plight. The music playing as **score** becomes source as the scene shifts to Dorota performing at a concert. She looks out to the audience for the doctor who finally has given her a definitive determination that her husband will die. Functioning again as source, the music concludes in the doctor's office as Andrzej, now out of danger, comes to see him.

"Remember the Sabbath day, to keep it holy" is *Decalogue III*. The story takes place on Christmas Eve, a holy night and a family night. Janusz (Daniel Olbrychski) dresses up as Santa Claus. During midnight Mass he sees his former lover, Ewa (Maria Pakulnis), who later contacts him for help to find her missing husband. Janusz lies to his wife to get out of the house. During the night, he learns that her husband left her three years ago after catching the two in bed. Ewa manipulates Janusz by saying she will kill herself unless they spend the night together. Janusz keeps his marriage vow holy as the commandment requires for the sabbath day and stays faithful to his wife.

The suggestion that Ewa's husband is missing is set up right from the opening. The camera slowly focuses on a drunk wandering into an accident. This narrative strand recurs through several scenes fortifying Ewa's story. Kieślowski takes full advantage of the emotional stress surrounding the holiday, when loneliness and failed relationships can make suicide an answer or a foil. The festivity of the night is captured in colored light but dimmed by Janusz's worry that he will lose something either way.

Decalogue IV, "Honor thy father and mother," concerns Anka (Adrianna Biedrynska), who discovers a note left by her deceased mother that Michal (Janusz Gajos) is not her biological father. This knowledge dramatically alters Anka's feelings toward him, but eventually she learns that his love for her, as with a natural parent, is unconditional. Honoring a mother and father goes beyond blood to true commitment.

The camera's ability to focus on elements within the frame is used to comment on the shifting nature of reality altered by learning a situation is not what it originally appeared to be. There are three major planes of action in a shot—foreground, background, and middle ground—where the characters often reside. For this episode, Kieślowski and his cinematographer, Krzysztof Pakulski, constantly shift the focal point, an aesthetic choice that visualizes the shifting moral choices that confront the characters.

"Thou shalt not kill" is *Decalogue V*, a harrowing depiction of a senseless murder followed by a hanging carried out by the state. The result of this powerful film is an unconditional interpretation of the commandment. By detailing the senseless and vicious murder of an innocent stranger and the obsession with carrying out the death penalty mandate, the sanctity of life is offended. The power to take a life does not belong to an individual or a group of individuals who call themselves a state.

Kieślowski and his creative team apply a different combination of aesthetics to this most serious episode. The overall color scheme has a yellow–sepia tone cast. The images are not sharp and clear but burnished. The design is timeless and less specific than any of the other films. This intensifies the brutality of the separate but related acts connected by a moral code. Many parts of *The Decalogue* feature days that are bleak, a combination of geographical and economic conditions. The murder of a cab driver (Jan Tesarz) is committed by the deadening anger of Jacek (Miroslaw Baka), a young man who lost his loving sister at a tender age. The bleak sky is a dramatic setting for the capital crime and a metaphor for the future of the man, his killer, and the society that rationalizes murder in the name of justice while ignoring the word of the Lord.

In *Decalogue VI*—"Thou shalt not commit adultery"—Tomek (Olaf Lubaszenko) falls in love with Magda (Grazyna Szapolowska), a beautiful woman whom he has spied on by peeping through a telescope into her apartment. His love is destroyed when Magda learns of his existence and tries to consummate the relationship. The boy then ends his obsession and falls out of love with her.

Voyeurism is the medium of communication here. Before the woman becomes aware of Tomek, the boy receives erotic pleasure by viewing her sexual exploits from afar, without interruption or intimacy on his part. When the connection is made, the two communicate through direct eyeline match and the viewer becomes a voyeur into both of their lives. The adultery theme is metaphorical in nature. By watching Magda have sex with other men, Tomek falls in love through a vicarious erotic experience. The symbolic adultery occurs when Magda falls in love with Tomek and violates his personal sense of commitment.

"Thou shalt not steal" is *Decalogue VII*. Majka (Maja Barelkowska) runs off with six-year-old Ania, who she knows is her biological child, taking her from her mother Ewa (Anna Polony), who took over Majka's motherhood role when the teenager had a baby out of wedlock with Wojtek (Boguslaw Linda), a young teacher at the time. Ania believes that Ewa, her grandmother, is her mother. Motivations are complex. Ewa was the headmaster of a school and came up with this solution to avoid scandal between one of her teachers and a student who was also her daughter. Majka is convinced Ewa wanted another child but couldn't so she co-opted Ania. Stefan (Wladyslaw Kowalski), her father, understands the rift between the two, and Wojtek has mixed emotions about his relationship with Majka, Ania, and Ewa.

Wojtek had long since given up his dream of becoming a writer and runs a stuffed bear business. In Kieślowski's poetic hands, this becomes part of the ironic fabric of the story. When Majka and Ania arrive, his room is filled with stuffed bears. Ania falls asleep among the sea of bears. When Majka suspects Wojtek is trying to send them back home, they leave. Majka gives Ania a toy bear to appease the child, saying it was left for her by her father.

The sin of stealing is double-edged. Ewa stole the baby from Majka because of social pressures. Majka stole Ania away from Eva because of her anger. In the end Ania is reunited with her "mother," but Majka takes action to separate herself from everyone. Stealing is a loss of incalculable repercussions.

Decalogue VIII is based on the commandment "Thou shalt not bear false witness against thy neighbor." Zofia (Maria Koscialkowska), a professor, is visited by Elzbieta (Teresa Marczewska), a younger woman who confronts Zofia's past by telling her that she was a Jewish child rejected by her during the war after Zofia had first promised to adopt her. The professor who teaches ethical issues learns of the tremendous hurt she has caused and tries to help Elzbieta as well as to make her understand the whole story. The price of bearing false witness is great for all involved.

Time is an important issue in this film and in all of *The Decalogue*. Here the sin was committed in the past and it altered Elzbieta's sense of time and quality of life. Both women had to spend the time of their lives with that event interfering with the course of their existence. Kieślowski and his editor on the series, Ewa Smal (*The Contract, Korczak, Nastasja*), emphasize gaps in the present time-line of the film with **time cuts**. The short-form film often requires the compression of time, so the episode cuts out the irrelevant and joins together the relevant. This technique is applied to most movies, but Kieślowski does it with such articulation. He moves the story through the moral time space, not only the reality of time past.

"Thou shalt not covet they neighbor's wife" is *Decalogue IX*. Roman (Piotr Machalica), a surgeon who has long been a womanizer, learns that he has become impotent. He implores Hanka (Ewa Blaszczyk), his loyal and loving wife, to find a lover. When she does, Roman becomes insanely jealous. When they finally are able to come back together, he misreads information, which makes him believe she is again off with her lover. He tries to kill himself but fails. All of these trials result in restoring their commitment to each other. Roman's dalliances and the encouragement he gave to his wife to seek an outside relationship almost results in the destruction of life and love.

The reflection of self through a mirror or other surfaces is a constant theme of *The Decalogue.* It can be a moral reflection of a character taking stock, or it can be self-confrontation. When the doctor returns from learning his fate, he wants to tell Hanka but she does not want to hear the story. He is reflected in the bedroom mirror and then in a bathroom mirror. Here, they remind him to face the truth but also represent duplicity, which he has practiced, an illusion that will fall apart when he sets the relationship into a tailspin by facing his wife with his version of the truth.

The final film, *Decalogue X,* "Thou shalt not covet they neighbor's goods," is a black comedy. Two brothers, Artur (Zbigniew Zamachowski) and Jerzy (Jerzy Stuhr), inherit an extremely valuable stamp collection when their father dies. When the men learn that their father secretly invested most of his life earnings into the collection and denied their mother, they rationalize their greed. In trying to quickly cash in on their inheritance, the brothers get caught up in a web of con artists. The result is a twist on the final commandment, because it is the criminals who benefit, and the brothers are the ones who are punished for their disrespect of the property of others.

The irony in this episode is in the creation of the characters. Artur is a popular punk rocker and Jerzy is a buttoned-down everyman. The brothers have little in common and have not seen each other for a long time. But the revelation that they may now be rich brings them together as siblings and partners and then divides them when paranoia sets in.

Kieślowski concludes his examination of the ultimate moral code with a light touch. The brothers haven't lost everything because they now have a greater love for each other and a shared passion kindled by their dad's secret obsession.

The Decalogue is not a religious film in the manner of Cecil B. De Mille's *The Ten Commandments* or John Huston's *The Bible,* but it is dedicated to the moral principles that govern mankind. They can be seen as ten short films about the complexities of human interaction. The Ten Commandments represent the word of God. *The Decalogue* translates them into human terms. It is Kieślowski's vision that penetrates all that is human in this watershed work.

Of Further Interest

Screen

Berlin Alexanderplatz
Three Colors: Blue
Three Colors: Red
Three Colors: White

Read

Double Lives, Second Chances: The Cinema of Krzysztof Kieślowski by Annette Insdorf
Decalogue: The Ten Commandments by Krzysztof Kieślowski and Krzystof Piesiewicz
Kieślowski on Kieślowski, edited by Danusia Stok
The Fright of Real Tears: Krzysztof Kieślowski Between Theory and Post-Theory, edited by Slavoj Zizek

Mythopoetic Film

Dog Star Man

This epic mythopoetic **experimental film** by Stan Brakhage (1933–2003) was photographed and edited from 1961–1964 and is structured into a prelude and four parts. *Dog Star Man* is a silent, 16mm, seventy-five-minute color work of artistic filmic creation that explores the cycles of existence and man's quest toward physical and spiritual ascension.

The critical classification of **mythopoetic film** was termed by **avant-garde** cinema historian P. Adams Sitney. In addition to Brakhage, practitioners of this school include Kenneth Anger (*Fireworks, Scorpio Rising, Invocation of My Demon Brother*), Bruce Baillie (*Quixote, Castro Street, Quick Billy*), and Gregory Markopoulos (*Twice a Man, The Illiac Passion, Bliss*). Through a visual language that governs the filmmaker's expression of thematic content, these works present the ventures of gods and heroes, organic elements, and animals as they impact the order of the universe.

Stan Brakhage was one of the most prolific, independent, and influential experimental film artists of the twentieth century with almost 400 challenging, handmade works to his credit. Brakhage's career-long quest has been to explore the manner and effect of how the human eye really sees. Brakhage has employed what he identifies as "the untutored eye" to the creation of his films. Traditional filmmaking developed compositional and editorial rules, a visual narrative vocabulary and cinematic conventions that were strictly adhered to so general audiences could easily follow the plot and meaning of the story. Brakhage rejected all of this

Stan Brakhage as the Dog Star Man during his mythopoetic climb to a mountain top in his watershed experimental film *Dog Star Man*. Brakhage utilizes mythic imagery and an avant-garde aesthetic to present the cycles of existence and man's desire for physical and spiritual ascension. Courtesy of Anthology Film Archives.

doctrine and sought out a pure non-narrative cinema, discovering a new filmic language in its wake.

No artist totally invents himself. In the cinema, Brakhage admired and studied the work of Georges Melies, D. W. Griffith, Sergei Eisenstein, and Carl Dreyer. His thematic pursuits grew out of a personal connection to the romanticism movement and the American tradition of poetry exemplified by Ezra Pound, Charles Olson, and Gertrude Stein.

During the long gestation and creation of *Dog Star Man*, Brakhage sought to record on film what he called "closed-eye vision," images imagined in the brain as light plays upon the shut lids of his eyes. After four years of intensive filming and editing, Brakhage's masterwork was complete. It tells a story through its own lexicon that is a tale for the ages, contemplating the grand themes of existence, man's relationship to the universe, and the search for self and purpose.

Prelude: Dog Star Man is twenty-six minutes. Faint shifts of light give way to swirling elements of fire, ice, and a timberland. The Dog Star Man's face, bordered by his dark mane and unruly beard, whirls by. Dark becomes bright, then blue, red, and pale yellow. Flames lick outward; headlights move forward as they sway. Alligatored textures become tilting ethereal skies, then hot white twisting reeds. Stars light the cosmos. The spiky hair and figure of the man's dog circuits with the reccurring elements, a white sun, and the ghostly face of his master. There is a flash of a nude female torso. White abstract branches speed by a field of brown. Explosive sun spots become a shimmering glacier, then burning embers. As abstractions consisting of light and color swirl around the film frame, the eye picks up fleeting moments of recognizable but layered and vividly animated images; a woman's vagina, the intense flickering of solar flares, a yellow sun, and a pearl-white moon. The vast expanse of space is depicted, as well of a constant stream of pure movement. Organisms, cells, and molecular structures multiply and disperse.

Superimpositions—the silence of clear light all interconnect in this universe with the elements of air, earth, fire, and water. The visions are fleeting, languorous, intense and passive, as are the rhythms of life. This is an experience, not a representation of how we really see through our outer and inner eyes. The world of the gods clashes with what man has made. Visible tape splices transport the visions.[1] Brakhage's physical editing of the celluloid, as well in-camera cuts performed by exposing rapid on-and off bursts of film frames through the lens of his Bolex camera, anticipate and reflect the connective visual membranes on the screen, much like they gather in the epicenter of the brain. These messages to the viewer's responsive eye include the surface of the moon, the landscape of a naked female body to signify sex and childbearing, the soft blur of birth, the focused reality of living, and the slow dim fade of death. The notion of home is established with visions of home, shelter, the organic comfort of nature, and the omens of tempest. Brakhage poetically creates expressive visions to capture the central issues of life, clarity, obscurity, myth, legend, existence, and evolution.

Celluloid grain is the DNA that pulses through Brakhage's film, an extension of his biological matter captured by exposing rolls of Kodak stock running through his hand-held Bolex camera that records his inner and outer senses.[2] *Dog Star Man* is the story of man and his total physical and spiritual environment. This is not **montage** but collage. Brakhage applies the camera more like a painter than a photographer. A hair caught in the camera gate becomes a twig twisting in the wind. Dirt on the surface of the film as it runs through the projector transforms into dust of the earth, particles in space. An anamorphic (see **anamorphic wide-screen format** in glossary) lens bends reality seen through animal and blessed eyes. A beating heart expresses humanity.

The nature of focus becomes an operating principle of *Dog Star Man*. In traditional cinema a sharp image is a correct image. Soft focus technique has limited narrative use and is only realized in comparison with a clearly rendered representation.[3] For Brakhage, clarity is not achieved by the rigidity of the camera lens or proper relation of focal length to subject but in the film artist's abilities to capture light, form, and movement through an organic function of his camera-tool.

The Dog Star Man (Stan Brakhage) is out in an open forest. The frame is filled with circular and equivocal shapes that expand the viewer's sight, not square or rectangular forms that confine it. The optical elements of the lens refract light. A zooming (see **zoom lens** in glossary) motion repeatedly creates depth from far to near, near to far. Transformation is attained by dense in-camera layering of colors and textures, not always by the collision of image through the physical editing process. The power and energy of sexual expression merges with the power and energy of the sun as a light and life source. The man celebrates the life of his child. Seasons change from winter, spring, and summer, to fall. Positive and negative printing symbolizes the yin and yang of the spirits. There is a period of night and then a new day bursts into being.

Dog Star Man: Part 1 is thirty-one minutes and begins with a white globe, the sky flickering with clouds passing over a tall mountain. The man, shouldering a long wooden handled axe, and his dog slowly climb the steep snowy mountain in a series of vignettes structured with long fades in and out of black. The surface of the moon and the burning embers return. The ice is now from his **point of view** as he slowly makes his way up the hilly path and confronts the outdoor forces. The air bubbles and dark marks from the adhesive tape splice create texture and set the images back in time. Brakhage simultaneously reminds viewers that they are watching a film and allows them to experience the aesthetic beauty actualized by the early stages of the editing process.

The Dog Star Man climbs day and night. The trip is arduous, often illustrated by slow-motion imaging. The pace of *Part 1*, like the climb, is slow and deliberate. As the man trudges upward, he proceeds through fire and ice, reproduction, and the bearing of the fruit of his offspring. He encounters religion represented by stained glass imagery. His long stringy hair and beard are at one with the bare branches of the trees all around him. A lactating breast is followed by a negative film, full-figured image of the man, then cuts back to a positive print as he struggles to mature. He gets nearer to the tall trees but falls and struggles with the dog for his survival.

Dog Star Man finally reaches a tree and chops it down with his axe as snow and ice tumble down on him. Light emits a prismatic rainbow. The felling of the tree is visceral and proceeded by a period of black visual silence. The tumult continues as fire and ice collide. The graphic patterns of snowflakes burst forward; then the rapid flow of protozoan life forms. The tree is down and the forest settles. The dog is on the side of nature as the axe flies through the air. The man continues his ascent; the dog follows as the man falls from the slippery footing. He is on his back—blood is seen pumping through his rapidly beating heart. Black. The Dog Star Man rises and climbs again. He falls again. Stately columns represent architecture. The climb commences. A microscopic view of a tree trunk bleeds a red, pointillist river.[4] Black.

Dog Star Man: Part 2 is six minutes. The climb is accelerated in fits and starts interwoven with sparkling geometric patterns. A baby emerges and experiences life, represented by ever-shifting patterns, colors, and changing ambient factors. The infant cries, blinks, stares, sleeps, and, by representation, is fed by the milk of a breast. The man begins to descend, sees a sexual apparition, and lies back. A flame burns, then turns to a pale yellow field.

Dog Star Man: Part 3 is eight minutes. In it, the Dog Star Man has a vivid sexual dream: Skin, a nipple, a woman in arousal, intertwining bodies, the man's face, the woman's face, and hands exploring flesh are flashed in a whirlpool of imagery cycled from his earlier experiences. Internal organs ooze and pulsate. It is frenetic, rapid, and densely abstruse.

In *Dog Star Man: Part 4*, which is seven minutes, Dog Star Man arises. He is bare-chested and shakes off his sexual dreams, religion, architecture, and the woodlands. There is a period of dense abstraction and then a baby comes forth from the birth canal. The mountains are receding from view as the homestead approaches. Fire. A crawling toddler. A hand holds a finely honed tool. On the ground, Dog Star Man, his axe shouldered once again, turns to look at the world around him. He rolls on the ground as the sun bathes him and then sets. He kneels in the snow, then walks around in glory as memories of chopping the tree spark in the cognitive sectors of his mind. The picture turns waves of gray—then black.

Dog Star Man is a landmark of cinema that has astonished and confounded critics, filmmakers, and audiences worldwide from its first public showings in lofts and cine showcases, to its enduring presence in museums, academic institutions, and private collections. It is synonymous with the notion of avant-garde art, and it influenced generations of filmmakers, who look to the mavericks for new vistas, as well as television commercials, music videos, and commercial feature films looking for unique images and cinematic techniques. In our image-driven culture, *Dog Star Man* is less inclined to infuriate, as it once did those who insisted film should be a traditional narrative medium. For Stan Brakhage the medium is the message and image is its messenger.

Notes

1. Visible tape splices were part of Brakhage's aesthetic on *Dog Star Man* and other films. The traditional completion method is to cut the negative in a checkboard A-and-B roll method by using liquid glue and a hot splicer that allows for a seamless join between images. Brakhage printed the cut made with tape splices so the joins can be seen, and the lines and texture caused by the tape add visual texture and a repetitive graphic pattern that become part of the viewing experience.

2. The Bolex 16mm movie camera was developed by the Paillard S. A. Company of Switzerland in the early 1930s. The Bolex, which has been the camera of choice for avant-garde and experimental filmmakers since the 1940s, can be operated by a built-in, hand-cranked, spring-driven power or by accessing an electric motor. It is easily hand-held or mounted on a tripod, shoots from eight to sixty-four frames per second, can photograph a single frame at a time, and performs in-camera fades, dissolves, and superimpositions.

3. Soft-focus technique is an aesthetic choice in which the image is not in a sharp focus but slightly or dramatically out of focus to soften or abstract the image being photographed. Traditionally, soft focus is used subtly to create the atmosphere of beauty and to remove age lines from an actor's face. In its more radical application, soft-focus technique attempts to explore new ways of seeing in which shape, color, and form dominate over line and definition.

4. Pointillism is a painting technique best associated with Georges Seurat's *Sunday Afternoon on the Island of La Grande Jatte*, in which small touches of pure color create a vibrant effect when the work is viewed from a distance.

Of Further Interest

Screen

By Brakhage (Criterion DVD)
Quick Billy
Scorpio Rising
Twice a Man
Wavelength

Read

Brakhage Scrapbook: Collected Writings 1964–1980 by Stan Brakhage
Essential Brakhage: Selected Writings on Filmmaking by Stan Brakhage
The Films of Stan Brakhage in the American Tradition of Erza Pound, Gertrude Stein, and Charles Olson by R. Bruce Elder
Film Culture Reader, edited by P. Adams Sitney
Visionary Film: The American Avant-Garde 1943–2000 by P. Adams Sitney

17

Political Objectives through Cinematic Storytelling

Do the Right Thing

There is a social history concerning race relations in America that precedes Spike Lee's *Do the Right Thing*, released in 1989, takes place in Brooklyn, New York, on the hottest day of the year. As this fateful cinematic day dawns, the characters are well aware of catastrophic events that have shaped their lives and motivated their thoughts and behavior. Years before *Do the Right Thing*, which takes place in the late 1980s, there were the murders of three civil rights workers, James Chaney, Andrew Goodman, and Michael Schwerner in Mississippi, summers of race riots, the assassinations of Martin Luther King and Malcolm X, and the deaths of Eleanor Bumpers, Michael Griffith, and Michael Stewart, victims of racial injustice to whom the film along with others is dedicated.

The shift from the belief that nonviolence is the way to achieve peace among the races to advocating violence as a means of self-defense is the lynchpin of *Do the Right Thing*. The film concludes with statements from Dr. King and Malcolm X that define these diverse positions and the moral posture of the film. A photo of these two powerful leaders smiling together connects the idea that in the future, African American life must be ruled by both philosophic positions and not polarized.

Do the Right Thing may be the most important American film ever made about race. It is filled with nerve endings, open wounds, moral and ethical quandaries, a minefield of hatred and misunderstanding—it is a time bomb about to go off.

Spike Lee (in the Dodgers shirt) as Mookie and Ossie Davis (center) as Da Mayor in *Do the Right Thing*. Depicted is just one of many confrontations that take place in a Brooklyn neighborhood on the hottest day of the summer. The physical heat becomes a metaphor that expresses a socio-political situation about to boil over. Courtesy *Photofest*.

Heat is the central metaphor of *Do the Right Thing*. The sun is relentless and the streets are sweltering. Tempers boil over—there is no escape. The **color palette** is comprised of red, orange, coral, yellow, and warm browns. Ice cold beer, an open fireplug spewing a waterfall onto loosely dressed neighborhood children and teens, cold showers, and even ice rubbed on a naked body can't cool off this cross-section of New York in Bed Stuy. The costumes by Ruth Carter (*Rosewood, Amistad, Love and Basketball*) celebrate ethnic pride and diversity. The original music **score** by Bill Lee (*She's Gotta Have It, School Daze, Mo' Better Blues*), Spike's father, recalls jazz, Negro spirituals, and the poignancy of Gershwin's *Porgy and Bess*.

Do the Right Thing was shot on location in Brooklyn. The production was given a cordoned-off area where production designer Wynn Thomas (*Malcolm X, Analyze This, A Beautiful Mind*) built a pizzeria directly across from a Korean market also created for the film. A block of brownstones went through major rehabilitation that repaired structural damage to the exteriors and provided new paint jobs to sustain a controlled color palette of desert colors. A radio station was built in an abandoned building so that a large window front faced the universe of the story.

Do the Right Thing, like many of Spike Lee's films, is theatrical in style and intention. Wynn Thomas was reminded of Elmer Rice's *Street Scene* and *Porgy and Bess*, two theatrical works in which all the characters and circumstances are self-contained and converge during the course of the story. The cinematography by Ernest Dickerson (*Brother from Another Planet, Mo' Better Blues, Malcolm X*) emphasizes the theatricality of the design and torrid color scheme with rays of white light, combining cool and warm compositional areas to provide contrast that makes hot hotter. The result is a Brooklyn that is a representation of the real world, not as dirty and gritty but as romantic and passionate. Below the surface are misconceptions, prejudice, fear, and hate. This is a neighborhood of people who cannot keep the larger forces of their combined histories out of their homes and streets.

The characters in *Do the Right Thing* are a sampling of urban city life. Before the sixties, neighborhoods were contained and everyone "knew their place," but the social upheaval that began in that significant decade sent everyone looking for liberation, self-expression, representation, and respect. Sal (Danny Aiello) is the proprietor of Sal's Pizzeria. Sal is old-school, decent, and hard-working. His business is not a pizza place or a pizza joint; it is a *pizzeria*. He takes pride in the food that has fed the children and people of Bed Stuy. The neighborhood has changed since he first opened decades before. His clientele were once Italian Americans who shared his ethnicity and values. Now, the young blacks of Bed Stuy are expressing their own culture. Sal tries to handle potential clashes with dignity, but he is the boss with rules that cannot be broken. Sal represents a white man who, when pushed beyond control of his turf, will resort to primal instincts to protect his own—his family business. Sal has two sons. Pino (John Turturro) is an angry racist. He openly displays his hostility. He wants Sal to sell the pizzeria and open one in their neighborhood, where they would be with their own kind. Pino admires Eddie Murphy, Prince, Michael Jordan, and other black celebrities. His racism convinces him that these men are not black. Vito (Richard Edson), his younger brother, is low in intelligence and self-esteem. Vito does have a good heart and does not harbor hatred. He freely associates with blacks in the neighborhood and abhors the violence between the races. Da Mayor (Ossie Davis), like Sal, is of the old school, but too much alcohol has eroded his standing in the community. He is willing to sweep Sal's sidewalk for a couple of bucks but spends the money at the Korean grocery on beer. He is openly hostile to this new wave of immigrants. Da Mayor walks his streets and tries to do good. He doesn't have the respect of the new black generation, but he keeps his title even if in name only. Da Mayor is not a politician, just a black man from a time when elders and those with community values were respected; now he is a shadow sustained by bottle after bottle of Miller High Life. Mother Sister (Ruby Dee) is a black woman who sits in her open window giving counsel from her motherland. She is treated with respect but also is no longer who she once was. She dresses in beautiful African garb, gives good advice but often sounds preachy, and is accused of practicing voodoo. Buggin Out (Giancarlo Esposito) is a new, proud black man. His braided and twisted hair draws jibes from many of his color. He is a street revolutionary looking for a cause. He finds it in Sal's when he confronts the owner about his Wall of Fame, featuring pictures of Italian American performers Al Pacino, John Travolta, Frank Sinatra, and other heroes of Sal. Buggin Out demands that Sal put pictures of black people up on the wall. He is ejected and begins a boycott that lights the fuse on a day so physically and emotionally hot that not much of a spark is needed.

Mookie (Spike Lee) is a central figure in *Do the Right Thing*. He works for Sal delivering pizzas. He is one of the family but is not treated equally. Mookie lives in both worlds. He knows everyone, and kind words are exchanged. He has a son out of wedlock with Tina (Rosie Perez), a Hispanic woman who lives with her mother in a railroad flat. Mookie is supported by his sister Jade (Jolie Lee) because he only earns $250 a week. Mookie tries to relate to everyone, but he is an outsider in his own world—a man not ready to take responsibility. Mookie is trapped in the stereotype of a lazy, no-show by Sal and Pino. Everyone has Mookie's ear and when he speaks his mind openly for the first time in the film's explosive conclusion, he is ready to move on to self-reliance.

Radio Raheem (Bill Nunn) is a powerfully built, game-face young black man with a boom box that establishes and maintains his rep. He blasts Public Enemy's "Fight the Power" everywhere he goes. He is angry but cool—a loner known to everyone and respected out of fear. When he draws the line with Sal over his music, the consequences are deadly. The corner men, ML (Paul Benjamin), Coconut Sid (Frankie Faison), and Sweet Dick Willie (Robin Harris), all African American, sit on chairs in front of a brightly painted orange wall that defines their role as Shakespearean commentators. They disrespect each other, Buggin Out, the police, the Koreans—they have something to say about everyone and everything. They want respect and they hate foreigners running stores in their neighborhood, but they are mostly talk. The police, Officer Ponte (Miguel Sandoval) and Officer Long (Rick Aiello), are indifferent, even hostile, to Charlie (Frank Vincent), an Italian American man who is guaranteed safe passage with his "antique" Cadillac but is set up by the local kids who flush him down with a Johnny pump geyser. The officers are doing their job, but they show brotherhood to Sal and hatred toward the corner men, and are responsible for the murder of Radio Raheem.

Mister Señor Love Daddy (Samuel L. Jackson) is an ultra-cool black disc jockey who watches the day from his microphone. Sitting in the window, Love Daddy is super smooth, preaches love, embraces the totality of black music, soul, R&B, rap, traditional jazz, fusion, pop, and everything in between. His roll call of respect toward the performers of this music is a salute to black culture and is scenarist Lee's message that culture should be embraced, not fractured. Love Daddy is involved but aloof; the day after the melting pot boils over he is back with his rap call for love.

A series of characters make up the diversity of communities struggling to live together in Bed Stuy. A group of black youths talk the talk but are looking for their way. They eat and hang at Sal's. They can be cruel, as young people can be to their own, especially to Da Mayor, whom they taunt and disrespect. They are waiting for a leader, an incident to define their future. The Hispanic group likes to drink beer, they stick to their own, and they dance their own dance to Latin rhythms. When it is time to stand up, they stand against Sal and the police although they may share more history with them than they are willing to admit. The Korean grocery owner, Sonny (Steve Park), and his wife Kim (Ginny Yang) work hard at their business. They mistrust the blacks and the blacks outwardly display hostility toward them. The owner is anti-Semitic. When sides need to be taken, he is "black" rather than white. This is business, and fear protects an owner's livelihood. Smiley (Roger Guenveur Smith) is a mentally challenged black man who carries pictures of Dr. King and Malcolm X whereever he goes. He is a loner who is acknowledged by everyone but only taken seriously by Buggin Out, who manipulates him into radical action. Tina, Mookie's girlfriend and mother of his child, wants her man to be a man—take care of his family, be responsible and available to her.

Spike Lee is as even-handed as is humanly possible toward his characters, given the rage, hatred, and prejudice that engulf them. Lee has imbued his characters with pride, self-knowledge, and the will to follow their emotions regardless of the cost. The result is an honest look at what is tearing urban America apart. He offers no clear-cut answers; things happen because they are the destiny of a country that would like to do the right thing but is unwilling to look at the problem through the eyes of each neighbor.

Do the Right Thing is a dramatic film based on close observation of real events concerning racial unrest. The 1986 incident in which a black man was murdered by white youths in Howard Beach simply because he asked for directions to a pizza place that the mob claimed as their turf was the flash point that inspired Lee to write the film. Claiming rights to turf is a theme that transforms this family neighborhood into a battle zone. A young black girl draws a happy house and a joyful sun in white chalk on the street. Bed Stuy is home, but whose home is it? The whites moved out long ago. Sal has stayed; he built the tin ceiling old-world pizzeria with his own hands, but he is convinced he does not have any other place to go. His white neighborhood is too competitive, and besides, the people of Bed Stuy have grown up on his food. In Sal's Italian American culture, food is the great healer, a mode of communication, a way of sharing love. The neighborhood has long since transitioned into a black community. When a white yuppie, Clinton (John Savage), buys a brownstone, he represents gentrification and threatens the young blacks who claim it as their own even though Clinton tells them this is America. The corner men resent the fact that there are not any black-owned businesses. They can't fathom why the Koreans are successful entrepreneurs, but their righteous criticism becomes just another rap. Sal's is the designation of the turf war. Sal owns the pizzeria. He runs it his way. His Wall of Fame celebrates his heroes who happen to be Italian Americans. When Buggin Out demands Sal put black faces on the wall, the fuse is lit.

Do the Right Thing is honest and truthful but prismatic in its point of view. All audience members are reflected in the drama and will see right and wrong in their own way. The answer to prevent disaster is Love Daddy's call to chill out and love each other, but that has not been the rule in American's urban areas. For their own reasons, Smiley, Buggin Out, and Radio Raheem bond in solidarity. They each have an axe to grind. They demand their rights but do not walk into Sal's with the premeditated determination to destroy. "Fight the Power" is blasting. Sal's rule is there is no music in his restaurant. When the line in the sand is drawn, Sal makes the first move and smashes Raheem's precious boom box with a baseball bat, a traditional Italian American equalizer. To the black men, Sal has symbolically murdered the radio, but he has done something more primal. His anger toward the disrespect caused by the music tears away his last layer of control—with deep and florid rage Sal shouts, "Nigger." The bystanders are outraged and the trio is incensed.

No longer able to control his rage, Raheem, who has demonstrated a tough exterior but no sign of physical violence, attacks Sal. It is now too late. Everything is in place for the worst in humanity to boil up to the surface. Mookie is forced to make a decision about which side he is on. When Raheem is murdered by the police, who choke him to death with a nightstick, Mookie's sense of outrage against brutality spurs him to action. Out of defiance, not rage, Mookie marches across the street, picks up a metal garbage can, and then, as all sides watch and wait, Mookie bashes down the glass separating Sal's ownership from the people who pay his rent. This action begins a riot in which no one is rational. The pizzeria is looted, ransacked, trashed, and burned to the ground. Through the flames the photos of Sal's heroes are incinerated, and Smiley claims the ground by mounting the picture of his black leaders.

During a coda that takes place the next morning, Mookie demands his pay and throws back Sal's charity. Both men accept that they have to do what they have to do. Mookie picks up the money and moves on. He has come of age. He has seen the evil that men do and the anger in himself, and it has empowered him to take responsibility for a life that will be lived after the film ends.

Do the Right Thing is not the first movie about the black experience, but it is a landmark, a call to arms for a black-controlled cinema, in which African American voices can speak freely and the truth of urban life seething with hate and anger drives the races apart. *Do the Right Thing* is boldly politically-incorrect. Lee's characters—black, white, Asian, and Latino—speak how they feel. Spike Lee was brave enough to define a truly black cinema, one that began in the late 1980s and grew during the 1990s. Other filmmakers, including John Singleton, Julia Dash, the Hughes Brothers, Charles Burnett, Reginald Hudlin, Warrington Hudlin, and Ayoka Chenzira, followed and formed a new black cinema. Blaxploitation put black faces on the screen as super heroes and urban legends, but those films were sponsored by white media.[1] *Do the Right Thing* is one of the most important films of the 1980s because it defines its time—and it shatters myths. When Spike Lee as Mookie hurls that garbage can through the window of Sal's Pizzeria, he symbolically smashes the plate glass of every multiplex in America.

Notes

1. Blaxploitation films were low-budget movies made in the 1970s that starred African American performers and featured action, sex, and violence. The films tapped a market that had been ignored by the Hollywood establishment. Blax-

ploitation entertained ethnic, urban audiences but perpetuated racial stereotypes. Primarily, they were black versions of tried-and-true exploitation themes and formats. The genre includes *Shaft* (1971), *Superfly, The Mack, Cleopatra Jones,* and *Truck Turner.*

Of Further Interest

Screen

The Battle of Algiers
Get on the Bus
JFK
Jungle Fever
Z

Read

Spike Lee Interviews, edited by Cynthia Fuchs
The Cineaste Interviews: On the Art and Politics of the Cinema, edited by Dan Georgakas, Lenny Rubenstein
Do the Right Thing by Ed Guerrero
Reel to Real, Sex and Class at the Movies by bell hooks
Do the Right Thing: The New Spike Lee Joint by Spike Lee with Lisa Jones
Political Film: The Dialectics of Third Cinema by Mike Wayne

Film Noir

Double Indemnity

A man on crutches shown in silhouette walks slowly and straight into the camera. We do not know who he is. When we do meet him, he has no trouble walking on his own two feet, but later we learn of a broken leg, an accident on the job. We see the man, Mr. Dietrichson (Tom Powers), get into his car on crutches. He is murdered while driving to catch a train. As part of a plan to collect on a life insurance policy he has unwittingly signed, his killer boards the train wearing similar clothes and walking with crutches. Who did we see in the opening—the man, his killer, or the ghost of the dead man, tracking down the doomed Walter Neff (Fred MacMurray), an insurance agent obsessed with lust and greed?

This presence of a moral conscience in pursuit begins Billy Wilder's (1906–2002) *Double Indemnity* (1944). It is what we see while the credits run. The movie begins before the beginning.

Double Indemnity is a **film noir**. This overused, misunderstood term has a specific reference and meaning that continues to blur when applied in broad strokes by contemporary critics and the public. It has become a common label given to any film that embraces crime as a theme or deals with subject matter from the dark side of the human personality. The derivation of film noir is French. Its precursors are *serie noire* and *fleuve noire*, two critical terms used to categorize translations of the American hard-boiled detective fiction of Dashiell Hammett, Raymond Chandler, James M. Cain, Horace McCoy, and others. After the start of World War II, French film critics discovered many narrative and thematic tendencies of

Fred MacMurray as the doomed Walter Neff in *Double Indemnity*. This landmark film noir contains the designating properties of the "dark film" style: low key lighting, expressive camera angles, a femme fatale (played by Barbara Stanwyck), and a relentless sense of the hopeless fate of the protagonist. Courtesy *Photofest*.

that literary fiction form in particular American movies. The literal translation of film noir is black film—motion pictures that are both physically dark in application of aesthetic properties and dark in content.

Disillusionment, loss of identity, paranoia, guilt, McCarthyism, and the nuclear threat all contributed to the vision of an obsessed America shaken by world war. The soldiers returning from overseas were in a period of readjustment. There was an overwhelming alienation in urban life. Freudian anxiety and the predestined fate of existentialism replaced mom and apple pie.

Although film noir eventually evolved into **neonoir**, future-noir, and noirs aplenty over the decades, the classic period as designated by the French runs from just prior to World War II to just after the Korean conflict. Because film noir is not a standardized genre, critics differed in pinpointing this cycle of films. There is general agreement concerning the years 1944–1950; others specifically bookended it by citing *Double Indemnity* as the beginning and *Sunset Boulevard* as the end—both of which were directed by Billy Wilder. Other directors associated with film noir are Otto Preminger, William Dieterle, Fritz Lang, and Robert Siodmak, but not one of them set out to make a film noir. Actors, cinematographers, designers, and others were unaware they were contributing to the film noir genre. Film noir was not like the Western or musical—there was no official rulebook. The results found in these films later quantified by critics and theorists were cinematic expressions—a crazy mirror reflection of American culture at a point in time. The atmosphere was doom-laden; the action, at night. A woman defined as a femme fatale was the eventual cause of the protagonist's downfall. Crime and vice dominated. The films were photographed in **high-key lighting** on black-and-white stock. German expressionism in painting and the cinema was a central influence (see chapter 10). Oblique and vertical lines dominate the compositions in opposition to the horizontal line of the classic Hollywood Western. Interiors are devoid of natural light. Ceiling fixtures are hung low; table lamps are set less than five feet high, motivating jagged light shapes: trapezoids, triangles, and vertical slits. The streets are empty and there are long shadows. Docks, piers, alleyways, and gin mills are all part of the noir universe.

The hard and tough story of *Double Indemnity* was double-boiled, first by James M. Cain in the original novel and again during the screen adaptation by Billy Wilder and Raymond Chandler. Insurance salesman Walter Neff is lured into murder when he immediately falls in lust with Phyllis Dietrichson (Barbara Stanwyck), who suckers him into killing her husband so they can split the pay-out from a policy with a double indemnity clause that the victim signed without knowledge. This relationship conceived in hell falls apart, as does the so-called perfect crime. Neff's boss, Barton Keyes (Edward G. Robinson), is relentless in pursuing the truth of the crime but only learns of Walter's involvement when the wounded, guilty man completes his audio confession back at the office.

Double Indemnity is a perfectly structured work. The main action is immediately set in the past by beginning near the end. Neff is suffering from a bullet wound as he tells Keyes (by dictating into a recording device) and the audience (via voice-over narration) that he murdered Mr. Dietrichson. *Double Indemnity* is not a whodunit. Revealing what only he can know and how he knows brings the audience directly into Neff's netherworld of greed and obsession. Knowing the path of Neff's destiny stimulates our curiosity to take what Keyes repeatedly calls a nonstop trip to the graveyard, traveling, as promised throughout by Neff and his femme fatale, straight down the line.

Once Walter, in flashback, takes the bait from the two-timing Phyllis, the narrative constructed by the screenwriters leads Walter and Phyllis and their illicit plot to devastation and destruction. Their plan was to beat the system—the screenwriters made sure that the dark side of human nature and not justice would be responsible for their demise. This is an existential destiny set in motion by Walter and Phyllis.

Supporting Keyes's metaphor, the story unfolds like a ride from which the passengers can not get off. The dialogue is tough, spit out with conviction. The characters are cynical. No one is likeable. This is not Hollywood where dreams come true and there is always a happy ending, nor is there moralizing about evil. This is a cinematic representation of an America that has lost its way. Optimism has been replaced with cynicism and despair. There is a deadpan, macabre sense of humor as the characters crack wise. *Double Indemnity* oozes with sex that is delivered with innuendo and symbolism rather than through graphic depiction. When Phyllis shoots Neff with one shot but is unable to finish the job, she embraces him and for the first time really tells him that she is in love with him. Neff bitterly returns his sentiments with two quick bullets as the moment plays like a final orgasm.

Present time in *Double Indemnity* takes place as Walter continues to record his confession. It is the exposition of what has happened before the film started. The **flashbacks** show what has occurred in a linear sequence. At intervals we return to Walter in the office, a reminder that time is running out as he tells the story from his point of view. This narrative of a doomed man moves ahead until it catches up with the here and now. When that moment arrives so does Keyes, and the present is finally allowed to move forward.

The bond between the two men takes an ironic twist. Neff tells Keyes that he is heading to the border to avoid the gas chamber. Keyes replies that Neff will not make it to the elevator. Fate has caught up with Neff. Keyes doesn't have to lay a hand on his colleague and friend. The moral conscience represented by Keyes signals the end of the line for Neff, who collapses right outside the office. As Keyes reverses a match-lighting ritual established through the film between the two men, Walter tells the master fraud investigator that Keyes was too close, just across the desk, to see his guilt. "Closer than that, Walter," Keyes replies. The last words of *Double Indemnity* are spoken by Walter Neff: "I love you too." Keyes was the one person Neff could trust. Phyllis Dietrichson deceived him. Walter Neff was guilty of double murder and the moral crime of deception. He deceived Keyes, the man he most respected. Neff was also guilty of self-deception. The wisdom of his mentor, Barton Keyes, taught him that no one could get away with a murder that robbed the pockets of the system. Walter Neff submitted to the urges of the night. The fool he suffered faced him in the mirror.

The cinematography by John Seitz (*The Lost Weekend, Sunset Boulevard, The Big Clock*) provides the contrast of light and shadow that gives *Double Indemnity* the darkness of night and the glare of truth. The application of lighting goes beyond the verisimilitude of natural and artificial illumination. The light is a visual representation of the film noir. This is a world that has lost a moral compass. The dark allows the criminal code to flourish. The light streaming through venetian blinds does not cleanse the inner world of Walter Neff. It paints him with black stripes, reminding us that he is a man headed for prison. The Dietrichson home gets darker with each appearance until the final murder, when the light is dim and murky like the soul of Walter Neff. As she begins to reveal her cold-blooded intentions, Stanwyck's face and figure are gradually diffused by light and soft focus until she is one of the shadows waiting in the dark. Throughout the film, Wilder and Seitz composed shots that juxtapose a character with a place to hide from another. Phyllis is positioned hiding in a hallway behind the open door of Neff's apartment as Keyes tells Walter about his suspicion of her. Walter stands in the back of Keyes's office, trying to avoid Mr. Norton (Richard Gaines), the only person who could prove that Neff was on the train posing as Dietrichson while he is questioned by the investigator.

The production design by Hans Dreier (*The Great McGinty, Ministry of Fear, The Blue Dahlia*), Hal Pereira (*Shane, Funny Face, Rear Window*), and set decorator Bertram Granger (*The Lost Weekend; Sorry, Wrong Number; Peyton Place*) is anchored in Neff's office. There are custom-made file cabinets with long rows of small drawers designed to store and organize the individual policy records. All the data and facts of each claim are secured here, a vault of records that Neff has attempted to scam but has failed. The rays of a banker's lamp cut through the night. Neff has sealed his fate by talking into a dictaphone, a machine that records his memo, a confession that now is evidence. The image is of a man being grilled under the hot lights. This is not a police interrogation room, but Walter's place of work. Neff has cracked and is spilling the beans, but he does the job himself. An ashtray is the source for smoke; everybody smokes in a film noir—it defines the characters and fills the air with a dense atmosphere during the confessional.

The Dietrichson home is spacious and done in a Spanish style. There are heavy door panels, an iron-railed staircase, and white stone arches. For Neff the estate is a palace of sinful pleasure, his escape from his boring, low-rent life. For Phyllis it is a prison where a bad marriage confines her existence.

Walter and Phyllis have clandestine meetings at a food market to plot the murder and its aftermath. Rows of shelves are stacked to perfection with canned goods. The top pyramids of cans, as well as all the others, have their labels facing out. Precisely stacked, they frame the doomed couple, trapped in their own private tomb.

The interior of the insurance company provides a visual subtext to the narrative. The space is huge, exaggerated in scale to express the power and might of companies that collect money readily but dole it out very carefully. The office is a two-level set. The main floor is structured by uniform desk setups where the employees do the detail work of the company. The space is open—there is no privacy. The upper level is a balcony that runs around the entire office. This is where the powerbrokers can keep watch. The brass are physically on top while the workers toil below. The managers have instant access to their spacious offices and a bird's-eye view of the bureaucratic operation.

Double Indemnity is a model of the film noir style, universally considered one of the best of the cycle. It is also a great movie that happens to be a film noir. Too often films are judged, understood, and analyzed using narrow criteria concerning genre, personal opinion, and the politics of aesthetic and narrative issues. A great film expresses its intent through visual storytelling and by translating the text through the film crafts. *Double Indemnity* should be studied because it defines film noir, utilizes cinematic language to tell a compelling story, and because, as with all important works of art, its magic is timeless.

Of Further Interest

Screen

Kiss of Death (1947)
The Lady from Shanghai
Night and the City (1950)
Out of the Past
The Postman Always Rings Twice (1946)

Read

Somewhere in the Night: Film Noir and the American City by Nicholas Christopher
Film Noir: The Dark Side of the Screen by Foster Hirsch
Dark City: The Lost World of Film Noir by Eddie Muller
More Than Night: Film Noir in its Contexts by James Naremore
Film Noir: An Encyclopedic Reference to the American Style, edited by Alain Silver and Elizabeth Ward

19

The Personal Film

□ ◆ □ ◆ □ ◆ □

$8\frac{1}{2}$

Federico Fellini's (1920–1994) *8½* (1963) is an autobiographical film that inspired Paul Mazursky's *Alex in Wonderland;* Woody Allen's *Stardust Memories;* Bob Fosse's *All That Jazz;* Richard Pryor's *Jo Jo Dancer, Your Life is Calling;* and Martin Scorsese's first New York University short film, *What's a Nice Girl Like You Doing in a Place Like This?* It is one of the most significant films ever made concerning a movie director and the motion picture creative process.

8½ is not the first film in which a director draws upon his own life for the narrative content; *8½* made its mark by probing the soul and psyche of the principal character, a film director, through an expressionistic interpretation of the feelings, experiences, and ruminations of an actual film director—Federico Fellini. *8½* gave audiences a peek inside the mind of a creative filmmaker. Its wider inspiration was to stimulate filmmakers all over the world to make personal films in which their lives were a source of creation.

8½ is the story of Guido Anselmi (Marcello Mastroianni), a prominent Italian film director who is enmeshed in a deep struggle in his personal and artistic life. Guido's producer (Guido Alberti) sends the director to a health spa for revitalization so that he can make the decisions necessary to take his next film out of planning-stage limbo and into production. As he undergoes a "cure," Guido encounters journalists, actors, his crew, wife, parents, and the many women in his life, and experiences a series of memories and fantasies that become the movie he wants to film. Ulti-

Marcello Mastroianni as Guido Anselmi, a blocked film director who can't get his next movie started, in Federico Fellini's *8½*. This influential personal film placed the film director at the center of the movie, not just as an auteur but as the flesh and blood inspiration of all of his work. Courtesy *Photofest.*

mately the project, including a full-scale rocket-launcher set, is scrapped. Guido finally achieves clarity and discovers his directorial persona as a cinematic circus ringmaster with all the "actors" of his life joyfully celebrating in a hand-in-hand circular dance while Guido, megaphone in hand, is in full control of the movie that is his life.

The title *8½* refers to the fact that this film is Fellini's eighth-and-one-half film. He had directed seven feature films and "The Temptation of Dr. Antonio" episode for *Boccaccio '70*. In a fantastical manner, Marcello Mastroianni, the film director in a midlife crisis, is a screen-in for the off-screen Fellini. There are references connecting Mastroianni to Fellini, including a facsimile of the maestro's hat, similar glasses, and graying hair.

8½ has both fascinated and eluded audiences since its initial release in 1963. For viewers who demand a linear logic and must know what the story is "about," the film seems overstylized and full of symbols that make it incomprehensible. At the other extreme, there are those who analyze *8½* to the frame. Fellini pokes fun at both of these responses toward the cinema throughout *8½*.

In *8½*, Guido, like Fellini, is surrounded by journalists and photographers—the paparazzi (a term coined in Fellini's *La Dolce Vita* with the character Paparazzo). They demand to know his views on God, nuclear war, and death, and badger him with endless questions concerning the "meaning" of his films. Everyone wants a part in Guido's new film. Many address the camera directly as if they are speaking to Fellini next to the camera. Federico Fellini began as an Italian neorealist (see chapter 6) and then departed from that style by exploring his dreams and fantasies. Fellini adored the circus and cartooning. The outrageous spirits in his characters are like caricatures come to life.

The movie within *8½* is never made, but it is the subject of the entire film. Dream sequences and Guido's fantasies are clear references for the story-line of the film stuck in preproduction. These fantasy sequences are triggered by the people in Guido's life and signs, symbols, and actions that mentally transport him into a Fellini-esque world—a delightful blend of surrealism, theater of the absurd, low comedy, metaphysics, and the bunkum of a carny huckster.

Most films about filmmaking concern the power and control possessed by the moneymen. The glamour, backstage politics, sex, romance, and the contrast between the glitz and desperation of moviemaking are often the focus of the narrative. The physical process of making movies is usually a backdrop for the drama played out through the interrelationships of the characters. The movie being made is often uninteresting or not plausible. *8½* is about the process of making a film seen through the reality experienced by the director. That is what makes *8½* so daring. To Guido, the movie and his life are so interconnected he cannot completely separate them. At the time of making *8½*, Fellini was suffering a creative block and was trying to understand himself, his method of making films, and the extreme reactions he received from the public, critics, and the press.

The director of a film is the constant center of attention—everyone wants something from him or her. There is always someone in the director's face asking for favors, looking for answers—wanting something the director does not always have to give. The director's mind is continually in the movie. Film directors have strong needs. They demand constant companionship—in Guido's case, an endless series of women from his mother, to his wife, to his mistress, to aspiring actresses and hangers-on who would like to know him.

8½ is presented totally from Guido's point of view. The audience sees his world through confused sensibilities. His past and present life become artistically and physically entwined. At the opening of *8½*, Guido is asleep at a spa where they are administering a cure with water baths and other therapies to calm his frazzled nerves and to allow his mind to operate clearly and decisively. But what we see in the opening sequence is Guido trapped in a car that is stuck in a massive traffic jam. Nobody is moving. People stare at Guido. He looks over to a bus and sees headless hanging bodies. A vapor comes into the car along with the sound of gas or some sort of emission. Guido slams on the windows, his hands squeak down the glass. Then, suddenly, Guido is released from the car and flies over the traffic and into the clouds. There is a tower in construction in the distance, which we learn later is a reference to his unfinished main set. Guido is attached to a rope held by a man on the ground and then falls into the water. From the outset, the critical extremes Fellini experienced are at work. What does the opening signify? The nightmare has elements that most moviegoers have experienced, but this is a film director's dream, one that admirers recognize as Fellini-esque. Guido wakes up from his nightmare at a health spa, to the constant attention of doctors working to get him well. The bill is paid by his producer, who is only supportive because his capital is at risk. So the surrealistic visual dynamics are heightened. Guido is trapped—blocked—the real life nightmare of any artist. People stare at him. In his celebrity life, everywhere Guido/Federico turns people are looking at him. Suffocation overwhelms him because everyone demands something from him. When Guido is free from the car and flying, it is a potent symbol for liberation. The rope represents the bonds that confine him in real life. Guido falls to the ground because he is not really free but chained down by personal relationships, his professional responsibilities, and the 24/7 demands of a celebrity filmmaker.

Often narratives that contain nightmares as a means of understanding the inner life of a character make stark contrasts in style between the dream and waking states; *8½* does not. Film directors see the reality of the world through their own perceptions. Their films reflect the worldview or vision they possess. Fellini was at the height of his powers during the golden age of international cinema in the 1960s. Contemporaries such as Ingmar Bergman, Michelangelo Antonioni, Luis Buñuel, Jean-Luc Godard, and Akira Kurosawa created bodies of work that could be comprehended as one continuous film, as each director explored the world and culture in a cinematic language refined for themselves. Camera, design, sound, and editing were all part of their lexicon.

So *8½* is an interpretive and expressive autobiographical film. For Fellini, it represented his emotional and subconscious life through which he filtered some reality of his actual existence. Combing *8½* for clues to the real Federico Fellini is a treacherous endeavor. Experiencing *8½* as a visual feast that probes the very essence of how a film director feels, sees, and interprets stimuli is not only rewarding, but like Guido's quest, it liberates the viewer from the shackles of attaining an absolute meaning.

Like Luis Buñuel (*Viridiana, Simon of the Desert, Belle de Jour*) Fellini was a Catholic film director who infused his films with a devilishly satiric criticism of the church. In *8½* he demonstrates the church's dominance over Italian society by presenting an eminence that has all the answers and lords over the content of films. Nuns take part in administering the spa's cure, and at one point Guido wears a priest's collar to equate the film director with God and the priesthood.

Guido is preoccupied to the point of distraction with the women in his life. Claudia (Claudia Cardinale) is a muse of whom he fantasizes as a nurse. He is intoxicated with her natural beauty and brings her to the set, desperately hoping she will cure his creative stagnation. Carla (Sandra Milo) is Guido's mistress. He puts her up in a hotel to hide her from his wife, Luisa (Anouk Aimée), but he really wants them both to be friends so he can have both his mate and playmate. During a memory trip, Guido remembers La Saraghina (Edra Gale), an earthy woman who entertained his pals when the boys visited her at a remote spot outside the city. To the young Guido, La Saraghina is pure sex with a bountiful figure, long disheveled hair, and layers of thick makeup. Guido has more issues than he can handle when he traces back to both his parents, especially his mother (Giuditta Rissone), who is ashamed when he is caught dancing with La Saraghina by a priest. Luisa wants Guido to bury his past. He can't live with or without his mother and wants her to allow him to be free. Guido wants the women in his life all to be actresses in his life movie. He tries to direct them to his every whim but has lost his authority. The metaphor of the director as ringmaster blatantly expresses itself in Guido's attitude toward women when at one point he is actually using a circus bullwhip to tame the female animal. For Guido, when women reach a certain age they are banished to the upstairs of his life, away from the main stage. He tries to cast actresses for the women in his real world for the film he can not seem able to make. The real female "cast" begins to hound him en masse, along with the paparazzi.

The content of *8½* and Fellini's cinematic style are directly linked. In concept, all of *8½* looks like Guido/Federico directed it; reality, recalled memories, dreams, and fantasies are subjectively rendered through the vivid, theatrical, surreal vision of the creator Guido, by way of Fellini. Two distinct areas of the visualization complement each other. There is the physical production and the cinematic representation commonly known as **mise-en-scène** (see chapter 39). The production design by Piero Gheradi (*Big Deal on Madonna Street, Juliet of the Spirits, Burn!*) and Vito Anzalone (*La Dolce Vita, Juliet of the Spirits, The Queens*) appears as if out of a director's notebook. There are graceful curves in the architecture and globe shapes for practical light fixtures. The spa has large Roman steps and elegant rooms. The countryside is spare and untouched by the fanciful design of the city.

In every Fellini film, there are those faces that fascinate him. No other filmmaker has captured such a wide range of humanity from the grotesque to the average to the beautiful. To Fellini, a person's face is his or her character. Some can be considered stereotypes, but all capture the viewer's eye as they have for the director, whose legendary casting process took him on a journey from town to town in Italy searching for the faces to fit the characters he dreamed of, and to create characters for the faces he found through the process of welcoming the family of man into his world. Makeup and hair are exaggerated and flamboyant, representing how characters want the world to see them.

8½ is brilliantly photographed by Gianni Di Venanzo (*Salvatore Guliano, Eva, La Notte*). The tonal range is wide—from the whitest of whites to the deepest blacks. The gray scale is so delicately rendered, it evokes a vivid **color palette**.

Fellini makes effective use of Wagner's *Ride of the Valkyries*. This adds an operatic input to the large gestures, extreme faces, and fantastical events. Much later, John Milius would write this music into the script for the *Apocalypse Now* (see chapter 3) helicopter battle. In *8½*, Fellini utilizes it to accompany a sequence of hordes of the psychically lost as they are taken through the regimen of the spa's cure.

The music by Nino Rota (*Romeo and Juliet, Fellini Satyricon, The Godfather*) is deliciously Italian, buoyant in orchestration—one almost feels the presence of the musicians sitting right outside the frame. The circus metaphor is directly carried into the score. The themes do not underscore action or attempt to generate dramatic emotion as much as create an atmosphere for the scenes to take flight in. The sound design for *8½* by Alberto Bartolomei (*Indiscretion of an American Wife, The Battle of Algiers, The Bird with the Crystal Plumage*) and Mario Faraoni (*Don Camilio in Moscow, Juliet of the Spirits, Senza Sapere Nieto di Lei*) is sparse and very subjective. The principal aural element is the sound of wind, interpreting both the space and movement of freedom as well as the threat of losing one's bearings.

The physical staging and camera choreography of *8½* is fluid and draws inspiration from opera, ballet, and classical theater. The character movements during long takes generate the realization of the mise-en-scène. Scenes and sequences have little interscene editing. Actors move cameras. Fellini's staging of the actors is assured and controlled, as if the director were conducting an orchestra, stage managing an opera company, or acting as ringmaster of the Cirque Du Soleil. When the camera dictates the movement of an actor, the recording instrument becomes the star. In *8½*, Di Venanzo's camera gracefully moves on a character's entrance, or to follow one to another, or travels in search and then dances a sublime dance locked in on a character's movement, gesture, and attitude. The camera movements in *8½* are subtle because the lens becomes the viewer's eye, and our thought process is given over to Guido/Federico for the course of the film.

Fellini-esque has become part of the international vernacular. Federico Fellini was a film director with more than just a cinematic worldview. Film was the viaduct for communicating his thoughts, feelings, and emotions about a world in which only he lived. It is shared by audiences every time they experience one of his films. *8½* is the film in which the maestro intimately let us in on what it was like to be Federico Fellini struggling with artistic and personal issues. Or was he just being Fellini-esque?

Of Further Interest

Screen

Alex in Wonderland
All That Jazz
Fellini's Roma
Jo Jo Dancer, Your Life is Calling
Juliet of the Spirits

Read

The Cinema of Federico Fellini by Peter Bondanella
Fellini's Films by Frank Burke
I, Fellini by Charlotte Chandler
Fellini on Fellini by Federico Fellini
Federico Fellini by Christopher Wiegand

Animation and Music

□ ◆ □ ◆ □ ◆ □

Fantasia

When *Fantasia* was released in a limited **roadshow** presentation in 1940, it was considered an oddity. Sitting in front of this daring cinematic experiment today, it is conclusive that its creator, Walt Disney, was not only ahead of his time, but also understood applications of the medium that would link animation and live action, narrative and **nonnarrative films**. With *Fantasia* Disney married music and moving images to create a film experience that operated simultaneously on many aesthetic and emotional planes.

Fantasia is a concert film. In fact, before the term fantasia, signifying a musical composition with improvisational character that explores a common theme in a free and fanciful manner, became the official title, early paperwork on the project identifies it as a concert film. The genesis of the project had been built around the Walt Disney Studios superstar, Mickey Mouse. The beloved character had been evolving, becoming more childlike with expressive facial and physical attributes. Disney was looking for different story situations for his creation, considered by many as a Disney alter ego. A short subject of Mickey as Paul Dukas's Sorcerer's Apprentice was the initial idea that began *Fantasia*'s long journey to the screen. Disney writers and artists crafted a story in which Mickey would be dressed in a red magician's robe and borrow the blue pointed hat with stars from his master. Tired of the drudgery of schlepping his broom and pail, Mickey casts a spell that brings the broom to life to facilitate his cleaning assignment. This spell quickly gets out of the amateur conjurer's

An animated image of Hell inspired by German Expressionism set to Moussorgsky's "Night on Bald Mountain" in the concluding segment from *Fantasia,* Walt Disney's brave experiment merged what were formally considered cartoons with classical music, proving the enormous dramatic potential of the medium. Courtesy *Photofest.*

control. Mickey tries to stop the broom, which is flooding the sorcerer's lair with pail after pail of water, by chopping it up with an axe, but hundreds of broom clones come to life and create a flood of biblical proportions. The master finally arrives with the power to end the procession started by his apprentice, who disrespected the gift of magic. To conduct the segment, Disney approached famed conductor Leopold Stokowski, who was dedicated to expanding the popularity of classical music to the masses. In addition to his accomplishments as a conductor, Stokowski was well-known to radio audiences, and his distinctive facial profile commanded respect as a musical authority and celebrity.

The enthusiasm of the two men led Disney to take a bold and unprecedented step. Instead of one short subject, he would commit the Disney Studio to a massive project and produce a concert film to present many pieces of music. Audiences attending this film would not only hear great classical works but see visualizations that ranged from abstract to representational expressions of the music.

At this time, popular animation was considered to be pure entertainment. The Disney Studio maintained a strict aesthetic of traditional narrative projects, many based on well-known fairytales and stories made palatable for Hollywood consumption. Disney was a man whose imagination had no bounds. The commercial and artistic desires of his imagination were often in conflict, because unlike smaller studios and independent experimental animation artists, Walt Disney was responsible for a corporation while being a dedicated risk taker.

The Stokowski–Disney partnership was forged at a time when Disney had access to the finest artists, animators, technicians, and innovative technology. Deems Taylor, a composer, author, and music critic who had advised CBS and was popular as a narrator for classical music radio broadcasts, was brought onto the team. The three men spent weeks behind closed doors going over the classical canon to select the program for the concert film.

The development of the multiplane camera in 1937 by William Garity, who led a team of Disney scientists and technicians, gave the team the ability to explore three-dimensional design ideas. The technique, which was awarded a special Academy Award, had been used on Disney's first feature animation project, *Snow White and the Seven Dwarfs*. It allowed different elements of a scene to be drawn and painted on separate plastic or glass cels. They then were placed at specific distances apart on different planes so that when photographed together the combination of images created the illusion of depth. Knowing the capabilities of multiplane animation expanded the stories and images that could be imagined and captured on film. Through innovation in this area, special effects, and film sound reproduction, the concert film team had few limitations on their ambitions for the project.

Animation had been developing as an art since 1832, long before live-action photography appeared on the scene. Although it was established and pigeonholed by the larger industry as a form of entertainment for children and families, the concept of drawings, objects, photographs, puppets, silhouettes, figures, places, and images, registered a frame at a time to create the illusion of movement, presented unlimited possibilities for moving picture art. Walt Disney was notable for creating mass-produced, assembly-line cartoons and feature films. Although the Disney name was synonymous with animation, there were many other pioneers with other aesthetic and narrative concerns as their mission. Winsor McKay and Max and Dave Fleischer had a less conservative, more adventurous approach to animation. In the early 1920s, Hans Richter, Fernand Leger, and Walter Ruttmann were avant-garde filmmakers who experimented freely with the medium. Disney was adventurous, but the risk of failure loomed as a high cost of maintaining his empire and the respect of his audience. Disney had created an animated universe of cute, cuddly animals and figures. He was fiercely loyal to American ideals. A man in conflict, the artist in Disney knew no boundaries; the businessman, however, guarded his sacred investment in the studio and what it stood for.

There was no precedent for *Fantasia,* only a prehistory of animation, live action, and the concert hall format. No one had combined them in the way Disney and his collaborators envisioned. They were starting from scratch and writing their own rules.

Everything emanates from the concert film concept. The viewer is positioned in an imaginary concert hall. The seats are our movie theater chairs or the home sofa. In front of our view, chairs and music stands for the orchestra surround a conductor's podium. *Fantasia* begins as if the audience is seated politely waiting for the program overture. It is not established whether this is a day or evening performance. It is almost like a concert performed in cyberspace—necessary elements are in place; others, like windows or the architecture of the hall, are not. Before a blue background the musicians assemble and begin to warm up. The atmosphere is serious but amiable. The musicians are in silhouette, most in dead black while a thin layer of light penetrates others. They are in concert dress. Tuning and warm-up exercises proceed in an airy and convivial manner. This is a concert for everyone. Deems Taylor makes his entrance and explains that he will be our host. Taylor explains that there will be three types of presentations: a distinct story interpreted by the artists from a narrative within the music, others in which the artists paint representational pictures of what the music stirs in them, and to open the program, the most challenging—music for its own sake with absolute music and abstract images to accompany it. Maestro Stokowski enters and takes his place at the podium. The opening piece is *Toccata and Fugue In D Minor* by Johann Sebastian Bach. The lighting changes on the conductor; a pink ball forms behind him. Color fields of subtle light pour over the sections of the orchestra. The tympani drums are struck with a mallet and the instruments emit light. This happens to the French horns and other sections that make up the symphonic orchestra. A **dissolve** transforms the scene to the animator's canvas. There are abstract clouds and a series of light streaks. *Fantasia* is forging pure sound with pure images. The abstractions are inspired by the nonrepresentational work of painter Oskar Fichinger, known for his experiments with geometric shapes. Disney has laid down the gauntlet by beginning *Fantasia* with the most extreme form of music combined with nonfigurative images. Disney the representationist can't resolve his conflict. The battle between art and commerce takes place in this sequence. The abstractions are defined as violin strings, rolling hills, mountains as towers in the sky. The result is radical for its time as a work meant for the popular audience—it would be left to others to pick up the pure abstraction work. Disney may have compromised, but must be commended for such a bold demonstration that could have lost the audience. There would be something for everyone in *Fantasia*, but only the open-minded, the curious, and those seeking adventure through art could stay the course on this premier journey into the reaches of animation.

Stokowski returns to conclude. There is no sign or sound of the audience. Do we clap in the movie theater, at home, even if alone? Why not? This is a concert and applause is a release of pleasure and an acknowledgement of enlightenment even if the performers can not hear it. This real-time act on our part completes the concert experience.

Deems Taylor introduces each new piece of music. He is the prototype for the Leonard Bernstein Young People's Concerts that years later would delight and educate a generation of baby boomers about the classical repertoire. Taylor never talks down to the audience. He gives them background and roads to follow. He never takes too much of our time, but without him this would be an incomplete experience, just a series of strung-together short subjects. Stokowski is the concertmaster, but Taylor is the teacher and guide. The live-action images of these two men and the orchestra feature bold graphics. This is not a realistic, **documentary** presentation that we leave periodically for flights of fantasy. This concert film is taking place in a very special hall, a perfect place where no one will whisper, chew gum, or say "excuse me" as they block your view. It is perfect because the experience travels directly from the screen to our eyes and ears to stimulate our imagination. Image and sound combine in *Fantasia* to delight the artistic soul and satiate the desire for cultural nourishment.

Tchaikovsky's *The Nutcracker Suite* is reimagined with dancing flowers, mushrooms, and a twinkling fairy. Snowflakes dance and there is a Russian dance, ice skating, and bubbles. The sequence is a celebration of nature in all its grace and beauty, achieved with gentle humor and delight. Each segment was assigned to a different team, part of the Disney factory method. The results are nuanced in line, color, figure, and abstraction.

The Sorcerer's Apprentice is the most celebrated sequence in *Fantasia*. It is both cute and spooky. We encourage Mickey's impish curiosity, but our worst nightmares are realized as the army of possessed brooms becomes the ultimate Halloween scare. Before *Fantasia*, Mickey was a star—now he is an icon—a master Hollywood performer like Paul Muni, Bette Davis, Fred Astaire, and Judy Garland.

Stravinsky's *The Rite of Spring*, which caused a music hall riot when it premiered in 1913, is interpreted by the audacious *Fantasia* team as the evolution of the earth. Film critic and Entertainment Tonight regular Leonard Maltin recalls public schools showing just this segment on a 16mm projector in science class as a legitimate educational tool. The growth of life as it evolves is exhibited as science, not the imaginative interpretation of the artist. A single cell becomes amphibious life; then the dinosaurs before the dawn of man appear. As creation evolves, the ocean and the cosmos form and volcanoes erupt from the bowels of the earth. The dinosaurs act out the survival of life—a story to be repeated endlessly by man throughout human history.

A fifteen-minute intermission is announced; it is a time to stretch, absorb, and prepare—a civilized ritual of the theater. A curtain closes. The title *Fantasia* appears. The curtain opens for the second portion of the program. The musicians again take their places. This time the warm-up is a spontaneous jazz improvisation that begins with a bass riff.

Deems Taylor introduces us to the soundtrack. To make a connection between the music and how it is delivered from the optical track on the film, there is a demonstration of what sound looks like.[1] Colors and wave patterns change; it is humorous and entertaining but close enough to the truth to be educational. The Disney artists found another way to display the relationship between music and images. These sounds and the patterns they make on the soundtrack are the ingredients for limitless possibilities that can be achieved by the marriage of sound and motion pictures. Musical instruments that produce both high and low timbre display what they look like, in color, hue, and undulating shape.

Beethoven's *The Pastoral Symphony* is visualized as Mount Olympus. This mythology play features centaurs, unicorns, Bacchus, Apollo, Zeus, and Morpheus. The sequence is graceful, painted in delicate watercolors, majestic, idyllic, and symmetrical. There is no central story here—we experience the passage of time and weather, rain, thunder, clearing, sunset, the moon, and a time for sleep.

Dance of the Hours by Amilcar Ponchielli is a musical war-horse that the Disney crew decided to send up. This ballet is danced by ostriches, elephants, hippos with tutus, and crocodiles. It is satire, but the artists studied and drew real dancers in preparation for the piece and we come away with a real respect for classical dance. The segment is about movement and interaction.

The powerful conclusion of *Fantasia* is the combination of Modeste Moussorgsky's *Night on Bald Mountain* and Franz Schubert's *Ave Maria*—the profane and the sacred, evil and good. This is adult animation. It begins with a depiction of a winged creature presiding over skeletons and ghosts he has commanded from graves. It can be read as the devil in Hades, but the sequence is primal, not biblical. Daring imagery includes naked female bodies, skulls, flames, and molten lava. A series of chimes send the bad spirits away. We rise to the sky as *Ave Maria* takes over from the maniacal *Night on Bald Mountain*. Day breaks. There are clouds, then a procession of the faithful carrying yellow globes of light as they steadily move across the land and over a bridge; the scene is reflected in a pool of water. As the procession moves through tall elegant woods, the trees become a cathedral. We are lifted above, see shafts of blue light, and move into a beautiful garden. The focus shifts our eyes to a blue sky and the sun rises—then the image fades to black. *Fantasia* has concluded; we are shaken with its beauty. We do not have to leave the concert hall or go anywhere—the music and the images are within us.

Notes

1. An optical track is a photographic recording of sound that is printed on the edge of a release print next to the picture area. A bulb in a projector scans the light and converts it to sound that is amplified during the screening of a film.

Of Further Interest

Screen

Akira
American Pop
Gerald McBoing Boing
Pinocchio
Toy Story

Read

Animation: The Whole Story by Howard Beckerman
Animation: From Script to Screen by Shamus Culhane
Chuck Amuck: The Life and Times of an Animated Cartoonist by Chuck Jones
The Animation Book: A Complete Guide to Animated Filmmaking, from Flip-Books to Sound Cartoons by Kit Laybourne
The Animator's Survival Kit by Richard Williams

21

An American Musical

□ ◆ □ ◆ □ ◆ □

42nd Street

Before there was Bob Fosse, or Joe Gideon, his on-screen persona in *All That Jazz,* there was Julian Marsh and *Pretty Lady* in the black-and-white musical *42nd Street* (1933). Marsh (Warner Baxter) is Broadway's greatest musical–comedy stage director. He signs a contract to direct *Pretty Lady,* a deal the producers make because they are convinced Marsh's name on the dotted line will ensure a hit. Marsh is edgy, short-tempered, and desperate. He should be rich and living off the wealth of his success, but Wall Street has drained all his cash. It is the early 1930s, the Great Depression has taken its toll on the country. The Broadway musical distracts Americans from their pain and is an escape for a nation in despair. Pretty faces, leggy blondes, catchy tunes, snappy dance numbers, and uplifting fantasies are just the ticket.

Marsh is bitter over the "gulch" that is Forty-second Street, which has emotionally, physically, artistically, and financially sucked him dry until all he has left is a good suit and a stiff brim hat. Accessorized with a lifetime supply of cigarettes, this is Marsh's uniform as a hard-driving, tyrannical director who will deliver a hit show by any means necessary.

42nd Street finds Julian Marsh at a low point in his life and career. He agrees to direct one last show—an all-or-nothing gamble. In addition to heading toward financial ruin, Marsh has a history of nervous breakdowns. His doctor advises against the new assignment. Marsh is a Type A perfectionist who exists in a constant state of agitation. No singer, dancer, or crew member is ever good enough for Marsh. He is warned by

Warner Baxter—as the driven, half-crazed, disheveled, mortally ill, and theatrical genius Julian Marsh—demands discipline and perfection as all eyes of his Broadway musical troupe listen in fear and anticipation. The two rows of dancers maintain a precision of depth perspective in *42nd Street*—the paradigm for New York, and the backstage American musical. Courtesy *Photofest.*

his physician that another mental collapse might trigger a fatal heart attack. Marsh rolls the dice and turns *Pretty Lady* into a Broadway hit—a toe-tapping entertainment wrapped in the delirium of the times that takes place in New York, the city that gives Marsh his razor's edge.

42nd Street is a New York movie filmed on a Hollywood sound stage. The pulse of the city is established during the opening credits. The Vitaphone Orchestra plays the theme music as if they had been up all night smoking, drinking, and carousing. The music is raw, hard, brassy, and played at a tempo just short of overdrive. There are shots of the city, mainly defined by a wide view jittering with excitement, and a **montage** of street signs, including the most famous one in America: Forty-Deuce—the boulevard of broken dreams, where careers are made and shattered. On Forty-second Street hope is turned into fame if the swarming crowd stops moving just long enough to acknowledge a diamond in a mountain of coal. There is always someone next in line on Forty-second Street.

Like the *N.Y. to L.A.* musical within *All That Jazz*, *Pretty Lady* combines glamour with grime. After a cute "Shuffle off to Buffalo" number concerning newlyweds and precision dance choreography, sex, and sophistication, the title song becomes a production number that goes beyond entertainment to a dance that celebrates the glory and danger of the city that never did sleep. A backdrop brings the street to the stage so show-biz can mingle with the dangers and manic energy of the Great White Way. Peggy Sawyer (Ruby Keeler), the kid who comes back a star, taps her heart out and then we jump to the top of a cab—we are on Forty-second Street. A subway entrance leads to the underground terrain of the city; a barber and a nanny with a baby do their jobs to the pounding song that pays tribute to the toughest real estate in America. Immigrants close up their fruit and vegetable carts to play golf; shoes are shined to the beat of dancing feet. A woman is mauled by her man through the window of a seedy hotel. There are gun shots and she leaps to the street and is caught and danced by a New York tough until the boyfriend, now behind her, stabs this dame to death. The stage becomes a sea of cardboard sky-scrapers tilted back and forth by a sea of dancers. When the show ends, the audience streams out of the theater on to the next New York minute. They celebrate Sawyer. A star is born as the denigrate Marsh sits on the back steps. He has directed his last show. He is exhausted. The exiting theatergoers dismiss his triumph and credit the star. John Q. Public is convinced Marsh is dispensable—the final insult from the town that made him and now breaks him. We do not see Marsh die, but he is a dead man spiritually if not physically—the city swallows him up.

42nd Street embraces the sudden passion of New York City, where ambition can lead to prosperity, celebrity, or disaster. Martin Scorsese, John Cassavetes, Sidney Lumet, Spike Lee, Woody Allen, Abel Ferrara, Bob Fosse, and a hundred B-movie directors have walked the Deuce, where promise of romance, the fear of the unknown, and the wrong place at any time have inspired the genres of drama, musicals, and comedy. Scorsese shot *Mean Streets* primarily in Los Angeles, but that film, like *42nd Street*, never lost its edge. It is the attitude—tough, funny, abrasive, crude, and elegant, it is the one place on the planet that is the litmus test to prove whether you can make it there, and so then, anywhere.

Cinematic technique is applied to *42nd Street* for expressive purposes. The **crane** shots shake, the montage is spit out, and the art direction is background for the human drama; the naked rehearsal stage and squalid backstage is home. *42nd Street* is a documentary fantasy, as if the dames and con men, the gents, the regular Joes, the shop girls who read *Photoplay*, the hustler hawking for a buck, and the street cops could all sing and dance.

42nd Street is a backstage musical, a story about show people: their desires, fights for survival, the tedium of their lives, the parties, the endless auditions and practice, and the ever-changing cast of lovers, moneymen, stage managers, chorus boys and girls. Abner Dillion (Guy Kibbee) is a kiddie-car magnate who backs the play to wine and dine Dorothy Brock (Bebe Daniels), a star who in turn is really in love with Pat Denning (George Brent), a performer with less luster. The fresh face kid Peggy Sawyer, a babe in the woods surrounded by cynical pros who have seen it all, becomes romantically involved with Billy Lawler (Dick Powell), one of Broadway's better juveniles. Marsh's right-hand man, Andy Lee (George E. Stone), is a yes man with a pencil mustache, who keeps things moving and is a father figure, brother, best friend, lover boy, diplomat, and taskmaster all rolled into one. Thomas Barry (Ned Sparks) and Mac Elroy (Allen Jenkins), curmudgeons always cracking wise, are permanent members of the Broadway grind. The songs by Harry Warren and Al Dubin are the score to *Pretty Lady*, performed in the context of the show as it is rehearsed and at the end, performed at its premiere. No one breaks into song as part of the narrative development in *42nd Street*. The film audience watches as Marsh shapes what the temperamental director considers a leaky musical into an entertainment machine that never quits. As he directs the show, Marsh perpetually chain-smokes cigarettes, rubs the back of his neck, scowls, gives speeches, throws out routines, and drives the cast to the breaking point. When he gives them an hour break or sends them home for a night's rest, he demands that they relax.

42nd Street perpetuates the myth of the director as dictator beating his cast and crew into submission. Marsh gives several tear 'em down, build 'em up speeches that are among the finest of the backstage genre. He is a no-nonsense man without agendas. He does not party, does not pick a chorus girl to share his bed each night. All he cares about—more accurately, obsesses over—is the work. Julian Marsh is not only the prototype for Bob Fosse or Joe Gideon as a genius slave driver, he is Hollywood's image of the director as a force of nature. As Marsh, always ready to explode, twists himself into his hardwood chair on the precipice of the stage, his presence on the screen is a tribute to Otto Preminger, Cecil B. DeMille, Joseph von Sternberg, and Eric von Stroheim. Warner Baxter inhabits all these men. His Julian Marsh is the life-blood of show business. The stars achieve celebrity, but it is the director, the man you love to hate, the entertainment machine that lives on sawdust, about whom the legends are written.

42nd Street was directed by Lloyd Bacon (1890–1955; *Knute Rockne All American*, *Give My Regards to Broadway*), who handled the dialogue scenes.

The Julian Marsh behind Julian Marsh's extravagant, glitzy, and delightfully excessive vision was Hollywood's choreographic genius, the one and only Busby Berkeley (1895–1976).

Berkeley was a stage baby—his father was a theater director and his mother was an actress of the boards and the screen. When he was three, Busby's family moved to New York; at five, the boy made his debut as a stage performer. Schooling at a military academy and service in World War I as a field artillery lieutenant instilled in Berkeley the discipline and precision he would later bring to his innovative work in film. By the end of the Roaring Twenties, Busby Berkeley was known on Forty-second Street as one of Broadway's best dance directors—a reputation he shared with the fictional Julian Marsh. Samuel Goldwyn brought Berkeley to Hollywood in 1930 to choreograph musical sequences featuring the mogul's star, Eddie Cantor. In 1933, he began to work at Warner Brothers, where Berkeley was empowered with the technology and the technicians to realize his vision of that seminal American decade.

Two major forces pulled America out of the misery of the Great Depression: President Franklin Delano Roosevelt and the Hollywood dream factory. For the suffering, public entertainment was a powerful healer. On the giant screen they could see glamour and beauty and for a few hours could escape from poverty, joblessness, soup kitchens, and a broken economy.

During the 1930s, Busby Berkeley seized the time and did more than just distract his countrymen. His delirious, extravagant, sexy, frenetic, and decadent concoctions raised the spirits and contributed to the delightfully vulgar American pop culture. His metaphor was a celebration of the populace. The production numbers in *42nd Street* are filled with a procession of humanity, configured in rows and circles moving in every direction of the compass. Going beyond the individual, past the pair to the masses was part of Berkeley's more-is-more philosophy.

The "Shuffle off to Buffalo" number in *42nd Street* is set in a sexually provocative context. The young marrieds are on a honeymoon train to Niagara Falls. As they skip through the cars, the packed train of the initiated smirk and chirp at the innocents, knowing what will come next. The number appears to be light and innocent, but there is erotic intensity when from behind the curtains of their berth the bride extends her arm to put her shoes out onto the train hall floor. With her arm up and fully extended, holding her shoe, Berkeley intimates the sexual rapture behind the curtain.

Berkeley is most associated with female dance configurations in abstract geometric patterns. Here his concept is stark black and white and a circle in an inverted V formed by the spread-eagle gams of the dancers. The women are linked arm-to-arm and circle on a turntable to the music of "Young and Healthy." The camera moves in between their legs and finds the juvenile and a platinum blonde lying down on the shiny reflective surface heads up and smiling. The abstraction of the limbs transcends the potential tastelessness of the visual image. This is the point of view of an abstractionist who uses live flesh as his medium, not the perverse daydream of a dirty old or young man—although maybe it is both.

Berkeley ends the play within the film with social commentary. The musical dance number that concludes *42nd Street* may be his masterpiece. The man who was Broadway's hottest dance director in the 1920s with a record of twenty-one hit shows returns to the Big Apple without leaving the Hollywood soundstage to present the street as microcosm of high and low life. The elite and the proles intermingle. A society of rich and poor, the rich own the town and pick all of its riches, but the underclass survives here too, off the wealth of the upper class. They can thrive in spite and because of the rich. The street is democracy. The street is desire and fear. Decades before Sam Peckinpah, Busby Berkeley turned horror into ballet. A woman's leap to the street, an act of desperation is also a moment of courage and bravery—she, for getting to safety; her rescuer, for his strength and command. Life is fleeting though, as the knife in the back proves, and as in life, both the high and the low pulse by without a turn of the head from the masses.

Ironically, Berkeley's radical application of formation, syncopation, and Dadaist absurdity still maintains the sanctity of the proscenium stage. In traditional musicals before and after Berkeley, the camera stays on the audience's side of the view to maintain the relationship with the stage and its performers. Movie musicals were designed to be theater on film with a modest breaking of the rules regarding dividing line between the audience and the stage. This was mostly done through composition and camera movement. Not until Bob Fosse's *All That Jazz* was the line totally broken down. The viewer was hurled inside the dance through cinematic means. Berkeley turned the text and aesthetics of the musical through his choreography of dancer and camera, but his roots on the Broadway stage did not allow violation of the old rule. He would create a circle and turn it but not circle the camera so it became the **point of view** of performers on the stage. Berkeley did transcend the 180-degree rule with the **top shot**, where the camera looks straight down on the choreography in a kaleidoscopic view—a vista of new possibilities he explored in much of his work. The top shot became part of the contemporary cinematic idiom when Martin Scorsese, who grew up worshiping Berkeley and the American musical, applied the idea boldly in *Taxi Driver*. D. W. Griffith may receive most of the credit for the close-up and other aspects of movie grammar, but the top shot, also known as God's point of view, or an overhead, is pure cinema.

42nd Street speaks to our primal desires to make it big, to get that one big chance. The movies are an expression of the individual and a gift to the masses. Julian Marsh is the voice that tells us there is nothing nobler than giving yourself to your art for the sake of others.

For Further Interest

Screen

Cabaret
Fame
Footlight Parade
Oklahoma
Singin' in the Rain

Read

Hollywood Musicals: The Film Reader by Steven Cohan
42nd Street (BFI Film Classics) by J. Hoberman
The American Musical Film Song Encyclopedia by Thomas S. Hischak
Our Musicals, Ourselves: A Social History of the American Theater by John Bush Jones and Sheldon Harnick
Can't Help Singin': The American Musical on Stage and Screen by Gerald Mast

22

New York Filmmaking

The French Connection

The modern era of moviemaking in the United States began after the mighty classical Hollywood studio era came to a close during the 1960s. As a movement, the American New Wave of the 1970s produced the next generation of filmmakers, who applied an evolved aesthetic to content derived from a rapidly changing social and political culture.

In 1969, the last year of the Aquarian decade, three American films, *Easy Rider, Midnight Cowboy*, and *The Wild Bunch* (see chapter 49) implanted reproductive seeds to generate what became filmmaking's second golden age. This trio of films challenged the moral code of the traditional school by altering motion picture vocabulary to bring once taboo screen subjects to realization.

Many complex factors merge to form an artistic epoch. The most audacious and controversial works receive the lion's share of attention and reputation for their pioneering accomplishments, but it is the total application of a nascent aesthetic to the standard mode of operation that produces a quantitative and lasting transformation. *The French Connection* (1971) could have been another cop and gangster film if it followed traditional conventions in its approach to narrative, visualization, and structure. By applying a new language and style to what, on the surface, seemed familiar, *The French Connection* became a model of the new cinema; this cinema produced movies for general release, popular films that honestly reflected the age in which they were created.

Three principal characters in *The French Connection*: French drug kingpin Alain Charnier (Fernando Rey, right), Marcel Bozzuffi (Pierre Nicoli), his hit man, and New York City. The gritty crime drama was shot on location on New York streets in what would later be called run and gun style, heralding a new era in East Coast filmmaking. Courtesy *Photofest*.

The genesis of *The French Connection* was the true-life story of New York narcotics detectives Eddie Egan and Sonny Grosso, who made the largest heroin bust of their era. In 1968, author Robin Moore chronicled these events in a nonfiction book. Through an unusual series of events that included signatures on a cocktail napkin by an industrious third party, producer Philip D'Antoni (*Bullitt, The Seven-Ups*) acquired the film rights for *The French Connection* and was bankrolled by 20th-Century Fox.

D'Antoni chose thirty-five-year-old William Friedkin as director. The producer considered Friedkin's impressive **documentary** work an asset for a film based on a real incident. In addition, the director had completed two fictional television films and four theatrical features; *Good Times*, starring Sonny and Cher; *The Night They Raided Minsky's*; and stage adaptations of Harold Pinter's *The Birthday Party* and *The Boys in the Band*, written by Mart Crowley. Friedkin's goal was to apply a documentary style to *The French Connection* that was fueled by his admiration of Costa Gavras's *Z* and the creative daring of Jean-Luc Godard's *Breathless*.

Several screenplays were commissioned and rejected. Finally D'Antoni and Friedkin hired Ernest Tidyman (*High Plains Drifter, Report to the Commissioner, Street People*), a New York Times crime writer and author of the novel *Shaft*, to write his first screenplay, as he had impressed them with his background and ability to write in a credible street vernacular. To get what they wanted, the two men spent mornings acting out each scene for Tidyman, who would spend afternoons committing it to paper until the script was complete.

For Friedkin, who more than thirty years later still claims never to have read Moore's book or to have given Tidyman's script much consideration, the story could only come from the original source—"Popeye" Egan and "Cloudy" Grosso. Friedkin and the actors portraying the detectives, Gene Hackman and Roy Scheider, went out with Popeye and Cloudy on actual drug raids all over New York. Astounded by what he witnessed, Friedkin paid meticulous attention to everything the two cops said and did. This on-the-job research was incorporated directly into the film's narrative and gave the story an impression of verisimilitude rarely achieved in the genre.

The French Connection opens in France as Alain Charnier (Fernando Rey), an industrialist turned drug trafficker, is planning to smuggle a major shipment of raw heroin to New York by concealing the giant stash in a luxury automobile. Back in the Big Apple, Sal Boca (Tony LoBianco) is the middleman in the criminal transaction who is spotted by Popeye Doyle and Cloudy Russo. The two narcotics officers follow the trail and through dogged, unorthodox police work, they finally break the landmark case.

No sets were built for *The French Connection*. The film was shot on location in France, Washington, D.C., and on the streets of New York during one of the coldest winters in memory. The film's images are a series of contrasts opposing the famed Copacabana with the town's grimiest gin mills, a curbside slice of pizza with the elegance of a fine restaurant, a Brooklyn candy store with a chic hotel, the seaside of Marseilles with a low-rent housing project, and the elegance of a dapper criminal strolling on Madison Avenue with fedora and umbrella contrasted with a street cop topped by a pork-pie hat in a drab police precinct.

The cinematography by director of photography Owen Roizman (*The Exorcist, Network, Grand Canyon*) is immediate and realistic. The majority of *The French Connection* was shot with a handheld camera and natural lighting. Locations were lit to appear as if the practical sources of the sun, moon, and artificial fixtures provide the illumination. Friedkin rarely called for more than two takes of a particular shot and the action was either improvised or rehearsed in private. The camera operator followed the actors as the drama unfolded in much the same way as news and nonfiction footage is captured.

Hollywood traditionally postdubbed sound for scenes shot on location, but production sound recordist Chris Newman (*The Godfather, Amadeus, The English Patient*) brought back a production track that resonated with the vibrancy of the city.[1] It was later sweetened with sound effects that completed a veritable city soundscape.

Film editor Jerry Greenberg (*Kramer vs. Kramer, Scarface* [1983], *The Untouchables*) paced *The French Connection* with a brisk rhythm that balanced character, motion, and story. His contribution to the chase scene made it a benchmark of action cutting that continues to influence practitioners of the genre.

The performances by the entire cast are models of naturalistic acting. Each character is multidimensional with specific personality traits. Relationships and emotional drives are defined as are the motivation and intent of these vigorous, flawed, and very genuine screen people. Many of the background characters are played by nonactors who lived the life of the actual story, and residents of New York, instead of hired extras, filled the streets. Conflict and contrast are the stuff of drama. Popeye is instinctive and volatile. Cloudy is morose, loyal, and careful. Boca is ambitious and defiant. Charnier is urbane and crafty. Many action films contain one-dimensional characters and are powered by nonstop physical events. *The French Connection* balances the relationship between character development and the results of their actions by constantly investigating how the characters are reacting to their environment and circumstances.

Before *The French Connection,* musical **scores** had functioned primarily to finesse an audience's emotional reactions and to indicate the mood of a scene. Don Ellis, a jazz artist known for his experimental approach to melody and time signatures, created an atmospheric and psychologically penetrating score for *The French Connection*. The music is spare and effective. The score articulates Popeye Doyle's obsessive nature by musically addressing his thought process as he continually returns to his mania to catch the bad guys. Ellis also underscores the tensions controlling Popeye with a deep-toned riff that is at the same time halting and relentless.

The "music" of the chase involving a car and an elevated subway train is the sound of a speeding car, the pounding on wooden tracks, tire squeals, and a blaring auto horn. A dynamic use of parallel editing juxtaposes the pursued and the pursuer, emphasizing the cat and mouse chase, a narrative theme expressed throughout *The French Connection*, first on foot, then through hard-charging vehicles. Greenberg cuts back and forth as congested traffic and the train crew simultaneously complicate the quests of Doyle and Charnier's henchman, Pierre Nicoli (Marcel Bozzuffi). The intercutting keeps both lines of action "alive" by arriving and returning at just the right dramatic moments.[2] In editing circles this scene is often compared with the Odessa Steps sequence in Eisenstein's *The Battleship Potemkin* (see chapter 5). One of the heart-stopping moments during *The French Connection* chase also involves a mother, child, and a baby carriage. The Russian montage masterwork belonged to an early era of cinema, the American montage-style of *The French Connection* to modern times, but they are linked by the fertile concept that a collision of shot units is so much more than a sum of its parts.

In the case, Egan and Grosso made the big bust, but the Frenchman escaped to France and was never prosecuted because he had been a resistance fighter with Charles de Gaulle. However, the film ends on an ambiguous note. As they search for Charnier in the bowels of an abandoned ruin on Wards Island, Doyle tells Russo that he has seen the Frenchman. Doyle charges off, gun in hand, and runs through a doorway out of camera view. A gunshot rings out—cut to black—and the end credits roll.

Did Doyle get his man? Did Charnier kill Doyle? Was this the beginning of another episode that continues even though the film is over? With few exceptions the happy ending had always been the backbone of the American film. The original studio movie moguls had decided long ago that the resolution of drama was congruous with the victory of democracy over tyranny. That all changed by 1969. *Easy Rider* and *The Wild Bunch* end in slaughter; *Midnight Cowboy* concludes in death and desolation. The bullet without a discernible target in *The French Connection* implies that life continues without explanation or justice. The American film was finally liberated from a convention that prevented movies from being a mirror of reality, a concept long understood by international cinema.

Before Los Angeles became the industry's capital, moviemaking in America was located in New York. In Hollywood, New York had been depicted on soundstages, and occasionally on a brief location visit, the gritty streets would be transformed into Hollywood gloss. There had always been a New York school of filmmaking—an independent cinema of realistic dramas, documentaries, commercials, industrials, and personal and experimental works. These films reflected the urban pulse of the metropolis but were outside of the mainstream of commercial releases that shaped the nation's celluloid image.

The French Connection changed all that. Popular success and many awards including the grand jewel—an Oscar for Best Picture—focused attention on the New York state of mind. Since the 1970s, the New York film has earned its place in the canon of American cinema. The works of Woody Allen, Edward Burns, Nick Gomez, Spike Lee, Sidney Lumet, Martin Scorsese, Susan Seidelman, and Whit Stillman have grown the New York school into a graduate conservatory. These accomplishments have roots in personal and cultural history, but the organization of film history demands the identification of a prehistory, somewhere to start tracing the birth of movements. In that spirit, *The French Connection* is as good a place as any to decree.

Notes

1. The production sound recordist is responsible for recording the production track during the shooting of a film. Newman prefers this term to the more commonly used production sound mixer. The job is the same. The dialogue and other sounds produced during the shooting process are recorded. Tracks are not mixed together. On most productions, several microphones record actors in the scene either on separate or multiple tracks at the same level. Mixing occurs near the end of the postproduction process during the re-recording mix when all the tracks are blended together to achieve a desired effect.

2. "Alive" is an editing term that refers to keeping all of the characters or actions active in the mind of the audience by returning to them periodically to show their relationship to the story and to the other characters as the narrative progresses.

For Further Interest

Screen

Dog Day Afternoon
Laws of Gravity
Manhattan
Smithereens
Taxi Driver (1976)

Read

William Friedkin: Films of Aberration, Obsession, and Reality by Thomas D. Clagett
To Free the Cinema: Jonas Mekas & the New York Underground, edited by David E. James
Projections 11: New York Film-Makers on Film-Making, edited by Tod Lippy
Celluloid Skyline: New York and the Movies by James Sanders
Hurricane Billy: The Stormy Life and Films of William Friedkin by Nat Segaloff

Period Comedy

The General

The Beatles or the Rolling Stones? Vanilla or chocolate? Boxers or briefs? Chaplin or Keaton? There was a time in the 1960s and 1970s when the answer to this last question determined the nature of your silent film comedy personality. You could not like both, although secretly many film buffs did. The camp you put yourself in identified your position—sentimentality or surrealism. Among the Keatonites, *The General* (1927) is considered by most critics and historians to be his greatest achievement. The film consistently ranks high on lists lauding the greatest movies ever made. Esteemed film historian David Robinson states on the DVD case for the Kino release that *The General* is the most accurate and vivid visualization of the Civil War, even taking into account *The Birth of a Nation, Gone with the Wind,* and *The Red Badge of Courage.* All this, and *The General* is a seriously funny movie to boot.

The glossary contained in André Breton's *What is Surrealism?: Selected Writings,* edited and introduced by Franklin Rosemont, identifies Buster Keaton (1895–1966) as "objectively surrealist" (p. 493). The popular movie press of his time dubbed him "Old Stone Face." Charlie was the Little Tramp; Keaton was a determined and resolute young man who persisted through circumstances that required otherworldly athletic ability that Keaton executed effortlessly. Keaton's face was not stone. He was impassive because of the hyperreality in which he found himself. His eyes were expressive enough to influence every inch of his strangely handsome, boyish face. Keaton's head was in perpetual motion when his body

Buster Keaton and two young friends squat alongside the star of *The General,* a Civil War era steam engine train after which this meticulously rendered period comedy is named. Courtesy *Photofest.*

required it. His stare was mesmerizing, communicating befuddlement with innocence and intelligence. In a generation of comic masters known for the art of the single or double take, Keaton transcended technique and embraced the notion that life just can not be all that real.

The General takes place in Marietta, Georgia, during the Civil War in the spring of 1861. Our hero, Johnnie Gray (Buster Keaton), is a Southerner who is pressured to enlist in the Confederate army to impress Annabelle Lee (Marian Mack). He is summarily rejected because the military brass feel he will be more useful in his civilian job as engineer of a train that travels along the borders of the conflict between the states. The title has a double meaning; it is the name of Johnnie's train, and at the film's conclusion, when it is finally acknowledged that he was responsible for the winning of a major battle, Johnnie is promoted to that respected rank. A Union plot to hijack the train is the narrative motor of

The General. With little distraction, the majority of the film is a chase scene involving the train in various lengths, configurations, and directions North and South, with the controlling parties switching between the Northern army and our lone hero, representing the South. These amazing sequences are performed live with a real period train that is actually moving on working tracks. There are no special photographic effects or plates. The background and foreground are not art directed. The verisimilitude heightens the thrill of the action and allows the comic elements to soar just past reality.

Although the Civil War was still a delicate topic in 1927 when *The General* was released, the film is apolitical. Keaton and his cowriter and codirector Clyde Bruckman, a longtime screenwriting collaborator, turned the North and South into generic good guys and villains. With Johnnie on their side, the Confederates are the underdogs with a genteel tradition. The issue of slavery is never raised. Northerners are portrayed as bad guys because they steal the Southern train through deception. The Yankees are one-dimensional baddies who are there so Buster can conquer them with a purity of intent that allows him to be respected and loved by his hometown.

Although *The General* is not overtly political, it is certainly one of the most accurate visual depictions of that historical time. The design of the film has consistently been compared with Matthew Brady's photography, the primary documentary record of the Civil War. The interior sets are typical of the average silent film. There is not much attention to dimension or texture. The sets look more like theater flats and primarily serve the purpose of indicating the scene locations. But interiors make up a small part of *The General*, which takes place out in the open country, surrounding the tracks on which the train travels. The terrain never smacks of art direction; every tree, rock, and grain of dirt appears real. A sense of distance and travel is accomplished by photographing from the moving train. One of the most remarkable shots in the film, and of the entire silent era, shows Buster so busy chopping wood to feed the steam engine that he is unaware there are troops from the North on one side and the South on the other—on horseback, in wagons, and on foot—speeding toward battle. This shot creates kinetic multidynamic movement and parallel action in the fore-, mid-, and background. Within each line of action there is a multitude of detail specific to the objective of the activity. The viewers—and only the viewers—are able to see the entire situation that is really happening on the screen. The result is funny, thrilling, and oddly real, as if Buster Keaton were in the middle of the actual Civil War. There does not appear to be any trickery here. The shot plays as if it were virtually staged, not achieved through **rear-screen projection** or a matte shot.

The other major location is the town of Marietta, Georgia. The environment looks like the sort of small village that would be featured in an average Western. But rather than the archetypal town that represents the romantic perceptions of the audience, Keaton, Bruckman, and designer Fred Gabourie (*Seven Chances, Steamboat Bill Jr., The Cameraman*) achieve a dusty, handmade, impermanent realism that reflects the early development of America from the open plains era to the establishment of towns and cities.

Keaton is objectively a surrealist because his films portray an ordinary man in extraordinary circumstances, many that defy the logic of reality. A René Magritte painting features a street scene where the sky is bright blue and illuminated by the sun, but in the lower portion of the composition the houses and street lamps are shadowed in the light of the moon. Buster sees a large wood tie on the tracks before him. The front of the engine scoops him up and he pitches another tie to knock off the offending one like a child playing pick-up sticks. The organic physical nature of this and other actions create a surreal environment. This is not cinema magic but filmed reality altered by the unexpected and seemingly impossible feats. Extraordinary alongside the ordinary was the operating principle of the comic character Mr. Mum, who appeared to be the only one seeing the unusual in his everyday reality. Of course, what made Mr. Mum surreal in the same way as *The General* is that there is one extra level of perception—that is, the audience watching an everyman deal with the ridiculous while acting sublime. Unlike surrealist painters Salvador Dali or Max Ernst, Buster Keaton did not function as part of an organized movement or follow the doctrine of a manifesto—it was the way he saw the world. Keaton's physical abilities allowed him to enter the super-real. Chaplin was balletic and moved with grace. Keaton was a human rag doll, master gymnast, stunt man, contortionist, and a performer without fear or guile. Johnnie is a pure heart who strives to do good against all odds, hazards, and literal roadblocks. He also plunges on even though he does not understand why he was rejected in enlisting in the cause. The audience witnesses an officer coldly telling the clerk that Johnnie is more important as a train engineer. The gruff dismal man leaves the young man puzzled but even more determined to serve his cause.

The train named General is a major character in the film and a loyal relationship with Johnnie is formed. The General travels from South to North so it plays a military purpose as well as being an unconditional friend to the young man, who is stalwart but underestimated by both sides in the war. Johnnie loves his girl and his train. He sets out to defend the honor of both in the name of the Old South.

Many of the set pieces concerning Johnnie and the General are memorable and part of his complex association with his job and his mechanical ally. Two of the most celebrated are when Johnnie sits dejected on a steel cross-piece connected to the wheels, which rises up and down when the General is in motion. Lost in his woes, Johnnie is unaware he is traveling and rising up and down until the train enters a tunnel. A perfectly timed double-take is executed just as the light from the tunnel falls upon Johnny capping the improbability of his situation. A cannon with a mind of its own turns from its enemy target toward Johnnie, who, as usual, is busy with other business when he is in the most danger. This sequence has forever been associated with the deadpan humor of Buster Keaton.

The General begins whole, but throughout the struggle against the North, the South's precious transportation equipment reconfigures its format and changes direction. At times the train may seem to have a mind and a life of its own—the General is always in command even when its persistent engineer Johnnie is distracted or presented with overwhelming challenges. It is hard to imagine that Sam Peckinpah didn't have *The General* in mind while planning and executing the spectacular scene in *The Wild Bunch* (see chapter 49) in which a bridge is blown up, sending the pursuing posse, horses, and all into a river. *The General*'s most breathtaking moment concerns a wooden trestle bridge that is on fire. In one dramatic extreme full shot, the train, now led by the North, tries to pass through the burning structure, which can no longer stand. The train derails and plunges a frightening distance down into the drink. There is nothing funny about this action. The viewer is reminded that Keaton breaks the comedy contract of always providing good clean fun where it appears that no one gets really hurt. *The General* once again becomes a Civil War film in which there is much at stake.

Keaton was a master visual storyteller. There are very few **inter-titles** in *The General*. Only what is absolutely necessary is presented in brief text. Many silent films presented dialogue sequences in which the actors mimed lines translated by the cards. *The General* cannot completely avoid this convention, but Keaton's command of cinematic language, portrayal of action, story, and especially character directly communicate with audiences who enjoy spending time in a world that appeared to mirror their own but was just beyond reality.

In addition to Keaton's surrealist tendencies, he also became a cinematic icon of the postmodern film movement in the 1980s and 1990s, influencing films such as *True Stories* (David Byrne), *Desperately Seeking Susan* (Susan Seidelman), and *Stranger Than Paradise* (Jim Jarmusch).

The General and Keaton's body of work clearly fit into several defining aspects of postmodernism. Keaton struck out against ideology. His film did not embrace or promote any specific political tract. Keaton was skeptical about society's advocacy of high art over popular culture. Although his films contain sophisticated aesthetic and stylistic concepts, they were accessible to the populous and were created for a general audience. Keaton's trademark flat pancake hat belongs to popular culture while holding a place in the existentialist landscape of Samuel Beckett (Keaton was featured in *Film*, the playwright's only foray into the cinema). Buster Keaton's embrace of hyperreality traces his direct lineage to the postmodernists. The perfect actualization of reality on film is a simulation of experience—that is the principal mission of postmodernism. The visualization technique applied by Keaton and Bruckman rejects the **montage**-driven frenetic style fashionable at the time. Long shots rather than close-ups are employed to frame the simulation of the period, the action, and the comic take on a historical event. It is camera placement that makes Keaton's visual ideas work, not editing, which here is a delicate structural device that controls the flow of cinematic events.

The General is a feat of filmmaking and performance that goes beyond stunt work and a "how did they do that?" attitude from the viewer. It is a unique blend of realism and vision—an elegy to filmmaking magic based on mechanical feats of wonder, not chemical or digital wizardry. Keaton's cinematic vision made the movies dreams to watch while awake.

For Further Interest

Screen

Brighton Beach Memoirs
A Connecticut Yankee in King Arthur's Court
History of the World—Part I
A Midsummer Night's Sex Comedy
Some Like It Hot

Read

Keaton by Rudi Blesh
Keaton: The Man Who Wouldn't Lie Down by Tom Dardis
My Wonderful World of Slapstick by Buster Keaton with Charles Samuels
Buster Keaton Remembered by Eleanor Keaton and Jeffrey Vance
Buster Keaton: Cut to the Chase by Marion Meade

Parallel Storytelling

□ ◆ □ ◆ □ ◆ □

Intolerance

The indelible, sweeping artistic and aesthetic influences of D. W. Griffith's (1875–1948) *Intolerance* bestowed the essence and syntax of cinematic structure on the feature film. The bold application of **intercutting** and **parallel storytelling** demonstrated the cinema's potential to visually link ideas and thematic strands into an intellectually connective, interactive narrative unit.

Intercutting, also called **crosscutting**, is often confused with parallel storytelling. Although the two editorial techniques have the ability to compare and contrast two separate actions to create a dramatic relationship, they serve different purposes in their practice. Intercutting occurs when shots or scenes in a simultaneous frame of reference are edited together in alternate sequence. Parallel storytelling occurs when two or more shots or scenes that do not have to be taking place at the same time or place are cut in alternating sequence.

Historically, crosscutting was employed by William S. Porter in his 1903 film *The Great Train Robbery*, and by Griffith and other moviemakers prior to *Intolerance*, but the notion of telling more than one story in a single film was considered to be impossibly confusing for audiences to comprehend.

It is widely recognized that in *The Birth of a Nation* (1915), D. W. Griffith, along with his master cameraman Billy Bitzer (*Broken Blossoms, Orphans of the Storm, America*), wrote the essential language of the American film. As an important cinematic accomplishment, it is indisputable that *The Birth of a Nation* led to the development of the moving image medium

The largest, most ornate movie set ever built in Hollywood for just one of four stories told in parallel during D. W. Griffith's *Intolerance*. Courtesy *Photofest.*

with a defined use of the close-up, dramatic sequencing, intercutting, editorial pace, and the storytelling abilities of the motion picture camera. However, the story being told and the directorial point of view harbored by Griffith are detestable. This adaptation of Thomas Dixon's novel *The Clansman* is a glorification of racism in which the Ku Klux Klan triumphs over African Americans, many portrayed by Caucasian performers in blackface, who are considered a threat to the country's honor.

The Birth of a Nation was an enormous financial success, but the torrential backlash toward its content saddened and angered the director. He then created *Intolerance* as a response to the personal criticism (that continues into the twenty-first century) of his values and core beliefs.

The central theme of *Intolerance* is the fundamental conflict between hatred, prejudice, love, and compassion throughout the ages. Four stories are tied together by the image of a young woman (Lillian Gish) rocking a baby lying in a wooden cradle. The scene is tinted deep blue. A heavenly shaft of light halos them as three women cloaked in black sit hunched over in the background. A preceding card quotes Walt Whitman, "Out of the cradle endlessly rocking," from his epic poem "Leaves of Grass." For Griffith, the recurring shot symbolized human pain, passion, and sorrow. A bound book with the title "Intolerance" slowly opens to two pages of text signifying that the film story is about to unfold.

The first story takes place in modern day, which at the time of *Intolerance*'s release was in the teens of the twentieth century. Three female social reformers interfere with the lives of a young couple as unjust circumstances lead the man to a life of crime and to leave his wife and baby destitute, ultimately threatening his very existence by the hangman's noose of an uncaring society.

The second story is set in old Jerusalem as Jesus Christ is betrayed and then crucified. Griffith recalls the spiritual awakening of the Holy Bible's passion play. The next tale reveals the events leading to the religious slaughter known as the Saint Bartholomew Massacre in 1572 A.D. in Paris, France.

The fourth story is the fall of Babylon in 539 B.C. This opulent grandeur and decadence plays out on one of the most spectacular film sets ever built. The scale and attention to breathtaking detail of this ancient world that mirrors the flawed times about which Griffith was moralizing has become a symbol of the cinema's potential for visual audacity.

Scenes are tinted sepia, blue, magenta, earthy green, and other tones to delineate a time, mood, or psychological state. **Inter-title** cards offer explanatory text and dialogue in the tradition of the silent film. Because of the adventurous and somewhat confusing multilayered narrative, Griffith gave the cards for *Intolerance* special attention as a means to inform the audience of time, place, and plot during the time-tripping excursion. Cards for the Jerusalem segments display a background of a stone tablet with writings carved in Hebrew. The text for the Babylonian scenes is over a stone wall topped with chiseled hieroglyphics. Fonts are changed appropriately. Footnotes give data and attest to the supposed historical accuracy of Griffith's research. The open-book pages of "Intolerance" appear throughout the film as a constant reminder that these many tributaries form one story.

What is behind the director's grand scheme? What motivates a shift in time in *Intolerance*? Griffith's idea was to connect the stories much in the way that they would be connected in the associative annals of the mind.

Griffith's parallel storytelling milestone is significant because he possessed the vision to attempt what even those in his inner circle deemed unworkable.

He did not begin with a scenario. Actually, no script was ever written for *Intolerance*; the director kept notes as the film evolved and expanded day by day. There was pressure for Griffith to follow *The Birth of a Nation* with another major, long-form work and not the short films he so abundantly produced in the past. He had just finished *The Mother and the Law*, a short film that would eventually become the modern-day story at the center of *Intolerance*. After screening the film, Griffith and his company agreed that it should not be released to follow his big success and he began to conceive of a multistory narrative that would be an even bigger extravaganza than *The Birth of a Nation*.

The Mother and the Law required revision, and the plotting for the three new stories was developed in stages as Griffith conceived new ideas and ordered extensive research to be conducted for each one. His reputation for the illusion of historical accuracy coupled with his fervor to restore his good name drove each story to the brink of hysteria with the message that intolerance threatened world peace.

The four narratives were not created equally. Although each story is intercut throughout the almost three-hour cinematic colossus, Griffith immersed his attention in the modern-day and Babylonian stories. The French segment established how powerful monarchs betray their subjects for political expediency. The crucifixion of Christ is the personification of the triumph of good over evil. The two longest and most intricate stories strike the moral tone Griffith is preaching: Universal justice will be served to reward the righteous and punish the wicked, but only God can redeem all.

Griffith's grand experiment resulted in a flurry of connective associations that pound at the director's singular cry for tolerance against unrelenting evil forces. The pace steadily accelerates hour by hour, pulsating with excess and a flood of emotion. The overall velocity of *Intolerance* is driven by Griffith's finely honed sense of spectacle and theatricality. The constant collision of action and ideas produces both an exhaustive and exhilarating response in the viewer.

The editing within each sequence is further dramatized by intercutting that builds suspense and dramatic dynamism. Shots are photographed straight on; angles and the inference of perspective is achieved by pivoting the positions of the actors. Griffith and his editor Rose Smith (*The Birth of a Nation, America, Orphans of the Storm*) do not use a large number of shots or a complex **montage** style to accelerate the rate of his propulsive drama. Momentum is attained by the juxtaposition of content. The train and car chase to save the boy from the gallows are alternated with mass suicide and the impending demise of a decadent civilization. The parallel stories intertwine internally and with each other, culminating in a frenzied conclusion.

Intolerance ends in a hysterical and bombastic coda. Men with knives attached to the barrels of their rifles stand poised to do battle on an open field. The resurrection of Christ has brought a gathering of angels from above. Their holy presence spreads a white glow of peace, and the men throw down their arms to gaze up at the heavenly miracle as a cross of light is formed over the scene. To the contemporary viewer, the battle may appear to be a recreation of the Civil War, but the director's intent was a conflict occurring during the film's most current time-frame in a major urban city such as New York. Acceptance of the grace of God and rejection of the perils of intolerance is achieved during this stunning visionary climax.

Griffith added another notable piece of film grammar that became associated with Hollywood studio moviemaking—the **crane** shot. The innovative director was looking for a way to shoot the massive Babylonian set in a way that would capture the expanse and splendor of the outdoor creation constructed by designer Frank "Huck" Wortman (*The Birth of a Nation, Remodeling Her Husband, Orphans of the Storm*) and his art department. It stood 150 feet high and stretched out for about three-eighths of a mile. The **crane** shot did not exist, so there were no commercial camera cranes. The solution was to build a dolly 150 feet tall, six feet square at the top, with a sixty-foot-wide base mounted on six four-wheeled railroad car trucks and an elevator in the center. A track was laid so the dolly could be pushed forward by one crew as another crew operated the elevator, which had to descend at a specified speed to create a fluid movement. This new sweeping camera gesture would be a mainstay in countless Hollywood musicals and epics for decades to come.

The legacy of D. W. Griffith's *Intolerance* is reflected in the directorial expression of expansive (some would say excessive) visions of American New Wavers: Francis Ford Coppola's *Apocalypse Now* and *One from the Heart*; Dennis Hopper's *The Last Movie*; Steven Spielberg's *1941*; Martin Scorsese's *New York, New York*; and Michael Cimino's *Heaven's Gate*.

Parallel storytelling also became a part of the cinematic repertoire. Notable examples include *Grand Hotel; The Best Years of Our Lives; It's a Mad, Mad, Mad, Mad World; The Last Picture Show; Nashville; Hannah and Her Sisters; Night on Earth;* and *Magnolia*.

Since the 1990s, movies as a whole have become more episodic, less plot and subplot driven. Related and seemingly unrelated narrative threads come together in the conciousness of the audience—much in the way they first came to the man often credited with fashioning the grammar of film—D. W. Griffith.

Of Further Interest

Screen

The Great Train Robbery (1903)
Kids
Magnolia
Time Code
A Wedding

Read

Story and Discourse: Narrative Structure in Fiction and Film by Seymour Chatman
D. W. Griffith's Intolerance: *Its Genesis and Its Vision* by William M. Drew
Thinking in Pictures: Dramatic Structure in D. W. Griffith's Biograph Films by Joyce E. Jesionowski
Story: Substance, Structure, Style, and the Principles of Screenwriting by Robert McKee
D. W. Griffith: An American Life by Richard Schickel

French New Wave

□ ◆ □ ◆ □ ◆ □

Jules and Jim

In the 1950s, the influential French film magazine *Cahiers du Cinéma* was revolutionizing critical thought by expounding on the **auteur theory**, which elevated Hollywood studio directors to the exalted status of artists with aesthetic and thematic vision. The French New Wave began when a number of these film critics started to make films. When François Truffaut, Jean-Luc Godard, Eric Rohmer, Claude Chabrol, Alain Resnais, Jacques Rivette, and others made films that both embraced and rejected the traditional cinemas of France and America, they reinvented cinematic grammar and storytelling and inspired change in international motion pictures. François Truffaut's (1932–1984) *Jules and Jim* (1961) encapsulates the vitality, daring, and artistic courage typified by the French New Wave.

What created the French New Wave? French film was stagnating. Past masters had died, gone into retirement, or were hopelessly repeating themselves. There was a new generation of filmmakers that came from different backgrounds than their predecessors. As a critic, François Truffaut understood how great directors like Alfred Hitchcock, Howard Hawks, and John Ford interpreted themes with images. The innovative critical work and filmmaking of his French colleagues stimulated a spirit of adventure and created a climate to grow their work as individuals into a movement.

A key contributor to any new wave is the cinematographer. New directions require a new look, a different set of aesthetics and conventions. The American New Wave of the 1970s (which grew out of admiration for

The blocking of the ménage et trois of Jules (Oskar Werner, left), Jim (Henri Serre), and Catherine (Jean Moreau) in François Truffaut's *Jules et Jim* communicates that the woman represents attraction and independence to the two smitten lovers. Courtesy *Photofest*.

the French New Wave) was godfathered by two Hungarian cinematographers, Laszlo Kovacs and Vilmos Zsigmond, who defied the rigid rules of Hollywood photography. Their role model was the man known as the general of the French New Wave, Raoul Coutard (*Breathless, The Soft Skin, Z*).

Raoul Coutard was responsible for providing Godard and Truffaut with a fluid **handheld camera** and the verisimilitude of natural light—a reaction against the Hollywood studio look in which artificial light defined character, created beauty and villainy, and set the mood out of the artifice of light and shade, photographed by a carefully controlled, stabilized camera.

Jules and Jim takes place at the beginning of the twentieth century, but it reflects the early 1960s, during which it was made. Truffaut was interested in the emotional, psychological, romantic, and sexual drives of the three main characters. By reflecting their needs and desires toward each other, Truffaut examined and explained the changing mores of the 1960s by revealing a prehistory of a revolution in human relationships.

The principal narrative of *Jules and Jim* is a simple one from which emerge complex characters and intricate consequences for all. Jules (Oskar Werner) and Jim (Henri Serre) both fall in love with Catherine (Jeanne Moreau), a woman with a mercurial personality filled with passionate motivations and a swirling disposition totally dedicated to her needs and desires. *Jules and Jim* is not just a ménage à trois; the relationship among the three is an investigation into the nature of love, sex, respect, individual freedom, the bond between two and three people, and the strength and fragility of connections.

The key to Truffaut's visualization of the special relationships between Jules, Jim, and Catherine is in the compositional placement and choreography of the three characters within the frame. The actors give penetrating performances, and the screenplay by Truffaut and Jean Gruault (*The Nun, Le Sex Shop, The Green Room*), based on the novel by Henri-Pierre Roché, provides the motivation and behavior. The staging and blocking interprets the manner in which Jules, Jim, and Catherine react to each other, with the camera capturing the way they move, stand and walk as pairs and as a trio. While bicycling, Jim catches up to Catherine and Jules, who are ahead of him. Later, Jules asks Catherine to marry him. Next, while the men ride their bikes together, Catherine is bicycling ahead of them to signify that she is in control of the relationship of the trio. Two-shots between Jules and Jim or between one of them and Catherine reveal the intimacy between two people, but throughout the film Truffaut and Coutard make detailed use of the three-shot to track the delicate balance as Catherine expresses her needs for each friend with very different limits and expectations. Often Catherine is physically in the lead if they are photographed in profile. Shots taken directly in front or behind the three often place Catherine in the center. The former represents her power over the two men who consider Catherine to possess all that a man looks for in a woman. The latter is Catherine's message to Jules and Jim that for her they represent two halves of a whole. Catherine respects Jules's loyalty and Jim's passionate nature. Jules commits himself totally to Catherine, but Jim holds onto his relationship to Gilberte (Vanna Urbino). Ultimately, the two men are symbolic of one man who would fully satisfy the physical and emotional requirements of a complete woman. Jules and Jim both agree that their attraction to Catherine goes beyond the surface. To these men she is not the most beautiful or intelligent, but she is a woman. It is that elusive quality and also what a woman wants from a man that Truffaut explores in *Jules and Jim.*

The French New Wave set out to create a new language culled from American and French cinema heroes (Jean Renoir was a major influence) that visually defined the characters, story, and textural themes. From D. W. Griffith, Truffaut borrowed the technique of the **iris shot**, where part of the image is on screen in a field of black and then the image widens to fill the screen. The shape of an iris is varied. This technique, associated with early silent cinema, ties *Jules and Jim* to earlier film traditions and is aesthetically appropriate because Truffaut mixes the old and new in the pre-World War I period film.

Jules and Jim is photographed in a widescreen format that references black-and-white CinemaScope films of the 1950s. This **aspect ratio** is also effective in presenting the three characters in a single locked-off (see **locked-off camera** in glossary) or moving shot while anchoring them in their environment. This especially applies to vital scenes in the countryside, where they are free to explore their social experiment.

The fluidity and pace of *Jules and Jim* is linked more to American than French cinema, but Truffaut departs from Hollywood by relying on a handheld and moving camera and the rhythm of action and dialogue rather than montage. The editing punctuates moods and emotional states with jump cuts, or a series of angles cut together to express the inner life of the characters. These moments do not interfere with the overall languid pace of *Jules and Jim* that establishes the movement of life in an earlier time. Editing accentuates Catherine's independent spirit and the way Jules and Jim react to her.

Before Steven Spielberg in *Jaws* and Martin Scorsese in *GoodFellas*, Truffaut and Coutard executed what has come to be known as the *vertigo* shot, named after Hitchcock's technique of tracking (see **tracking shot** in glossary) in and zooming (see **zoom lens** in glossary) out or vice versa to inject and heighten a sense of uneasy movement in the viewer's mind and stomach. Truffaut uses this technique as a sign of profound recognition when Jules and Jim visit the Adriatic Islands and find a statue that reminds them of the face of a beautiful woman who later takes the human form of Catherine.

The French New Wave was a bridge between the classical cinemas of France and the United States—the evolution of the medium that progressed throughout the 1960s, resulting in a new generation of filmmakers who flowered in the 1970s. With *Jules and Jim*, François Truffaut challenged the morality portrayed in traditional cinema and liberated the camera from the restrictions of the tripod and studio lights. However, the **dissolve**, the classical article of grammar where one image **fades in** while another **fades out** to suggest the passage of time, is used throughout the film.

In *Jules and Jim,* the freeze frame is applied in a playful and insightful manner within the body of the film (a favorite cinematic gesture in a Guy Ritchie film). Truffaut did not invent the **freeze frame** with the ending of *The 400 Blows*. Frank Capra used this editorial technique in *It's a Wonderful Life* to stop the action so the narration could comment on the story. The freeze frame was later used by Scorsese in *GoodFellas*. Dziga Vertov employed freeze frames to stop the kinetic action in *Man with the Movie Camera* (see chapter 28). The renowned freeze frame of Antoine Doinel, which ends *The 400 Blows,* influenced editorial grammar so thoroughly that it became a popular aesthetic choice for a film's conclusion. By holding Antoine in our gaze, Truffaut stopped the motion but allowed the viewer to continue to ponder the boy's future and fate. During a domino game between Jules and Jim, pans passing by all three characters are punctuated with freeze frames of Catherine's facial expressions as her alternating moods are contrasted with the exuberance demonstrated by the men.

Throughout *Jules and Jim,* a third-person narrator was woven in between scenes and when Truffaut found it necessary to switch to an informed observer's point of view. The **narration** anoints Jules and Jim with a literary voice to connect the film to its novelistic origin. The narrator is able to supply information and insights that the characters and action cannot. The voice of the narrator becomes linked with the musical score as an interlude to bridge time and to understand the emotional rollercoaster of feelings that shift constantly through the intricacy of the trio's relationships. The narrator is another reference to the cinema of the past, a favorite device of classical Hollywood movies, combined with the daring aesthetic technique that defined the French New Wave.

The performances by Oscar Werner, Henri Serre, and Jeanne Moreau are fresh and real. The approach to acting represents a rejection of Hollywood movie star gloss and the mannered plunging of emotions found in the method style (see chapter 32). The performances emphasize the range of emotions conveyed with the complicated love relationships shared between the characters. All three actors are specific in their portrayals while demonstrating a sense of fun, romantic spontaneity, and the sixties zeitgeist that drove the New Wavers during this period. Werner and Serre are absolutely convincing as two very different men who share friendship and love. Moreau achieves exactly what Jules and Jim say about Catherine: Her inner beauty, intelligence, and mystery imbue Catherine with the indefinable qualities that Jules and Jim say embody their ideal woman.

The lessons and achievements of *Jules and Jim* and the French New Wave are lasting. Truffaut and his colleagues invigorated the cinema with a resonance that reflected the vibrant era in which they lived and created a new aesthetic paradigm that paid homage to the past while opening new vistas for future generations of filmmakers.

Of Further Interest

Screen

Breathless (1959)
The 400 Blows
Last Year at Marienbad
My Night at Maud's
Zazie in the Underground

Read

Truffaut: A Biography by Antoine De Baecque and Serge Toubiana
Screening the Text: Intertextuality in New Wave French Cinema by T. Jefferson Kline
The French New Wave: An Artistic School by Michel Marie
The New Wave: Truffaut, Godard, Chabrol, Rohmer, Rivette by James Monoco
A History of the French New Wave Cinema by Richard Neupert

26 The Epic

Lawrence of Arabia

David Lean (1908–1991) was a director's director. After a career as a prominent film editor, the British Lion directed eleven feature films starting in 1942, including *Brief Encounter, Oliver Twist, Hobson's Choice,* and *Summertime*. In 1957 with *The Bridge on the River Kwai*, David Lean began a period of filmmaking in which he directed just four more films over three decades: *Lawrence of Arabia, Doctor Zhivago, Ryan's Daughter*, and *A Passage to India*. This work set a benchmark for epic filmmaking and defined the very role of the motion picture director at the highest level of the profession.

David Lean was well-respected by his peers. To all film directors, regardless of their affinity with the content and style of his films, David Lean represented freedom—the freedom to make a movie with the money, resources, time, and methodology it required, and with no limitations.

David Lean's scope of cinematic vision embraces the historical and visual. *Lawrence of Arabia* (1962) is the story of T. E. Lawrence, a British Oxford-educated scholar who learned Arabic, became entranced with the region, and envisioned a unified Arab state. During World War I, the timeframe of the film, Lawrence planned and led Arab rebellions against the Turkish Empire, which was allied with Germany. Lawrence of Arabia, as he became known, led guerrilla campaigns by organizing and uniting warring Arab tribes. Their first major victory was in 1917 when they took Aqaba. In 1918, after Lawrence was captured and escaped from the

Englishman T. E. Lawrence (Peter O'Toole) leads an all-Arab unit of guerrilla fighters, by sheer passion and the barrel of a gun, deep into the desert in David Lean's masterful epic *Lawrence of Arabia*. Courtesy *Photofest*.

enemy, his troops made it into Damascus, a strategic stronghold, but even at this moment of victory the fragile coalition crumbled into a bitter, fractured alliance, and French and British concerns prevented Lawrence's dream of a united Arab nation from materializing. T. E. Lawrence retired from the military and declined all decorations.

The themes of Lawrence's life and those explored by Lean in the film are epic: claiming a homeland, the search for ethnic and personal identity, the power of an empire, peace, war, the impact of violence on the individual, the nature of dissent, the impossibility of unity, the cult of personality, and the sweep of history.

The 217-minute running time of narrative (227 minutes including the overture, Entr'acte during the intermission, and exit music for its initial **roadshow** release) gave David Lean and his scenarists Robert Bolt (*Dr.*

Zhivago, A Man for All Seasons, The Mission) and Michael Wilson (*The Bridge on the River Kwai, Planet of the Apes, Che!*) a large enough canvas to explore a story that demanded breadth. The story structure embraces Lawrence's single-minded mission, driving himself away from the proper British tradition, and obsessively and methodically bringing fractious, warring Arab tribes together in solidarity to overthrow the Turkish Empire. The narrative is carefully constructed. The time compression is so well planned that the combination of character, **exposition**, action, and transition scenes modulate across the running time, which is almost twice the length of an average feature of the time. What could have been an unwieldy, repetitive story instead is finely tuned entertainment with purpose and bold showmanship.

Through careful collaboration and supervision of the fine screenplay, David Lean emerged with a blueprint he would visualize in a grand manner worthy of his grand subject. Staging and filming in desert locations present so many technical and logistical problems that earlier filmmakers had avoided going and settled for studio art-directed sand or location terrain just outside of civilization. Lean knew that approach could never capture or represent the vastness of a Middle Eastern total desert environment and shot all the desert sequences on location.

Lean took on this enormous challenge with cinematographer Freddie Young (*Goodbye Mr. Chips, Treasure Island, Solomon and Sheba*), whom Lean had met when he was an editor. Their relationship continued through every Lean film save *A Passage to India* when Freddie Young's advancing age made the grueling process too difficult for him. David Lean directed every shot of *Lawrence of Arabia*; there was no second unit. Lean was in on the planning and execution of each shot. Young was the ideal cameraman for Lean. He was one of England's most accomplished photographers and a confident man who relished an intense relationship with a meticulous director.

David Lean wanted the desert to have the pink tinge that sand masses reflect in intense sunlight. He envisioned the microscopic sharpness he could see as billions of individual grains of sand-formed dunes, waves, and a bed of glistening grains as far as the eye could see. Lean decided *Lawrence of Arabia* would be photographed in 65mm. To achieve a greater definition of the image, Lean and Young used the 70mm film stock developed for the Panavision cameras used on the production, which produced a much finer grain pattern than standard 35mm film. The wide-screen format would give him the perfect compositional structure for the epic form, and the horizontal width that stretched out across the large screen was what he needed to create shots full of space, detail, and the landscape of legend.

The experience of life in a desert with the hot, glaring sun beating down created a mirage—the illusion of a shimmering, liquidy reflection that can be seen by the human eye but doesn't really exist. As Freddie Young was going through the Panavision equipment at their plant, he came upon a 500mm lens. The compression captured by the long lens would create the mirage effect on film. In practice, the lens was photographing the long distance between the camera position and the subject and shooting through layers of air, dust, sand, and light reflections that cause a mirage when the sun is at a particular intensity. In the desert Young observed that mirages appeared at the hottest time of every day, so those sequences were planned accordingly.

The first mirage sequence ever put on film is the spectacular entrance of Sherif Ali ibn el Khrarish (Omar Sharif), who appears as if from infinity on his camel and slowly and steadily rides up to defend the water well of his tribe. Sharif was 1,000 feet from the camera and ten minutes of a continuous take was shot, concluding with him at the well. Carefully planned cutaway shots and the environmental sounds that include the steady clip-clopping of the camel's hoofs all combined to give the viewer a desert mirage experience that added a magical quality to Ali's character and demonstrated the illusion of space and time in an environment place without boundaries.

The desert sequences in *Lawrence of Arabia* are absolutely breathtaking. The technical problems that confront a movie company filming in the middle of a desert are enormous. The cameras were constantly in repair; sand penetrated everything. Maintaining the natural surface of the sand for each shot involved teams of workers rolling and smoothing out vast areas. Logistics were critical in keeping the large cast and crews from soiling zones that were supposed to look virginal. The sun was so hot during the day that cameras constantly had to be cooled down, and nights were so cold that warming blankets were utilized to keep the delicate equipment from freezing.

It has been said that a David Lean film expresses love for the camera. He was a **visualist** of the highest order, but the images were there to serve the story. Lawrence was a passionate and iconoclastic man brought up in proper British tradition who fell deeply in love with the desert and had an obsession with the Arab cause. This led Lean to a **mise-en-scène** that always connected Lawrence to his environment. The vast desert is an awesome sight, especially to Western audiences. If a forest or an ocean setting can imbue a scene with spirituality, demonstrating how infinitesimal man is on planet earth, the desert represents a timeless stretch of land without borders to the naked eye. It references biblical times, an ancient world before man, one that will survive for centuries and that expresses romantic poetical beauty rarely experienced in films.

The musical **score** by Maurice Jarre (*Dr. Zhivago, The Man Who Would Be King, Dead Poets Society*) soars. The main theme, which refrains, is reinterpreted and swells with emotions throughout the length of *Lawrence of Arabia*. The score sings of the region, the sun, wind, and sand as the film moves across the desert and echoes the human condition of man trying to cross and survive it. The music is as responsible for the impact of the look of *Lawrence of Arabia* as the production design by John Box (*A Man for All Seasons, The Great Gatsby, First Knight*) and Young's cinematography. Without it the film would be a series of pretty pictures. With it the audience endures the physicality of Lawrence's journey and is exhilarated.

Peter O'Toole's inhabitation of Lawrence is one of the great screen performances, ranking with Marlon Brando in *On the Waterfront* (see chapter 32). O'Toole burns with a special light that comes from within and radiates through his marine blue eyes and his blond-on-blond locks. The performance contains so many great moments: Lawrence breaking tradition by insisting an Arab boy be served a glass of lemonade in a British officers club; his delight at wearing his Arabian robe for the first time; the inner and then outer explosion before a massive campaign, the words "No prisoners! No prisoners!" shouted as he leads a cause both personal and political, not only a military charge. O'Toole plays Lawrence's homosexuality outside of the text with confidence. The tenor and strict censorship of the times would not have allowed much more of Lawrence's sexual feelings in the text, but O'Toole maintains the integrity of Lawrence's complex nature. This is a film about Lawrence's historic contributions that does not deny his most intimate knowledge of himself and the expression of his emotional, intellectual, and moral character.

Film editor Anne V. Coates (*Becket, The Elephant Man, Out of Sight*) is responsible for one of the most famous **time cuts** in cinema history. Lawrence blows out a match and in one cut we are transported to the desert. This remarkable and highly cinematic transition was written into the screenplay by Robert Bolt, but Coates made the cut. The two graphic and evocative images perfectly capture the light-as-air trip to the desert. The cut contains the poetry of the wind, and the magic that is in store for us in this almighty sight. Achieving the mystical connection between these two images is far more complex editorially than it looks on the surface. When do you exit the first shot and enter the next? Do you cut right on the blow out or find the spot as Coates does to blow us to, not just cut to, the next shot? When should the sun rise—right on the cut, or later? If later, as it is in the film, how much so? Just long enough to give the viewer the experience of watching the sun rise on Lawrence's first time in his beloved desert. Coates gives *Lawrence of Arabia* pace, context, and the perfect rhythm for each scene. The editorial style, some of which originates from the screenplay, is filled with time cuts. Coates takes us from one place in this massive story to the next, never overstaying her welcome or leaving too soon.

David Lean achieved an epic grandeur in *Lawrence of Arabia* by orchestrating all of the narrative, character, and craft elements, which were painstakingly chosen, detailed, developed, and then choreographed within the camera's frame. Shot by shot, *Lawrence of Arabia* is beautiful and perfect.

The legacy of *Lawrence of Arabia* is deep. It is an Oscar champion, consistently on critics' lists. The film inspired the American New Wave of the 1970s and is responsible for motivating the modern blockbuster, the Hollywood holy grail founded by Steven Spielberg and George Lucas.

David Lean made his films with concrete cinematic elements that are no longer practical or affordable. The romance and adventure of *Lawrence of Arabia* is solid, not electronic smoke and mirrors. David Lean may be the last film director who went out and *made* movies. He started in the confines of an editing room, but the film frame led him to exotic places. *Lawrence of Arabia* is a timeless film created in the classical manner. Its well-made screenplay, forceful performances, and consummate craft represent a unique set of aesthetics. It is not a consumer product or digital wizardry to amuse. *Lawrence of Arabia* will live on forever because it makes us forget film as a business while we are in awe of its art.

Of Further Interest

Screen

Ben Hur (1959)
The Bridge on the River Kwai
The Fall of the Roman Empire
How the West Was Won
Spartacus

Read

David Lean: A Biography by Kevin Brownlow
Lawrence of Arabia: A Film's Anthropology by Steven C. Canton
Sam Spiegel by Natasha Fraser-Cavassoni
The Hollywood Epic by Foster Hirsch
Lawrence of Arabia: The Official 30th Anniversary Pictorial History by Robert L. Morris and Lawrence Raskin

The Political Thriller

The Manchurian Candidate

The Manchurian Candidate (1962), a watershed political thriller directed by John Frankenheimer (1930–2002), based on the novel by Richard Condon and adapted for the screen by George Axelrod, is a finely constructed dramaturgy that is effective because of its narrative triggers and design. The production design by Richard Sylbert (*Who's Afraid of Virginia Woolf?*, *Chinatown*, *Reds*) not only interprets and complements the taut story and vivid characters; it provides the primary source for visualization of the key event in the film. The audacious and disturbing scene involves a brainwashing, mind-control, programming session. The participants are Russian and Chinese Communist officials who manipulate captured American soldiers during the Korean conflict. The sequence shows a mix of reality, the soldiers' perceptions of their ordeal, and a ladies' garden club meeting seen from the point of view of two of the captives. It is so particularized that a black soldier sees the garden ladies as African American and the Caucasian men see the women as white. Their personal views are maintained as their brains are rewired to suit a diabolical purpose.

The design of a film goes beyond art direction, costumes, and the physical décor. When a total filmmaker like John Frankenheimer is the director, it extends to composition, shot and scene structure, visual cues, metaphors, intertextual relationships, blocking, and the choreography of the actor's contribution to the story.

Laurence Harvey as the brainwashed Raymond Shaw, carrying a disguised rifle case and dressed as a man of the cloth. Patriotism and hysteria are about to meet in a final showdown in the original *The Manchurian Candidate* directed by John Frankenheimer. Courtesy *Photofest.*

In a **pretitle sequence** that takes place in Korea, 1952, a unit of U.S. soldiers are set up by a Communist spy and captured. Unconscious, the men are airlifted out of the area. After the titles, a solemn narrator (see **narration** in glossary) explains that Raymond Shaw (Lawrence Harvey) is to receive the Congressional Medal of Honor for saving the lives of his unit while under enemy attack. When Bennett Marco (Frank Sinatra) is plagued by sweaty nightmares that recall distorted pieces of his tampered memory, he begins to understand that there is something very wrong with Raymond Shaw. When Marco is asked how he feels about his sergeant, he goes into a trance and is compelled to say, "Raymond Shaw is the kindest, warmest, bravest, most wonderful human being I've ever known in my life," even though rationally he states that Shaw was intensely disliked and unloved.

The programming of the men, who were swept off the battlefield as part of a fiendish Communist plot to manufacture an assassin, relies on convincing others, especially in Washington, D.C., that Shaw was so revered that he would be above suspicion. The incongruity of that sentiment sparks an investigation that uncovers Shaw as a perfect killing machine who will murder at the will of his operators.

Shaw appears to behave with free will, but he has been rewired to obey commands as if he were an automaton when he hears the phrase "Raymond, why don't you pass the time by playing a little solitaire." Shaw then methodically plays the solitary game, a metaphor for a lone assassin, a role that has been designated for him. When the red Queen of Diamonds appears, a mental switch is thrown and Shaw is left without free will. He will do as he is told regardless of his personal morality. This trigger is narrative, word-driven, and provocatively visual. The film is in black and white, but the deadly significance of the red Queen's appearance throughout the film plays as vivid red in the viewer's imagination. The color red dominates *The Manchurian Candidate*. The red stripes of the American flag represent the fanatical patriotism that threatens democracy in the hands of the villains. It is also a symbol of Communism, an ideological force dedicated to crushing the American system. Red, of course, also signifies the blood of the victims murdered at the hand of the brainwashed Raymond. During a demonstration of the brainwashing shown in **flashback**, Raymond coldly shoots to death the company "mascot," a young soldier. The blood (most likely chocolate syrup, the substance of choice at the time for blood in a black-and-white film) splatters all over a poster of Joseph Stalin. The result of Raymond's horrible act is more terrifying when shown as if it were a detail of a Jackson Pollock painting, and like the recurring red Queen, it registers as red in the mind's eye because in human experience we know blood is red.[1] *The Manchurian Candidate*, like *Psycho* (see chapter 34), would have been unbearable in color. The black-and-white images are able to directly translate to color through the viewer's recollection of emotional life experiences.

Variations on the red Queen theme build the tension and intensify the drama. Jocie Jordon (Leslie Parish), the love of Raymond's life, comes back to him even though his mother's evil machinations had kept them apart. Drawing this development into her heinous plans, the mother manipulates Jocie to wear a Queen of Diamonds outfit at a costume ball. The visual image of Jocie standing with the huge card across her body heightens the sense of impending crisis. The operatives employ a magician's deck of cards that to the eye looks like a standard pack of fifty-two, except every other card is cut to a slightly smaller size and has the same face so that the magician can always identify the right card. This trick deck can be purchased in a wide range of choices for the duplicate. Here it is the Queen of Diamonds, a symbol for the domineering mother he despises to ensure that Raymond will get to the prompt card and go into his trance quickly. When Marco attempts to deprogram Raymond, his most powerful tool is to fan out all the Queen of Diamond cards. The impact of seeing the platoon of trigger cards could be the final short-circuiting of the evil mechanism inside Raymond. The ending of the film both confirms and points to a deeper psychological issue operating in Raymond when his anger is finally turned toward the genuine source of his pain.

The trigger line about solitaire is not always under the total control of the operatives. In one scene Raymond goes to Jilly's (a New York bar made famous by Sinatra and his Rat Pack cronies). Raymond hears the bartender inadvertently say the line in conversation with other customers. He asks the barkeep for a deck of cards. When Raymond sees the red Queen he hears the bartender, who while telling patrons a story says a phrase about jumping in a lake. Obeying the command, Raymond goes off to Central Park and does so. Marco follows him. This advances the plot in making contact between Marco and Shaw and establishing that something is very wrong.

The villain of *The Manchurian Candidate* is Raymond's mother, played to perfection by Angela Lansbury. She is Raymond's American operative. Her plan unfolds like the concoction of a most elaborate assassination buff. She has sacrificed her son, who hates her. This makes Raymond susceptible to brain laundering and makes the Queen the perfect symbol–stimuli. His mother's second husband is Senator John Iselin (John Gregory), an alcoholic nobody who allows his brilliant and commanding wife to shape him as a political demigod. Iselin is a totally undisguised representation of Senator Joseph McCarthy, the red-baiting senator whose abuse of power and finger-pointing lit the match for the dreaded blacklisting era, one of America's darkest moments as a democracy. Iselin accuses the innocent of being Communist spies, always bellowing names, numbers, and threats. His campaign is televised and black-and-white monitors are filled with images right out of McCarthy's reign of terror. And then there are those words, "Point of order, point of order," a mantra for the senator known as tail-gunner Joe, which grabs the attention of a duped American public. Iselin is positioned to receive the nomination for vice president of the United States. Raymond's mission is to assassinate the presidential nominee during the convention so Iselin can step in, rally the party, and become president under control of the Chinese and Russians. But Raymond's mother resents that she has been taken advantage of. As a Communist disguised as a right-wing zealot, she was forced to destroy her relationship with her son. When she realizes she has been suckered, her plan becomes to get Iselin into the Oval Office so she can hunt down and destroy her former comrades for revenge.

The principal performances are riveting. Sinatra is tough, vulnerable, human, and heroic as Marco. Laurence Harvey is mesmerizing as the ill-fated Raymond Shaw. His handsome, fine-lined face is haunted with familial pain and the zombielike trance over which he has no control. He is an unloved man and is devastated that he has been denied happiness. Viewers who only know Angela Lansbury from her hit television series *Murder She Wrote* are in for a rude awakening. This first-class actress portrays pure evil. The complex character uses diplomacy, power, manipulation, and deception for the means to her objective to control the United States government and strike back at her enemies around the world. James Gregory has done his homework in bringing a perfect portrait of the McCarthyite senator, a drunk, led by the nose by other concerns, a man of no conscience and only blind ambition.

John Frankenheimer had been a tireless voice against the blacklist. Although not directly affected by the scourge himself, *The Manchurian Candidate* gave him a direct potshot at the absurdity and danger of what the morally bankrupt senator had done to his country. For his film *Seconds*, Frankenheimer hired many blacklisted actors and crew members well before other producers and directors were doing so.

Raymond's purpose is to assassinate a presidential nominee. *The Manchurian Candidate* was released in 1962, a year before the assassination of President John F. Kennedy changed America forever. This context makes *The Manchurian Candidate* even more fertile. It is more than just a good thriller but approaches art in making a statement about the violent nature of the country and the fragility of democracy, a theme Frankenheimer would explore again in his next film, *Seven Days in May*, about an attempted coup d'état by the U.S. military.

The Manchurian Candidate is not always solemn, but peppered with gallows humor. When Raymond shoots his boss, a powerful newspaper magnate, the man is in his bedroom dressed in his wife's fuzzy nightgown. This absurdity makes the killing tragic and nuanced. The man explains he is wearing it because the garment is warm but the cross-dressing point is made as well as the ridiculous image of a powerful media giant wearing feathers. Raymond shoots Jocie's father, Senator Thomas Jordan (John McGiver), a political enemy of Iselin, through a milk carton the man is holding in front of his chest. In such a highly charged movie about the

American way, milk is the perfect symbol for the purity of the country. It also replaces a bloody moment with an ironic one. Then Frankenheimer turns the film back into high drama as Jocie enters and is also shot to death by Raymond. A two-shot of father and daughter lying dead on the floor is sobering and a sign that Raymond may be beyond the point of no return. Jocie was the love of his life and her father was a role model of a caring parent, a fact of life denied to Raymond.

The final sequence resonates with the dark side of American history. Raymond is given his command to assassinate the presidential nominee. He is in a perch high up in New York's Madison Square Garden, where the convention is being held. Raymond is dressed as a priest so that he will not be noticed. There is the irony of a man of the cloth wielding a rifle. He is shown from many perspectives—inside looking down and from the floor looking up. A **point of view** angle through the rifle scope is the most disturbing, and it is through this shot that the shocking climax occurs. After 1963 it was impossible to watch *The Manchurian Candidate* without striking an emotional connection with the list of leaders who were taken down by the assassin's bullet.

The Manchurian Candidate is a film to be studied for the physical excitement generated by director and production designer. There are statues and images of Lincoln strategically aligned with Iselin to disguise his fascist nature. Senator Jordan has a large spread-eagle plaque over his fireplace. At one point when he stands, it appears that the wings are coming out of the sides of his body. His character embodies liberty. The amphitheater where the brainwashing exhibition took place and the solarium for the hotel garden party were two sets on real railroad tracks, which allowed for a 360-degree pan to go from one set to another without cutting the camera. The detailing in the interiors is rich and reflects the political power of the characters. There are several variations of wood-paneled walls, arches, elegant décor, and old American style.

The Manchurian Candidate is the model for the contemporary political thriller. It is intelligent, pregnant with meaning, and sheds insight on the fragility of a democratic society. John Frankenheimer was a director with a strong social conscience. He was politically astute and a natural-born filmmaker. He entertained and sent a message. It did not come from Western Union, as the old saw goes. When John Frankenheimer wanted to send a message, he made a movie that was entertaining and that made you think. He believed that the cinema should reflect society and embraced the notion that movies should move—in every sense of that word.

Notes

1. Jackson Pollock (1912–1956) was an action painter who splattered, dripped, and poured paint as he stood above the painting surface on the floor.

Of Further Interest

Screen

Fail Safe
Patriot Games
Saboteur
Seven Days in May
State of Siege

Read

John Frankenheimer: A Conversation with Charles Champlin by Charles Champlin
The Thriller; the Suspense Film from 1946 by Brian Davis
The Suspense Thriller: Films in the Shadow of Alfred Hitchcock by Charles Derry
The Cinema of John Frankenheimer by Gerald Pratley
The Films of Frankenheimer: Forty Years in Film by Gerald Pratley and John Frankenheimer

Self-Referential Cinema

□ ◆ □ ◆ □ ◆ □

Man with a Movie Camera

The cinema has always been fascinated with itself. There are countless films about the making of a movie—*The Bad and the Beautiful, Contempt, Day for Night, Day of the Locust, Boogie Nights, The Last Movie,* and *Alex in Wonderland*—or those concerned with the film business—*The Big Knife, The Last Tycoon,* and *Barton Fink.*

Audiences are lured to these films because they appear to show the backstage glamour and drama associated with moviemaking as well as insights into the process. Some of these films are truthful and perceptive, others are not, but all use the narrative and aesthetic techniques consistent with the traditional mode of filmmaking.

Since the 1970s, filmmakers have referenced or quoted other films by recreating a shot, repeating dialogue, or replicating visual characteristics. This practice has been a dominant stylistic element in the films of Peter Bogdanovich, Martin Scorsese, Brian DePalma, and Quentin Tarantino.

An entirely different movement is the self-referential film, a cinematic work that refers to itself. A self-referential film is not about the making of another film—it is concerned with the one that is currently being watched by the viewer. One such film is *The Projectionist,* which incorporates the concept of a daydream film within a film to capture the fantasy life of the main character. Morgan Fisher's *Standard Gauge* examines the very physical properties of motion pictures.

Man with a Movie Camera (1929) is an early and daring experiment in self-referential cinema. Dziga Vertov (1896–1954) brings two concepts to-

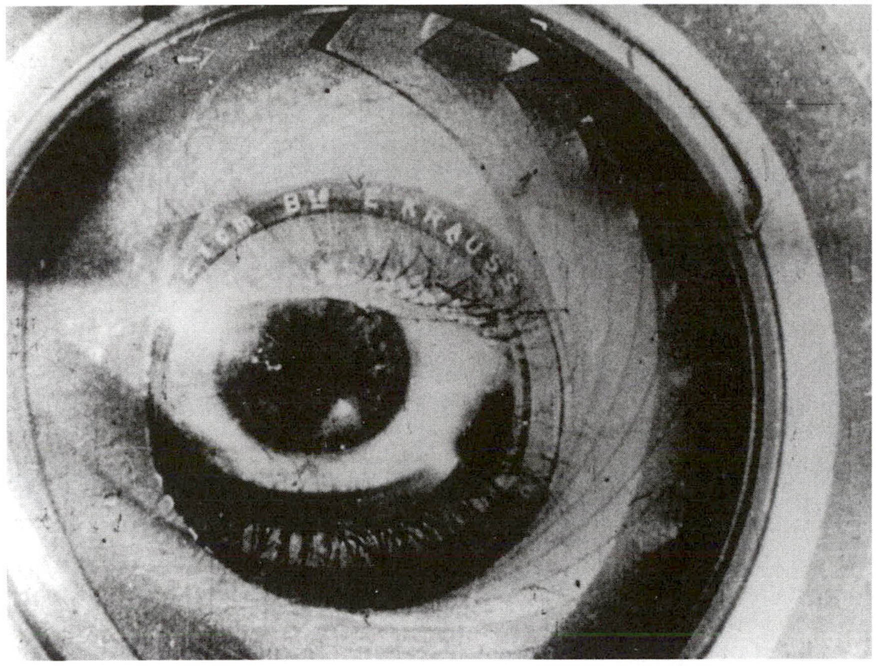

A literal camera-eye observes all in Dziga Vertov's experimental documentary, a film that constantly refers to itself. Courtesy *Photofest.*

gether—his celebration of the cinema and the workers of his country, the U.S.S.R. This **nonnarrative, nonfiction, avant-garde film** follows an intrepid motion picture cameraman as he carries his camera and tripod to film city life in Moscow, Kiev, and Odessa.

Man with a Movie Camera also fits into the critical classification of a *city symphony*—films that present the characteristics of life in a specific metropolis within the structure of a day from morning to night. This movement began during the 1920s. Along with *Man with a Movie Camera, Nothing but the Hours,* directed by Alberto Cavalcanti, and Walter Ruttmann's *Berlin: Symphony of a Big City* are considered classics of the form.

Vertov celebrates filmmaking by making the man with the movie camera a heroic figure. Undaunted, he takes his camera high and low to capture the vitality in front of his lens. Socialism is the subject matter here:

happy productive workers at the job, at play, keeping physically fit, and moving effortlessly by means of the state's active transportation system.

Is *Man with a Movie Camera* a propaganda film or the reflections of an enthusiastic citizen? Both apply. For Vertov, the film was a manifesto for a cinema empowered with the responsibility of capturing life through the nature of the medium. *Man with a Movie Camera* is not a documentary. The images are poetic and captured with cinematic innovation. *Man with a Movie Camera* opens as a day-in-the-life-of-a-city film is about to be shown in a movie theater. Wooden chairs magically open by themselves through a form of **stop-motion photography**, an audience files in, and we see the projectionist ready himself for the show. The sparking of an arc allows the projector to present images through light on the screen, which is the movie being made by the cameraman. At the conclusion of *Man with a Movie Camera*, Vertov again returns to the movie theater to show the film ending on the screen. The last image is an eye reflected in the camera lens that signifies that the camera is all-seeing.

During *Man with a Movie Camera*, as the man is shown filming the city, an editor begins to go through what is supposedly the footage being shot. She catalogs, cuts, and splices the film. The concept that the film we are watching is being edited by this on-screen editor ratchets up the self-referential intentions.

As seductive and exhilarating as this notion becomes, there is another reality taking place here. Another man with a movie camera, the one who is not visible to the audience is photographing the man with the movie camera as he appears to shoot the film we are watching. With the exception of **point of view** shots that are editorially linked to the on-screen cameraman's actions, this is an illusion. The editor could not possibly be editing what we see on the screen in real time. It is the result of detailed **intercutting** that creates the relationship between the shots of the on-screen editor editing and the edited footage presented in *Man with a Movie Camera.*

The day is organized in sequences that depict the movement of the city as it goes through a daily cycle. At first the city is at rest. The man with the movie camera is visualized on screen, but in reality Vertov and his chief cameraman and brother, Mikhael Kaufman (*Kinoglaz, Moscow, Odinnadtsatyj*), show empty streets, a trolley depot, machinery at rest, and empty shops. A surreal quality is achieved by several images of dolls or mannequins on display. They represent the culture and the omnipresence of the Soviet worker.

Intercutting and **montage** techniques create editing patterns to connect several categories or movements of action at the same time. A young woman is asleep, then wakes and readies herself for the day while the city slumbers, then begins to come alive for the day as shops begin to open. This editorial relationship personalized the film by allowing the audience to relate to the woman's morning ritual of washing and dressing while linking her to the city and the masses, made up of other individuals who gather, work, and play in the city.

It is the choice of what to shoot and the order and rhythm in which the shots are edited that creates the cinematic experience of the man with the movie camera being omnipresent as the day progresses. A factory sequence stresses the harmony between the mechanical and the human. Machine parts spin, pump, and revolve. Workers start up and maintain the machines. A rapid montage of a woman forming cigarette packages by a series of manipulations depicts her dexterity, efficiency, contribution to society, and her pride as a Soviet worker. Vertov uses associations to connect ideas. The on-screen film editor has similar qualities. She performs her job with great speed and purpose. The former serves the Soviet people and industry. The latter supports art and history by becoming part of the documentation process in this vital social and political order. This sequence communicates other aspects. Gender equality is stressed throughout the film. This woman captured on film by Vertov and edited by Yelizavita Svilova (*Kinoglaz, The Fall of Berlin, Parade of Youth*) is shown to possess the ability to slow down and freeze images by her manipulation of the editing process. The slow motion and **freeze frames** for the film were accomplished by the cinematographer and the laboratory, but intercutting of the editor working on strips of film with full shots of those very frames moving, slowing down, and freezing gives the impression that the editing produces this result. The speed in which the editor selects and splices shots creates the illusion that to produce a film with quick, dynamic editing like *Man with a Movie Camera,* the editor must move at the speed of the real-time unfolding of the film.

An effective editorial strategy is establishing an intercutting pattern between individuals and an action, such as the sequence in which onlookers are shown in close-ups reacting favorably to intercuts of athletes performing a variety of Olympic decathlon sports. Just when the viewer feels comfortable that they understand the context, the relationship changes so the onlookers are now observing and reacting to something entirely different. This principle is known as the Kuleshov effect after the Russian filmmaker Lev Kuleshov (*Three Day's Life, Taras's Dream, The Great Consoler*), who discovered that intercutting could produce a specific emotional response based on the intended purpose of the filmmaker. The viewer's own response to the stimuli influences the reaction to a character or subject's feelings.

Man with a Movie Camera is transformed into an avant-garde film by several aesthetic devices employed by Vertov. **Multiple exposure** is a process by which the film is run through the camera more than once, giving the filmmaker the ability to combine separate images to form a whole. This technique is applied throughout the film and utilized in two specific ways. A distorted perspective is achieved by shooting one side of a street scene on a right angle and then shooting the other with an opposite angle, forming a graphic pattern that resembles a mountain or an image that has been broken in half. Interspersed during the overall structure, this effect contributes a delirious atmosphere of the cameraman dizzy with enthusiasm in filming the bustling activity around him. Multiple exposure is also used to place one view of the city above another, a split-screen effect popular in the films of Brian DePalma. This presents multiple views of the city in one frame, demonstrating the relationships without editing. It also contributes to the topsy-turvy vision Vertov presents of a city so full of vitality it is whirling beyond reality.

The man with the movie camera is able to travel instantly to wherever the action is. He rides in a car during an emergency, filming from a fast-moving vehicle that seems to be at his command when necessary. Editing is his prime means of transportation. The cutting allows Vertov to place his man almost anywhere, including high atop the city by placing his figure up there via multiple exposures. The point of view is constantly shifting from first person as seen through the camera lens, to third-person views, to the viewer's point of view staring directly into the camera. The human eye that is reflected in the lens is a metaphor for the human eye behind the camera and the human eyes viewing the film.

Stop-motion live-action animation allows a lobster to dance; a hand-held camera places the viewer in the middle of a basketball game. Vertov brings the audience into this cinematic trip by using techniques to directly engage them in what the cameraman is experiencing. Often Vertov reveals how the man with the movie camera is achieving a shot, such as digging a hole so vehicles can pass over him while he is filming, or exactly where he and his camera are in relation to what we have seen or are about to see. A close examination of *Man with a Movie Camera* uncovers that this logic is constantly violated. What we see the man with the camera doing is not always directly connected to how the previous or forthcoming shots were filmed.

As posted in the opening credits, *Man with a Movie Camera* is an experiment in cinema. It is a joyful one, full of fun and exhilaration for the potential of the medium and for the positive portrait it shows of the Soviet people and their city. Many cities were used to create a unified composite of a Russian city, just another illusion and principle of what the act of filming and editing motion pictures can create.

Man with a Movie Camera can be seen as a propaganda film, a cinematic demonstration film, documentary, art film, sociology, anthropology, history, and a nonnarrative narrative. It is all these and more. Dziga Vertov was not just ahead of his time; he clearly understood the artistic properties of the cinema in presenting the point of view of its creator by examining the aesthetic issues the medium embraced. It may be the first and only motion picture to attempt to take viewers on an expedition through the filmmaking process while at the same time they are watching a film. The mind boggles at the possibilities contained in *Man with a Movie Camera*. One can only hope that the grand experiment begun by Dziga Vertov will never cease.

Of Further Interest

Screen

Coming Apart
David Holzman's Diary
The Last Movie
The Lickerish Quartet
Standard Gauge

Read

Coming Apart by Milton Moses Ginsberg
The Language of New Media by Lev Manovich
Kino-Eye: The Writings of Dziga Vertov, edited and with an introduction by Annette Michelson
The Man with a Movie Camera (The Film Companion) by Graham Roberts
Allegories of Telling: Self-Referential Narrative in Contemporary British Fiction by Lynn Wells

Architecture in Production Design

Metropolis

Historians have designated *The Cabinet of Dr. Caligari* (see chapter 10) as the first German expressionist film and *Metropolis* (1927) as the last. Robert Wiene conceived *The Cabinet of Dr. Caligari* in reaction to the social and political morass in the Germany of his day and at the beginning of the German expressionist art movement. As German expressionism was in gestation, Fritz Lang (1890–1976) was refining his architectural vision of the cinema. His Wagner films developed lofty themes and presented the visual power of the masses. In these films, Lang's abilities to use structural and graphic images emerged and were employed to advance the narrative and to envisage content on the screen. *Metropolis* is a warning about the future—a warning that the brains that create machines must have a heart for a society to survive. Lang foresaw a Germany driven by mechanization and was inspired by the accomplishments of Wiene, F. W. Murnau, and the German expressionist painters to reinvent science fiction when the cinema was still in its youth.[1] Lang had the nascent technology available—**miniatures, superimpositions, glass shots**, and other cinema technology that already existed or was just coming into use—but it had never been combined for a single purpose. *Metropolis* is not just a science fiction film but a film with a message, point of view, and the visualization to support it and create a cinematic experience that eight decades later can still astonish.

Lang employs architecture as a means to present and articulate themes concerning political dominance, caste struggles, the decadence of the

In Fritz Lang's *Metropolis*, futuristic architecture towers over a city of workers who provide blood and sweat labor underneath this playground of a rich, god-like class who dominate the upper and lower depths. Courtesy *Photofest*.

powerful, the suffering of the underclass, the dangers of science, and the healing of spiritual power. *Metropolis* is set in the future, where Art Deco buildings rise up to the heavens and lofty roadways soar past ultrasky-scrapers. The city is lorded by Joh Fredersen (Alfred Abel), who oversees every detail from his massive office, where he give orders to control the power source that runs electricity, water, transportation, and everything necessary to provide a productive life for those who live in this metropolis. Fredersen's son Freder (Gustav Fröhlich) resides in the Club of the Sons, located high above the city, where the privileged few exercise in a stadium worthy of an ancient Greek Olympics and have their pick of feminine delights from a Garden of Eden.

Freder falls in love with Maria (Brigitte Helm), an angelic young woman who cares for children and secretly gives solace and hope to their parents, the workers who keep the metropolis vital. Conflict between father and son begins when Freder learns that workers labor in an underground power station and live in dwellings comparable to contemporary housing projects. Freder goes far below the city, where the workers toil sweat and blood under brutal, inhumane conditions so that the well-to-do can live extraordinary, progressive lives. Freder joins the workers in the cause, and his father turns to the evil Rotwang (Rudolf Klein-Rogge) to create a clone of Maria (also played by Helm), who turns her spiritual power and message of hope into a fury of maniacal decadence, so that Fredersen can retain his dominance over the classes. In a spectacular climax, the workers' city is flooded, but the people are saved when good, in the form of the true Maria and Freder, triumphs over evil.

The screenplay by Lang and Thea von Harbou (*Spione, M, Journey to the Lost City*) provides the thematic context that connects German expressionism in *Metropolis* to a country speeding towards oblivion. This metropolis is a fascist state in which one man and his perfect race live off the suffering and sacrifice of others who are offered no choice but to be loyal slaves to the state. A constant metaphor in *Metropolis* is that the brain and the hand must have a mediator—the heart. Maria preaches this to the oppressed. Joh Fredersen is the brain, actually the authoritarian figure beholden to the mad genius Rotwang, who performs evil deeds and provides the leader with the technology to keep the metropolis safe from a growing resurgent anger. This anger threatens to disrupt the paradise above the hell of the workers who provide life to the city. When Maria gives her sermon to the workers and talks about a mediator who will come and end their misery, she appears to be referring to the coming of God. Freder becomes an earthly flesh and blood mediator between his father and the workers after much destruction leaves the two sides even further apart. At the conclusion of *Metropolis*, it is Freder who takes responsibility for this enormous task and brings his father together with Grot the Foreman (Henrich George) to fulfill Maria's prophecy. Good and evil are clearly defined. The ultimate evil is Rotwang's corruption of Maria's purity by defying God's will and creating a life form dedicated to destroying the moral will of the people.

Seen today, the visualization of *Metropolis* is remarkable, a unified vision of a futuristic world composed of heaven and hell. Like *Blade Runner* (see chapter 7), *Brazil*, or *Dark City*, *Metropolis* creates a convincing future city with scope and detail. The workers are dressed in black with matching caps. They pass through tunnels of low arches and are packed into massive elevators. Symmetry imprisons the men who work below the earth. The masses are choreographed to walk slowly, heads down, in lockstep that causes them to sway right to left, left to right, in the tradition of ancient slaves. The center is dominated by a mechanical beast that must be labored over at all times to keep the city running. It is a machine that looks like a face with open mouth and an insatiable appetite. This is achieved by dynamic application of industrial design principles. The metaphor becomes a nightmare reality for the men when the machine's needs get ahead of the human ability that cannot possibly keep up with it. Moloch, an epic mythic monster comes alive and swallows up the workers who have lost control of their master and oppressor.

Fredersen's office is a vaulting space. The height is four to five times that of a man, so high up that the frame cannot contain it in shots of the colossal doors that guard and protect it. Mechanization is at the fingertips and allows Fredersen to run this city of light. The technology is created by the brute strength of men with arms outstretched as they race the arms of an oversized clocklike gauge matching the ever blinking lights.

Rotwang's house is shaped like a barn in a dark fairy tale and tucked into the modernist city, visually representing a dark, magical place of danger. His laboratory is the definition of the mad scientist's lab, with boiling beakers, neon coiling, machines, and contraptions everywhere. The occult symbol of a pentagram, a five-pointed star designed with alternate points made by a continuous line, is on the wall, indicating the dark angel's presence and evil blessing—Fredersen's pact with the devil to consummate his position of power.

The original inspiration for the look of the city came to Lang when he first saw the skyscrapers of New York City. Other design influences came from a close collaboration with his art department. The production designers Otto Hunte (*The Blue Angel, By Rocket to the Moon, The Spy*), Erich Kettlehut (*The Thousand Eyes of Dr. Mabuse; Berlin: Symphony of a Great City; Asphalt*), and Karl Vollbrecht (*The Hound of the Baskervilles; Die Nibelungen: Siegfried; The Testament of Dr. Mabuse*) meticulously researched the project and began to design the city much as a city planner would work on designing a real, working city. The cinematographers Karl Freund (*Dracula* [1931], *The Good Earth, Key Largo*), Günther Rittau (*Die Nibelungen: Siegfried; The Blue Angel; Lady Killer*) and Eugen Schüfftan (*The Horror Chamber of Dr. Faustus, The Hustler, Lilith*) had the technically difficult job of putting the images on film.

Lang built physical movement into *Metropolis* through blocking and action and camera movement and also through photographic and editorial effects. The Art Deco concept led to angular and other graphic shapes that move, transition, and multiply to create an architectural, mathematical scheme that brought futurism to the visualization of the film.

Rendering the imagery by using existing technology meant embracing state-of-the-art equipment and processes as well as applying the tools and grammar of cinema in an innovative manner to produce startling new results. Germany and UFA studios[2] pioneered and refined the expressionist style. It was an extremely progressive cinema, but Lang and his team looked to Hollywood for aspects of production developed by the mecca of movies. Freund and Rittau made the pilgrimage, met with veteran cinematographer Charles Rosher, and returned with two Mitchell cameras, the premier Hollywood photographic tool for several decades. While in Hollywood, Lang saw a process that allowed background drawings to be animated frame by frame, adopting this for the dynamic opening title sequence of *Metropolis,* in which a mountain of buildings rises into a city. The sequence incorporated 1,000 separate drawings. This technique was also used to give the illusion of movement to 300 scale model cars racing along a sleek sky freeway. Eugen Schüfftan was also a painter and architect who had developed the Schüfftan Process, which Hollywood embraced for created movie magic. The Schüfftan Process allowed models of the city architecture and other design elements to be combined with a background. By reflecting the model onto a live-action background by means of a forty-five degree angled mirror, Lang and his creative team were able to create the illusion of the giant stadium used by the sons, and an enormous statue dedicated to Hel, Freder's mother.

The layering of several images together to create either a collage of visuals that produces a thematic, narrative, psychological, or atmospheric relationship, or to form a consistent image, was accomplished not by printing several negatives together but by **multiple exposure**. For the fantastical shot of the mechanical woman coming to life as the evil Maria, a single **negative** was exposed in the camera, rewound, and exposed again thirty times, each run adding one of the details to create this supernatural effect. Each pass through the camera had to be perfect in execution of action, registration, exposure, and lighting. One mistake could have ruined the shot during this in-camera, not postproduction, effect.

In addition to his architectural contributions to the cinema, Fritz Lang also exercised the power of opera and theater in *Metropolis*. The characters are openly expressive in both their facial expression and in their ability to project intense feelings through body movement toward the constantly shifting relationships and the stage of film—the frame. Each character is clearly defined in relationship to good and evil, but *Metropolis* fascinates with the complexity of its morality. The biblical tale of the Tower of Babel is the centerpiece of the film's philosophical tract. Not only are the towering buildings and hedonistic lifestyle warnings for the futuristic society and a metaphor for biblical prophecy; Lang actually visualized the parable. The prophets of the Tower of Babel are a direct allusion to Fredersen, and the slaves who build the tower refer to the subterranean workers in the story. This film within the film is as visually detailed as is all of *Metropolis*, and it sets the downward spiral of the future city in a doomed context. Maria is portrayed as both good and evil. Her pure beauty glows in one and her sexual depravity reigns in the other. Fredersen is a character burdened with the weight of his responsibility. As played by Alfred Abel, he is not purely driven by ambition and lofty ideals. From his very first appearance, he is absorbed by guilt over the loss of his wife and his inability to love his son unconditionally. This can be seen in his strong but sad eyes and his furrowed brow. This moral shading turns the plot in the climax when Freder as the mediator brings together the head—his father—and the hands—Grot the foreman. Freder's heart is touched by Maria's devotion to peace and humanity and the message that only the mediator of the heart could save *Metropolis* from the disaster represented by the Tower of Babel.

Lang's understanding of cinema language is masterful. To show the initial attraction between Maria and Freder, he intercuts (see **intercutting** in glossary) full screen **point-of-view** shots of their faces. Handheld shots are used to show the chaos of working with the monster machine, and another point-of-view shot of Freder is dramatically rendered by including his outreached arm in the shot so that the viewer experiences life as this character for the length of the image. Lang moves from big shots of the city to the smallest human detail with ease, all at his disposal in the **mise-en-scène**, which creates the science fiction world of *Metropolis* and is a comment on the rise and fall of great societies.

With *Metropolis* Fritz Lang brought a maddening, expansive vision to the screen, attempting to tackle philosophic issues of human existence. He reached out beyond entertainment and traditional drama and employed the alchemy of the cinema to take us into a future he hoped we could avoid.

Notes

1. F. W. Murnau (1888–1931) was a German film director who worked in the German expressionist style in such classics as *Nosferatu* (1922), *The Last Laugh* (1924), and his first American film, *Sunrise* (1927), considered by many to be not only one of the finest achievements in silent film history, but possibly the greatest film of all time. The German expressionist film movement evolved from German expressionist painting, which is noted by its favor toward distortion and exaggeration of color and shape to express the artist's emotional response to his

material. Prominent painters in German expressionism include Emil Nolde, Oskar Kokoschka, and Ernst Ludwig Kirchner.

2. UFA (Universum Film Aktien Gesellschaft) was a giant film production studio created in Germany in 1917. Created from the combination of several major studios and helped by government funding, UFA's mission was to create a positive image of Germany and its politics to counter Hollywood's impact on Europe during World War I. In 1937 UFA became owned by the state. In 1943 *Münchhauseni,* the most spectacular film of the Nazi era, was released, but by 1945, with the end of World War II, UFA no longer existed.

Of Further Interest

Screen

Dodsworth
Eclipse
The Fountainhead
The Hudsucker Proxy
Things to Come

Read

Designing Dreams: Modern Architecture in the Movies by Donald Albrecht
Fritz Lang by Lotte Eisner
Fritz Lang: The Nature of the Beast—A Biography by Patrick McGilligan
Film Architecture: Set Designs from Metropolis to Blade Runner, edited by Dietrich Neumann
Cinema & Architecture: Méliès, Mallet-Stevens Multimedia, edited by Francois Penz, Maureen Thomas

Roots of Documentary Film

□ ◆ □ ◆ □ ◆ □

Nanook of the North

Robert Flaherty (1884–1951) was not the first documentarian, but his inaugural effort in nonfiction filmmaking, *Nanook of the North* (1922), is considered to be a starting point for creativity and substance in the genre. The **documentary** is a film form governed by many philosophies. From the beginning theorists and practitioners were divided as to whether documentary films needed to have a social–political purpose or be the result of an objective journalistic effort. A search for the truth motivates those working in **nonfiction film**. Filming real circumstances is a component of a nonfiction work, but how real are documentaries? What impact does the presence of the camera and filmmaker have on the way reality is captured? How can editing preserve or replicate the truth?

Robert Flaherty was not a trained or experienced filmmaker, but he got many aspects of the documentary right. The subject of *Nanook of the North* evolved out of four major expeditions Flaherty had taken over a period of years to prospect the region east of the Hudson Bay. This effort began in 1910, when Sir William Mackenzie contracted Flaherty to explore this vast area for its potential for railway development and for its natural resources. During these excursions, Flaherty became fascinated with the survival skills and spiritual strength of the Inuit people, popularly known as Eskimos.

Flaherty was not an anthropologist or ethnographer. His original intent was to produce a film for commercial exhibition. In terms of structure and style, Flaherty felt strongly that his audience would be accustomed to the

Nanook, an Inuit who fights for survival in a frozen wilderness, is seen here comforting his son. Robert Flaherty's landmark documentary film proved manipulation and cheating of reality were necessary to create the illusion of truth in documentary filmmaking. Courtesy *Photofest.*

conventions of fictional films—a position that would inform many of his decisions as a filmmaker.

The filming of *Nanook of the North* was arduous; conditions of the landscape made motion picture production close to impossible. Traveling with the Inuit people, Flaherty dealt with cold, ice, snow, and lack of provisions. At one point well into the process, the film **negative** was destroyed during an accident. A determined Flaherty headed north and began again, and this time he returned with the material that he and his wife Frances, the film's editor, would structure into *Nanook of the North.*

When Flaherty met Nanook, he knew he had found a man who embodied the spirit of the Inuits. Nanook had tremendous survival skills, indomitable fortitude, and the force of personality to engage an audience in a narrative departure from what had been seen during the early development of the cinema.

Even in the media-savvy world of the twenty-first century, the general public tends to believe what it sees in nonfiction, including documentary shorts and features, as well as television news. "Seeing is believing" continues to be a powerful concept. In understanding *Nanook of the North* or any nonfiction work, it is essential to comprehend several critical truths about filmmaking. No film can literally capture real life. Issues such as composition and creative manipulation of images during the editing process make the absolute truth in motion pictures unattainable. The best documentaries are either objective or subjective in an honest attempt to bring what the filmmaker has found to the screen. Filmmakers must manipulate material to get it on film and structure it. Here the word "manipulate" does not necessarily imply deceit or a predetermined agenda—it defines the process. It is through this process of orchestration of cinematic devices that the filmmaker, working with integrity and without a preconceived interpretation, can create a nonfiction work that captures some eternal truths.

Do not believe everything you see. The family shown in *Nanook of the North* was not Nanook's actual family—they were brought together by Flaherty for narrative purposes. The clothing worn by the Inuit people in the film was not their actual clothing, but a wardrobe provided by Flaherty. When Nanook struggles to capture a seal, the scene is a simulated recreation. The seal, in fact, was already dead before the camera rolled and what appears to be a fight between man and mammal was actually men off camera pulling Nanook's hunting line.

The walrus battle that is the climax of *Nanook of the North* was a real and harrowing experience for Nanook and the men. The exciting and dangerous action allows the viewer to feel that the battle could possibly be lost by the Inuits. In truth, Flaherty filmed the event with a rifle at his side. The conflict continued for so long, the men pleaded with Flaherty to stop shooting film and to utilize his rifle to end the fight. The filmmaker ignored their cries and kept the camera running. The result is one of the great documentary sequences in film history, but the cost could have been deadly. This more than any issue concerns the morality of some documentary filmmaking methodology. The truth of the total situation occurring when filming commences, not just what is projected in the dark, is a reality that documentarians must face: Does the end justify the means?

Flaherty engaged Nanook's complete trust and cooperation in participating in the film. During the shooting, Flaherty screened the raw footage for Nanook and made the subject a collaborator in the documentary process by discussing what to shoot next. Instinctively, Flaherty adopted a working method that would become a tenet of **anthropological** and **ethnographic film** creation.

The narrative of *Nanook of the North* follows the logic of life in the wilderness. The family is introduced. A trip to the trading post shows how Nanook supports them by trading pelts. The majority of the film follows Nanook and his family as they travel by dog sled across the vast snow environment, build an igloo, hunt, survive, and resettle after a new search for food and merchandise to trade. The structure is a visual passage through the life of an Inuit, in which heroic energy is required to provide and survive.

Flaherty takes great pain and pride to present Nanook's spiritual nature and the heroic skill he applies in order to endure in his dangerous environment. Flaherty's prime motivation for making the film was to document and preserve a way of life he was concerned would soon vanish. Seen in a contemporary context acquired through a history of traditional narrative films, the point of view of *Nanook of the North* presents a happy ending: Nanook and his family go to sleep at the end of another day in the wilderness. The impression is that life will go on. The film is a document of life as it is but also a poetic romantic view that shields the audience from the real dangers the Inuits face. If Nanook and his family have survived through what we are shown in the film, why would this life not continue on? A year or so after completing the film, Flaherty learned that Nanook had starved to death on a hunting expedition. Earlier prints of the film ended with a card that stated Nanook's passing. On a first viewing this was a shocking fact. Although Flaherty clearly depicts the life of an Inuit as difficult, the viewer becomes attached to Nanook as a man who can conquer any challenge.

Flaherty successfully tells Nanook's story through images. Each sequence demonstrates clarity in action and point of view. The compositions are straightforward and direct. Flaherty filmed the action in front of him without a conscious attempt to create artful frames or to apply the camera in an interpretive role. The camera has tremendous power in placing figures in relationship to their environment by emphasizing distance, height, and scale as is demonstrated in masterly fashion in the cinema of Michelangelo Antonioni (see chapter 4). Flaherty's approach is the opposite of this camera application. The documentary camera is filming Nanook, who is in the environment. This direct recording is a step forward from amateur home movie application. The naiveté of this relationship takes on a poetic innocence. **Interscene editing** is minimal.

Flaherty moves the camera when logistics require a change of angle. Often, Flaherty shoots in front of a scene without changing angles. **Jump cuts** are used to continue a sequence when there are no other angles or **coverage** to cut to. The technique is a phenomenon that causes a jump in continuity when there is no angle change or the ability to match action. For Flaherty the jump cut was a necessity, not a creative tool as applied during the postproduction of Godard's *Breathless*. Flaherty is not consciously trying to fracture the notion of time and space. The lack of Hollywood conventions signal to the audience that they are watching real life in action, when in reality they are watching film structured during the editing process to create a narrative flow that is uninterrupted, even if transitions and continuity are abrupt and crude. This is precisely the fascination with Nanook—the audience obtains the rarified privilege of going where it would be too difficult or impossible to go.

All nonfiction sound works attain information delivered either through interviews, narration, or unfolding scenes with dialogue. A silent documentary has two modalities in addition to the visuals: inter-titles and a musical **score**. The current music by Timothy Brock available on the film's release to DVD serves Flaherty's original purpose of distributing *Nanook of the North* to general audiences. In terms of documentary integrity, the score does add an artificial emotional control over the images. Often intrusive, the music manipulates the viewer's feelings rather than allowing a more objective, atmospheric approach. The titles are also intrusive. Written in elaborate prose, the cards interrupt the viewer's relationship with the visual storytelling. They are very wordy and overwrought with suggestive information that turns a pure human story into a literary experience heavy with meaning and an authorial view.

It is the images of *Nanook of the North* that fascinate. Flaherty transmits his sense of awe and respect as his camera watches Nanook build an igloo. Each snow brick is precisely cut by Nanook's knife, then positioned in place. A hole is cut for a door and a window. An ice block is carved to size as a window. Soft snow becomes the mortar for the constructed blocks to seal the home from the elements. The sequence is so perfectly executed that there is never a thought about recreation or the imposition of the filmmaker. The seal hunt we now know is a simulated recreation of past encounters. There are no visual cues that the igloo building sequence was created for the sake of the film, but the assumption is that Nanook was acting for the camera and not captured in the process of being himself in an actual circumstance. Elsewhere in *Nanook of the North,* Flaherty became aware he had to signal the audience that Nanook was involved in the making of the film. He achieves this by having the man address the camera during several sequences. This occurs in circumstances similar to the home movie—moments of frivolity, like when he is playing with his children. It never occurs in sequences in which Flaherty wants us to believe the camera was an objective observer or when the action is of a serious nature, such as the sequence when Nanook deals with his warring dog team.

Robert Flaherty's *Nanook of the North* is a humanist documentary. The intrusion of the filmmaker was intended to maintain realism and not distort it to communicate the artist's point of view. The film is a testament to what documentaries could become and to the moral ambiguities that confront the nonfiction film each time out. It is informative, inspiring, exciting, educational, and historical. With *Nanook of the North*, Robert Flaherty became a founding father of the nonfiction movement. It was not his original intention; he was first motivated by his curiosity and admiration for a man living as people did before modernism began changing lives. *Nanook of the North* is world and film history—a simultaneous feat rarely repeated.

Of Further Interest

Screen

Berlin: Symphony of a City
The City
Man of Aran
Night Mail
The Plow That Broke the Plains

Read

Documentary: A History of the Non-Fiction Film by Erik Barnouw
Nonfiction Film: A Critical History, edited by Richard Barsam
The World of Robert Flaherty by Richard Griffith
Documentary Film: The Use of the Film Medium to Interpret Creatively and in Social Terms the Life of the People as It Exists in Reality by Paul Rotha, Sinclair Road, and Richard Griffith
Robert J. Flaherty: A Biography by Paul Rotha, edited by Jay Ruby
For Documentary: Twelve Essays by Dai Vaughn

31

Multiplot, Multicharacter Narrative

□ ◆ □ ◆ □ ◆ □

Nashville

Many films have attempted to define America at a point in time on a grand scale: *Gone with the Wind*, depicting life during the Civil War; *The Best Years of Our Lives*, after World War II; *Easy Rider*, the late 1960s; and *Magnolia*, the 1990s. Robert Altman's *Nashville* (1975) is a laser beam on the United States as it approached its 200th birthday—the bicentennial.

Joan Tewkesbury's (*Old Boyfriends, A Night in Heaven, Strangers*) screenplay, based on a research trip to Music City in Nashville, connects the lives of twenty-four characters representative of the country music scene; they embrace politics, power, wannabees, insiders, and outsiders. They are twenty-four characters in search of the soul of America.

The characters are linked narratively through profession, romance, music, sex, political causes, and commitments. Together they form a cross-section of an America largely neglected by the east and west coasts. In the elusive search for America, Altman found the character, values, ambition, tragedy, and survival of the country in Nashville, Tennessee.

Nashville is constructed as an intricately woven pattern of **parallel storytelling**. There is a plot line and subplot for the characters that connects them as they maintain relationships and forge new ones. The results are complex. Lives crossing other lives becomes a metaphor that defines democracy at a moment when the power base of the United States was being redefined by President Jimmy Carter and country music was replacing rock and roll as the national anthem.

The framework created by Joan Tewkesbury and Robert Altman is or-

The twenty-four actors of *Nashville* in search not of an author but of the truth about America at its bicentennial birthday. The connections between characters create a multi-plot narrative that is both exhilarating and exhausting in its ability to mirror the breadth of the nation through examination of the home of country music. Courtesy *Photofest.*

ganized by events that converge in a shocking finale. Hal Philip Walker is running for president of the United States on the Replacement Party ticket. His campaign van, equipped with loudspeakers, is the narrative voice for the character and serves as political satire of the two-party system. Altman returns to a device that proved effective in his antiwar film *M*A*S*H*. The loudspeakers get the word out. They also create an additional thematic layer and allow improvisation. Scenes of the omnipresent vehicle were photographed and the commentary was written but still fluid and ripe for elaboration during postproduction. Hal Philip Walker is not a physical character in the film. He is seen in the flesh only once in an extreme long shot, just before the benefit concert in his name is to begin. When the concert turns into a violent tragedy, his motorcade suddenly drives off.

John Triplette (Michael Murphy) is Walker's advance man who is in Nashville to get the country music industry on board for his candidate. Hollywood once had great influence on the political scene, but their liberal message was no longer considered to be mainstream. The courting of country superstars to support Walker symbolizes Music City's connection to the American political machine. In organizing the concert, Triplette receives help from Delbert Reese (Ned Beatty), whose purpose is to establish a relationship between Nashville's elite and the new political force. The politicians are not interested in music; the performers are not interested in politics. They are connected because the music reflects their political views and is the key to real power over the hearts and minds of the American people.

Nashville is a musical, with Richard Baskin (*Welcome to L.A.; Buffalo Bill and the Indians, or Sitting Bull's History Lesson*) serving as the music supervisor. Altman required that each of the actors portraying singers write their own songs. The music is the best kind of parody. The ersatz country songs so capture the style and intent of the elder statesmen of country music that it is difficult to separate the performances from the real thing.

Altman began experimenting with sound early on in his career. The aesthetics of Hollywood studio sound demanded that spoken voices be separated in dialogue scenes. Overlapping dialogue was rare. Characters did not speak while others talked, although in life there are cross conversations, interruptions, and discussions while crowds and other ambient sounds are heard. By the time Altman made *Nashville,* the maverick director had found the ideal production sound mixer in Jim Webb (*All the President's Men, One from the Heart, Down and Out in Beverly Hills*). Webb came to the project with expertise and experience in multitrack recording. Applying music recording technology to film sound allowed for each of the twenty-four-plus voices to be recorded on separate tracks. During the editing and mixing processes, the choreography of dialogue could be controlled to perfection. The rerecording mixer, Richard Portman (*The Godfather, Funny Lady, The Deer Hunter*), was able to place each voice in its correct zone on the screen and in the proper aural perspective.

Altman's keen sense of casting is connected to his philosophy toward acting. Robert Altman adores actors. He allows them the freedom to improvise within the structure created by the director and screenwriter. Throughout his career Altman has created a stock company that grows with every project. For *Nashville* Altman chose many actors from television, some known for their character parts in feature films, some of his own discoveries, and established players, who, for Altman, dispensed with actorly mannerisms, personas, and conventions that the director felt constrained the craft. Altman gave the cast of *Nashville* his unconditional trust to develop their multifaceted roles, which gained nuance with every interaction and unfolding situation.

Haven Hamilton (Henry Gibson) is royalty in Nashville. In public he is an ambassador and diplomat; in private he is a tyrant with ambitions beyond music. Lady Pearl (Barbara Baxley) puts the political context of *Nashville* into perspective. She pines for the days of Camelot when John F. Kennedy was president. His assassination had changed America forever and moved the country into a darker, more cynical cycle. Barbara Jean (Ronee Blakely) is based on Loretta Lynn, the country music queen whose life was chronicled in *Coal Miner's Daughter*. Lynn had suffered from psychological stress that made it difficult to perform for a period in her career. Altman uses Barbara Jean as a cult of celebrity figure who intersects with the majority of the characters. The country music world revolves around her. Her fragility and unstable behavior is a crack in the American Dream. Barbara Jean is held together by her husband–manager, Barnett (Allen Garfield), who is at odds with everyone trying to exploit his wife.

Another central character is connected to a number of *Nashville*'s women. Altman comments on the sexual politics of the music scene through Tom Frank (Keith Carradine). This lothario is a member-in-standing of the "Me Decade," only interested in his own pleasure. Tom juggles affairs with Mary (Christina Raines), who is married to Bill (Allan Nicholls), all of whom are part of a contemporary trio act; Linnea Reese (Lily Tomlin), Delbert's wife and mother of their two deaf children; Opal (Geraldine Chaplin), a BBC reporter who is reporting on the Nashville scene (through whom we see Altman's European perspective on American life); and L.A. Joan (Shelley Duvall), a groupie in town to visit her dying aunt.

The political wing of *Nashville* uses sex to buy support for Hal Phillip Walker. Sueleen Gay (Gwen Welles) is a sweet and naïve but talentless waitress who aspires to sing at the Grand Ole Opry. An insensitive bartender delivers her to Triplette and Reese, who book her for a gathering of men, known as smoker, where she is deluded into performing a striptease for potential campaign contributors. The scene quickly loses the humor of the terribly off-key chanteuse singing badly to a roomful of button-downed men. When they yell for her to "take it off," Sueleen is humiliated but she strips, losing all self-respect, and is cheered by the crude male chorus. Altman delivers the final blow to Sueleen's abuse when, after driving her home, the normally affable Delbert Reese becomes an out-of-control predator.

Barbara Jean is another female victim, but of a more extreme sort. *Nashville* must be seen twice to observe the subtle clues and motivation of her assassin. During a first viewing, it is shocking in its recall of the memory of JFK on that tragic day in Dallas. The assassination of John Lennon in 1980 in front of his home marked another descent into madness. In *Nashville* the murder of Barbara Jean reflects the dark side of the decade, which followed a hopeful period of belief that a new generation would remake the world in its own image. Altman concludes his film masterfully with a straight dose of reality but is able to make another turn during the tragedy. Throughout the film, Albuquerque (Barbara Harris), an unknown country singer, struggles to get her big break in the Nashville music scene. The tragedy becomes her moment and the film concludes with Albuquerque's galvanizing vocal performance to the stunned crowd and a film audience who now realizes *Nashville* is more than a satiric romp—it is a microcosm of a young country experiencing growing pains.

The superstructure of *Nashville* is a series of set pieces. The airport arrival of Barbara Jean is a story convention to create the superstar's mystique and to reveal the motives of the swirl of people around her. The spectacular multicar pile-up that stops traffic allows for character development and reveals aspects of the twenty-four as they interact when they are thrown together by happenstance. The recording session that opens *Nashville* establishes the power of Hamilton Haven and the studio as a symbolic seat of government. Club scenes present the characters at play as they continually strive for ambition and look for love after hours. The concert at the Parthenon is the location of the assassination and a scene toward which the film builds throughout its development. Triplette and Reese are constantly organizing for it. The performers are courting for the event, Barnett is trying to protect his wife from appearing, and the fans ready themselves for a country music Woodstock disguised as a political rally. The Parthenon is a copy of Greek architecture that represents a great society in ruins.

The cinematography by Paul Lohmann (*Time after Time, California Split, Mommie Dearest*) is crisp and employs Altman's trademark use of the **zoom lens** to bring an immediate sense of near and far as well as a **documentary** patina to the film. On the surface, the tableaus of *Nashville* do not have intricate **interscene editing**. Much of the **intercutting** that enjoins characters and story-lines is the result of the editing by Sidney Levin (*Sounder, Mean Streets, Norma Rae*) and Dennis Hill (*Quintet, Major League,*

Powder) that tightly controls *Nashville* so it can appear to be improvisational and free-form. The maestro of *Nashville* is Robert Altman, who choreographs the music, drama, and satire for the purpose of defining America.

Altman had been preparing for a film of *Nashville*'s magnitude his entire career. *M*A*S*H* was a satirical statement about America's involvement in Vietnam, filtered through the story of a medical unit in Korea. *Brewster McCloud* captured the nature of American eccentricity. *McCabe and Mrs. Miller* began serious experiments in overlapping sound and realistic aural backgrounds. *California Split* celebrated gambling as an American sport, part of the country's evolving morality. All of these films featured a growing cast of actors that developed a freewheeling ensemble style open to expansion as the film was shot.

Nashville is a solid candidate for the great American movie. It captures the imagination through parody and firmly and surely is a portrait of America on its 200th birthday. In its specificity concerning Nashville and country music, it is a film that embraces the totality of America itself. A good film is bigger than what it appears to be. *Nashville* is a film about the country music industry that allows us to inspect and reflect the democracy's past, present, and future.

Of Further Interest

Screen

Baby Fever
Gosford Park
Short Cuts
Slacker
Welcome to L.A.

Read

Reading for the Plot: Design and Intention in Narrative by Peter Brooks
Robert Altman: Jumping off the Cliff—A Biography of the Great American Director by Patrick McGilligan
Robert Altman's Subliminal Reality by Robert T. Self
Robert Altman Interviews, edited by David Sterritt
The Nashville Chronicles: The Making of Robert Altman's Masterpiece by Jan Stuart

Method Acting

On the Waterfront

Film acting has evolved over the course of cinema history. Theater acting styles were first applied to the new medium, and the silent film required its own acting technique to communicate story, action, emotion, and character. During the sound era, the Hollywood studio system employed actors under contract and had its own program of training performers to act on screen. The star system made a tremendous impact on the craft. Projects were created for particular actors as vehicles, and supporting players who often specialized in particular roles were part of the ensemble.

Early notions of screen acting were based on elocution, poise, and theatrical blocking. Many actors captured the imagination of audiences with their personas, iconic qualities, and association with particular genre characters and attitudes: Greta Garbo, Cary Grant, Bette Davis, James Cagney, Joan Crawford, and Humphrey Bogart. There was a distinction between personality actors such as Gary Cooper, John Wayne, and Rita Hayworth, who played roles close to themselves, and transformational actors such as Paul Muni, who became his characters.

The nature of screen acting changed when method acting moved from its experiments and practice on the stage to the medium of film. The method, as it was called, was an Americanization of the teachings of Konstantin Stanislavsky. The tenets of method acting, taught and practiced by the Group Theater, Harold Clurman, Cheryl Crawford, and Lee Strasberg, were based on the concept of being the character and not just play-

Karl Malden (left), Marlon Brando, and Eva Marie Saint don't act but "be" the characters of Father Barry, Terry Malloy, and Edie Doyle in *On the Waterfront*. This attainment of realism launched a new era in motion picture screen acting that influenced most American films to follow. Courtesy *Photofest*.

ing the character outwardly. The training involved learning to understand the character's history, motivations, and emotional life.

Director Elia Kazan (1909–2003) brought method acting to American filmmaking. *On the Waterfront* (1954) features the finest examples of this influential acting technique that inspired generations of actors who followed.

Great acting evolves out of great writing. *On the Waterfront* had a long gestation period. Kazan first worked with playwright Arthur Miller for a project about corruption on the New York waterfront. When they parted company over personal and artistic differences, Budd Schulberg (*A Face in the Crowd, Wind across the Everglades*), a writer with a lineage of Hollywood royalty, immersed himself in the subject.[1]

Key to the creation of *On the Waterfront* was Kazan's and Schulberg's personal cooperation with the House Committee on Un-American Activities (HUAC). After naming names, Kazan found himself in a moral quandary. He had been a member of the Communist Party as a young man and now reversed his position. Kazan's colleagues in theater and film questioned his motives and declared that he named names to save his own career at the expense of others. Schulberg also named names. To Schulberg and Kazan, *On the Waterfront* was not only about mob corruption against the dock workers. The subtext of *On the Waterfront* is a defiant rationalization of informers. Kazan tries to justify his dubious moral judgment, which continued to cause animosity toward him to the end of his days. Kazan sought vindication, turning the protagonist of *On the Waterfront*, a character identified with the director, into what we now would call a whistleblower. To those who suffered as a result of the blacklist, and to their families and supporters, Elia Kazan was and remains an informer, a squealer, a rat.

On the Waterfront moves swiftly with decisive dramaturgy. Terry Malloy (Marlon Brando), a washed-up prizefighter and the brother of Charlie the Gent (Rod Steiger), is ordered by union mob boss Johnny Friendly (Lee J. Cobb) to set up Joey Doyle, a member of the local union who is about to testify to the Waterfront Crime Commission. Terry manipulates Joey to go up to the roof where Friendly's thugs are waiting. Terry was led to believe they would just "lean on" Joey, but Friendly's orders were to silence Joey by throwing him off the roof.

Terry becomes involved with Joey's sister Edie (Eva Marie Saint), and his conscience and deep guilt lead him to take on Friendly by testifying against him and the corrupt union. Although the thugs beat Terry into submission, he is able to walk into work, thus breaking the criminal dominance over the decent working man. When Terry says "I'm glad what I done to you" to Friendly, it is clearly the voice of Kazan galvanizing his defenseless HUAC position against his fellow actors, writers, and directors. Terry was noble; Kazan continued to defy his inquisitors.

Marlon Brando's performance as Terry Malloy has long been acclaimed as one of the finest on film. He brings to Terry brutality and tenderness. Malloy is a man willing to play deaf and dumb as part of the system he has been born into, but his social conscience battles right and wrong until through guilt and Edie's love he is radicalized. When Terry and Edie walk in a park on a bitterly cold winter day, she accidentally drops one of her white gloves. Brando picks up the glove and puts it on his hand. This action is separate from the dialogue about their past and Terry's growing attraction for Edie. The glove exchange was not just a planned piece of business; actually it was not even in the script—it was Brando's improvisation. What seems like a way of teasing Edie becomes an associative act.

As they talk, they each have on one glove. The gesture is a feminization of Terry that eventually gets him to open to his feminine side to gain the inner strength to fight a fierce enemy.

Brando takes advantage of the strong dramatic blocking by Kazan. While waiting in a crowd of longshoremen to see who will work on a particular day (a dehumanizing procedure called a shape-up), two investigators approach Terry; one, played by Leif Erickson, is to his right and the other, portrayed by Martin Balsam, is behind him in the center. Terry refuses to cooperate with them. He directly answers questions from Erickson's character, but when Balsam's character makes a comment Brando turns all the way around to screen-left to rudely dismiss him. The dynamics of the gesture indicate Terry's rebellion and defiance of law enforcement, which will later evolve into motivation for Terry's cooperation with the authorities.

It is the emotional honesty in Brando's performance that empowers Terry Malloy. A product of mean streets and failed dreams, Terry is used as muscle for the mob, but his conscience and support from Edie and a maverick priest (Karl Malden) turn him toward a more just and noble life.

Edie had been at a Catholic school preparing for the sisterhood. Her hardworking father, "Pop" Doyle (John Hamilton), wants his daughter to be far away from the ugly and brutal life of the neighborhood. Edie becomes a crusader for the truth about her brother's murder. Eva Marie Saint, in her first film role, was the perfect physical type for Edie, with her thin, under-nourished looking, and delicate features as well as long blond hair, but it is the inner life of Edie that is the stuff of conflict and drama. She is defiant against those who turn their back on justice. Edie stands up to the priest, holding him to his word and reminding him that hypocrisy is just as wrong as noncommitment. Edie's relationship with Terry is complex. As a young girl, Edie took in stray cats to her family home to nurture. She sees Malloy as someone who with care and encouragement could do good but has had the wrong influences in his life. She expresses revulsion upon learning that Terry was involved in Joey's death but ultimately believes he was duped and supports his courageous one-man army against Friendly's regime. Saint gives a performance that is sincere and human, without actorly pretenses.

With his portrayal of the priest, Karl Malden breaks decades of screen stereotypes. Actors often portrayed men of the cloth as devoid of a social consciousness, as witty moralists, or as pious figures without conviction in the real world of their parish. Malden embodies the bravery of the father as he puts himself on the firing line in his battle against the mob, which is destroying his parishioners. Malden is emotionally specific, showing us exactly when the priest makes this commitment. It occurs when Dugan (Pat Henning), one of the workers who agrees to testify if the priest will go shoulder-to-shoulder with him, is killed. Of the many powerful moments in *On the Waterfront*, one of the most memorable is when the priest is summoned to the hull of a ship to give last rights to Dugan, who has been murdered to silence him. During his powerful oratory, Friendly's goons taunt him. Malden continues on. One of the thugs throws a can which hits the priest on the head. Without pause the priest finishes his message to Dugan's killers, then gets on a platform with the body as a winch pulls the netted base up to the deck. The symbolism of rising out of the ashes is palpable, genuine, and pure theater.

Rod Steiger plays Terry's brother Charlie, a chief counsel for Friendly. Dressed in menswear finery, Charlie has taken the road traveled by his father, who was killed because of mob business. Charlie loves his brother and takes care of him by getting him a cushy longshoreman's job with Johnny Friendly. Charlie's warning about the dangers of going against power is clearly defined and projects the passion he has toward his brother. In one of the most expressively rich scenes in American film, Charlie and Terry take a cab ride that is either the end of the road or a turning point for Terry. On instruction from Friendly, Charlie is mandated to make sure Terry is on the right side or else one brother must be the impetus for the demise of the other. As Charlie tries to deliver the message, Terry gives his essential monologue in which he tells his brother that Charlie's decision to throw a critical boxing match took away Terry's dream and an opportunity to be a contender. The boxing term here is symbolic for the following line, "I could have been *somebody*." As with the majority of characters in *On the Waterfront*, Charlie is at a crossroads. He chooses to save his brother and to sacrifice himself instead. Later, Terry and Edie find Charlie dead, hung up on a meat hook. In this film about Catholic morality, a crucifixion is witnessed.

Lee J. Cobb plays Johnny Friendly as a powerhouse of greed, corruption, and abusive power. His mere presence and his fierce shouting voice intimidates and presents him as an indomitable force. When Friendly learns a Greenpoint grifter has handed in a short cash count, Friendly slaps the helpless man around like a rag doll. Friendly has a tender spot for Terry and feeds the fighter's memories of former glory. Johnny gives Terry a cushy job out of respect for Charlie, and because Terry is a boxer, Friendly has someone to possess and nurture. Friendly's connection with Terry brings him closer to a sport identified with his milieu. Friendly's transition occurs upon learning that Terry will cooperate with the Waterfront Crime Commission's investigation. In the dramatic conclusion of *On the Waterfront*, Terry physically takes on Friendly and is beaten to a pulp by the goons and their boss. The last human challenge of *On the Waterfront* is for Terry. If he can walk into work on his own power, he can prove to the big bosses that the Friendly era is over. Brando eschews all movie conventions and in time gets himself to his feet. The walk is arduous. Bleeding, badly limping, and eyes blurred with blood and tears, Terry steadily makes it to the entrance on his own. Friendly becomes a screaming fool when he realizes no one will listen to him. He is tricked into falling into the river—a bully is rendered impotent.

Kazan's dynamic direction of the actors and his staging skills heighten the physicality of the emotional drama. Kazan's extensive work as a stage director and on social documentaries of the 1930s and the influence of **Italian neorealism** (see chapter 6) of the 1940s contributed to the visual style of *On the Waterfront*.

On the Waterfront was photographed by Boris Kaufman (*L'Atlante, 12 Angry Men, Splendor in the Grass*), the brother of Dziga Vertov, creator of *Man with a Movie Camera* (see chapter 28). The cinematographer also defied Hollywood conventions by methodically stripping away all prettifying photographic devices like diffusion and soft backlight for high-key realism (see **high-key lighting** in glossary) and the flat and gray actuality of life during a bitterly cold winter on the docks of New York.

Although much of *On the Waterfront* was shot on location, the production design by Richard Day (*How Green Was My Valley, A Streetcar Named Desire, Tora! Tora! Tora!*) realistically emphasizes the squalor and degradation of the environments in which the characters were forced to reside. The union office is positioned just off the main dock area to symbolize that it has a separate rather than unifying purpose. The bars, apartments, and streets are dehumanized and in disrepair. The workers toil to survive, not to create or maintain a decent lifestyle. The physical world of *On the Waterfront* is as decayed as the moral climate of life there.

On the Waterfront unfolds as a well-constructed straightforward drama, but the motor of the film is in the moral context that heightens the narrative. Every gesture, look, and piece of body language communicates to the audience's emotional receptors. The film is layered with Catholic symbolism. A television antenna on the roof where Joey was murdered appears as a cross. Brando's brave walk to end the mob's tyranny recalls the image of Jesus taking his last walk, which ended in crucifixion, then transcendence. The text, dialogue, action, and plot are just one aspect of *On the Waterfront*'s communication with the audience. By creating a new acting language that did not rely on conventions long since developed by Hollywood to manipulate emotions through indication, Kazan's search for the truth of each scene gave *On the Waterfront* an inherent power to capture the trust of the audience.

On the Waterfront is a significant film in many ways. It was a seminal East Coast production, one that used social issues for its content, presented without artifice. The film was a highly influential work for Martin Scorsese and for a new American cinema that emerged during the 1960s and 1970s. Terry's pained words, "You was my brother Charlie, you should have looked out for me a little bit," gives *On the Waterfront* timeless significance. They signify hope that the human spirit can conquer oppression. The fact that *On the Waterfront* was directed by a less than moral filmmaker is significant to the terrible legacy of the blacklist. Whatever the artist's intentions, *On the Waterfront* is about a standard of American ethical courage the country strives for but does not always achieve.

Notes

1. Budd Schulberg is the son of B. P. Schulberg, who was a screenwriter and publicity director for Rex Films. The elder Schulberg joined Adolph Zukor's Famous Players at their outset, discovered Clara Bow as an independent producer, worked as a producer at Paramount, and in 1928 became the studio's general manager of West Coast Productions.

For Further Interest

Screen

Bus Stop
East of Eden
Raging Bull
Somebody up There Likes Me
Splendor in the Grass
A Streetcar Named Desire

Read

On Method Acting by Edward Dwight Easty
A Method to Their Madness: A History of the Actors' Studio by Foster Hirsch
Elia Kazan: A Life by Elia Kazan
On the Waterfront: The Final Shooting Script by Budd Schulberg
An Actor Prepares by Constantine Stanislavsky

The Close-Up

The Passion of Joan of Arc

This 1928 black-and-white silent film directed by Danish master Carl Theodor Dreyer (1889–1968) has been identified as a transcendental film by director and film scholar Paul Schrader (*Mishima, Hardcore, Auto Focus*) in his landmark book *Transcendental Style in Film.* By its very nature the film-going experience transports the viewer to another state of consciousness. Some films allow the audience to enter a dream state; others are time machines that carry viewers to another time period or situational space. Entertainment films and blockbusters can relieve the audience of cares and woes, providing an escape until the lights come up.

The experience of watching a transcendental film presents an opportunity for the viewer to transcend worldly reality and enter a spiritual state. Robert Bresson (*Diary of a Country Priest, Pickpocket, A Man Escaped*), Dreyer (*Day of Wrath, Ordet*), and Yasujiro Ozu (*Late Spring, The Flavor of Green Tea over Rice, Tokyo Story*) were filmmakers who consistently attained transcendence in exploring holiness. Content is not enough. Nontranscendental films about spirituality ground the audience in a prosaic reality or just never take divine flight. In a transcendental film, the cinematic technique expresses the atmospheric, psychological, and emotional lives of the characters and the story. The performers become the characters. The camera style, art direction, and editing of the work form a totality that communicates with the conscious, subconscious, and unconscious existence of the viewer.

The Passion of Joan of Arc is based on actual trial records concerning the

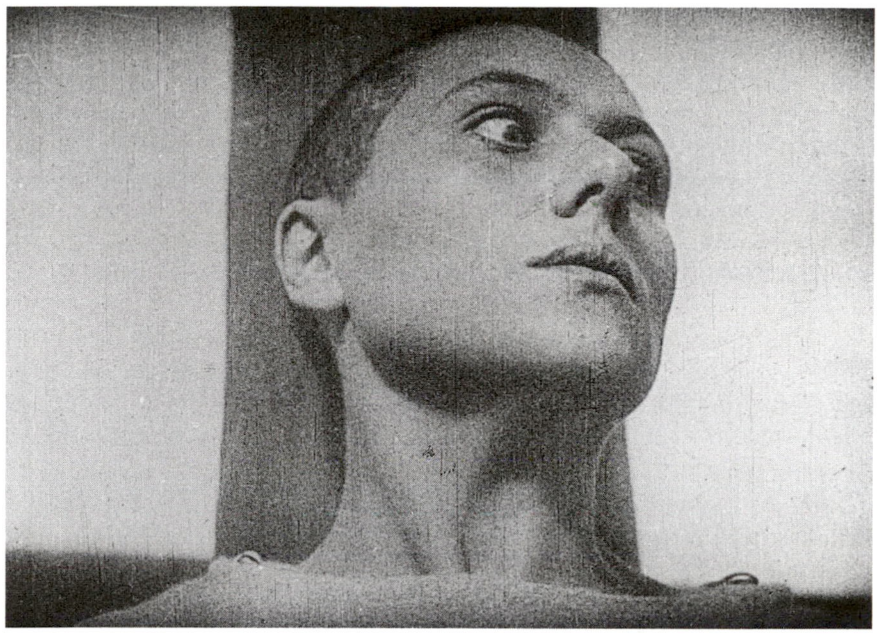

Renée Falconetti as Joan of Arc in Carl Dreyer's silent masterpiece *The Passion of Joan of Arc*. The use of the close-up transcends the traditional use of this shot unit, which usually features a character by bringing them intimately close to the viewer, by attaining a state of faith, grace, commitment, and acceptance of Joan's faith that has been judged by the oppression of an organized religious authority. Courtesy *Photofest*.

fourteenth-century French teenage military heroine who claimed that the voices of Saints Michael, Catherine, and Margaret compelled her to save France from England during the 100 Years' War. After successes on the battlefield, she was captured and sold to the English, who put her on trial as a heretic and burned her at the stake after she repeatedly refused to recant that her actions has been inspired by messages from God. She was canonized as Saint Joan in 1920.

Joan of Arc has been portrayed in many films throughout cinema history. With the exception of *The Trial of Joan of Arc*, another transcendental film with a totally different artistic temperament directed by Robert Bresson in 1962, Joan's heroic efforts in war, as well as her physical beauty, is often stressed in mainstream cinema, literature, and painting.

Transcendental films address the holy. By structuring the narrative in *The Passion of Joan of Arc* around the trial and subsequent execution, Dreyer placed the action and romantic dramatics of Joan's military actions before his story, one that investigates the persecution of Joan of Arc's belief that she was a messenger of God. Her accusers, church officials, go beyond decency and morality to force her to confess to being duped by the devil himself, turning the actual text of the trial (with some artistic deviation) into a test of faith. To achieve a pure state of spirituality, Joan suffers physically and mentally in defending her deeply felt beliefs.

To achieve his narrative and thematic goals, Dreyer made many radical stylistic decisions in this silent film. The most controversial, and proven over time to be highly effective, was the extensive use of close-ups. Many of the shots are so tight that they fill the screen with Joan's anguished face, magnifying her myriad reactions of pain and suffering to the evil, misguided injustice forced on her by the priests.

First there are the faces themselves. In casting the film, Dreyer rejected the suggestion to select Lillian Gish, one of the silent screen's most accomplished actresses. After a long search, Dreyer selected Renée Falconetti, an actress known in France for her stage performances in sophisticated comedies. The creator of the Theater of Cruelty, Antonin Artaud, was given the role of a young compassionate priest; his very presence gives the film authenticity in presenting drama out of the suffering inflicted by the ignorant, callous, and self-serving violent nature of man.[1] For Dreyer the actors had to both look the part and transform elements the director observed in their own natures in order to become rather than act their roles.

The unprecedented decision not to use any cosmetics on the actors' faces allowed the camera lens to record and capture every pore, wrinkle, and facial muscle as the actors moved through a complex series of turbulent emotions. A technical innovation allowed this choice. Orthochromatic film stock, which had a limited sensitivity to translating the color palette to the gray scale and was especially limited in recording red and yellow to black-and-white film, had been the available celluloid medium when Dreyer mounted his production. Dreyer and his cinematographer, Rudolph Maté (*Dodsworth, Gilda, D.O.A.* [1950]) chose to photograph *The Passion of Joan of Arc* on panchromatic film stock, which first became available at this time and rendered the gray scale with fine attention to tonal detail. Every artistic decision Dreyer made was based on achieving a sense of spiritual truth. The sensitive film stock more accurately captured the realities of the face and the inner emotions conveyed by the actor's instrument because it was photographed directly from lens to flesh, not through filtration or distortion of the lens or by the mask of makeup.

The Passion of Joan of Arc is a study in the art, power, diversity, and intensity of the close-up. Dreyer's directorial concept was to engage Joan and her inquisitors in constant confrontation. Every word and feeling expressed during this assault against religious freedom and for the power of conviction can be felt through the inescapable juxtaposition of the men who question and badger as Joan's indomitable beliefs endure and ultimately conquer the hypocrisy against her. Through a wrongful and painful death, she transcends her earthly role and takes her rightful place beside God at the end of her spiritual journey.

Many were critical of Dreyer's bold choice in designing the film through the expansive use of this specific shot. They argued that the close-up should be used sparingly to make a dramatic point during a scene that was covered in myriad shot sizes, in combinations of long and medium shots. This statement ignores the breadth, power, and diversity of what may appear to some as a singular entity. What does blue mean to a painter, the word white to an Eskimo, and sweet, salt, hot, or sour to a master chef? *The Passion of Joan of Arc* is a masterpiece of the close-up. The open-minded, open-hearted viewer will observe that each shot is composed for the moment and suddenly reveals blue as a range of colors and hot as spicy, tangy, or smoky, as a burst, an aftertaste, a constant presence, or a recurring series of taste-bud experiences that retreat and endure.

Dreyer blocks and composes the faces right, left, up, and down. The relationships of the characters to arches, to white space, and to each other are constantly changing. Some shots are framed with faces in the extreme lower quadrant of the image. Dreyer rewrites the rules of **eye-line match** cutting, the guiding principle of cinematic technique, for his directorial purpose. The rule states that when two characters are speaking to each other, looking or reacting to another person in a close-up, the direction in which they are looking, the eye-line, must match the gaze of the other person when the reverse angle or associative shot comes on screen. Joan is in a heightened state of emotion, agitation, and holiness throughout the course of the interrogation, sentence, and her martyrdom. Because she answers only to God, her eye-line is often turned heavenward, above the heads of the priests. In shots in which the eye-lines match in the correct direction, they do not always match in focus of attention. Joan looks at the others, but her mind is concentrated above the hostile proceedings; the eye-lines trace and connect, but Joan's mind and soul are elsewhere, underscoring DaVinci's pronouncement that the eyes are the windows to the soul.

At times the priests look directly at Joan or at each other, or they are in a deep inner monologue as they deviously plan how to trick this mortal woman they are convinced has crossed over to the devil's way. The intensity of the faces reaches the highest threshold of the viewer's ability to receive emotionality. The intimacy of the range of feelings is directly absorbed because every facial feature and the terrain of the human mask reveal the deep convictions of all the participants. The priests represent a range of personalities, but they are uniform in their insistence that Joan must confess at any cost. The expressions are honest and reveal truths of each character. During a shot, reactions to events and the feverish process of proving the church's honor speed from anger to false sorrow, real compassion, and devious manipulation from the men—some that is learned, and some that is petty, deceitful, and calculating. Joan cries, suffers deeply, experiences moments of spiritual bliss and many emotions representative of human frailty.

The Passion of Joan of Arc is made up of 1,333 shots and 174 **inter-titles**, a total of 1,517 separate edits. The average Hollywood silent film of this period contained 500 to 1,000 cuts, with a maximum of 1,300, which was rare. Silent films relied on visual storytelling to eliminate the need for dialogue. When necessary—and it was kept to a minimum—the characters spoke silently on screen and the text followed on a title card. In *The Passion of Joan of Arc*, the characters are constantly and fervently speaking. It was Dreyer's intention to project the film silent without any musical score. These decisions increase the intensity of the viewing experience. The audience is not asked to understand each word but rather to read each face, wherein the truth lies.

The original prints of the film did not identify any of the crafts people. The editing by Dreyer and Marguerite Beaugé (*Napoleon, Pépé le Moko, Abel Gance's Beethoven*) was influenced by the work of Abel Gance and Sergei Eisenstein's *The Battleship Potemkin* (see chapter 5). The rapid passages of montage stress Joan's agitated state and the aggressive behavior of the priests. The editing accentuates how at times Joan turns her head jarringly to see that there are priests all around her. The camera movement is employed to express emotional reactions. There are many **swish pans**, some in which the priests are looking in one direction and others in which the camera quickly moves down their faces. Extreme low angle shots, which were the essence of German cinema at the time, are used to emphasize the power and might of the priests and how they try to overpower Joan with their very presence.

For a film with a minimalist approach, the production design is curious and effective. Although only fragments and elements of gothic structures are in the film, Dreyer and his designers, Hermann Warm (*The*

Cabinet of Dr. Caligari, Train without Eyes, Vampyr) and Jean Hugo, devised and built a complete gothic environment for *The Passion of Joan of Arc*. The look was highly influenced by German expressionism (see chapter 10) and surrealism (see chapter 12). Arches dominate the architecture as a symbol of the church. Circular structures physically imprison Joan, who is able to spiritually escape the dominant architecture of the organized religion that represses her. Crosses and crosslike images in the details of the set and props bear the presence of the priest's notion of a wrathful God upon Joan. Warm and Hugo employed distortion of structure and perspectives to create a psychological atmosphere of unreality. Windows are off scale and angled. The many angled compositions balance and counterbalance the distorted environment of the set, which heightens the overbearing human and architectural power that dominates Joan. When light comes through the simply constructed windows with black bars, the shadow image of a cross appears on the floor to Joan as a sign that God hears her. Later, when one of the most deceptive priests walks past the crosslike shadow, it disappears, signaling to Joan and the viewer that God is no longer present.

The conclusion of *The Passion of Joan of Arc* is a powerful representation of religious strife. As Joan burns at the stake, the horrifying yet poetic images are intercut with the English soldiers launching an attack on the townspeople who witness the murder of their future saint. Dreyer was inspired by the work of Eisenstein (see chapter 5), and he employs a powerful example of how montage can generate unrelenting action, as destruction of life is everywhere. Eisenstein's philosophy as a Russian was to utilize montage as a celebration of the people and the unity of the masses for good and harm. Dreyer was interested in the individual; as the montage records countless deaths from one mass of people toward another, it is the central image of Joan's earthly form burning to ashes that prevails. The last shot is of the stake. Joan's body is gone—her soul is at the side of God.

The Passion of Joan of Arc is a challenging film for the viewer. Dreyer was relentless in the application of his austere aesthetic. The musical **score** provided with most presentations of the film eases the viewer's discomfort, but Dreyer was truly a silent film master. He communicated with silent images that created their own dialogue, sounds, and music. It is the images that provide the power of *The Passion of Joan of Arc*—those unforgettable close-ups of Falconetti, her hair shorn to the scalp, desperately trying to transcend the oppression of life on earth. Through the cinematic artistry of Carl Dreyer and his artisans, the viewer witnesses a spiritual event—the soul leaving the body and achieving heavenly bliss. This is done without special effects. It is accomplished with the most profound instrument of emotion and expression—the human face.

Notes

1. Antonin Artaud's theories, applied to what he called the Theater of Cruelty, were intended to liberate his audience from the negative effects of society and to free intuitive instincts. He proposed to create theatrical spectacles that presented human suffering, pulsating lights, and oversized puppets to shock the audience. His writings and ideas influenced many avant-garde movements including the Living Theater and the Theater of the Absurd.

Of Further Interest

Screen

Faces
Husbands
Pickpocket
Tokyo Story
The Trial of Joan of Arc

Read

The Films of Carl Theodor Dreyer by David Bordwell
Speaking the Language of Desire: The Films of Carl Dreyer by Raymond Carney
My Only Great Passion: The Life and Films of Carl Th. Dreyer by Jean Drum and Dale D. Drum
Transcendental Style in Film: Ozu, Bresson, Dreyer by Paul Schrader
Dreyer in Double Reflection: Translation of Carl Th. Dreyer's Writings about the Film, edited by Donald Skoller

Dark Side of American Cinema

Psycho

During the 1960s, American film mirrored the society it represented and metamorphosed to challenge traditional values and conservative comportment. The Hollywood studio era was rapidly coming to a close, and a new generation was looking to the movies to reflect its needs and desires. Ironically, three lions of the old system opened the decade with films that led the way to the development of a new American cinema that evolved over the following twenty years. *The Apartment*, directed by Billy Wilder, presented a frank portrayal of sexual morality. John Huston's *The Misfits* examined the dissolution of the American Dream and the human desolation left in its wake. The third stalwart director harnessed the powers of pure film to reinvent the conventions that were the lifeblood connections between a movie and audience expectations. Alfred Hitchcock's *Psycho* crossed a line that represented what movies should be, and there was no turning back. It also scared the heck out of everyone who saw it.

Psycho (1960) was adapted from the novel by Robert Bloch, who used the real life of brutal murderer Ed Gein as an impetus for the story of Norman Bates, a psychopath who killed out of a murderous rage harbored in his split personality. Joseph Stefano (producer and writer on the landmark speculative fiction television series *The Outer Limits*) crafted a screenplay that Alfred Hitchcock (1899–1980) considered a blueprint for an experiment in cinematic storytelling. The camera would tell the story. Hitchcock was celebrated for his enormous contributions in shaping the contemporary suspense thriller. *The Man Who Knew Too Much*, *The Wrong*

One shot from the infamous shower murder sequence from Alfred Hitchcock's *Psycho*. The screen space to the left of Janet Leigh, as the ill-fated Marion Crane, is designed to create tension in the viewer's consciousness as well as a position for the knife wielding Mrs. Bates. Courtesy *Photofest*.

Man, *Vertigo*, and *North by Northwest* brought him to the dawning of the 1960s. He always respected his audiences and made their participation a part of his creative process. With an instinctive awareness of what contemporary audiences craved and the audacity to go beyond the acceptable in content, form, and implementation, Hitchcock stepped out into a brave new world.

Psycho defied two narrative conventions and forced the viewer to abandon preconceived expectations nutured by traditional filmic formulas. One-third into the film the main character, Marion Crane (Janet Leigh), is murdered. Audiences had been trained by Hollywood to believe that a movie star was invincible until the conclusion of a movie. The role of protagonist then switches to her sister, Lila (Vera Miles), and Marion's boyfriend, Sam Loomis (John Gavin). *Psycho* begins as a caper film. Marion steals forty thousand dollars cash from her employer's client in a desperate attempt to bring happiness to her clandestine relationship with her financially burdened lover. When Marion is suddenly and savagely knifed to death by a deranged killer in a motel shower, Hitchcock has without warning switched the genre to a psycho-thriller. Marion's death in the first act creates fear and anxiety in viewers. They are no longer sitting comfortably in the dark; Hitchcock has destroyed their cinematic belief system—they are in his diabolical hands.

Hitchcock transforms the audience into a total state of voyeurism during *Psycho*'s opening sequence, as the camera's gaze takes viewers across a cityscape and through a hotel window to pry into the lives of Marion and Sam, who have stolen an afternoon for carnal engagement. We witness an illicit, private act, with many more to follow. This conditions the audience to be detached toward the characters and to fixate on watching their behavior and actions without becoming emotionally involved. We like to watch. We are attracted to the dark side. The price paid is giving up the innocence preserved by a cinema of carefree fantasy, role playing, and happy endings.

None of the characters in the *Psycho* universe are particularly likeable. Marion and Sam are self-involved. Her boss, Mr. Lowery (Vaughn Taylor), is dour and tiresome. Cassidy (Frank Albertson), the client with the cash, is boorish. The highway patrolman (Mort Mills) who finds Marion sleeping in her car is suspicious and has a lack of affect. California Charlie, the used car salesman (John Anderson), is facile and skeptical. Arbogast (Martin Balsam), the private detective, is cynical and mostly business. The personalities of murderous Norman Bates (Anthony Perkins) and the inherited one of his dead mother within him are fascinating, intriguing, and delightfully perverse. First we find ourselves rooting for a swindler to get away with her crime of passion, then take morbid enjoyment in watching Norman cover up his devious deeds driven by acute psychosis.

Norman's psychotic impulses are illustrated in the opening titles designed by Saul Bass (*Anatomy of a Murder*, *Spartacus*, *The Age of Innocence*). Gray horizontal and vertical lines and white lettered credits dart from right to left, left to right, and up and down as they converge and shatter—a graphic representation of Norman's fractured psyche. The signature musical **score** by Bernard Herrmann (*Citizen Kane*, *Vertigo*, *Taxi Driver*) directly penetrates the nervous system of the listener. Composed for and performed only by string instruments, the piercing, throbbing themes replicate the actual stabbing and the jangled thoughts of a mentally disturbed mind. The score creates a sonic invasion on vulnerable viewers as they watch the picture. Herrmann's music is the sound of neurosis, terror, and murder.

Hitchcock's primary implement in filming this lurid and vivid story is the daring application of the motion picture camera in *Psycho*. A **rack focus** shot of Marion changing clothes in her room indicates her plans as the camera slowly pans left from the envelope with the forty thousand dollars, across the bed, to an open packed suitcase. After Marion overhears an argument about her between Norman and his "mother," she walks out of the door of her cabin. The camera swings around, framing her from behind on the right side, from which Norman eventually enters around the corner frame-left, carrying a tray with milk and a sandwich for her. As he approaches her, the camera again swings over until they are in a profile-two shot. Norman keeps his distance and we can see a second image of him in front. The reflection in the window is a visualization of his dual personality. While Arbogast is going through the Bates Motel register looking for clues, Norman, in a low-angle close-shot, watches intently, nervously chewing on candy. When the detective says that he has discovered her alias, Norman turns his head and strains to see what was found, as the camera moves below his jaw, now working furiously, to reveal a dark moving shadow down his neck. As the camera continues to glare, the image becomes a Rorschach blot that looks like an animal or perhaps, a bird, like one Norman stuffs. The knifing of Arbogast on the stairway inside the old house is shocking because of the element of surprise. Through the use of **rear screen projection**—also known as a **process shot**—Hitchcock filmed the scene from the **point of view** of the killer stabbing the man as he helplessly falls backwards. Later Norman walks up the stairs and goes into the bedroom where he has an off-screen argument with "mother." The camera steadily cranes up over the doorway and around to the other side of the wall until it is shooting down at the staircase from an extreme high angle. The sound of the argument has been continuous. Now Norman comes out carrying the old woman and takes her down the steps as she bitterly complains about being carried to the fruit cellar. When Lila approaches the house to investigate, Hitchcock again employs point of view, this time to establish mood and anticipation. Two moving camera shots are crosscut (see **crosscutting** in glossary) to create tension between the intimidating, creepy house and the frightened sister concerned about what she might find inside. One is a high angle looking up at the house on a hill that continues to get nearer. The other is a down angle on the worried Lila as she gets ever closer. Lighting is a potent tool throughout *Psycho*, used to create atmosphere and presence. During Sam's struggle with Norman, now dressed as his mother, a naked hanging light bulb swings back and forth. A close-up of the mother's corpse sitting in a corner chair is eerily animated as the light and shadow pattern sway across her decrepit face.

Décor is employed to communicate Norman's demented condition. His hobby is taxidermy. There are stuffed birds mounted on the walls of his room. Varieties of birds have been associated with the horror genre and contribute to the general creepiness of the locale. The owl is all seeing, a metaphor for the voyeur. Marion's surname is Crane; she, like the feathered creatures, becomes a victim of Bates. During her search, Lila finds a room furnished with an old wooden rocking chair, Norman's childhood toys, a bed with a handmade comforter, and a record of Beethoven's *Eroica* symphony on the turntable of an antique Victrola. This disturbing clash of Norman's multiple personalities increases the tension and rouses the sister's worst fears that something terrible has happened.

The adroit practice of **montage** by Hitchcock and his film editor, George Tomasini (*Stalag 17, The Time Machine, North by Northwest*), utilizes pace, juxtaposition, and precise dramatic timing to transform meticulously planned shots into sequences of heightened, unrelenting suspense. The celebrated shower scene is so much more than an assembly of the **storyboard** in which Hitchcock and Saul Bass designated each shot in sequential order. It is the actual act of editing that propels each shot logically to the next. Tomasini and Hitchcock often use an edit as a practical and metaphoric tool to create the illusion that Marion is being stabbed, even though the knife never really enters a human body. The editing positions the viewer at just the correct place and time to witness the horror of the attack, constantly shifting from position, angle, and shot size for the optimum visceral force. Less acknowledged and equally effective is the application of editorial technique in every scene of *Psycho* to sustain the balance of pressure and release, and to deliver the nuances achieved by the screenplay, acting, directing, and cinematography.

Sex and violence have always been components of movie narratives. The degree of daring and explicit imagery asserted has been governed by the will of the film director and the standard and practice of the censor. With *Psycho* Hitchcock expanded the envelope in both areas. In the real world, murder and sexuality had often both expressed themselves outside the definition of "normal" established by the moral arbiters of society. It was time for the screen to grow up and to reflect the times. The dark, personal side of life needed to take its place alongside its sunnier disposition. The sexual persona of the girl next store is displayed in the voluptuous torso of Janet Leigh. First she is seen in a white brassiere and half-slip; then, when she becomes a bad girl contemplating stealing the money, her preference of lingerie switches to black. The shower sequence mixes a dangerous combination of voyeurism, (the impression of) casual nudity, and (the illusion of) graphic violence. Viewers are titillated, shocked, and then saddened by the events before coming to the unsettling conclusion that the prior logic of the story has been swept out from under them. The slaughters of Marion and Arbogast set the precedent for things to come.

Whereas Hitchcock used staging and montage, technology would soon allow for direct representation of acts of horror. Hitchock chose to photograph *Psycho* in black and white because he was well aware of the shocking impact the violence would make on audiences. For the director, the shower scene would have been unbearable in color. But the master of suspense began the 1960s by opening a pandora's box of explicit screen violence, allowing filmmakers to explore subjects with graphic, violent content. After *Psycho,* America would witness political assassinations, riots, unrest, and serial murders captured by a new American cinema that would mirror history—and the blood would then flow red.

During the 1970s and 1980s, a new genre evolved out of the traditional horror film and from the prehistory of Alfred Hitchcock's *Psycho*. Slasher and splatter films like *The Texas Chainsaw Massacre* (also inspired by the misdeeds of Ed Gein) and *Friday the 13th* were filled with gore and a celebration of amoral violent acts. *Halloween*, directed by John Carpenter—a landmark of the style—actually starred Janet Leigh's daughter, Jamie Lee Curtis, who became known as the teen scream queen, picking up the modern tradition her mother championed.

Eventually the unthinkable fell upon the film world. Three sequels were made to cash in on the *Psycho* legend and the fine filmmaker Gus Van Sant had a monumental lapse of judgment when he directed what he described as a shot-by-shot recreation of the original. For the curious only, view this freak of cinematic nature after the one and only. For the purists, concerning *Psycho* (1998), repeat to yourself over and over, "It's only a movie, it's only a movie, it's only a movie. . . ."

Of Further Interest

Screen

The Apartment
The Birds
In Cold Blood
Midnight Cowboy
The Misfits

Read

Hitchcock's Notebook's: An Authorized and Illustrated Look Inside the Creative Mind of Alfred Hitchcock by Dan Auiler
A Long Hard Look at Psycho by Raymond Durgnat
Psycho: Behind the Scenes of the Classic Thriller by Janet Leigh with Christopher Nickens
Alfred Hitchcock: A Life in Darkness and Light by Patrick McGilligan
The Dark Side of Genius: The Life of Alfred Hitchcock by Donald Spoto

Subtext in Personal Expression

□ ◆ □ ◆ □ ◆ □

Raging Bull

Although *Raging Bull* (1980) is a biopic of the middleweight fighter Jake La Motta, it is not really about boxing. Director Martin Scorsese was never a boxing enthusiast, but the La Motta story gave Scorsese a framework for a theme that permeates his work and life—redemption.

Robert De Niro, Scorsese's longtime collaborator and on-screen conduit of the director's inner life, read La Motta's book and saw it as an ideal vehicle for the duo's explosive gifts. When De Niro brought the project to Scorsese for consideration, the director was suffering emotionally from the failure of his large scale musical, *New York, New York*, and he was also in a hospital bed. Martin Scorsese had been an asthmatic since childhood and was abusing cocaine, a drug that had grabbed many affluent baby boomers by the throat in the 1970s. Doctors told Scorsese that a brain hemorrhage could explode at any moment and kill him. As he contemplated the project, Scorsese envisioned a film that could redeem his cinematic and personal sins. Scorsese was convinced it would be his last picture—but not because of his tenuous health situation. He was convinced that when people saw what he put on the screen in *Raging Bull*, he would never be allowed to make another film.

Raging Bull subverts the boxing film genre in every imaginable way. Although it contains many boxing matches and scenes concerning career struggles and mob infiltration into the sport, which are all conventions of the fight film, it is not really about boxing but the redemption of a man who has consumed himself with anger, fear, and self-doubt.

During one of his grueling, soul-destroying boxing matches, the self-tortured Jake La Motta (Robert De Niro) is portrayed as a Christ figure. The ring rope symbolizes the crucifixion cross, De Niro's physicality symbolizes the body of Jesus, and the bright light from above symbolizes the voice of Heaven. Courtesy *Photofest*.

Jake's rage is complex and his furious behavior is unrelenting. He tells us he is angry when a steak is overcooked, that his hands are too small so he can never fight the legendary heavyweight champion Joe Louis. He taunts his brother Joey (Joe Pesci) through intimidation and ridicule and goads him to punch him in the face. Jake despises the organized crime figures that can help him win the title and the law enforcement officers who arrest him when he weakens and throws a fight badly. Jake later goes on to accuse Joey and his own wife Vickie (Cathy Moriarty) of having an affair and ultimately loses everything meaningful to him. This evokes references to Jake La Motta as an animal, a charge that leads to Jake's redemption and slow journey back to prove to himself, and to the world, that he is not an animal but a human being.

Scorsese is a film scholar as well as a master filmmaker. In studying the boxing genre, he observed that boxing matches in feature films were rarely visualized by employing the totality of expressive film grammar to transform them from the form in which the actual sporting events were historically televised. Sound had not been adequately explored as a method of creating the physical or psychological experience of two men in a ring competing for dominance over their opponent.

Scorsese made an artistic choice to shoot *Raging Bull* in black and white. In the classic studio era of Hollywood movies, the boxing genre film had been done in black and white. The golden age of televised boxing was during the 1940s and 1950s when transmission was black and white. Black-and-white images linked Scorsese and *Raging Bull* to the period being recreated, also a time when the majority of motion pictures were produced in black and white. Color is utilized in two exceptions. The main title image of *Raging Bull* is a slow-motion black-and-white shot of De Niro as La Motta in the ring alone, throwing punches with all his strength. This iconic image does not only express the poetic beauty of the sport but also the intensity of La Motta's rage. The main title letters are blood red. In a montage that depicts the marriage, honeymoon, and early life of Jake and Vickie, the images are shot to appear as home movies on Kodachrome color film stock—this evokes a powerful memory of a generation that shared in this postwar amateur film tradition.

As is his practice, Scorsese storyboarded every shot in *Raging Bull*, collaborating with cinematographer Michael Chapman (*Taxi Driver, Personal Best, The Fugitive*). The results of the boxing sequences are astonishing. Each is based on a historic bout and is dramatized to reflect Jake's personal state of mind. Scorsese is loyal to the aesthetics of personal filmmaking rather than the conventions of the sport or how it had been captured on television and the movies. Long before digital technology made it easy and commonplace to ramp (see **ramping** in glossary) the frame rate up or down, Scorsese goes into slow motion or advanced speed within a shot. Angles are employed to fully express the defined space of the ring. The camera moves almost constantly and shifts in its point of view according to what Scorsese is trying to investigate inside La Motta's mind and the way he sees, hears, and feels while he is boxing.

The sound design of *Raging Bull* puts the viewer inside Jake La Motta's head, a mind tortured by demons, unrelenting rage, severe paranoia, and a crippling anger. Scorsese first worked with Frank Warner (*Little Big Man, Close Encounters of the Third Kind, Being There*) on *Taxi Driver*. A genteel man who began his career in radio and television sound, Frank Warner credited Stanley Kubrick, whom he worked with on *Spartacus*, for mentoring him in the important contribution sound brings to the cinematic experience. Throughout *Raging Bull*, Frank Warner created aural backgrounds that set the mood for each scene and contributed to the palpable sense of time and place. For the interior scenes, Warner evoked the volatility of streets outside with voices, music, and traffic that waft in through the open windows.

Frank Warner called the sounds he created to identify La Motta's emotional and psychological states "the *Raging Bull* effects." The ingredients—animal noises, transportation sounds, and the crushing of fruits and vegetables—are less important than how the sounds express the internal turmoil of Jack La Motta. Inside the ring Jake focuses his attention on his opponent. His perspective changes from hearing the **diegetic sounds** of the crowd, the fight bell, the referee voice, and his cornermen, to a distorted cacophony as he is overwhelmed by his extreme mental condition. Jake does not hear voices in a clinical sense, but the low and pounding rumbles, screeches, and thumping, and the flashbulbs that sound like explosions; the slowed-down aural stretches demonstrate the depths of his mental deterioration. Elements of these *Raging Bull* sounds follow Jake throughout his life until he reaches what for him could be called a stage of inner peace.

Catholic imagery defines Jake's persona. This obsessive theme in Scorsese's oeuvre is depicted here with crucifixes hanging over the beds of the principal characters and framed religious images hung on the walls. During one of Jake's most brutal fights, a sponge filled with blood bathes his torso, associating the fighter with the figure of a crucified Christ. Even the pummeling he receives from Sugar Ray Robinson will not allow Jake to give up his dignity. Losing the fight, Jake proclaims "You never got me down, Ray," a subtextual message about how his soul cannot be taken from him.

After his boxing career is over, La Motta continues to slide into Dante's hell. He opens a nightclub where he serves underage girls liquor and leads them to a life of depravity. When he is arrested and dragged into isolation in a Florida prison, La Motta pays his penance by banging his head repeatedly into a concrete wall, pounding it with fury as he emotionally collapses into tears chanting, "I am not an animal." This is the bottom. Jake begins the long road to redemption. To repent for one's sins is a centerpiece of Catholic theology. Redemption can be attained by prayer and devotion, but for Scorsese the sins of life must be exorcised, not just spiritually but physically. Jake's punishment in the ring was linked to a cycle of anger that destroyed everything that was good in his life—his reputation, wife, brother, and the pride of his individuality. Jake fights as a man at war with himself. His insane jealousy and suicidal attitude bring more sins and more pain, and leave him spiritually bankrupt. After serving jail time, La Motta plays dive bars where he tells self-deprecating jokes, insults hecklers, and emcees for strippers. By chance Jake sees Joey walking to his car. The brothers had not spoken for many years. Jake tries but fails to reconcile; Joey barely responds as Jake begs for a hug and to be let back into his brother's good graces.

Raging Bull ends where it began, in 1964 in a New York City hotel dressing room as La Motta prepares for an evening in which he will perform monologues from Tennessee Williams, Rod Serling, Shakespeare, and Budd Schulberg. In a final act of redemption, Jake rehearses the "You was my brother" monologue from *On the Waterfront* (see chapter 32) directed by Scorsese's hero Elia Kazan and written by Schulberg. De Niro plays the scene as if Jake is just running the lines, leaving La Motta's actual performance of the monologue off screen after *Raging Bull* concludes. The words of the speech relate directly to La Motta. Terry Malloy was a down-and-out fighter whose brother sold him out to the mob but loved him enough to sacrifice his life to protect Terry. Jake's brother Joey sacrificed everything to devote himself to Jake. Both men learned their brothers loved them unconditionally when it was too late. When Jake says Terry's words, "You should have looked out for me," he is lamenting that Joey should have saved him from his worst enemy—himself. Jake then physically works himself up to go on stage by rapidly throwing punches and saying "the boss" repeatedly as his mantra. "That's entertainment" is Jake expressing that he must move on. He accepts the realization that by taking life so seriously and letting his dark side rule, he missed the fact that everything does not revolve around him. Now Jake La Motta can go on without the demons.

Raging Bull is a uniquely Italian American story. Scorsese layered the film with autobiographical touches and an insider's understanding of La Motta's cultural identity. La Motta's pride, stubborn nature, and volatile temper were all common traits for his generation of Italian Americans who considered themselves to be outsiders to the culture of the United States. During the 1940s and 1950s La Motta was a force to be reckoned with in boxing. At the time it was difficult to get into the championship arena without compliance with organized crime, which controlled the sport. La Motta was fiercely independent to a fault. His macho dominance over family and business affairs was traditional in the male role in Italian American households. Scorsese has revealed at length in interviews that the pressure and influence of Italian American cultural traits appear in his body of work. The dominant one is irrational anger. During the period in which *Raging Bull* was conceived and produced, Scorsese experienced severe bouts with anger. A generation raised on global social change clashed with the tradition of Old World upbringing. This phenomenon transformed Scorsese with an awareness of identification and compassion with La Motta, a man who demonstrated outwardly what the gentleman director felt inside. Scorsese would use not his fists but the cinema to express his inner rage through Jake La Motta's story. *Raging Bull* is a movie about redemption by a film director who had to prove after the failure of *New York, New York* that he could still make the kind of personal movies to which he was dedicated.

The vision and concept of *Raging Bull* is a personal interpretation from Martin Scorsese as a director and creator of the film. Scorsese's longtime editor Thelma Schoonmaker (*GoodFellas, Casino, Gangs of New York*), who won the Oscar for her work on the film, heightened the manic energy Scorsese imagined, felt, designed on paper, and executed on film through Michael Chapman's probing, hard-charging camera. Every craft decision, image, edit, and sound, is inspired by the sinful soul in Robert De Niro's brilliant portrayal of La Motta. The actor became skilled as a middleweight contender under the tutelage of La Motta himself. Much has been said about the weight De Niro gained to play the older La Motta in search of redemption, his anger and sins transferred from the physical to the spiritual, destroying and distorting his physique by eating himself into oblivion. For De Niro, gaining the weight was more than just an actor's stunt; it physically matched the emotional transformation the actor created to serve the subject and the personal intentions of the director.

When a film director is in perfect harmony with his or her subject, the results transcend drama and become an experience that exposes truths about the subject and the creator. *Raging Bull* is the model for that paradigm.

Of Further Interest

Screen

The Hustler
The King of Comedy
The Pawnbroker
The Swimmer
Ulee's Gold

Read

Martin Scorsese: Interviews, edited by Peter Brunette
Untouchable: A Biography of Robert DeNiro by Andy Dougan
Martin Scorsese: A Journey by Mary Pat Kelly
Raging Bull: My Story by Jake LaMotta with Joseph Carter and Peter Savage
Scorsese on Scorsese, edited by David Thompson and Ian Christie

36

Multiple Point-of-View Narrative

□ ◆ □ ◆ □ ◆ □

Rashomon

With *Rashomon* (1950) director Akira Kurosawa (1910–1998) challenged the notion of a single-person narrative. *Citizen Kane* (see chapter 13) created the portrait of a man through the perceptions of those who knew him. *Rashomon* investigates a tragic event from the points of view of its participants. Kurosawa employed the elements of high drama to explore a universal theme that truth is in the eye of the beholder. Regardless of any single witness's account, something has occurred in *Rashomon* that has had a profound effect on all involved and that is an essential truth.

The story is set in eleventh-century Japan at the crumbling gate of Rashomon, which guarded the entrance of a court palace. Everything is in ruins. From the first frame, it is not just raining; the sky has opened up and there is a torrential downpour. A light warm rain can be a cleansing metaphor, but Kurosawa set the scene for high and profound tragedy. First two men, then a third, take refuge from the relentless hard rain. Kurosawa, a student of Shakespeare who adapted the bard's work throughout his career, understood the elements of Shakespearean tragedy. A once great society guarded by a magnificent structure now ripped apart by unrest is a shadow of its former greatness. The men are dwarfed by the environment—damaged architecture with a wide set of stone steps that lead to the platform where the men are physically confined to be protected from the constant storm. As the rain falls it becomes part of the visual tapestry. The image of a former power symbol and of two men trapped in fear and horror at what they have seen and learned about

In 11th century Japan a commoner (Kichijiro Ueda, left), a priest (Minoru Chiaki, center), and a woodcutter (Takashi Shimura, right), are at the crumbling gate of a former court palace. *Rashomon,* directed by Akira Kurosawa, investigates a past crime against humanity told through multiple points-of-view. Is the truth in any one of the many accounts or in the sum of all? Or is reality only in the mind of the individual who experiences it? Courtesy *Photofest.*

themselves is repeatedly pelted and stained with wrath from the heavens.

As the men speak above the sound of the bombarding rainstorm, the story begins. There has been a rape and murder. The priest (Minoru Chiaki), the younger of the two, fears he has lost his faith. What has occurred is so horrible that it overshadows war and plague. Man's sins are crushing his soul. A third man, a commoner (Kichijiro Ueda), comes out of the rain, and after some provocation the woodcutter (Takashi Shimura) begins his story.

Rashomon had a seismic impact on audiences raised on traditional linear storytelling. Kurosawa defied the single point-of-view narrative to embrace what was experienced in life—the fact that there are many sides to a story. The violence inflicted on a samurai (Masayuki Mori) and his wife (Machiko Kyo) in the forest on a clear and sunny day is told four different times, each reflecting a view of the truth for the teller. In a search for what really happened, Kurosawa made profound insights into the facets of human perception, the reality of the self, and universal truths.

The structure of *Rashomon* is deceptively simple. The stories begin in the present and unfold in **flashbacks**, but Kurosawa plunges deeper into the unknown territory of nonlinear storytelling by creating variations on the narrative voice he employs. The techniques utilized included cutting directly to the flashback—a daring device for a medium that often signaled a return to the past by blurry shimmering **opticals** and musical cues that indicated that time shifts were about to occur. The **direct cut** was a bold editorial choice. Kurosawa used the text dialogue to make it clear when a **backstory** was about to begin. Some of the recollections are presented in story and through dialogue; others are elucidated while underway by the **voice-over** of the teller. Each story has internal credibility. This is not a detective mystery but an evolving human drama. The stories take place in the same forest setting with the samurai and his wife. As they progress, aspects of the story clearly reveal what has occurred, as when it is learned why the woodcutter found a woman's hat, rope, and other items. But larger truths are left to the audience by allowing viewers to make a value judgment concerning the veracity of the teller. A bandit (Toshiro Mifune) is introduced in the flashbacks, and he becomes one of the four reporters of the facts. To accomplish this, Kurosawa presents a trial held to examine the crime. The tribunal appears in several of the flashbacks with the witnesses directly addressing an unseen judge and jury. By staging these scenes with the witness seated directly in front of the camera, viewers become the judging body. The witness speaks directly to the lens and at times responds to unspoken questions that come from this **off-screen** authority situated in, and among, the audience. The purity of the images from the recurring trial sequences is concise and transcendent. The witnesses are seated on the ground. After the initial testimony, each one takes his or her place to the back right of the frame against a low wall in the background. The composition acquires depth as the physical presence of other viewpoints are visually represented and contrasted by each teller of the tale.

The bandit is the last of the participants to appear. He is introduced by the man who captured him and his view reflects negatively on the bandit's character. This allows the bandit, who is tied with rope much like the victim, to report a story about which only he knows the most salient aspects, because the voice of the victims cannot be represented in present time.

Each time Kurosawa returns to present time the rain continues. The ferocity of the storm is so intense both visually and aurally that it appears as if it will never end as long as this murder and rape go unsolved and remain wrapped in a tissue of truth, half-truths, and lies. Kurosawa returns to present time at key narrative moments to conclude a character's story and to introduce the next speaker and their point-of-view. But the contrast between the story taking place at the ruins and the one taking place in a sun-dappled forest creates a stark metaphor. The society is in decay because it has embraced evil and is being punished by the gods. The sanctity of the woods and the tradition represented by the samurai and his elegant wife signify the end of civility when the primitive urge for dominance and the emotions of lust, jealousy, greed, and wrath, representative of the seven deadly sins, erupt into a physical and psychological violence that brings on the end of a dynasty.

Kurosawa was a master of camera and editing. The cinematography by Kazuo Miyagawa (*Sansho the Bailiff, Floating Weeds, Zatoichi the Outlaw*) captures the contrasting moods with an acute attention to light. For the present, the intensity of the rain is created by an effective angle of the light source. The texture of the wooden ruins, stone steps, and grounds are detailed but layered in gloom and dark sheets of light. The forest is speckled with strong sunlight. The beauty of the woman is enhanced by the light revealing her face underneath a hat and through a white veil. The trial is photographed in an even light that does not make an atmospheric judgment about the characters, their testimony, or the sincerity of the facts they present. The compositional style subtly shifts to illustrate the mood of the major segments. The present-time scenes are shown in full shots that incorporate the ruined gate, the men, and the turbulent environment. These shots have an epic sense featuring jutting elements of architecture and a large canvas of rain so that the characters are both dwarfed and confined by the images as defined by the framing and as identified by the narrative context. The forest sequences are poetic, contrasting the beauty of the woods, and the tradition and elegance of the couple with the archetypal villainy of the bandit. There are shots of the sky and sun intercut with the drama unfolding on the ground. There is a larger degree of coverage during these scenes to build interrelationships between the characters and to accelerate the rhythm, tension, and action during all versions of the story. The trial is photographed in a wide shot that is distinguished from the **intercutting** throughout the other scenes. The framing of the witness in the minimalist setting with the characters addressing the camera brings a heightened interest to their every word. The setting and simplicity of the camera presentation creates an aura of truth, just another layer of complexity in this moral film about honor, integrity, and human desires.

Kurosawa is an editing director, a filmmaker who conceives and produces his films with the notion that the editing process will drive and interpret the vision of the cinematic narrative. Kurosawa has always been involved in the editing of his films and has been credited on screen for some of them, including *Rashomon*. The most memorable edits in *Rashomon* are of the bandit running through the forest at top speed. Kurosawa cuts from one take to the next, with the bandit in the same zone of the frame. This technique is known as a **match cut** because the bandit's body in movement is matched from one cut to the next. It is also a **jump cut** because the background is advanced from cut to cut and does not match. Both shots contain trees, so it gives the illusion of a match, but close inspection reveals that the background action jumps forward with each of these cuts, advancing in time.

When all the stories have been told, the scene returns to present day. The third man is revealed to have stolen a valuable dagger used during the tragedy. He runs back out into the rain where he first made his appearance. The woodcutter and the priest take care of a crying baby they have found. A series of **dissolves** indicates the passing of time as the two men ponder the future. Mercifully the rain stops. The baby cries in the arms of the priest, who is ashamed he is so suspicious of others. The woodcutter has six children of his own and takes the child from the priest. The baby stops crying. There is a traditional bow of respect between the two men, and as the camera tracks back, the woodcutter walks off with the responsibility of the child as the priest looks on from an ever fading perspective point in the background. The recognition of responsibility in the men appeases the gods and now they can move on. *Rashomon* ends in the present, but the excursion through the events of the past has moved the story forward. Kurosawa used a complex nonlinear (see **nonlinear storytelling** in glossary) structure to make the philosophic point that truth is not in what people say but in what they find out about themselves and the actions those revelations can bring.

The legacy of *Rashomon* is enormous. After decades of linear storytelling, filmmakers began to understand the cinema's capacity for structuring time and space. Time in motion pictures defines the medium. Eventually, telling a motion picture story in a nonlinear fashion became a viable narrative form. Kurosawa's accomplishments have not only influenced countless movies, television programs, and commercials, but also contributed to the lexicon. The title of his movie is often evoked when trying to describe situations where the multiple points of view make it seem impossible to arrive at a single truth. *Rashomon* is so much more than a clever story structure—it is a life lesson. All people see the world in their own fashion, often driven by their own agendas, human limitations, or emotional needs.

Rashomon is a classic film that happens to be Japanese. Kurosawa has often been identified as the most Western of Japanese filmmakers. This is a quibble. He was a Japanese man with insight into the world that went beyond his culture to a universal worldview. *Rashomon* has been remade by many filmmakers, sometimes in recognizable ways and sometimes in spirit. *Rashomon* is the cinema—a place where time is timeless, specific, interchangeable, compressed, expanded, reinvented, and erased. It is where many come to find the truth and learn it is hydra-headed. With *Rashomon,* Akira Kurosawa sent back a dispatch in the form of a film that is a paradigm of what narrative structure can contribute to the noble search of eternal truths—if one is willing to look deep inside first.

Of Further Interest

Screen

Amores Perros
Hero (2002)
The Outrage
Seven Samurai
Velvet Goldmine

Read

The Emperor and the Wolf: The Lives and Films of Akira Kurosawa and Toshiro Mifune by Stuart Galbraith
Akira Kurosawa and Intertextural Cinema by James Goodwin
Rashomon (Rutgers Films in Print, Vol. 6) by Akira Kurosawa, edited by Donald Ritchie
Something Like an Autobiography by Akira Kurosawa
The Films of Akira Kurosawa by Donald Ritchie

37

Widescreen Filmmaking

□ ◆ □ ◆ □ ◆ □

Rebel Without a Cause

Directed by Nicholas Ray (1911–1979), *Rebel Without a Cause* (1955) is a teenage psychodrama saturated in symbolism, metaphor, social–political content, and visual expression. The film stars James Dean as Jim Stark, a young man looking for the emotional support of his father; Natalie Wood (Judy), who is painfully making the transition from girl to woman; and Sal Mineo (Plato), who is desperately lonely and searching for a nuclear family. This drama has been classified by critics as a juvenile delinquent or J.D. film. With the exceptions of *The Wild One* and *Blackboard Jungle*, most of the genre targeted the growing youth culture of the 1950s and landed on the trash heap of B, C, or D movies that were confined to drive-ins and very late night television.

Rebel Without a Cause is an emotive and artistically demanding film from a script by Stewart Stern (*The Rack; Rachel, Rachel; The Ugly American*). The story opens as Jim, Judy, and Plato are brought into the local police precinct. This meeting of three teen strangers sets up the triangle of youths that becomes emblematic of an alienated generation who can only turn either within or to each other. Stark is the new kid on the block and is taunted by a gang that calls him chicken. Jim is attracted to Judy, whose boyfriend, Buzz (Corey Allen), is leader of the pack. A class trip to the planetarium is disrupted by wisecracks that lead to an outdoor knife fight and then to a disastrous chicken run between Buzz and Jim, which ends with the death of the leader. Jim, Judy, and Plato are further disaffected as they hide from the gang that is looking for revenge. They

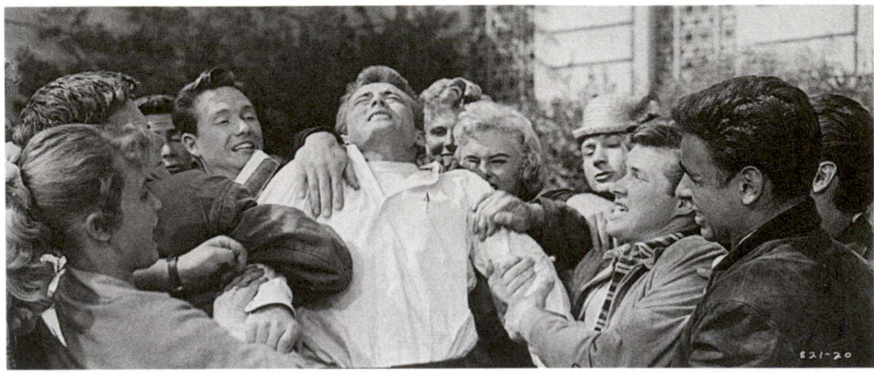

After the invention of the widescreen motion picture image, it was Nicholas Ray's *Rebel Without a Cause* that finally utilized the dimensions of the screen as a vital aspect of presenting the narrative and its troubled characters. Courtesy *Photofest.*

form a nuclear family with Jim as dad, Judy as mom, and Plato, a boy emotionally abandoned by his parents, as their surrogate son. They take residence in an abandoned house they call a castle. When the gang arrives, the trio escapes to the planetarium where the tragedy began. In reaching out to Plato, Jim comes of age and gets Plato to surrender after he wounds one of the gang and fires a gun at a police officer. When the police see the gun (that has been stripped of bullets by Jim), they shoot and kill Plato. The film concludes as Jim proudly introduces Judy to his parents and father and son finally reunite in their proper roles. Now the father is the father and the son is the son.

Nicholas Ray brought the theme of disaffection to *Rebel Without a Cause* with every major directorial decision he made. The most significant was photographing the film in CinemaScope. The widescreen format was created to compete with the growing popularity of television, but filmmakers were perplexed with how to compose and block for the aspect ratio that was much wider than its height. Directors working in the epic genre were able to fill the frame with landscapes, troops, and other large masses. Interiors, dialogue scenes, and close-ups were especially problematic.

Ray applied great artistry to the CinemaScope format for his drama. For the director, the widescreen frame was ideal to depict the temporal alienation of the characters. In the opening scene in the police station, Jim, Judy, and Plato are physically separated: Jim and Judy are distanced from each other by a glass partition, and separate sides of the room set Jim and Plato apart from each other. Every shot of *Rebel Without a Cause* places the characters solidly in their environment while stressing their alienation from their surroundings. The knife fight is inherently dramatic, but Ray and director of photography Ernest Haller (*The Roaring Twenties, Mildred Pierce, Lilies of the Field*) use the curved cement path and the California landscape high in the background to create tension between the natural and man-made world of the story. Ray, who had worked with architect Frank Lloyd Wright as a young man, applied dynamic expressions of space throughout the film. The widescreen frame is also used to present the full figure of Jim with Judy at his side. Then, a **reverse angle** reveals her torso, completing the composition. Ray was well aware of how close-ups left large areas of space to fill in the frame. The most common solution in these early days of widescreen photography was to counterbalance a shot with a piece of furniture or a zone of space. These and many other techniques wasted the power of the format and filled in the rest of the frame with much window dressing. Ray utilized space in a dynamic force that addressed the content of a scene and the overall narrative artistic intent of the filmmaker.

Space in *Rebel Without a Cause* is either in control of the adults who run society or in the domain of the alienated teens. The police station is old-world, wooden, and bare—a place to process crime. When Jim, along with his family, is taken in to talk to Juvenile Officer Ray Fremick (Edward Platt), Jim and Fremick are seated in the foreground on opposite ends of the frame. They are separated by his family standing in between them in the fore and background as the officer works at his desk, physically and emotionally isolating himself from the troubled boy. Later they talk tough in a separate room from where Jim's parents are waiting. At first Fremick is forced to physically handle Jim when the boy lashes out and attacks the officer. After some communication, Fremick allows Jim to take out his aggression on a desk and watches as the boy attacks the furniture—representing authority—with the full force of his entire body.

The familial homes of Jim, Judy, and Plato do not meet their emotional needs. They serve as a way station as the youths search the night for relief from their unrelenting loneliness. The abandoned house Plato has found is a respite for comfort and freedom. The disrepair represents the destruction of the order, confinement, and repression of their parent's world. The empty pool is a surrealistic hole in the ground where family fun once took place. Now it is a playground for wayward youths, a setting where the three can act out against their parents through parody informed by a hunger to be accepted. It also becomes a trap for Plato, who fights off the marauding gang members.

Rebel Without a Cause is about stress within the family unit. Jim wants his father to stand up to his domineering mother. Judy wants her father's love as it was before she entered her teens. Plato is abandoned by his natural parents and cared for by an African American woman. Before the three role-play as a family unit, Plato demonstrates homoerotic feelings for Jim, who seems compelled but confused by the troubled boy.

Ray designed and applied color in a bold manner that also heightened the psychodynamics of the narrative and characters. Red has an expressive purpose throughout the film. The main and end titles, Jim's jacket, and Judy's coat, hair, and lipstick are red, signifying rebellion, anger, sexuality, violence, and self-expression. Jim wears a white tee shirt and blue jeans—the uniform of American youth. Plato wears a dark blue sweater, white shirt, and black tie, signifying his morose nature.

The colors of the adult world are cool and drab. A room in the Stark residence is a dull, grayed green. The contrast expresses the dissatisfaction the teens have toward straight society, and the colors represent the positions of the fractured family structure and a generation gap between the youths and their parents. The **color palette** represents a collision between outward rebellion and the status quo.

The camera angle and movement of the lens work in concert with the design, format, color, and staging to comment on the dynamics between the teen and adult worlds. In the police station sequence, there is an up-angle on Jim in a chair as his parents and grandmother are reunited. The impression of Jim rising above his parents, who are incapable of understanding the boy, further distances the family emotionally. Later in the scene, Ray juxtaposes an up-angle of Jim and his family with an eye-level shot to contrast the two divergent points of view of rebellion and repression. While Jim is lying on the family couch with his head near the floor, feet up on the wall, Ray cuts to Jim's **point of view** of his mother coming down the stairs. As she comes closer, the camera turns in a circular movement until she is upright. Then a cut to Jim shows he has gotten up a bit. Jim's position does not match the upright position of his mother in the point-of-view shot, but the message concerning a reversal of power occurring is abundantly clear. **Dutch** or **canted angles** had been part of the cinematic vocabulary, but Ray on several occasions tilts the camera from a stable position to create a psychological tension between the characters. The dynamics of power are experienced by the audience who view through this interscene tilting Jim's struggle against his parents and a world that does not accept him for who he is.

The musical **score** by Leonard Rosenman (*East of Eden, Barry Lyndon, Star Trek IV: The Voyage Home*) gives an aural interpretation to the context of *Rebel Without a Cause*. For the most part, Hollywood composers stayed within the conventions of interpretive music that restated the drama of the story on screen. Music that addressed the psychology of a character was rare, that of Bernard Hermann (*Citizen Kane* [see chapter 13], *Vertigo, Psycho* [1960; see chapter 34]) being a notable exception. The main theme repeated throughout the film does not indicate but evokes the terrible loneliness of the three main characters. The majority of the music engages the inner torment of neurosis. Music scores for contemporary films of this era found it necessary to establish time and place, but Rosenman allowed the visuals to create those on their own. The music operates on a psychological level that speaks to the emotional disturbance, anxiety, and frayed nerves of the characters.

James Dean's performance as Jim remains iconic in its depiction of a 1950s troubled youth. Dean is best remembered and associated with this role. To millions of admirers Dean was Jim Stark. Dean's otherworldly gifts for portraying emotional pain as well as a confident sense of cool are on display in the three films he left behind upon his early death in 1955 at age twenty-four.[1] But Jim Stark was a character that a generation alienated by postwar culture understood, and they empowered Dean to represent them. The James Dean cult of personality tends to dominate *Rebel Without a Cause*, but the entire cast gives honest, memorable, and nuanced performances. Casting Jim Backus as Jim's father was a shrewd decision on the part of Nicholas Ray. The man then known as Mr. Magoo and now as Thurston Howell III from television's *Gilligan's Island* brought empathy and recognition as a man unable to reach out to his son or to stand up to his overbearing wife. Edward Platt, associated with the television culture classic *Get Smart*, embodies the burden of a law enforcement officer who understands the generational divide. Natalie Wood and Sal Mineo are as compelling as Dean. Wood embodies the conflict of not being accepted at home and of the highly charged sexuality of a teenage girl. Mineo may have the most complex role of the three. Rejected by his parents, Plato acts out through violence, a confused sexuality, and distorted self-image. There is no hope in this tragic figure unable to resolve the situation he finds himself in.

The nuclear age is a subtext that permeates *Rebel Without a Cause*. During the class trip to the planetarium, the main characters see a demonstration of how the world may end through natural science, and it strikes terror into young lives already stressed with cold war worries. The end-of-the-world theme takes on both political and religious meaning throughout the film for Jim, Judy, and Plato, who are strongly affected by an unstable world that holds a dim future for them.

The legacy of *Rebel Without a Cause* flows through decades of American films that followed. It was the prototype for the youth culture film of the 1960s and the American New Wave of the 1970s, and responsible for the acceptance of the widescreen format that has been a presentation choice of filmmakers for the last thirty years. *Rebel Without a Cause* should no longer be classified or viewed as a cult film. It is a motion picture containing the DNA for the American cinema of the latter half of the twentieth century.

Note

1. Dean's other two screen appearances are in *East of Eden* and *Giant*.

Of Further Interest

Screen

Bigger Than Life
The Blackboard Jungle
East of Eden
River of No Return
The Robe

Read

Widescreen Cinema by John Belton
Teenagers and Teen Pics: The Juvenilization of American Movies in the 1950s by Thomas Doherty
Nicholas Ray: An American Journey by Bernard Eisenschitz
The J.D. Film; Juvenile Delinquency in the Movies by Mark Thomas McGee and R. J. Robertson
I Was Interrupted: Nicholas Ray on Making Movies by Nicholas Ray, edited by Susan Ray

Camera Movement as Metaphor

□ ◆ □ ◆ □ ◆ □

La Ronde

La Ronde (1950), directed by Max Ophüls (1902–1957) and based on the play by Arthur Schnitzler, is a master lesson in the art of the moving camera. The one constant influence director Stanley Kubrick acknowledged was the films of Max Ophüls. Kubrick and countless others are in artistic debt to Max Ophüls for his use of camera choreography to inform the heart and soul of a film story and its characters.

To Hollywood cinematographers, light is the principal tool for photographic expression. In European cinema, it is the combination of movement and light that powers the **mise-en-scène** of a film. The cinema of the 1990s and the early twenty-first century continues to apply camera movement as a potent and essential tool. However, current attitudes favor camera movement for its own sake. Moving the camera in contemporary film has become an aesthetic in itself, not always connected to the story in a direct or metaphoric manner.

In *La Ronde*, set in Vienna in 1900, the merry-go-round is both a physical object and poetic symbol signifying life—specifically, love life that goes around and around. The circular passage is constant; the characters, their needs, and agendas come and go, but the world continues to turn.

Our guide is the Raconteur (Anton Walbrook), who addresses the camera in a theatrical gesture to introduce the characters and their stories. In trying to explain his role in the story, he suggests "I am you." But he is more than just an informed bystander. The Raconteur also takes roles in the multipart narrative while wearing various disguises. The theme is the

Anton Walbrook as the Raconteur and Simone Signoret as Leocadie, the Prostitute, in Max Ophüls, *La Ronde*. The merry-go-round is a metaphor for life, which goes round and round. Fluid camera movements also address the concept of life in constant motion. Courtesy *Photofest*.

elusive nature of romantic and physical love. The characters in the sketches are searching for love. The words "I love you" rarely link physical love with the emotional, spiritual, marital, and total love sought by both the male and female characters. The act of sex changes the momentum of each relationship. The quest for love as demonstrated by the characters seems endlessly complicated. The result is not consummation but another turn of the merry-go-round of life. The Raconteur tells us that the past is more reliable than the future. He tells us about events that have either happened or are about to happen, and his power to influence them is at work. To introduce the first story, the Raconteur pulls a young lady off the turntable. In *La Ronde* the past may appear a more reliable indicator of the veracity of events that have taken place, but in fact, the reality of an unfolding present and future may be no different. The Raconteur foresees the future and tells the woman that fate will be kind to her in two months. In the next scene that part of her story unfolds. A bell rings at significant moments, often before a new event in the story.

La Ronde is both theatrical and cinematic in nature. The Raconteur/participant who is the host, ringmaster, narrator, and guide is theatrical in style and delivery. There is a stage on the main street and a clothing pole on which to hang his various disguises and a dress tuxedo with top hat. The sets by Jean d'Eaubonne (*The Blood of a Poet, Lola Montès, Charade*) are elaborately designed and decorated, but their architectural structure is predicated on narrative connections and provides easy access for the fluid camera. The movement of the camera often reveals and heightens the theatricality of *La Ronde* through cinematic application of cinematography, music, and art direction. The potent symbol of a spiral staircase—like the merry-go-round, a circular image—contributes to perception of the romantic environment. The film was richly photographed in black and white, but when a character compliments the blue of a woman's blouse, we begin to sense the color of the scenes as perceived by the characters.

Ophüls and his director of photography, Christian Matras (*Le Plaisir, Paris Blues, The Milky Way*), use two guiding principles to motivate the dolly shots in *La Ronde*. As Gordon Willis (*Klute, The Godfather, Annie Hall* [see chapter 2]) once explained, "actors move cameras." Ophüls's staging involves characters and couples strolling, so a dolly shot that follows their journey is logical and experiential. The viewer travels along as characters move through the atmospheric environment and the rhythms of the developing relationship. The extensive use of the long take or plan sequence also necessitates a moving camera. There are many reasons for a long take. A **plan sequence** brings a dancelike and theatrical feeling towards the material. In a long take, time is not compressed or structured by edits. The relationship between the characters and their spatial environment is explored, so the viewer can be acutely aware of its physicality. Camera movement in a long take can direct the eye right, left, up, down, forward, and back within the frame. Edits can achieve all the same results, but the method of a cut presents images by ending one and beginning another. The relationship between shots produces spatial changes. Camera movement within a long take carries the eye through scenes, so many revelations concerning a composition in constant transition can be observed. A scene fades to black and the next fades up from black. Ophüls and his editor, Léonide Azar (*Bitter Victory, The Lovers, The Battle of Austerlitz*), also employ intercutting, **wipes**, and **direct cuts** to structure the episodes into a form.

In *La Ronde* Ophüls and Matras move the camera so that the thrust of a character's energy is encapsulated in the camera's every nuance. Over-the-shoulder (see **over-the-shoulder shot** in glossary) dialogue scenes do not separate the characters as using **shot–reverse shot** technique would; they record the interactions between characters, and edits often occur during the moving composition to preserve the emotional and physical connections. A waltz is the major musical theme. There is dance in the narrative as well as the physical grace of the character's movement. The **plan sequence** connects all of these directorial objectives: the metaphor of the merry-go-round, the magic of the theatrical experience, and the ability to transport the viewer inside the lives of the lovers.

Content determines style. *La Ronde* is an honest, satirical look at how men and women pursue sexual and romantic relationships. The characters, many of whom are connected by relationship or situation, span a variety of social types. Cynical for its time but faithful to the emotional complexity that governs human needs, each segment of *La Ronde* has the games of pursuit, the passion of desire and lust, and the change in perspective the morning after. Are we obsessed with pursuit but looking for the unattainable?

The exterior scenes often take place at night. The streets, town square, and park roads are old world, layered with fog, and decorated with an atmosphere to spark a chance meeting or a planned rendezvous under a bridge or on a park bench. The interiors are lavish, expressing wealth, comfort, and status.

There are mirrors ready to capture a reflection when the camera glides into position. Some mirror moments catch the audience unaware until the symbolic image is revealed. Others express duality or a reflexive impulse within the composition, framing the characters.

Ophüls orchestrates the mise-en-scène of *La Ronde* with other applications of the camera. Tilted shots, also known as **canted** or **dutch angles**, are often used in horror films, melodramas or for an extroverted psychological impact. In *La Ronde* Ophüls and Matras do not just tilt the camera pointed at a squared-off location or blocking; the staging and design are created to complement the tilted shot so it can express the intoxication of *amour*. The softness of the lighting is layered by the many finely woven drapes and curtains in the rooms and boudoirs. Before sophisticated filtration for lights and lenses became available, cinematographers would put a woman's stocking over the lens to accomplish diffusion across the entire frame. The curtains and drapes in *La Ronde* function as elegant décor, and when the camera moves into position so that the image is treated with partial organic filtration, the result is multitextual. The camera is proactive, with the architecture, sets, and décor moving into relationships with shapes, light, and shadow to create the essential mood for each scene.

Other **locked-off camera** shots do not employ angles but feature precise framing to comment on a scene. To convey that a couple has a marriage of convenience, the camera shoots from the foot of their separate beds, framing a perfectly symmetrical composition (which Kubrick would later use in another homage to Ophüls) that demonstrates their physical and emotional distance. Shooting through the decorative wooden design in the bed's structure and at times with an ornate clock in the foreground, the visuals show what the characters reveal emotionally and what the text indicates in action.

The Raconteur is not a traditional film narrator (see **narration** in glossary). He appears on camera and addresses the audience directly, which signals an active relationship between the viewer and the character in the film. His observations about love and life take on weight because of his authoritative presence. He tells us up front that he will be wearing disguises throughout the film. These are costumes that identify him to the other characters as a member of their environment. During the sketches his involvement in the story and with the characters has a direct impact on their actions and reactions, so the Raconteur takes on magical romantic powers. At times he takes on the role of film director standing behind a slate that identifies the next sequence. This is the most overt technique used by Ophüls to tell us we are watching a movie. On another occasion he directs a light onto the set that can represent theater, cinema, or both.

La Ronde is structured around sketches that are indicated by titles announced by the Raconteur. They are named plainly and clearly identify the situation, such as "The Young Man and the Married Woman" and "The Poet and the Actress." However, *La Ronde* is a unified cinematic work, not an anthology or compilation. This is achieved by Ophüls's understanding of Schnitzler's theme—the search for love as a continuum and not as a means to an end—and his observation that the human libido and the human heart search for different dreams.

Every aesthetic decision concerning staging, décor, and camera choreography realizes Ophüls's directorial objectives. *La Ronde* is an elegant waltz through the minefield of sexual politics. The act of love is always off camera; it is the joust and the gamesmanship that interests the playwright and director.

For Max Ophüls his sensitive, gliding camera was more than a stylistic device; it was a cinematic philosophy that grew out of the director's worldview. The beauty of *La Ronde* underscores the reality that love is complicated by status, gender, economics, and the endless search for an everlasting satisfaction, a love that just eludes our grasp while life continues to offer temptation and opportunity on a merry-go-round existence that is forever circling.

Of Further Interest

Screen

1900
Paths of Glory
The Round-Up
The Shining
Weekend

Read

Max Ophüls in the Hollywood Studios by Lutz Bacher
The Mobile Mise-en-Scène: A Critical Analysis of the Theory and Practice of Long-Take Camera Movement in the Narrative Cinema by Lutz Bacher
Mise-en-Scène: Film Style and Interpretation by John Gibbs
Making Pictures: A Century of European Cinematography by Imago, the Federation of European Cinematographers
Max Ophüls and the Cinema of Desire: Style and Spectacle in Four Films, 1948–1955 by Alan Larson Williams

Mise-en-Scène

Rules of the Game

Directed by Jean Renoir (1894–1979), *Rules of the Game* (1939) is a comedy about class distinctions, love, and friendship. The film maintains a high critical ranking because of its sophistication, honesty, and droll attitude, as well as the grace of its performances and direction. *Rules of the Game* is a model for excellence in **mise-en-scène**, a French theater term for staging. Later, the influential critics of the *Cahier du Cinema* adapted the phrase to identify filmmakers who combined production design, composition, and the movement of actors within a frame as an expressive cinematic technique.[1] The text of the film is a paradigm for the social comedy that prevailed during the studio system period and into the modern era. *Shampoo*, produced by and starring Warren Beatty and directed by Hal Ashby, was an updated American version of Renoir's masterpiece. Robert Altman's *A Wedding* and *Gosford Park* owe a debt to Renoir's satiric examination of society's mores. In Renoir's case, it was the mores of the French upper class; in Beatty's, the Beverly Hills set; in Altman's, WASPs and the English. Films as diverse as *The Big Chill, The Return of the Secaucus Seven, The Exterminating Angel, A Midsummer's Night Sex Comedy, Down and Out in Beverly Hills*, and Preston Sturges's *Sullivan's Travels* all follow the tradition of *Rules of the Game.*

The game is life. For these privileged French aristocrats and their circle of friends, needs are met by access to the opulence around them from birth or invitation. So the game of life here is not in chasing money or financial survival, but in the endless search for love and happiness and a

André Jurieux (Roland Toutain, left), a heroic aviator, and the wealthy Robert de la Cheyniest (Marcel Dalio) in the center of a room in Cheyniest's elegant home, in Jean Renoir's *Rules of the Game*. The décor, staging, composition, camera movement, and lighting are all part of the film's elaborate mise-en-scène. Courtesy *Photofest*.

constant struggle against the dreaded enemy of the wealthy—terminal boredom. The rules concern the acquisition of wives, husbands, and mistresses while maintaining superficial relationships recognized by society and the church. Everyone, male and female, in *Rules of the Game* wants someone who belongs to someone else. It is desire that drives them, motivated by status and divided by class structure.

In today's film nomenclature, *Rules of the Game* would be classified as a dramedy—a term that points out the limits of many film stories adhering to the artificial conventions of the Hollywood studio system. These narratives could only be identified as strictly funny or serious. Renoir and his coscenarist, Carl Koch (*Les Marseillaise, The Story of Tosca, Night of the Silvery Moon*), understood before others that life's comedy informs its tragedy and vice versa.

What does the film director utilize to create a style, a mode of production to present the narrative? *Rules of the Game* is story driven. There are many characters, intertwined plots and twists until the last shot of the film. It is also an actor's film. The performances are delicately graded and in depth. The performers appear to be free to inhabit their characters and their environment. The cinematographic style features luxurious sets that create a perfect stage for the story to unfold. The adroit utilization of the camera, staging, and blocking communicate the ostensibly careful existence of the characters. Their lives are riddled with anxiety, by lust and secrets, they maintain a patina of civility as passions run wild. It is a film with a grand theme. On the surface, *Rules of the Game* is about moral corruption of the ruling class. A line spoken by Octave, a pivotal character portrayed by the director, Jean Renoir, goes straight to the meaning of all human interactions when he explains that the sad truth of life is that everyone has his or her reasons; today we use the terms motivation and agenda. This philosophic observation, spoken by the director and cowriter of *Rules of the Game* through one of his characters, may be the most important theme concerning human behavior in the film. The drives of the characters and their lower-class staff are the same. The context changes with freedom from financial worry, but that only amplifies Renoir's point. Life is messy. It is the heart that rules and the mind tries to maintain order. *Rules of the Game* is a director-driven film—a masterwork of style and content and a timeless reflection on the search for status, love, and true friendship.

The narrative of *Rules of the Game* begins on the eve of World War II, placing it in a global political context. André Jurieux (Roland Toutain) is a dashing, heroic aviator who has taken a historic flight for his love of Christine de la Cheyniest (Nora Gregor), who is married to the wealthy Robert de la Cheyniest (Marcel Dalio), referred to as the Marquis. Andre has just landed when a radio interviewer and a slew of reporters and admirers mob him. The aviator is so distraught that Christine was not at the airfield to meet him that he goes into an emotional down-spiral. Andre and his friend Octave, a charmer who also adores Christine romantically and is embraced by Andre's rich company, arrive at the home of Robert and Christine. The complications between the married couple and the cast of romantic suitors play out their many tributaries. The main action of the film takes place at a country estate where Robert and Christine have invited their friends to a hunt, party, and theatrical extravaganza during which the games become serious and costly in human terms.

Rules of the Game is an ensemble piece in which characters interact and move freely, motivated by their desires and intricate cover-ups of secret liaisons. Renoir and his cinematographers, Jean-Paul Alphen (*L'Atlante, La Vie est à nous, La Marseillaise*), Jean Bachelet (*The Crime of Monsieur Lange, Poison, I Did It Three Times*), Jacques Lemare (*Maid in Paris, Dish-*

onorable Discharge, Échec au Porteur), and Alain Renoir (*They Met on Skis, L'Enfer des Anges*), often compose shots so that many characters are shown full frame in **deep-focus photography**. This anchors the characters in an environment acquired through birthright. The fullness of the space allows the viewer to observe how they react to each other, their body language, and the freedom in which they frolic and play games of love and deception.

Renoir's staging is masterful. The camera moves with or to characters and composes and recomposes groupings to capture the zest of the characters. Close-ups are used sparingly, assigning a real emotional weight when they occur. Two-shots are especially significant in *Rules of the Game* because they do more than satisfy the convention of relating to both characters in the frame as they talk; the framing defines spatial and emotional relationships—it captures the excitement of a clandestine meeting.

Renoir clearly depicts both the segregation of classes and the dependence of the upper echelon on the underclass. Aside from the duties the servants and house staff perform to make life free of chores and drudgery for the rich, there are emotional ties that put the servants on equal footing or even tip the balance with their employers. Christine and the lady's servant Lissette sa Camériste (Paulette Dubost), bond as women and support each other like girlfriends. Christine relies on Lissette for romantic advice, and when Lissette gets into a catastrophic situation Christine is there for her servant, saving her job and protecting her from a toxic marriage. Robert understands the rules of the game. He gives an opportunity to Marceau (Julien Careete), a poacher elevated to servant by the Marquis and a womanizer who is enchanted with Lissette, and defends Schumacher le Garde-Chasse (Gaston Modot), Lissette's husband who handles hunting and security issues for Robert, from a potentially serious criminal charge.

The story is further complicated by the fact that Christine is also interested in St. Aubin (Pierre Nay), who for a time seems to be in position for a tryst. Of course the Marquis also has a mistress, Geneviéve de Marras (Mila Parély), a friend of the couple, and Christine's young niece Jackie (Anne Mayen) pines for Andre; but these acts are Christine and Robert's obligation if they want to continue the game. Octave, a friend to all, learns he can never be equal to his rich friends, so as the game proceeds he leaves for Paris; friendship costs more than he can afford.

Rules of the Game is a charming yet caustic look at a self-serving society. Its morality is defined by the necessity to live by rules granted by status, and a license to legislate a proper exterior behavior even though the heart does not always comply. The shocking and surprising ending of *Rules of the Game* concludes Renoir's interpretation of the rules: Appearances matter, love is fleeting, and loyalty and friendship endure.

The production design by Eugene Lourie (*Grand Illusion, Limelight, Shock Corridor*) is the environment in which Renoir stages his intricate but light-footed mise-en-scène. The entrance hall of the country castle was central to the design. There are entrances to the house from the terrace, and the main staircase leads to upper floors and bedrooms. Another hall staircase leads down to the kitchen and servants quarters. The upstairs/downstairs metaphor is an effective one. The workers live and work below the main floor, and well below the upper-class accommodations on the upper floors. The hall also opens into a sitting room containing entrances to a spacious ballroom. On the other side of the hall, double doors lead to a gun room in which there is an entrance to a big dining room. Lourie also designed a side corridor open to all the rooms, providing staging possibilities for the climatic scene when Schumacher chases Marceau around the house with a gun after he learns of the poacher's carnal interest in his wife. Lourie used real materials for the floor of the castle set, not the traditional paper reproductions of stone slabs. There is real parquet in the bathroom and black and white checkered stone slabs for the other rooms. The checkerboard pattern creates a visual continuity that complements the constant traffic of people from room to room. It also is a chess metaphor for all the moves and entanglements of the participants. The materials give a look of authenticity to the viewer's eye and to the actors who inhabit it. Lourie created uncluttered sets to enhance the action and support the deep-focus photography.

By staying specific to the time period and to the culture of his country, Jean Renoir created a timeless film that was a precursor to the modern cinema. *Rules of the Game* is daring in what it reveals about emotional truth and the primal motivations that drive people. Jean Renoir's direction is seamless, as light as a soufflé, and as tart as the driest burgundy. *Rules of the Game* ages well as it continues to reveal its secrets about life, love, and the direction of movies.

Notes

1. The French film magazine *Cahiers du Cinema* appeared in 1951 and was coedited by André Bazin, who developed the auteur theory, which was its guiding critical principle. Many of the young film critics writing for the magazine became filmmakers in their own right, including François Truffaut, Jean-Luc Godard, Claude Chabrol, Jacques Rivette, and Eric Rohmer. In their writings con-

cerning the film director as the author of a film, they adapted the theater term mise-en-scène to establish how a director presents his or her personal vision of a film through the use of staging action for the camera. The contemporary definition and application of the mise-en-scène concept now includes the use of editing in examining how a director utilizes camera and staging to cinematically capture a scene.

Of Further Interest

Screen

Imitation of Life
Laura
Letter from an Unknown Woman
Lola Montès
Touch of Evil

Read

Jean Renoir by André Bazin
Mise-en-Scène: Film Style and Interpretation by John Gibbs
My Life and My Films by Jean Renoir
Renoir, My Father by Jean Renoir
Renoir on Renoir: Interviews, Essays and Remarks by Jean Renoir

Direct Cinema

Salesman

A brief history of the nonfiction film before the late 1960s is necessary to fully appreciate the achievements of Albert Maysles, David Maysles (1932–1987), and Charlotte Zwerin (1931–2004) in creating this **documentary** about traveling Bible salesmen. Early **nonfiction films** were without synchronous sound and were presented with a musical **score.** The advent of sound brought narration, sound effects, music, and limited **sync-sound** dialogue. The sound was limited because the cameras were bulky and unwieldy, and the sound recording consoles were not mobile enough for field use. The development of the Nagra, a portable sync-sound recorder, and lightweight cameras that could easily be handheld, led to the cinéma vérité movement in France; notably Jean Rouch's *Chronique d'un Été* (*Chronicle of a Summer*), which did not employ narration or talking head interviews. During the 1960s, several American filmmakers developed their own style of cinéma vérité commonly known as direct cinema. The Maysles brothers were at the forefront of this movement.

Salesman (1969) observes the lives of four Bible salesmen on the road through several U.S. territories as they go from snow to sun. The technique and method of filmmaking was to follow the men into the homes of potential customers, into sales meetings, countless motel rooms, their cars, and to the doorsteps of leads. There is a minimal acknowledgment of the camera almost too subtle for the average viewer to perceive; the results look as if we are watching real life unfolding.

Reality as filmed by Albert and David Maysles. Bible salesman Paul "the badger" Brennan uses his charm, patter, and take-no-prisoners approach to sell a woman a Holy Bible in her home as the filmmakers watched and recorded the action. Courtesy *Photofest*.

As in fiction, the men chosen as subjects have distinct characteristics, and their exploits create several narrative threads. *Salesman* resonates with many themes and insights into American life. On the surface, the film is about the business of selling Bibles door to door. As with many vérité filmmakers, the Maysles strived for objectivity and searched to find the story that unfolded during the extended filming process. The subjects themselves should reveal their motivations and the reality of the situation in a word, the truth as it can best be obtained. Just minutes into the film, it is clear that salesmen are salesmen regardless of the product they are selling. The Holy Bible is sold using every sales technique the viewer has experienced and then some. The men are not actually or particularly sacred or religious about their professions or lives. They smoke, gamble, tell ethnic jokes, and when away from the public do not demonstrate much good will toward their fellow man.

This dichotomy between the role of the salesman and the reality of the men as individuals is the engine of the narrative. The dual persona of each man sheds light on the other. The selling of God is a powerful aspect of this investigation. The salesmen are continuously giving the message that it is the material aspect—color, binding, the physicality of the product—that is more important than the words within.

During the film's initial theatrical release in 1968, *Salesman* revealed a surprising portrait of an America unchanged by New York–Hollywood sensibilities. *Salesman* was refreshing in its untrendyness. To most audiences the film reflected an American consciousness and lifestyle more of the 1950s than of the Summer of Love, hippies, LSD, radical politics, and headlines and buttons proclaiming "God is Dead."

Salesman is about men relating to men. As in a John Cassavetes film, these men are old school, rough around the edges, streetwise, and jaded about their societal roles. They take turns using a motel room phone to give their wives the impression that everything is fine as they face the harsh realities of the road. Their interpersonal communications are raw—not profane but crude and basic meat-and-potatoes talk. Like David Mamet's real estate salesmen in *Glengarry Glen Ross*, they constantly work their leads. The Bible salesmen are unconditional toward each other but show little affection for those marks they hard sell. Screened today, *Salesman* is both a period piece reflecting a kinder, gentler America and a record of the practically dead art of selling door to door. It also reveals truths not widely shared by homogenized histories of the 1960s. For the majority of the families in *Salesman*, a buck cannot be stretched. There is nothing swinging about these sixties. Male–female and parent–child relationships and ethnic attitudes seem untouched by consciousness raising. Most surprising is a sense of cynicism associated more with later decades.

Salesman is about work: attitudes toward work, the sacrifices, staying ahead of the competition, and the daily grind of keeping in the game. Work defines who these men are. *Salesman* is a uniquely American film that defines the Christian nation in the context of a free market system. Only in America can selling religion be accepted as honorable. By showing the process of hustling the world's best-selling book for hard cash, check, or by various installment plans, the thin line of separation of church, state, and the profit margin is exposed.

It is the salesmen themselves who are the heart and soul of the film. *Salesman* begins with the introduction of the four main subjects who become characters. Paul Brennan is nicknamed the Badger; Charles McDevitt, the Gipper; James Baker, the Rabbit; and Raymond Martos, the Bull. Each man is the focus of a short scene that reveals his nature—a technique that Martin Scorsese later applied to the opening of *Mean Streets*. Paul immediately emerges as the focal point of the narrative. We meet Paul at a critical moment in his life. Everyone speaks of Paul's great reputation as a top salesman, but times are hard for him now. No matter what pitch, be it hard or soft, he can not close a sale. When he does, the orders for the day and week are way below the goals of the company and of his own prideful standard. The men are supportive, but Paul is inconsolable. The scenes of him at work are fascinating. Paul says all the right lines and has all the correct comebacks, but the look in his eyes reveals depression, fear, and the sad fact that drive is seeping out of this salesman's soul. Paul's rapidly diminishing success has a devastating impact on his attitude. With each bad day, Paul becomes increasingly negative. Every night back at the motel room, Paul holds court, bad-mouthing the territory and the leads. He ridicules the people he has met on his travels. Paul is a Boston Irish Catholic, and he saves his most vicious barbs for his own, speaking in an exaggerated brogue as he rips into what he calls Mickies. In discussing an Italian American area, he makes disparaging remarks about their cuisine and refers to them as Guineas. If Paul was once a gentleman, his disillusionment has embittered him and he is spiritually lost. One devastating scene at the end of the film takes place in a home where the Gipper is trying to close a sale as Paul, detached, watches on. Then a spark hits and Paul goes into a closing pitch. They fail and the Gipper explains to the family that Paul has been a bit negative and down on his luck. Is the Gipper being honest about his despondent friend or is he trying to use sympathy to try again to close the sale? The Gipper tells the family that Paul just needs a spark. Paul says, more to himself than to the others, that sometimes it is not a spark you need but an explosion. Paul goes back to the motel and packs up. He is at the end of the line. As Paul looks outside in the last shot of *Salesman*, he could be a character in a Eugene O'Neill play.

The Maysles understood that it was essential to capture intimate, revealing, and honest material as it unfolded while they followed their subjects across the country. The Maysles also realized that the editing process would organize the material, define character relationships, and create the pressure, success, failure, boredom, and camaraderie of the salesmen's exploits on the road. Documentary film editors had long believed that nonfiction films were constructed in the editing room. It is the time when critical decisions are made concerning what to show, and when and who should communicate the story and point of view consistent with what the filmmakers experienced during the time they spent filming.

Because of her tremendous contribution to "making" *Salesman* out of the rolls and rolls of film shot in search of the story, the Maysles made editor Charlotte Zwerin (*Gimme Shelter; Running Fence; Thelonious Monk: Straight, No Chaser*) a codirector. So *Salesman* is a collaboration between a cameraman and soundman who directed during the shooting and an editor who directed while cutting the film along with the other filmmakers.

The foundation of *Salesman* is Paul Brennan. The scenes of Brennan driving that are woven throughout the film reveal the Paul only we see. It is here that we see a man personally, spiritually, and physically lost as he drives, endlessly trying to find the locations on his lead cards. Alone, Paul talks to himself and sings "If I Were a Rich Man" and Irish songs that he exaggerates into the arena of parody.

Well into *Salesman*, during the Miami segment, Paul directly addresses the audience through the camera, talking about his colleagues from his point of view. Paul speaks as a man who knows everything, although at the moment he is at a professional standstill. As he explains that each man is named after an animal and provides an analysis of their personalities and personal sales styles, there is an intercut (see **intercutting** in glossary) to a scene of each individual in action. This technique puts Paul above it all at a time when he is perilously spiraling downward emotionally. The motel room sequences develop Paul's humor, his coming to grips with failure, and the dark side of his personality, as he is unable to show grace toward others because he has lost the drive to sell, leaving him resentful.

As with the editing of a fictional film, Zwerin plays dialogue against reaction shots and uses close-ups of the salesmen with customers to focus on their attempts of dominance over the potential client and how they immediately shift when a dead end is hit. It is the editing process that transforms *Salesman* into the story of a man at the end of his career. The editing achieves empathy for Paul, who has hustled and conned his way into American homes with an all's-fair-in-business attitude that at times took unfair advantage of his prey, who for the most part were decent, hard-working people. The fact that Paul and his colleagues sell the Bible creates a moral quandary for the audience, but ultimately *Salesman* is about the tragedy of a man who has seen his best days pass him by. As Paul looks off in the sad final shot, there is no hope, only regret.

The Maysles and Charlotte Zwerin dramatically heightened their findings with the skills of their craft. Truth is in the telling. Truth is in the details. Truth is elusive but precious.

Of Further Interest

Screen

Chiefs
Don't Look Back
Gimme Shelter
Primary
The War Room

Read

Documentary Explorations; 15 Interviews with Film-Makers by G. Roy Levin
Robert Drew and the Development of Cinéma Vérité in America by P. J. O'Connell
The Documentary Conscience: A Casebook in Film Making by Alan Rosenthal
New Challenges for Documentaries, edited by Alan Rosenthal
Documentary Filmmakers Speak by Liz Stubbs

The Freudian Western

□ ◆ □ ◆ □ ◆ □

The Searchers

The screen story and thematic intentions of John Ford's (1895–1973) *The Searchers* have over time certified this 1956 American Western as one of the most influential movies of the modern era. Since the 1970s, *The Searchers* has been considered by critics internationally to be among the finest of the Western genre. *The Searchers* resonates because it tackles universal issues: the search for home, racial differences, the obsessions of love, hate, and vengeance, and the complex nature of the id. *The Searchers* is also a well-told tale with multifaceted characters that brims with conflict, plenty of action, dramatic meditation, warmth, and humor. Although based on a historical incident and adapted by screenwriter Frank S. Nugent (*Fort Apache, She Wore a Yellow Ribbon, The Quiet Man*) from the novel by Alan LeMay, *The Searchers* is the singular voice of John Ford in his mature years. With this film, the man largely responsible for writing the poetic mythology of the West-on-celluloid turned to the unchartered territory of the dark side of that American story. With Homer, Shakespeare, and Freud spiritually beside him, John Ford constructed the foundation for the next chapter in American film history.

The setting is Texas, 1868. *The Searchers* begins and ends with a view of Monument Valley from inside a homestead. The landscape is vivid: blue sky, deep coral mountains, the light sienna of the earth, and the green of the brush. The camera pulls back out of the black-framed doorway like a baby coming out of a precious womb. Ethan Edwards (John Wayne), once a member of the Confederate army, then soldier of fortune and wander-

Natalie Wood as Debbie, is protected by Jeffrey Hunter, as Martin Pawley, from an off-screen Ethan Edwards, played by John Wayne, who has hunted down his own kin abducted by Comanches when she was just a girl. To Ethan she is no longer pure blooded and therefore he must kill her. The John Ford film utilizes Freudian symbols to depict the tormented psychological state of Ethan Edwards. Courtesy *Photofest.*

ing outlaw, has come home. From the porch, his family watches him slowly ride in. Ethan receives a welcome from his brother Aaron (Walter Coy) and sister-in-law Martha (Dorothy Jordan). The sexual tension between Ethan and his brother's wife is clearly felt through the emotions they project. As they share dinner with Aaron and Martha's children, Ben (Robert Lyden), Lucy (Pippa Scott), and little Debbie (Lana Wood), Martin Pawley (Jeffrey Hunter), a young man who was rescued by Ethan after Indians massacred his family, is a late arrival. Ethan openly shows his racial hatred for Indians and the mixed blood he immediately recognizes in Martin. Although Martin has assimilated into his family, Ethan does not hide his disgust and deep-seated prejudice.

Ethan and Martin are deputized by the captain, the Reverend Samuel Johnson Clayton (Ward Bond), for a posse investigating cattle thieves. Out in the valley they discover that Comanches are responsible. Ethan has greater knowledge of his enemies than of his kin and tells the men they were lured out so that the Comanches could go on a murder raid.

During the orange light of dusk, the nervous flutter of birds indicates to Aaron that the Indians are not far off. When her mother blows out an oil lamp that Lucy is carrying, the young woman is overcome with hysteria. Extinguishing the light represents to Lucy that an Indian attack is imminent. As the camera swiftly moves in, Lucy, facing the camera, lets out a blood-curdling scream. It is an action that deromanticizes the Western legend. Lucy's chilling scream assaults the audience as it directly experiences the terror of the moment. The slaughter that then occurs is not shown on screen, only indicated by Chief Scar (Henry Brandon) blowing a war horn after he finds Debbie hiding in the family cemetery. What we do not see is far more unsettling than the genre's usual convention of showing violent action to build sympathy for the victims and hatred for the villains.

When Ethan returns home, tragedy flashes across his face before Ford shows us what Ethan sees—the house burning to the ground. His passion is no longer contained; he cries out repeatedly for Martha in the way a lover would. When Ethan discovers her dead body, we only see the loss on Ethan's face as the camera again shoots from within the black frame inside the house. When he finds Lucy's dress and Debbie's doll, Ethan knows that the Comanches have abducted them. The repellent thought that they might lose their ethnic purity sends Ethan into an obsessive fury.

During a posse search for the girls, a dead, buried Comanche is discovered. Ethan shoots out the Indian's eyes because he understands the Indian belief that without sight the native cannot enter the spirit world. With two thunderous blasts from his gun, Ethan pronounces an eternity of wandering between the winds on the soul of his foe.

After a battle with a Comanche unit, the posse breaks up. Ethan, Martin, and Brad Jorgensen (Harry Carey, Jr.), Lucy's sweetheart, continue on. While tracking on his own, Ethan finds Lucy's desecrated body. This information is revealed when Brad insists he's seen her alive traveling with the Indians. When the young man expresses doubt, Ethan, with bile, spews, "What do I have to do—spell it out for you!" The burden of proof is the terrible responsibility Ethan takes upon himself. This burden hardens his heart and continues to eat away at Ethan's humanity. Brad runs off in a fit of blind revenge. His murder is presented in the **off-screen** sound of gunshots while Ethan and Martin are left to persevere on their mission.

When snowfall prevents them from continuing, Ethan vows never to give up and that he will eventually be victorious. Martin only wants to rescue Debbie, but Ethan has now turned away emotionally from the girl because he is convinced she has lost her lineage. As they travel back to the Jorgensen homestead, the interior view is repeated, but this residence is brighter inside without the Freudian connections of the Edwards home. Lars (John Qualen), his wife (Olive Carey), and their daughter Laurie (Vera Miles) warmly greet Ethan and Martin.

More time passes and Ethan and Martin go off when they receive a new lead for Chief Scar's trail. More time passes again and Charlie McCorry (Ken Curtis) brings a letter from Martin to Laurie as he comes to court her. As she reads the letter aloud, Ford presents what has been occurring with Ethan and Martin. In a series of **flashbacks**, we learn that Martin was tricked into marrying an Indian woman during barter for goods he was selling. A lighthearted scene turns ugly when Martin kicks the woman away from his sleeping ground and Ethan harasses her for information concerning the whereabouts of Scar. By returning to Laurie reading the letter; Ford is able to continue the flashbacks and set them up through **narration** spoken by Martin. During another winter, Ethan wildly drives away a buffalo herd to deny the Comanches the white man's food. They come upon Scar's village, which has been terrorized by a calvary platoon, and take off to find the platoon in case its men apprehended the chief. Ethan is obsessed with killing Scar. They reach the calvary outpost and are brought to a room where white women kidnapped by the Comanches reside. As Ethan looks at the women who have been defiled and driven mad by his archenemy, Ford rapidly tracks the camera (see **tracking shot** in glossary) into a tight close-up of Ethan. The disgust and extreme hatred that burns in his eyes have made him half crazy over his anger toward what he truly believes is an Indian scourge against the supremacy of the white race. Laurie concludes the letter, bringing the story back to date.

Later Emilio Gabriel Fernandez y Figueroa (Antonio Moreno) sets up a meeting with Scar, for a price. Ethan and the chief finally stand eye to eye. Inside his teepee they see Debbie (Natalie Wood), now grown into a beautiful young woman. Scar tells them she is one of his wives. An older, paunchier Ethan is as determined as ever. Controlling his emotions, he tells Scar he will return to offer a trade.

Debbie runs down an embankment and Martin charges after her. She tells him it is too late—the Comanches are her people. Ethan unabashedly reveals his true intentions and draws his gun to kill his own kin because her bloodline is now contaminated. Martin protects her with his body as Ethan is shot by an arrow fired by an advancing Indian party led by Scar. Martin and Ethan manage to fend them off, riding to a cave where they hold their own in battle. The inside of the womblike cave is sanctified by a pure white light.

Back at the Jorgensen house, Laurie and Charlie are about to be married. Ethan and Martin return as unwanted guests. Charlie and Martin enter into a raucous fight over her that ends the chances of a union. Lieutenant Greenhill (Patrick Wayne) enters to tell the Reverend Captain that the army has located Scar.

Ethan, Martin, and the unit sneak up on the Comanche and his tribe in the night air of the valley. At daybreak Martin goes into Debbie's teepee unnoticed. She awakens and screams but then immediately embraces him. The regiment attacks when they hear the sound of Martin shooting an Indian who comes to stop him. Ethan rides directly into Scar's tent. The chief is dead and Ethan completes his self-determined mission by taking his knife to the Comanche. When Ethan leaves the tent, he spots Debbie and charges after her. Martin is unable to stop him. It is the moment of reckoning for Ethan. Debbie makes it to the mouth of the cave, again a symbol for the womb, the sanctity of the home and the unbreakable bond of family. Ethan sweeps her up in his arms and says, "Let's go home, Debbie," in a gentle voice that lets her know he accepts her as family. It is time to return home.

The Jorgensen family waits on their porch to receive them. Martin and Laurie are reunited. Debbie becomes part of their family. Ford returns to the safe black frame of the doorway, a representation of home as a place of inner peace. Ethan, now alone and fully whole, says goodbye, turns, and walks off to roam. The door closes—*The Searchers* has concluded.

John Ford was a master cinematic storyteller. This strong narrative, abounding with insight into the human condition, is cinematically rendered with elegiac and potent moving images. Director of photography Winton C. Hoch (*Joan of Arc, She Wore a Yellow Ribbon, The Lost World*) shot *The Searchers* in Technicolor and VistaVision. The color is deeply saturated and especially rich in capturing the red, blue, green, and earth tones that define the Western genre. VistaVision was a widescreen process in which 35mm film ran through the camera horizontally rather than by the standard vertical flow to create an image with an approximate **aspect ratio** of 1:85:1, the standard widescreen format for American films. VistaVision excelled in sharp definition. The extreme clarity of the process assisted Ford and Hoch in achieving a hyperrealism that expressed the extreme range of emotions attained by the characters in the story.

John Ford considered himself not a filmmaker but a film director. The difference may be semantics, but Ford was not a hands-on filmmaker such as Alfred Hitchcock, King Vidor, or Orson Welles. John Ford was a classicist, a Hollywood professional, and a cinematic poet. He directed with personal vision and by leadership. The insightful thematic treatment and engaging story sensibilities of *The Searchers* are translated and structured by images that serve their purpose with unpretentious virtue. Each shot is composed and staged to convey a sense of place, emotional truth, and dramatic fulfillment. Ford rarely moves the camera. When he tracks alongside the gallop of horseback riders or pushes in for a close-up, it is for a reason that has nothing to do with personal visual style and everything to do with applying the right technique for that moment in the story. There is a minimum of **interscene editing**. Ford cuts only when it is absolutely necessary to move to another view or angle. His choices are only dictated by the story he is telling, not artistic ego or personal expression. *The Searchers* may be John Ford's most personal film in which he probed the American psyche, but it is also a well-made movie, a paradigm for the classical style of the American film.

The Searchers made a lasting impression on the third generation of American film directors. The motifs of the nature of family, the racial politics of hate, and the journey for internal realization appeared in the work of many American New Wave filmmakers, emerging in many forms distilled by the perceptions of a diverse group who share respect for and a yearning to participate in Ford's search for the American character. Martin Scorsese's *Taxi Driver*, Steven Spielberg's *Close Encounters of the Third Kind*, George Lucas's *Star Wars*, and Michael Cimino's *The Deer Hunter* continued John Ford's tradition of making American films that go beyond genre conventions and speak to who we are as Americans.

Of Further Interest

Screen

Forty Guns
Johnny Guitar
The Left-Handed Gun
Taxi Driver (1976)
Unforgiven

Read

About John Ford by Lindsay Anderson
The Searchers by Edward Buscombe
Print the Legend: The Life and Times of John Ford by Scott Eyman
John Ford: The Man and His Films by Tag Gallagher
Searching for John Ford: A Life by Joseph McBride

42

Defining Theme, Metaphor, and Character through Color, Texture, and Environmental Design

□ ◆ □ ◆ □ ◆ □

Se7en

The narrative of *Se7en* (1995) concerns a serial killer who plans and executes elaborate, grisly murders that interpret the seven deadly sins: gluttony, greed, sloth, wrath, pride, lust, and envy. The film is directed by David Fincher in high visual style. *Se7en* is a **neonoir** set in an urban city that is never identified. It is constantly raining. The interiors are dark; long beams of flashlights held by law enforcement cut through thick, dirty air. Everything is aged, decrepit, and disintegrating like the immorality that produced a pathologically brilliant murderer hunted down by detectives William Somerset (Morgan Freeman) and David Mills (Brad Pitt).

Fincher, who learned his craft as a music video director, was highly influenced by Ridley Scott, especially Scott's *Blade Runner* (see chapter 7), a neonoir set in the future. Fincher, director of photography Darius Khondji (*The City of Lost Children, Stealing Beauty, The Ninth Gate*), and production designer Arthur Max (*Gladiator, Black Hawk Down, Panic Room*) applied Scott's aesthetic to *Se7en,* but interpreted it by their own enormous talents; they created the very detailed environments for the story of *Se7en*.

What makes *Se7en* unique is the elaborate library of journals produced by the serial killer chronicling the crime plans: text, photos, graphics, and the physicality of the crime scenes themselves with their ornate Grand Guignol architecture identified with each of the sins. The materials used by the killer include blood, feces, urine, flesh, bone, and gruesome props. Each crime was well planned, designed, and carried out over a period of time by one man. The artistic premise of these sequences that are the

Brad Pitt as detective David Mills in *Se7en*, directed by David Fincher. A serial killer commits a series of murders based on the seven deadly sins. By leaving elaborate and gory crime scenes the killer is narratively responsible for the environmental design he deliberately creates. Courtesy *Photofest*.

centerpieces of the film presented a challenge for Arthur Max, who designed these sequences as if they were created by the killer known as John Doe.

This unique perspective added narrative depth to the character and presented a formidable task for Arthur Max. How are the design ideas presented in these horrific crimes manifested from the character's state of mind? It is not until the last half hour or so of the film that we meet John Doe, played by Kevin Spacey. For the majority of *Se7en* we only see the results of his hellish deeds and learn about him indirectly. The detectives are constantly talking about him, witnessing his heinous handiwork, researching the clues he has left for them, and investigating the origin and nature of the deadly sins.

The detectives have conflicting philosophies concerning the killer's motive; their theories are directly linked to their diverse personalities. Somerset is highly intelligent, methodical, and well aware they are hunting a brilliant psychopath. His approach is to read Dante, Milton, and other literary sources to understand the mind he is tracking. Mills is a young, inexperienced, volatile hotshot with good instincts. Mills yearns for respect and works hard at straight police work to solve the case that defies conventionality. To Mills the John Doe killer is a dirt bag, a nut job, a psycho. He tries to give the impression that he is unwilling to afford the killer intellectual satisfaction, and at first dismisses the complex scholarly approach necessary to understand the fiendish plan linked to classical and religious imagery and beliefs. Mills is rough around the edges and tries to hide it. Eventually the two approaches come together and the killer is captured with calamitous results for both detectives.

The killer is highly intelligent—image- and word-oriented. The visual presentations of his crimes are an important motivation for him. His notebooks, numbering over 200, are works of depraved art, a library of anger, hate, and the destruction of humanity. The title sequence reveals the killer's skilled hands in creating the miniature hand printing, cutting and pasting of photos, and other Hadean graphic elements. When the detectives find his apartment from which he has escaped, they locate the raw materials utilized for his death art.

Arthur Max created the ideal metaphorical environment in which to breed these crimes. Buildings are old, **retrofitted**, and blighted with urban decay. New businesses reflect moral depravity; a leather shop featuring custom-made S&M gear becomes a plot point, as does a sex club that signifies the bowels of hell.

Max's design for John Doe's apartment and the murder sites are within the parameters of the overall look of the film. The personal touches that link these design elements to the killer's interpretation of each sin are the logistics and specifics of each action, victim, and the environment altered by the criminal's punishment for the designated sin.

Fincher carefully constructed clues and support for the sin of envy. The characters involved in this segment are meticulously created. The most audacious touch is the use of the color green, which is a selective thread from the opening shot of the film. Green is the color of jealousy and envy. Green becomes part of the **color palette**, first received as a color that depicts revulsion and disease. It may take more than one screening for a viewer to comprehend the careful symbolic use of the color green. The color is employed both as part of the emotional and psychological atmosphere of *Se7en* and as a deadly clue as to how envy and wrath will personalize the series of nightmarish atrocities even after John Doe is captured.

John Doe's composition books of planning information were created by a highly erudite criminal mind. They are a record of a serial crime so perfect, so contained and internal, it could never be solved without reading the books. The books are shelved in no discernible order and are found at a point when there is no time to disseminate information, only to find and capture the killer.

A separate team in the art department worked on this detailed graphic project. The massive micro-sized text was written by hand. It was not necessary to the technical or narrative requirements of the film that the words make sense or that they reflect the character of John Doe, but they were designed using the logic of the character as written in the script. The opening title sequence showing Doe's hands working on one of the volumes puts him right in front of the viewer, who can see the step-by-step process. As the movie is beginning, we can see inside his diabolical mind. The character comes vividly alive long before we meet him.

Se7en is about urban life. The weather conditions of constant wind and rain have led some to feel the film takes place in Seattle. New York and Chicago also come to mind, but Fincher and his design team went beyond, creating a generic city. The metropolis in *Se7en* is a conglomeration of many American cities because this disintegration of the American urban city is a salient theme. The collapse of civility and the rise of deviance, anarchy, perversity, and violence are consuming the cities. Fincher did not want to personalize *Se7en* by placing it in a specific geographic location; rather, he generalized what was happening to the country.

Somerset, a streetwise but civil man, is retiring to withdraw from the societal cancer surrounding him. David Mills and his wife, Tracy (Gwyneth Paltrow), have lived in rural areas of the country. For David, the city is the place where he can gain respect as a detective. Mills has a jaded point of view toward urban crime and knows little about the sophisticated procedures necessary to deal with it. Tracy is frightened by the city but is a dedicated marital partner, so she supports David and acts as a diplomat to bring the two diverse detectives together. The dinner scene is critical in better understanding Somerset and Mills as individuals—they are brought together by Tracy. Somerset and Tracy bond immediately because they share sensitivity and a sense of humor toward life. Later when Tracy learns she is pregnant, she confides in the detective and asks for his counsel. Tracy is not sure she wants to bring a child into this decaying society. Somerset advises Tracy not to tell David until she resolves this issue, knowing that his partner is a man who wants a family as well as to be justified in his role as a detective before he can be whole.

The screenplay by Andrew Kevin Walker (*8mm, Sleepy Hollow, Panic Room*) is tightly structured and has a seven-day timeframe dedicated to the seven sins. Each day is identified on screen with a text graphic. The week begins with gluttony, greed, and sloth from Monday to Wednesday, with one crime per day. Thursday and Friday are time units used to develop the story and characters. On Saturday lust is carried out in a sex club. On Sunday, a holy day, the man who has brought the seven deadly sins to contemporary life completes the cycle with the sins pride, envy, and wrath. The results forever impact the detectives, Tracy, and John Doe, as well as the future of human history. The Somerset **voice-over** that concludes *Se7en* is a chilling summary of mankind at the end of the twentieth century. Quoting Hemingway, Somerset says, "The world is a fine place and worth fighting for." Somerset ends with his own point of view: "I agree with the second part." Somerset has seen too much destruction during his career as a detective to remain an optimist.

The end credits do not crawl up from the bottom of the frame, the traditional direction for all films; they descend down from the top of the frame. *Se7en* is a journey through heaven and hell. The descent can be viewed as a symbolic visualization of John Doe going to hell. It can also represent hell on earth, a world where the dark side is gaining strength as we head for judgment day.

The musical **score** by Howard Shore (*Dead Ringers, The Silence of the Lambs, The Lord of the Rings*) and sound design by Ren Klyce (*The Game, Fight Club, Being John Malkovich*), Yin Cantor (*Rushmore, Waking the Dead, The Iron Giant*), and Patrick Dodd (*Red Rock West; The Crow: Salvation; Jakob the Liar*) combine to create a metallic, buzzing atmospheric soundtrack that aurally inhabits the evil within the city, within Doe's head, and in the caverns of hell.

In *Se7en* David Fincher and Darius Khondji brought the concept of dark- or low-light photography to a new level. Low-light photography developed during the 1970s after the demise of the Hollywood studio system. The Hollywood studio system demanded films brightly lit, an aesthetic that supported their generally escapist attitude toward the medium. Dramas would employ contrast and **film noir** took that concept further. With his daring work in photographing *The Godfather*, Gordon Willis (*The Parallax View, Interiors, Pennies from Heaven*) utilized very low levels of illumination for the scenes in Don Corleone's office, which contrasted with the bright sunny scenes of his daughter's wedding. By creating entire scenes that were physically photographed as dark, Fincher and Khondji visually interpret the dark context of the story. This low-light style was the ideal application for an American cinema that delved into the underside of human behavior.

Through a then-experimental laboratory technique, the prints of *Se7en* were developed with a combination of the black-and-white and color processes. The result left an imprint of black-and-white cinematography on the monochromatic color scheme. Visually, the photography creates a look of devastation, where the human glow of light has worn away layer by layer. The look of *Se7en* created by the production design and by the cinematography is the visual equivalent of the story content. The images supply their own narrative that communicates graphically to the psychological channels of the viewer. These cannot be separated from the sound, the story, or the performances. *Se7en* is a cinematic experience directed to envelop the viewer in a world corrupted long before John Doe, who takes us just a little bit closer to the fire and brimstone.

Of Further Interest

Screen

Clockers
Fight Club
Red Desert
Scarface (1983)
U Turn

Read

Interaction of Color by Josef Albers
Bright Earth: Art and the Invention of Color by Philip Ball
Se7en by Richard Dyer
The Elements of Color by Johannes Itten
Dark Eye: The Films of David Fincher by James Swallow

43

Symbolism in the Cinema

□ ◆ □ ◆ □ ◆ □

The Seventh Seal

During the golden age of international cinema in the 1950s and 1960s, Swedish film director Ingmar Bergman dominated the interests of American audiences looking for a meaningful experience at the movies. To those raised on Hollywood entertainment, the films of Ingmar Bergman represented a gateway into art cinema. A prolific body of work including *Wild Strawberries, Through a Glass Darkly, Persona, The Virgin Spring,* and *Hour of the Wolf* were a revelation that motion pictures could present serious themes about God, death, and existence. Bergman did not make films to entertain but to ponder human and spiritual issues. These brooding and liberating works did not fit the paradigm of the Hollywood drama. Bergman's vision of the world was expressed in poetic imagery rich with symbols, signs, and layers of meaning that required an intellectual and emotional commitment from the audience. In return, the films did more than satiate the need to pass time; Bergman's cinema was a central part of a canon that contributed to a new cultural era. Film, the medium of the twentieth century, took its rightful place alongside opera, classical music, and the literate and visual arts. Bergman helped to elevate the movies to an art in which images, text, and sound could deliver an experience that made a lasting and significant impact on the viewer.

The Seventh Seal (1957) is a landmark of international cinema. The thematic structure of the film and the poetic cadence and imagery in which Bergman presents and interprets the allegorical narrative would, over the decades, have an indelible influence on American film. A knight, Anto-

Antonious Block (Max von Sydow), a Knight who has returned from the battles of the Crusades, is confronted by Death (Nils Nittel). The man with the stone white face dressed in black and a game of chess to decide the fate of the Knight are some of the striking symbols in Ingmar Bergman's *The Seventh Seal*. Courtesy *Photofest*.

nious Block (Max von Sydow), and his squire (Gunnar Björnstrand) have returned from the Crusades, a centuries-long religious war. The land is ravaged by plague, the survivors fear doomsday, and zealots are about to burn a young woman (Maud Hansson) at the stake for consorting with the devil. The knight is weary from the long battle and seeks answers to eternal questions about the existence of God and the meaning of life. Antonious encounters a white-faced man (Nils Nittel) cloaked in black—the traditional Swedish image for death. Antonious challenges Death to a single game of chess to win a respite from destiny so he can continue his spiritual odyssey in search for answers that would justify his long suffering on the battlefield and the gloomy future he sees ahead. The spectacle of Nittel standing on the shore of the ocean announcing "I am Death" is one of the seminal moments of poetic cinema.

Bergman's art is imbued with symbols and metaphors. You can not just watch *The Seventh Seal*; you must also read it. The chess game between the knight and Death begins on a rock with the sea and a dramatic, turbulent sky behind them. Chess is a war game in which the opponents move pieces in the form of a knight, bishop, queen, king, castle, and pawns related to the traditional ranks of battle. Antonious is a knight; his wife, who appears in the last act of the film, can be seen as his queen. The religious symbol of a bishop is reflected in the religious fervor to rid the plague by destroying the devil in human form. All of the characters are pawns for the devil, God, or both. Antonious is heading for his castle, and a baby named Mikeal is a representation of Jesus, the Prince of Peace, son of the almighty, who could be recognized as the figure of a king. Chess is a game concerning territory, acquiring the enemy's matériel. When a player resigns or is checkmated, making it impossible for the king to escape enemy forces, the game is over. In chess one can win, lose, or draw if the players are equal in strength. The knight has no chance of defeating Death because it is an inevitability of human existence. The knight is looking to extend his time on earth to learn why human suffering persists. What is man's purpose? Chess is an intellectual game as well. The players use strategy and psychology of human nature. Intelligence and will are critical skills as is the ability to presage events. The players vie for which color to play, black or white, two colors with ages of iconography attached to them. White is an advantage because that player moves first, affording him an offensive lead, forcing black to defend, circumvent, or defeat the attacker. The knight wins the right to play white, and Death is comfortable with the color he says suits him. Death cannot lose but he allows the knight to play on and live long enough to discover that after the darkness of life there is light—another good and evil metaphor. A young silent woman (Gunnel Lindblom) repeats the last recorded words of Jesus, "It is finished." The phrase reveals insight into the knight's question about God's existence. Death and chess represent finality. But for the knight playing the game elevates him to a plane of spirituality that transforms the hard reality of death with the magical possibility of an afterlife. This is visualized by a signature shot of Death leading the knight, his squire, the girl, and others in a long shot in silhouette that pictures a hand-in-hand dance that liberates the characters. The final vision of Jof (Nils Poppe), who survives a storm threatening the lives of his family, is that this is not their time to leave the earth. Jof is a member of a troupe of actors touring the countryside. He represents another of *The Seventh Seal*'s potent symbols. Jof, his wife Mia (Bibi Andersson), and their baby son Mikeal are, in the screenplay written by Bergman, an actualization of Joseph, Mary, and the baby Jesus.

The acting troupe tries to spread joy during a time of great worry and strife. All through the film there is talk and there are signs that the end of civilization is near. To audiences who lived with the threat of nuclear annihilation during the cold war and a global society turning toward the dark side, the metaphor of the end of the world and a search for salvation was a powerful connection between the fourteenth and twentieth centuries. Throughout his career Ingmar Bergman assembled one of the great acting repertory companies of the cinema. In addition to von Sydow, Bibi Andersson, and Björnstrand, there were Ingrid Thulin, Harriet Andersson, Liv Ullmann, and Erland Josephson. To Bergman, his actors and crew were part of his family (he also had intimate relationships with several of his actresses). In *The Seventh Seal* there was a significant link among the director's acting company, the troupe portrayed in the film, and the wandering performers who represented the family of Jesus. The actors in the traveling troupe participate in a play within the film, which can also be seen as a film within the film. The troupe is a positive force that tries to uplift a society driven by fear and religious fanaticism. The actors have their own lives and interactions. Jof, Mia, and Mikeal are both symbols of the holy family and flesh-and-blood people struggling with the evil of the plague and the same cardinal questions of purpose as the knight.

The plague in *The Seventh Seal* is a physical illness that is ravaging the land, but Bergman uses it as a metaphorical device to represent a spiritual crisis. The disease is interpreted as a message from God as punishment for the sins of man. This use of the deadly, contagious disease as a religious sign of moral degradation and collapse that brings the world toward a day of judgment resonates throughout history. In the contemporary age, the rhetorical descendants of those fanatical in their religiosity have placed AIDS in this context.

The storm that is unleashed at the climax of the film when the knight reaches his castle is a dramatic element employed in many Hollywood movies to intensify or heighten a narrative situation. But in *The Seventh Seal* the storm does more than just add atmosphere; it is a representation of God's wrath and a sign that the end of the world has arrived. Although destruction of the modern world is predicted to be by fire, the Old Testament image of an impending flood is a symbol of washing away the ravages of disease and drowning the earth leveled to rubble by war. During this sequence, Jof and his family are out in the forest. The image of their vulnerability is intercut (see **intercutting** in glossary) with the young silent woman speaking the words of the Son of God. This demonstrates that the storm or the message from God is far-reaching and has engulfed all of the characters and, by inference, the world. The clearing of the sky at the end of *The Seventh Seal* is an indication that God has spoken and given mercy because belief was recognized.

Bergman is obsessed with the notion of death and the meaning of life. *The Seventh Seal,* like the bulk of his oeuvre, is solemn, morose, brooding, and deadly serious in examining man's nature. What is often overlooked however is a contrasting energy that enriches *The Seventh Seal* and many of Bergman's films with humanity and a zest for life. There is humor sourced from the squire and members of the acting troupe. Mikeal is a celebration of life as well as a symbol for the baby Jesus. The child brings hope, love, and happiness to his parents and to the world. The knight, even in his despair, shows great compassion for the young woman accused of being a witch. *The Seventh Seal* ends with the family moving forward as the world survives. The threat of the apocalypse is held in abeyance.

Bergman's cinematic vision evolved out of his response to the content he created. Over the course of a long career, Ingmar Bergman continued to explore psychological pain, the burden of organized religion, the familial past, and fundamental issues of life. His two principal cinematographers were Gunnar Fischer (*Monika, The Devil's Eye, The Magician*), who photographed *The Seventh Seal*, and Sven Nykvist (*The Silence, Shame, Persona*), who collaborated with Bergman from the 1960s through the 1980s.

The lighting of the black-and-white cinematography in *The Seventh Seal* accentuates stark blacks and shimmering whites. The tonal range highlights the textures of the natural environment: the beach, ocean, rock formations, and dense forest. There is little interscene editing in *The Seventh Seal*. Bergman uses long takes in which composition and staging bring power and visual dynamics to every frame. In a two-shot the characters often do not look at each other. By allowing the lens to observe both characters as they face in different directions, Bergman examines the strain of intimacy, the physical and psychological relationships they have with each other and with their environment. This approach also gives *The Seventh Seal* a measured pace that alters the viewer's sense of time. Most of Bergman's black-and-white films are in the ninety-minute range. But the intensity of the experience can make time seem interminable to the viewer watching a Bergman film. Sound is very specific. All the voices are post-synched and projected in an up-front perspective into the viewer's consciousness. Sound effects are limited but distinctive and used to identify place or mood or to evoke an emotion. There is music, but the overwhelming sound is silence. Viewers are put in touch with their own heartbeat, breathing, and inner thoughts.

The Seventh Seal is an essential film. Woody Allen's career was permanently altered by it, not only in his dramas *Interiors, Another Woman*, and *September*, but in the comedies *Love and Death, A Midsummer Night's Sex Comedy*, and dramedies such as *Hannah and Her Sisters*. American New Wave directors Francis Ford Coppola and Paul Schrader, who came of age in the 1960s and 1970s, were disciples who made the pilgrimage to each and every new Ingmar Bergman film. It is a film that fascinates adolescents who question their own existence. There is a stage when cineastes feel they have outgrown *The Seventh Seal* with its pronouncements concerning death and God. But that passes and we eventually arrive in a place that Ingmar Bergman has never left. It is a place where he plummets into his subconscious, conscious, and personal life for an answer he may only get after the light finally goes out.

Of Further Interest

Screen

El Topo
Fireworks
Interiors
Meshes of the Afternoon
Persona

Read

Images: My Life in Film by Ingmar Bergman
The Magic Lantern: An Autobiography by Ingmar Bergman
Bergman on Bergman: Interviews with Ingmar Bergman by Stig Björkman, Torsten Manns, and Jonas Sima
The Passion of Ingmar Bergman by Frank Gado
1000 Symbols: What Shapes Mean in Art and Myth by Rowena Shepard

Art of the B Movie

□ ◆ □ ◆ □ ◆ □

Shock Corridor

The American B movie is a subversive art form. During the studio system, B units produced lower-budget products to go out as support for the main production vehicle. Going to the movies, audiences were treated to a double bill of feature films packaged with short subjects, a newsreel, and cartoons. The Bs were genre movies with a second-, third-, or lower-tier cast. They were produced quickly without the intense scrutiny favored on an A-list release. As a result an American art thrived; the films were bold and an explosive cocktail of exploitation, expressive style, raw content and not-so-hidden messages. B-movie directors did not attain the prestige of John Ford, Alfred Hitchcock, Howard Hawks, or William Wyler, but they were able to make personal films in a factory system that engineered their product to entertain and weave concocted dreams. To the Hollywood moguls, the B movie was a classification. After the demise of the studio system, it became an alternative cinema, then a genre. B movies have always been a cinematic way of life for the maverick.

Samuel Fuller (1911–1997) is the quintessential B moviemaker. He was a New York street journalist, a tabloid newspaperman. Fuller was in the frontlines of World War II, and he wrote screenplays and novels. He called his stories yarns. A highly intelligent yet blunt man, his yardstick for turning a yarn into a book or movie was based on whether it gave him a "hard-on." Fuller hated phonies and was a truth seeker who always aimed between the eyes and socked one in the gut. He never had to make a speech or pen a position paper about radicalizing the well-made Holly-

Newspaper reporter Johnny Barrett (Peter Breck) goes undercover as a mental patient to solve a murder committed in an institution. Director Sam Fuller transformed the B movie into art with a stylized high key light, a set that represents infinity, a political/social agenda, expressive performances, and an inventive, highly charged plot. Courtesy *Photofest.*

wood production with its polite and instructive conventions—Fuller made movies the way he saw them.

Shock Corridor (1963) is a great movie title that, like a tabloid headline, provokes the viewer to "read" further. The story and characters assault the viewer with hard-hitting ideas, opinions, direct language, and no-nonsense action. The language is pulp grit—the central plot and the supporting reportage speaks for and to the proletariat in an uncensored voice.

Johnny Barrett (Peter Breck) is a newspaper reporter who decoys as a mental patient so he can solve the in-house murder of an inmate and win a Pulitzer Prize for journalism. With the help of Dr. Fong (Philip Ahn), who coaches him to pose as a sexual psychopath, Swanne (William Zuckert), his supportive boss, and Cathy (Constance Towers), his loving girlfriend and a leggy stripper who charades as his sexually harassed sister and is the impetus for his institutional commitment, Johnny lands on "the Street"—lingo for the mental ward's central hallway.

Johnny fights the strain to maintain his own sanity as he investigates three men who witnessed the crime. Stuart (James Best) is an American soldier who during the Korean conflict defected to the Communists and now believes he is a Civil War Confederate colonel. Trent (Hari Rhodes) is an African American who went mad from the pressures of integrating an all-white Southern college and now lives out the role of an Imperial Wizard of the Ku Klux Klan. Boden (Gene Evans) is a brilliant scientist who regressed to childhood when government pressures concerning nuclear armament shattered his sanity. Johnny solves the case and wins his cherished Pulitzer, but the price is a permanent state of catatonia. He has lost his most precious commodity—his voice.

Fuller realizes this powerful intention with a razor-sharp screenplay, forceful direction, a visual style that interprets the narrative, and a story structure that intensifies the emotional experience of the tragic protagonist.

The story is taut and economical. Not only is there no filler or fat, but most scenes end unpredictably at the height of action and emotion, like the erratic rhythm of a disturbed mind. Others go well beyond traditional dramatic endurance and bring the viewer into direct experience with the tedium and impulsive chaos that perpetually confronts the lives of the confined mentally ill. The dialogue and situations are surprising and candid. Fuller allows his audience to witness hate, shame, violence, humiliation, racism, betrayal, sexual obsession, and the mental and physical destruction of the human spirit without pity or any semblance of creative restraint. This yarn is outrageous, honest, over the top, and a warning to those who tamper with the mind. Fuller pulls out all the stops from beginning to end to make his prophetic point, one that may be the most significant metaphor that challenges human existence. *Shock Corridor* is relentless until the lights come up. It begins and ends with the words of Euripides in 425 B.C.: "Whom God wishes to destroy he first makes mad."

Shock Corridor brims with powerful and brutally effective performances. Most of the cast members were better known at the time for their work in television and other B movies. The acting is forceful, often played full out beyond melodrama and operatic intensity. The emotions are so outwardly projected, they pound away at the viewer's credulity in recognizing naturalism. With no contrast or rest from the relentless passion of the sane or the manic urges and irrationality of the insane, the audience enters a world where all is at stake in every nerve-stretched moment.

The Street is a lone, narrow hallway, the corridor to oblivion. The mouth of this limbo is centered in front of the camera eye. The perspective is infinity. This row of desolation does not end. The internationally renowned production designer Eugene Lourie (*Grand Illusion, Rules of the Game, Limelight*) created an exacting visual metaphor for total confinement, a prison of the mind with no escape in sight. To achieve what Fuller identified as "infinity in a finite space" and "invasive claustrophobia," Lourie employed **forced perspective**. At the far end of the set, he painted the endless horizon. Dwarfs dressed as patients paced before it to complete the illusion.

Shock Corridor is photographed in ultra-stark black and white by master Hollywood director of photography Stanley Cortez (*The Magnificent Ambersons, Night of the Hunter, The Naked Kiss*). Cortez lit the film with hard northern light. The visible source emanates from long ceiling fixtures that illuminate the Street—an upside down two-lane blacktop. The cinematographer redirected the harsh white light so that it was aimed straight and low across the frame. This created long black shadows and a cruel reality for this doomed community. Their faces and figures are not modeled in tonality but blasted with a cold bright intensity that leaves them partly in the scrutiny of light and partly lost in the dark. When the lens is far, the subjects appear to be trapped in the glare of an eternal sunrise. In close-up, the rays rake across the face so skin looks like a barren desert.

Fuller's direction is tough, blatant, and immediate. Johnny Barrett's inner voice is established at the get-go. The filtered sound of his thoughts serves as a delivery method of narrative exposition and a system to track Johnny's descent into madness. The psychodrama of this cautionary tale posing as a mystery is kept on edge by Fuller's command over the **mise-en-scène**. Some scenes are choreographed in long takes to emphasize the hopelessness of the men and the enormity of the reporter's quest. The camera can pan back and forth along the hallway, sit in one of the bleak rooms, or stop on the Street to stare as the men act out their frayed emotions. Without motivated provocation, the action can burst into spastic motion with abrupt changes in camera position, movement, or jump cuts that inflict illogic to the former tedium. Fuller's directorial method included firing a gun instead of shouting "Action!" and announcing "Forget it!" instead of "Cut." His sense of immediacy on the set was an extension of years chasing sordid but human stories on the streets of New York and dodging bullets in the theaters of battle during World War II.

This corridor shocks the senses. When the witnesses have their temporary mental breakthroughs to rational clarity, Fuller cuts to 16mm color footage that he photographed with his own camera during his many travels over the globe. The 16mm images are stretched out and distorted when presented in the wide-screen format, a strategy that effectively represents repressed memories of reality bursting forth through the madness of the characters. When Johnny's mind submits to the breaking point,

Fuller exposes the reporter's frightening breakdown by staging a full-blown lightning and thunderstorm on a soundstage that was not prepared for this effect. As Johnny screamed and thrashed through the water, the set was flooded. Fuller got the reality he wanted and the lightning bolt that rams into Johnny's helpless body was added optically in post-production. The studio proprietors cursed the director out as he jumped into his car and sped triumphantly away from the lot he treated as a battleground for personal expression.

Fuller and his editor, Jerome Thoms (*Pal Joey, The 7th Voyage of Sinbad, Underworld U.S.A.*), applied traditional editing transitions in a manner that was faithful to their original purpose as elements of film grammar, but they were redefined in the way a jazz improvisation could riff on a composed melodic structure. An **iris shot**, mostly associated with D. W. Griffith, pinpoints the infinity vanishing point of the Street, then opens to reveal the entire scene. Fuller establishes place and focuses the viewer's eye on a detail. By beginning with that existential concept, he opens the cinematic curtain with a metaphorical idea rather than information or dramatic narrative introduction. Many scenes end with a fade to black and fade up from black to begin the next. This is a common editorial device to create a passage of time and to situate the sequence of events, but it is only a device and is interpreted by text and context. The nature of time in *Shock Corridor* is determined by the behavior of the inmates, so the viewer is never exactly sure when events are really occurring or allowed to settle into a comfort zone with the narrative. The story is about the insane, told by a man who is slowly but surely moving into a state of mental illness. Superimposed (see **superimposition** in glossary) images can enter the fantasy life of a character or represent the character's imaginings. The sexually provocative image of Cathy in her stripper costume haunts and taunts Johnny when he is alone and inside his own head. Fuller goes so far with her imaginary presence, well past the time necessary to comprehend the impact this has on Johnny, that it becomes experiential—the viewer directly experiences his nightmares, hallucinations, and hears voices, the clinical symptom for psychosis.

Shock Corridor is a disturbing yet entertaining film. Samuel Fuller takes the audience in to see a **film noir**, a mystery that happens to take place in a mental institution. This is more than a plot device set in a particular location. The themes are reaching and important: the politics of hate, the destruction of love, the insanity of the battle, and the sanity of peace. When the order of the mind is disturbed through the stress of the extreme negativity of society, racism, war, and destruction, there is hell to pay. The issues that take these men over the brink threaten civilization. Insanity is evil; sanity is love. When the men snap they become their polar opposites. Johnny is a man of words; he is destroyed by losing his voice. Hate is action—love is compassion. If we cannot speak out against hate, we are doomed not to love. In Samuel Fuller's words, "If I've learned anything at all from writing all those stories, from fighting a world war, from making all those films, from being way up and way down, I've learned that everything—*everything!*—can be expressed in just four God-blessed words: *Love is the answer.*"

Of Further Interest

Screen

Gun Crazy (1949)
The Hitch-Hiker (1953)
The Naked Kiss
The Phenix City Story
The Wild Angels

Read

A Third Face: My Tale of Writing, Fighting, and Filmmaking by Sam Fuller
Sam Fuller by Phil Hardy
Kings of the Bs: Working within the Hollywood System: An Anthology of Film History and Criticism, edited by Todd McCarthy and Charles Flynn
B Movies by Don Miller
Sam Fuller: Film is a Battleground: A Critical Study with Interviews, a Filmography, and a Bibliography by Lee Server

Digital Filmmaking

□ ◆ □ ◆ □ ◆ □

Star Wars: Episode II—Attack of the Clones

During the 1990s, the cinema as we knew it changed forever. Until digital technology began yet another revolution in the development of motion pictures, the moviemaking process from the earliest days involved shooting with a film camera on sprocketed celluloid film stock as the medium that recorded the images. The evolution of the editing process began with scissors and holding the film strips up to a light, and progressed to a viewer, then to the Moviola, a mechanical upright editing machine used to edit at least ninety-five percent of the movies produced during the twentieth century. The flatbed editing table was a refinement but still relied on transporting film through a light source via sprockets. After many false starts by myriad companies (including George Lucas's Editroid), Avid Technology developed a software by which film could be edited digitally on computer. During the mechanical age, the film laboratory and the **optical printer** were the lifeline to visual effects and the final look of a film; digital technology changed all of that.

Every motion picture begins with an idea, a story that forms in the human imagination. Once the basic tools of the medium were invented and in practice, it was the thought processes, dreams, fantasies, and the ability to see images and an unfolding narrative in the mind's eye that led to the technical innovations necessary to realize them on film. The imagination and realities of "how to do it" are inextricably linked. Throughout history what could be done and how well or convincingly it was rendered rested on the tools and techniques that transposed the ideas onto the screen.

The all-digital Jedi Master Yoda in *Star Wars: Episode II—Attack of the Clones.* Courtesy *Photofest.*

When George Lucas originally conceived the *Star Wars* saga, he envisioned a multipart film that would tell the epic story he dreamt of in his thoughts. As he was writing the story before any of the films were made, he was aware that the technology needed to produce particular images and scenes was not yet available. The first film, *Star Wars,* released in 1977, was not limited in Lucas's abilities as a sci-fi dreamer and storyteller, but Lucas was limited in the application of the mechanical film technology that existed and the results it produced.

In the period from the release of *Star Wars: Episode VI—Return of the Jedi* in 1983 to the arrival of *Star Wars: Episode I—The Phantom Menace* in 1999, George Lucas and his companies Industrial Light and Magic (ILM) and Skywalker Sound had been at the forefront of digital sound and visual effects and electronic cinema. ILM had delivered cutting-edge masterful visual effects for a long line of successful films, and the Skywalker Ranch had become the state-of-the-art venue for digital sound design.

Star Wars: Episode I—The Phantom Menace gave Lucas and his team the first opportunity to apply the technology they had cultivated working on other projects onto a *Star Wars* film. *Episode I* became an experiment that allowed refinements in *Episode II.* It had taken twenty-five years for the tools to serve the creator's vision.

Lucas took a quantum leap by deciding to shoot *Episode II—Attack of the Clones* (2002) on digital video. The previous four films had to be photographed on film with motion picture cameras. Up until the creation of a digital video camera that could shoot the same frame rate as a film camera and improve in factors including definition and tonal range, video as a recording device for a commercial feature motion picture was unable to compete with the image quality of film. With the camera available, Lucas was able to place his entire production in the digital domain. This possibility allowed Lucas to create the intergalactic visions he imagined; it also ratcheted up the definition of control on a motion picture. Film directors had been struggling for total artistic control since the dawn of the medium. Electronic cinema demonstrated that it had the capability to allow changes to sound and image elements throughout the process with nearly unlimited possibilities.

As long as someone else is paying the bills, no filmmaker has total artistic control, so Lucas financed the entire production himself. Computer graphics can create and render digital backgrounds and virtual characters and can design compositions and camera movement with a virtual camera that can apply lighting and color effects as well. This liberated Lucas from creature makeup, mechanical monsters, conventional **matte paintings** on glass and extensive model and set construction—the computer could now generate them.

Although George Lucas put all his trust into a creative team of supervisors and their staffs comprised of small armies of artists and technologists, every detail and details within details of *Attack of the Clones* were personally approved by him; Lucas even had an actual stamp pad made up to put an imprint on drawings designating his graces to move ahead.

The process of electronic cinema is in many ways similar to traditional filmmaking, but it allows the director to manipulate everything in the frame at any time. This permits the director to make decisions and changes all throughout the major aspects of production: screenwriting, preproduction, production, and postproduction. Lucas had the vision of the story in his mind's eye, and on *Episode I* for the first time he could work more like a painter or a chef in adding a microelement at a time, selecting from a wide range of possibilities and having total control over the collaborative aspects of moviemaking. The visual effects supervisors would take their instruction directly from Lucas and relay it to the computer animators and graphic designers, who would do the work that would be presented by the supervisor to the director, maintaining the chain of command. Lucas would then sign off or give notes to continue the process until he was satisfied.

The original screenplay for *Episode II* had its genesis decades ago when

Lucas conceived and wrote out the full saga containing all of the episodes in his epic story. Production on *Episode II* began with a working revised screenplay but with the knowledge that new scenes or modifications to scenes could be added during production and postproduction. Traditional filmmakers like Woody Allen regularly conducted reshoots that were a total and complete process unto themselves. With digital cinema, elements could be reconfigured and new material more easily created and then composited (see **composite shot** in glossary) into the film. Lucas was in control and did not have to explain and trust his collaborators as in the traditional one-step process in which the film is shot and becomes the material the editor works with. Lucas was able to have the prerogative of dealing with or revealing what he wanted a bit at a time, and he set himself up as the ultimate, sole arbiter of the final work.

After the script was prepared, preproduction involved more than scouting locations, hiring actors and extras, and assembling a crew and creative team. It was at this stage that Lucas previsualized the entire production. To accomplish this, a **storyboard** was drawn for every shot in the film. Then Ben Burtt (*The Dark Crystal, E.T. The Extra-Terrestrial, The Empire Strikes Back*), a longtime Lucas collaborator and the film's editor and sound designer, directed and photographed basic shots depicting the characters (here played by ILM and Skywalker employees, family, and friends) on a simple makeshift set. They even used one of Lucas's old cars to represent a space craft. Digital **background plates** from earlier *Star Wars* movies were used to composite the images. Actors wearing an element of a creature or character on their head or body would walk through as reference.

This material was edited by Ben Burtt and his crew into a temporary version of the entire film. Next, Lucas worked with Burtt to go over each shot and get the timing, sequence, and structure refined. During the production process, this temporary version was referred to a scene at a time and a shot at a time to guide the crew and give Lucas the precise logistics of what he needed to shoot.

When Lucas made *Star Wars* in 1977, he had to put most everything he wanted into the shot before the film camera. On *Episode II* there was quite a bit of location shooting with the director of photography David Tattersall (*Con Air, The Green Mile, Die Another Day*) and his crew and a production sound team. There were physical sets or partial sets built on location and on stages in several countries selected for the properties to evoke the terrain of planets from another galaxy.

Much of the production work was photographed on a blue-screen (see **blue-screen shot** in glossary) stage. The environment consisted of large shapes that were colored blue, representing architectural and other elements. The actual visual design would be digitally created and composited later in postproduction. So the actors performed in a blue void when they were in a scene with a character or set elements that would be computer-generated at a later date. The actors did rehearse with a voice actor and shot at least one reference take with that actor or a stand-in. Then the actor, knowing the **eye-line matches** and choreography of the scene to be added later, would be the sole actor—or with other actors—on the take surrounded by a sea of blue, a color that allowed computer graphics to be composited into the scene later.[1]

The process of directing the actor here is similar to silent film technique because the director literally talks the actor through the scene while the camera is running. The actors were completely reliant on Lucas to direct their attitudes, emotional states, and physicality toward the action and reactions to the characters and environments they could not see. The performances could only be as good as Lucas's ability to communicate and the actors' instincts in applying their imaginations.

The definition of acting took on a new dimension in *Episode II*. Many more characters were digitally created after *Episode I*, including Yoda, who had previously been a hand puppet manipulated by Frank Oz (*The Muppet Movie, The Dark Crystal, The Stepford Wives* [2004]), who also was the voice of the Jedi master. The casting process involved approving drawings and sculpted models. Once selected, often by combining elements from several models in a sort of mix-and-match process, the computer animators would scan in the figure and begin to animate. Every expression, gesture, and piece of body language was analyzed and created to Lucas's specifications. Lucas's comments ranged from the movement of hairs on Yoda's ears to the speed of the walk of a digital alien in a crowd scene.

All traditional films are not only as good as just their director's ability to judge acting, photography, design, editing, music, and sound; the collaborators always make a substantial contribution and in many cases may be responsible for a major stylistic aspect that is defined as part of the vision of the film. Take as example Conrad Hall's cinematography on *American Beauty* and *Road to Perdition* for director Sam Mendes. Lucas's control is absolute. He functions as the only one who truly knows, and is treated as such by everyone who works with him.

An overview of what was accomplished digitally on *Episode II* includes putting the actual face of Christopher Lee portraying Count Dooku on a human double for many of the shots during the climactic light saber duel, creating the battle sequence by filming and editing one fighter, either human or virtual, at a time and layering them to get the desired choreography and scope; to adding architectural or prop elements to complete sets or computer graphics; to virtual camera zooms and jitters to simulate a live action camera responding to the tumultuous action. A romantic scene between Padmé Amidala (Natalie Portman) and Anakin Skywalker (Hayden Christensen) in a lush field was populated by actual bugs while they shot the scene on location. Digital artists painted out each insect by hand to bring serenity to the scene. For buglike creatures elsewhere, digital animators created their own intergalactic bugs.

In the long view, the possibilities of electronic cinema are in their infancy. The overwhelming majority of movies are still released on film after a match-back process in which the digital final is transferred onto sprocketed film and projected by a film projector onto a theater screen. The current process—with few exceptions including *Star Wars* Episodes I, II, and III, *Bamboozled, 28 Days Later, Full Frontal,* and *Timecode,* which originated on video—is to shoot on film, edit digitally, composite design elements digitally, and conform to and release on film. Very few theaters as yet are set up for video projection.

Most films have been transformed by digital technology, many not as radically as *Star Wars* Episodes I and II but as a way of enhancing, adding, and subtracting elements as necessary. Visual effect-laden films such as *The Hulk, Spider-Man, Terminator 2: Judgment Day,* and others take greater advantage and use of the technology. The aesthetics of digital cinema are writing a new language for the medium of motion pictures. **Ramping** speeds, **morphing**, and the new possibilities of image manipulation have begun to reinvent the grammar.

Ironically, George Lucas is harnessing this great technology to contemporize a narrative genre from the 1930s—the movie serial. His direction constantly relates to *Flash Gordon*, Clint Eastwood, Sergio Leone, and a backlog of classic movie references and moments. Lucas is a traditionalist storyteller who used technology to streamline the process and make a better production rooted in early Hollywood cinema.

As the tools become more accessible to artists who want to explore the properties of new media and apply it to stories that demand it, the nature of cinema will radically change. It is always the mavericks—Welles, Gance, Kubrick, Altman, Cassavetes, Antonioni, Fellini, and others—who seek new forms, structure, and methods of storytelling. Tools are just that—tools. The digital revolution offers the greatest opportunity for evolution of the medium since the creation of the motion picture camera. *Star Wars: Episode II—Attack of the Clones* is the prehistory of an exciting future for the medium. *Pong* was the first video game. It consisted of two digitally controlled white bars representing paddles hitting a digital ball. This digital tennis game was primitive but gave access to many imaginations and discoveries. *Star Wars* is also part of the global pop culture. George Lucas has used it to complete his vision; others are thankful and will travel many different roads. Without Edison, Porter or Méliès, we would not have had Griffith or Eisenstein. Film history is organized by the vision of filmmakers, those who supply the tools, and the progression of art as one artist is inspired and led by those that have gone before. The biggest challenge to the future of cinema is whether the ideas can match and surpass the tools—that is true innovation.

Note

1. The color green can also be used for the composite process.

Of Further Interest

Screen

The Anniversary Party
Bamboozled
Final Fantasy
Full Frontal
Time Code

Read

Digital Moviemaking by Scott Billups
$30 Film School: Write, Finance, Direct, Produce, Shoot, Edit, Distribute, Tour With, and Sell Your Own No-Budget Digital Movie by Michael W. Dean
Visual Effect in a Digital World: A Comprehensive Glossary of over 7,000 Visual Effects Terms by Karen E. Goulekas
Digital Filmmaking 101: An Essential Guide to Producing Low Budget Movies by Dale Newton and John Gaspard
Industrial Light + Magic: Into the Digital Realm by Mark Cotta Vaz and Patricia Rose Duignan

46

Birth of a Nonfiction Film Style

□ ◆ □ ◆ □ ◆ □

The Thin Blue Line

Errol Morris transformed the **nonfiction film** with *The Thin Blue Line* (1988). The story comprised hard documentary fact. Randall Adams was accused and convicted of murdering a police officer in Texas. Teenager David Harris was also a suspect, but law enforcement and the Texas justice system wanted to convict twenty-eight-year-old Adams so that they could execute him in the electric chair. To do so they cut a deal with the underage Harris who could deliver the ultimate punishment through his false testimony. This case was not about justice but retribution at any cost.

Under any circumstances this would have made an intriguing **documentary**, but Morris did not use the standard process of the form. *The Thin Blue Line* incorporates talking head interviews, **docudrama**, recreation, fictional and **avant-garde film** techniques, a postmodern sensibility, and illustrative images that range from **inserts** to **stock footage.** The hypnotic, repetitive, and cosmic **score** by Philip Glass (*Mishima: A Life in Four Chapters, Koyannisqatsi, The Hours*) transcends the traditional informative or dramatic purpose of a documentary film score to impart a point of view toward American justice as an impenetrable force. Errol Morris is not an objective filmmaker; he is out to find the truth and to cinematically proclaim that the unbalanced scales of justice continue to tip in the direction of abusive power. Morris does not achieve his political goals with in-your-face guerilla tactics as in Michael Moore's *Roger & Me* and *Bowling for Columbine*; rather, he employs a series of complex artistic strategies.

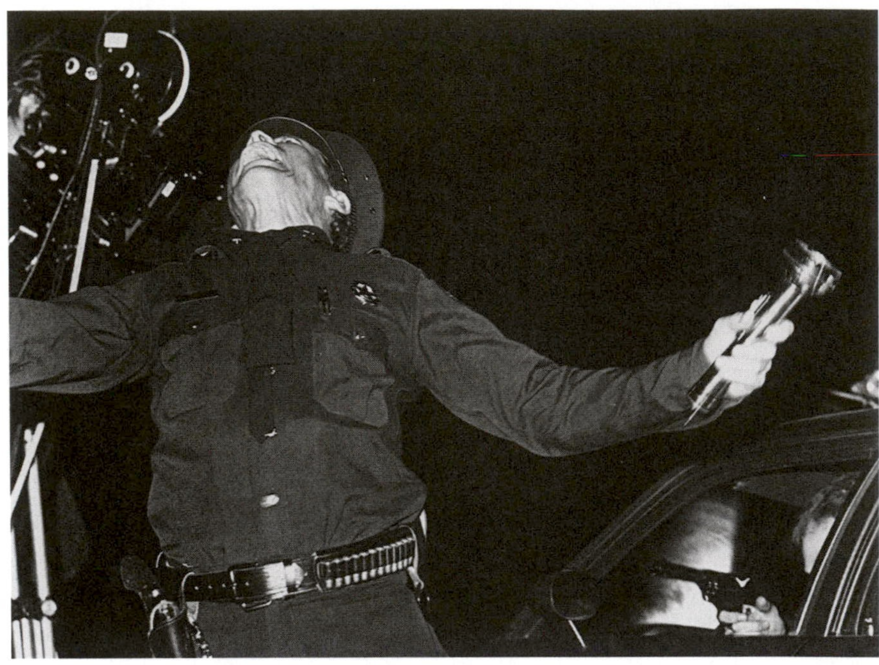

On set of *The Thin Blue Line* as a recreation of the murder of a police officer is filmed by director Errol Morris and his crew. The recreation is shown from many different vantage points throughout the film—stylized talking head interviews, post-modern inserts, and a hypnotic score by composer Philip Glass, transform this true-life story into a radically new form of documentary film. Courtesy *Photofest*.

The Thin Blue Line deconstructs the facts. Time cannot be stopped, but it can be reconfigured until reality begins to emerge through the lies and distortions, and almost mathematically, an answer appears.

The structure of *The Thin Blue Line* parallels the progression of the murder, investigation, trial, and outcome. The story is told by Adams, Harris, attorneys, the judge, witnesses, policemen, and detectives. Morris tells the story from a posttrial vantage point. Adams was convicted and sentenced to death, and the case was then overturned and manipulated by Texas authorities to a life sentence. Adams and Harris are interviewed in jail, the younger man incarcerated for another murder he committed. The others are in their offices, homes, and other nondescript locations recounting the story. Morris carefully questioned all the subjects so the story could be told in chronological order. Through the editing process the story unfolds in a **nonlinear storytelling** structure with all the twists and turns and points of view that are presented through word, image, and an ever-changing series of recreations of the policeman's murder.

The talking heads are interviewed skillfully, so they freely tell the story as they know and understand it with personal views intact. Morris gets them to speak and reveal themselves without a hint of directorial point of view. The interview subjects trust Morris, so they gladly tell their truths. They are not being overly manipulated by the interviewer's questions or altered by tough questioning that might put them on the defensive.

The photography of the interview subjects is also nontraditional. The art of the talking head interview has limitations, but many variations. The size of the image, close medium, the subjects' relationship to setting and environment, the coverage, camera movement, attention to body language, and lighting are all components. Morris and cinematographers Robert Chappell (*In Our Water, Robert Wilson and the Civil Wars, Jakarta*) and Stefan Czapsky (*Last Exit to Brooklyn, Edward Scissorhands, Batman Returns*) stylized the way the interviews were photographed as part of the postmodern approach to the nonfiction film. Locations are simplified to their essence. Adams's lawyer is seated, shelved law books on the left, table and lamp on the right. Adams is in prison whites with the cage of a cell in the background. Harris is in prison orange with a large tile wall behind him. Shots appear to be locked off with no overt interpretation by application of lens choice, composition, or movement. Of course, there is always some interpretation. No film can be truly objective, including documentaries. Morris seeks the truth in his own idiosyncratic manner. The relationship between subject and frame is established by the individual's persona and Morris's view of their truth. Adams's attorney is photographed from a slightly low angle looking up to give her authority. Adams is often in the center of the frame to represent his stability. Harris is framed off-center, positioned to the right of frame where the use of space is challenging his authority. The judge is photographed at a slight up-tilt and on an angle to give him distinction, but his words reveal a close-minded man looking for easy justice.

Color is used to transform the interview subjects from reality to an altered atmosphere that comments on the surreal absurdity of the Texas system of jurisprudence. The colors are all cool, like the blue car used in the crime. The backgrounds include pink, red, blue, and purple. The color scheme of the film is tied together by this palette and connects all the participants tonally, a unifying element to create the metaphor of a system controlled by powers that have imprisoned both Adams and the truth.

The stylistic elements that have the most impact on the attitude, point of view, and perception of the text are the illustrative shots intercut (see **intercutting** in glossary) into sequences of the subjects as they tell their stories. Most documentaries use this editorial technique. It visually presents what is being said, gives additional, supporting, or contradictory information, and allows the editor, in this instance Paul Barnes (*Pumping Iron II: The Women; The Civil War; Jazz*), to manipulate the original on-camera interview now being utilized as a voice-over narration. Off-point sections of the interview can be removed, and the order of sentences can be rearranged.

Morris's strategy is very different than the average documentarian. The visual illustrative material is rarely traditional or realistic. A postmodern sensibility expresses itself through the use of images. Shots presented to reveal the city of Dallas are artfully constructed to portray the unemotional power the buildings and city represent. They dominate over the city and its people. Maps take on a surreal quality linking the hellish events that Adams experienced. A shot of the motel where Adams and his brother stayed the night of the murder is not archival footage and does not look like a journalistic presentation, but rather appears as if it were out of a B movie. Photos of the murdered police officer and headlines documenting the crime are similar to those seen in most documentaries, but the context of the film's design alters our perception of them. When Adams discusses how he was pressured to sign a confession, Morris and Barnes cut to a slow-motion shot of a pen flung onto a typed confession. This is not archival. It could be considered a recreation, but the choice of slow motion and the fact that there are no people in the image transforms it into an interpretive gesture.

Time is a critical issue in the Adams case and to Morris as a filmmaker. As the interrogation of Randall Adams is covered by the interview subjects in the form of **voice-over**, there is a **jump cut** and **montage** of a watch swinging right to left, left to right. The image is photographed in a hyperrealistic style. The passage of time is indicated, as is a trancelike atmosphere. The police officer was hypnotized to clarify her testimony and Adams talks about the experience of being in a nightmare from which you can not wake. Time in *The Thin Blue Line* is relentless, mathematical, cosmic, and on the side of the law. There are so many discrepancies in the case's timeline. The absurd tragedy of Randall Adams's situation is that he is trapped in a time continuum, held by the authorities with little chance of ever being released. This seems to be controlled by forces larger than all the mortals involved with the case.

The chief eyewitness is discredited by a woman who speaks at length of the poor character and chicanery she has observed. This is a standard documentary editorial technique and the backbone of television's *60 Minutes* journalism. Before this, however, Morris gets the witness to speak about how she always wanted to be a police officer or the wife of a police officer. As she confidently explains how she never misses anything and suggests that her prowess as an amateur detective comes from watching *Boston Blackie* films as a child, Morris and Barnes cut to footage from the old films. The Philip Glass score then presents a satiric take on motion picture detective music that contributes to the denigration of the woman's integrity as a witness.

Overall the Philip Glass score does not operate to elicit specific emotional responses. The endless repetition of the chordal notes is sequenced by human hands playing keyboards. So the mathematical, Zenlike music takes the entire documentary away from tradition into a cinematic mindspace that creates a new modality for interpreting reality. Viewers are not so much emotionally led or influenced by the score as they are swept into a state of alternate realism.

If documentaries are manipulated to achieve a sense of truth, Errol Morris has opened up a new arena for the nonfiction film. The facts are correct; the texts of the interviews are reliable in representing the reality of each individual. All documentary filmmakers have a point of view usually expressed by the selection, juxtaposition, and structure of the facts. They utilize realistic imagery that may or may not be accurate. Morris moves in another direction, allowing the viewer to find the perception of the speakers and the truth of their statements through less obvious and restricted methods.

Re-creation of the murder recurs throughout *The Thin Blue Line*. Audiences are never sure if they are seeing what actually happened. What is stressed is a visual representation of what various witnesses say they saw and how investigators and lawyers insist on what happened. Basic elements remain the same each time they appear: the road, a police car, a male officer who approaches a blue car and is shot to death. Major discrepancies involve the number of people in the car, who was sitting in the driver's seat, and whether the female officer remained inside the police car or got out to pursue the shooter. Through repetition and the visualization of credible testimony from the speakers, truths do come out. They all make it unlikely that Adams could have been at the scene or committed the murder.

These recreations and multiple viewpoints are not shot and edited in a conventional docudrama format. They are never labeled, and they play as if they are B art movie accounts of the murder. The style is closer to **neonoir**. These sequences either play for the viewer's chance to deduce or are revelations, as when two different models of a blue car are intercut to demonstrate inconsistencies, or to place the officer eating inside the car where she would have been unable to see or get involved. A slow-motion shot of a milkshake cup flying through the air graphically but poetically illustrates the woman's response to hearing the gunshot from inside the police car.

The repetition and slight variations in the music and the repeated showings of the crime create the sense that nothing will ever be resolved—that somewhere in cyberspace this moment in time plays endlessly.

Errol Morris's dogged investigation into the Randall Adams case resulted in the filmmaker actually solving the crime. At the conclusion of *The Thin Blue Line,* Morris interviews David Harris one last time. This time no camera was present. During a montage of a microcassette tape recorder playing the interview, Harris clearly suggests his guilt and gives his motive for allowing and contributing to Adams taking the fall for a murder Harris committed.

The Academy of Arts and Sciences did not nominate *The Thin Blue Line* for best feature documentary. *The Thin Blue Line* is a nonfiction film and an experiment into the outer reaches of reality to find the truth. They say truth is stranger than fiction; the Randall Adams case proves that thesis, but Errol Morris showed the way that fiction—at least fictional artifacts—could lead to the truth. Randall Adams was eventually released as a free man because of a movie and an uncompromising and very idiosyncratic filmmaker.

Of Further Interest

Screen

Bowling for Columbine
Capturing the Friedmans
Crumb
Mr. Death: The Rise and Fall of Fred A. Leuchter
Sherman's March

Read

Making Documentary Films and Reality Videos: A Practical Guide to Planning, Filming, and Editing Documentaries of Real Events by Barry Hampe
Directing the Documentary by Michael Rabiger
Experimental Enthnography: The Work of Film in the Age of Video by Catherine Russell
Documentary Filmmakers Speak by Liz Stubb
The Search for "Reality": The Art of Documentary Filmmaking, edited by Michael Tobias

Experimental Narrative

□ ◆ □ ◆ □ ◆ □

2001: A Space Odyssey

Stanley Kubrick's *2001: A Space Odyssey* (1968) is a landmark film less for its pioneering contribution to the science fiction genre than for its impact on cinematic storytelling method and structure. From the inception of his career, Stanley Kubrick (1928–1999) strove to explode the traditional nature of film narratives. The catalyst was to transform the standard conventions of a genre such as **film noir** in *The Killing*, the war film with *Paths of Glory*, the political thriller in *Dr. Strangelove*, and the sex comedy in *Lolita* into a radical new form to express his iconoclastic vision toward the subject.

The first step toward narrative discovery in creating *2001* was in Kubrick's choice of collaborator and the manner in which they arrived at a shooting script. Kubrick's strategy was to first work together with noted science fiction/science fact author Arthur C. Clarke, a man internationally recognized as one of the finest minds in the field, to write a novel loosely based on Clarke's short story "The Sentinel" and then to adapt the novel into a screenplay. This process allowed Kubrick to create an original screen story in which literary prose and thematic elements were invented for the purpose of translation to a film grammar that would result in a cinematic experience for the viewer rather than a literary plot-driven Hollywood movie story.

Of course even an experimental process is still only a process. Ideas propel innovation, and those developed for *2001* reflected philosophical thought, science, religiosity, man's relationship to the universe, and the

American officials survey a monolith that has been excavated on the moon. Stanley Kubrick's landmark science fiction film accomplished the director's career-long mission to "explode" the traditional cinematic narrative. Courtesy *Photofest.*

existence of extraterrestrial life. Reducing the application of dialogue to the bare minimum and creating a framework consisting of separate but thematically related segments, *2001* communicates through action, visual signs and symbols, and expressive visualization.

The main title shot introduces the alignment of the moon, earth, and sun in space directly centered in the frame. This image of order represents celestial power and the symmetry of the universe. "The Dawn of Man" sequence of *2001* does not contain a single word of dialogue or the presence of a human being. The time is the prehistoric era, land is untouched, wild animals roam the earth, and the ape is the descendant of humanity. This section discerns the story of man's nature. The behaviors of the apes demonstrate the primal instincts of the future inhabitants of planet earth: territorial imperative, survival of the fittest, the protection of shelter, acquisition of resources, the strength of leadership, defense of the homeland, expansion of empire, and the constitution of violence and reasoning. The apes discover a marker from a civilization of higher intelligence. This black monolith is aligned with the sun and moon now shown from the earth's point of view. The great ape Moonwatcher (Daniel Richter) makes an important discovery in a bone, which he first implements as a weapon, then victoriously throws into the air where it transitions in a single edit to a tool—a spacecraft traveling in outer space.

The segment continues in the year 2001 and now concerns itself with Dr. Heywood Floyd (William Sylvester), who takes flights to a space station and then to Clavius, a region of the moon. Once there he boards a hover craft to an excavation where the United States has discovered a black monolith that emits a powerful, recordable energy that was deliberately buried four million years ago. When Floyd and his team inspect the momentous find, it emits a deafening high pitch and is shown from the perspective of the moon in its alignment with the sun and earth. The beings responsible for the markers link the sun and the moon, which serve the earth with light and life.

Eighteen months later, Astronauts Dave Bowman (Keir Dullea) and Frank Poole (Gary Lockwood) are traveling to Jupiter on the Discovery spacecraft. Three members of the crew are in hibernation until they reach their destination. Hal, a supercomputer (the voice of Douglas Rain), is fully responsible and in control of all on-board operations. After Hal openly becomes concerned with the mysterious mission, the computer uncovers an upcoming malfunction in one of the units. When it is determined by mission control that Hal is in error, Bowman and Poole try to discuss the situation in private but the all-seeing machine reads their lips to learn of his possible disconnection. Hal terminates the lives of Poole and the three astronauts in hibernation. After a battle of wits and wills, Bowman is able to regain command of the Discovery by, in effect, putting Hal to death. With his last surge of energy, Hal triggers a videotaped message from Dr. Floyd that was to be played when the entire crew was revived and ready to receive their mission assignment. Floyd reveals that the first sign of intelligent life outside of the Earth had been discovered on the moon. The origin and purpose of the monolith is a total mystery. The object is inert but emits a strong signal aimed at Jupiter.

In the next segment, a monolith moves through space and is part of an alignment of the sun, earth, moon, and Jupiter viewed from outer space. Bowman sets out in a space pod. The monolith disappears from its position in the galactic order and Bowman is propelled through a star gate into another universe. He lands in a Victorian room that is historically accurate except for a futuristic floor composed of large white illuminated squares. Bowman looks on as he ages toward death and then, through the presence and force of a monolith at his bedside, is reborn as a star child and takes his place in the cosmos.

2001 offers limited narrative facts and clues to its meaning, and many of the principal ones are open to interpretation. The film was conceived and designed to be a cinematic odyssey—"The Ultimate Trip" as the ad campaign heralded. Enjoyment and understanding of Kubrick's *2001* is attained by relying on the senses of sight and sound and less on the heart and mind. Movies activate our unconscious state of mind, so the deeper the viewers can allow this transformation to penetrate their imagination, curiosity, and spiritual life, the more satisfying and enjoyable this journey will be.

Narrative conditioning dies hard and many of what one would perceive as plot points are deliberately obscured in the film but clarified in Clarke's short story and the resultant novel. Kubrick intended audiences to search for their own meaning to the film, and he put his faith in the emerging visual grammar and cerebral explorations of the 1960s to reinvent the language of the feature film.

At its fundamental level, the monolith is a marker left by an intelligent civilization to announce its presence. It has the power to attract, influence, and communicate. The monolith can also be surmised as God, a supreme being, or higher power. Hal has been programmed to communicate with humans and to give the appearance of possessing emotions, but can he think on his own and what motivates his extreme behavior? It is established in the film's text that he had demonstrated pride. His words, inflections, and actions reveal egotistical pride toward his abilities, then paranoia and vengeance when he perceives a threat. He demonstrates sensitivity and care toward Bowman and Poole but will do anything to protect the secret that only he knows and Bowman learns after he shuts down Hal's digital brain and nervous system. What does Hal know about the origin and purpose of the marker? Is it fear or foreknowledge that influences his actions toward the men and mission? Why is it so important to Hal that he be in control of the ship until the mission is completed? Bowman enters another universe and lands in what appears to him to be a Victorian environment, but he knows because of the modernistic floor that this is not the case. In the novel Bowman arrives in what he recognizes as a hotel room, but when he examines it closely he finds a bible with scribble, not real text. It is explained that the extraterrestrials have envisaged this for Bowman to make him feel comfortable in their world. The viewer is left with an obtuse context and only the monolith as a sign or symbol of a higher life form. These are just some of the mysteries of *2001* presented to the intrepid members of the audience who tour Kubrick's brave new world of cinematic exploration.

2001 does create detailed believable environments that allow for immersion into the veracity of place and the totality of experience. Kubrick was disappointed with the results of all previous visual effects. The limitations of standard techniques inspired him to vastly improve available technology and in many cases to invent new cinematic tools and methods through the brilliance of his four special photographic supervisors: Wally Veevers (*The Guns of Navarone, Dr. Strangelove, Superman*), Douglas Trumbull (*Close Encounters of the Third Kind, Star Trek: The Motion Picture, Blade Runner*), Con Pederson (*Impostor* [2002], *Gods and Generals, Scooby Doo 2: Monsters Unleashed*), and Tom Howard (*Village of the Damned* [1960], *The Haunting* [1963], *Where Eagles Dare*).

Traditionally backgrounds were created by **rear-screen projection**, but the results lacked sharpness and increased the film grain pattern. Kubrick tested and then moved ahead with front-screen projection, a more complex and experimental technique that produced a more decisive image that could not be detected from the foreground. Kubrick even used this process to project what looked like computer graphic monitors in the spacecrafts and for visual elements within the architecture of the ships as well as the landscape for "The Dawn of Man."

Models animated by **stop-motion photography** had previously been employed in science fiction films but never as realistically detailed and graceful in flight as the magnificent spacecrafts in *2001*. Corporate, aeronautic, and engineering firms were consulted for input into the futuristic designs, which were then created and built by the art department headed by production designers Tony Masters (*Papillion; Buffalo Bill and the Indians, or Sitting Bull's History Lesson; Dune*), Harry Lange (*The Dark Crystal, Monty Python's The Meaning of Life, The Great Muppet Caper*), and Ernest Archer (*Nicholas and Alexandra, Superman, The Pirates of Penzance*). The interior of the Discovery was built in an actual centrifuge so that the illusion of Poole jogging inside the circumference could be achieved along with other feats of defying gravity. The star gate visions were created through Trumbull's Slit-Scan machine, which allowed graphic materials to be photographed through a gateless camera, creating abstract streaks of color to flow, ribbon, and race through space. Printing color records out of their correct match converted American landscapes into topography from another world.

The visualization achieved by Kubrick, cinematographers Geoffrey Unsworth (*Cabaret, Murder on the Orient Express, A Bridge Too Far*), John

Alcott (*Barry Lyndon; The Shining; Greystoke: The Legend of Tarzan, Lord of the Apes*), and the entire art and visual effects departments made it possible for the meditative aspects of the narrative (some would say **non-narrative**) to transport viewers into an unprecedented experience of the senses that allows them to enter the world and mind-space of the film. The critical point here is that *2001: A Space Odyssey* is not about space travel—it is space travel. This notion has been attested by real astronauts who have seen the film and by the millions who go along for the ride once they leave behind the resistant baggage of what a story and a film should or should not be.

This innovative benchmark film comes largely from the mind and vision of Stanley Kubrick, but no work of art comes out of a vacuum. The pristine, centered compositional style evolved from Kubrick's previous six feature films, as did the analytical point of view toward the various subjects he investigated. For a filmmaker who is often categorized as cold and detached, Kubrick was able to arouse the passions of the intellect, body, and spirit. The only director to have made a major stylistic impact on Kubrick was Max Ophüls (*La Ronde* [see chapter 38], *Letter from an Unknown Woman, Lola Montès*), mostly for the use of camera movement. On *2001* there were three specific cinematic inspirations that led to aspects of Kubrick's approach to the project. *Universe*, a black-and-white short film produced for the Canadian Film Board, astonished Kubrick with its depiction of heavenly imagery and pointed to possible technical solutions unavailable from the Hollywood school. The work of experimental filmmaker Jordan Belson, a West Coast Zen master and cinematic abstractionist, is reflected in the "Star Gate" sequence. Belson is acclaimed for his use of the optical printer to conjure up spiritual images of a cosmic origin. John Whitney, the pioneer of computer graphics on film, opened up a panorama of possibilities concerning consciousness-expanding visions that led Kubrick out of the conventional box of cinema-think.

2001 has made such an impression on film culture that Richard Strauss's majestic *Thus Spake Zarathustra*, composed in 1896, is commonly known as the *2001* theme. The concept of marrying music from the past with the visions of the future is one of the film's grand accomplishments. Kubrick understood that context was everything. The old-world grace of the *Blue Danube* waltz humanized space flight and turned science into pure poetry. Stanley Kubrick may have set out to just make "a really good sci-fi movie," but *2001: A Space Odyssey* is so much more than that. Stanley Kubrick did not live to see the first year of the new millennium, but that is okay—he had already filmed it for posterity.

Of Further Interest

Screen

Baraka
Koyannisqatsi
Nagoyqatsi
Powaqqatsi
Privilege (1990)

Read

The Making of Kubrick's 2001, edited by Jerome Agel
2001: Filming the Future by Piers Bizony
Kubrick's Cinema Odyssey by Michel Chion
Moonwatcher's Memoir: A Diary of 2001: A Space Odyssey by Dan Richter
The Making of 2001: A Space Odyssey, edited by Martin Scorsese, selected by Stephanie Schwam

The Essay Film

□ ◆ □ ◆ □ ◆ □

Weekend

> *es•say*: an analytic or interpretive literary composition usually dealing with its subject from a limited or personal point of view

Jean-Luc Godard is an essayist in the medium of cinema. Godard is a complex, movie-mad filmmaker who, like Pablo Picasso and Miles Davis, moved through specific artistic periods addressing concerns of the time. Godard was an essential part of the French New Wave, an auteurist (see **auteur theory** in glossary) film critic, and an independent creator who always went his own way.

Godard's undying love of cinema tradition and fervid political passions merge in his prolific body of work. *Weekend* (1967) was created at a time when Godard was about to break with commercial cinema. By the early 1970s, the French maverick had made a series of highly didactic films for the Dziga Vertov collective that dealt in content and aesthetics with Mao Tse-tung, Communism, and the evils of capitalism. *Weekend* (1968), one of Godard's most celebrated works, took mainstream international cinema as far as it could go before evolving into other more experimental forms.

The essay film has been practiced by few—most notably, Chris Marker (*La Jetée, Le Joli Mai, Sans Soleil*) and Ross McElwee (*Sherman's March, Time Indefinite, Bright Leaves*). Godard designed *Weekend* as a cinema essay with an intricate structure that is distinctively his own. The subjects for Godard's *Weekend* essay are all within a political context. The corruption

Radicals tote guns and play rock and roll in the woods during Jean-Luc Godard's *Weekend*, an essay on the corruption of the bourgeoisie, destruction, class decay, revolution, and the end of cinema. Courtesy *Photofest*.

caused by the bourgeoisie is illustrated in consecutive episodes identified by title cards. The plot, as it is, concerns Corrine (Mireille) and Roland (Jean Yanne), a married couple with plans to drive to Olinville to kill her father to get his money. The greedy get greedier. Their plans are immediately and permanently altered as soon as they get into their car. Corrine and Roland encounter a massive traffic jam, countless overturned and burning wrecks, class struggles, endless detours, the power of sex, the abuse of sex, unspeakable violence, and the loss of control over their lives as they slowly hitchhike their way to their destination. The automobile is a symbol of destruction and class decay. When Corrine and Roland finally arrive, her father is already dead (possibly due to the couple's long practice of poisoning him), and they murder her mother, become rich, and while returning home are captured by working-class revolutionaries who slaughter Roland and feast on him. This cannibalism is accepted by his wife, who in the closing seconds of the film informs the chef, who wears a bloody apron, that she will have more later.

But *Weekend* is not a mystery or a thriller film as intimated in the opening scenes. It is a philosophical essay on America's abuse of power and the diseased global spread of capitalism. Godard articulates his themes with tour-de-force long takes, monologues, and sequences that stand alone while amassing a cohesive statement about the modern world as seen from a radical viewpoint in the late 1960s. A structural device that informs the content is the extensive use of graphic full-screen cards with titles that express the sequence, often flashing and reconfiguring the words and their meaning.

Weekend is filled with references to history, politics, literature, and the cinema. The celebration of movies inherent in these references, common for a Godard film, pays off in the film's most surprising declaration. Godard's real shocker is not the final image of Corrine eating human flesh off the bone—it is the concluding card that announces "The End." Throughout *Weekend* Godard shuffles the words in title cards so that the meaning changes and comments on the events of the film. When the word manipulation finalizes "The End," it becomes "The End of Cinema." Godard waited until the last moment to announce that cinema as we knew it was over. Most thought it was just another Godardian stunt, but *Weekend* is audacious in demonstrating the limits of traditional narrative and aesthetic tools to articulate radical statements.

Godard's bold application of technique supports his personal views concerning the corrosion of modern society. His masterly use of long takes (also known as **mise-en-scène** or **plan sequence**) is more Brechtian than related to the masterly form of Max Ophüls and Jean Renoir (see chapters 38 and 39).[1] Godard makes the audience aware of the camera choreography to celebrate cinematic language in a didactic manner. A slow 360-degree pan switches direction. The famous **tracking shot** of the giant traffic jam demonstrates that camera movement can witness and interpret an event while providing an experiential cinematic vehicle for the viewer to become a participant and observer. The camera moves along its way, slowing up, speeding up, and even stopping to capture the action as it unfolds. The shot runs almost seven minutes and is interrupted once by a title card. After countless arguments and witnessing anger and death with indifference, the car carrying Corrine and Roland through the seemingly endless traffic jam finally gets to the end and they speed by. After traveling along the road parallel to the action for so long, the camera pans to follow them as they drive off to the right through a field, away from the apocalyptic main road of French and American life.

Characters address the camera directly, but it is not always their voices we hear but those of other characters in the scene. In this manner Godard was able to get in the rhetoric of many radical points of view, usually supporting the workers over the oppressors, so that the audience could listen to the words while confronted by another character looking right at them to make sure they were listening.

The color scheme of *Weekend* is as controlled as Dick Sylbert's Oscar-winning production design consisting of primary colors for Warren Beatty's *Dick Tracy*. The **color palette** here is limited to red, yellow, blue, and green. Red is the color of revolution, Mao, and blood. The blood in this film looks deliberately fake and is poured onto actors and locations to symbolize the blood spilled by capitalists and revolutionaries. The artifice is part of a continual effort to remind viewers they are watching a movie. We never see a camera, but characters refer to the cinema in general or to the movie that we are watching. Red, white, and blue are emphasized to evoke the flags of France and America, two countries that contain young radicals trying to undermine the capitalist credo. Green represents the earth. Sequences take place outside the city in the countryside where there is always a road, a sign of modern life. Green is also carried over into the dress of the revolutionary characters to link them to the purity of the environment.

Godard comments on the use of **score** in classical Hollywood cinema by positioning the music cues written by Antoine Duhumel (*Stolen Kisses, Belle Époque, Ridicule*) so that they are not invisible but deliberately intrusive. A traditional dramatic musical theme is employed in the scene when the woman is interrogated about a forced sexual encounter, but the music cue starts abruptly and concludes in what seems like random positioning. If that is not enough to call attention to a cinematic element, the music is mixed to rise so loudly, it competes with the audibility of her voice.

Theatrical and literary devices are brazenly applied to Godard's mise-en-scène. Characters portraying Emily Brontë (Blandine Jeanson), Tom Thumb (Yves Afonso) and Saint-Just (Jean-Pierre Léaud) walk into scenes in period costume while proselytizing social and political views. Godard's staging nods to the Theaters of the Absurd and Revolt.[2] When Corrine's mother is murdered, a close-up of an animal's head fills the screen as quarts of stage blood are poured over it. Corrine and Roland keep going on their road trek by taking turns carrying the other in piggyback fashion as the laborer counts to a proscribed number signaling the switch. As a ploy to stop cars for a ride, Roland encourages Corrine to lie on the road with her legs spread open in the direction of the oncoming traffic. These theatrical strategies draw attention to the heightened polemics Godard is espousing. For example, Corrine is obsessed with finding designer clothes on dead accident victims. The couple's embrace of capitalist ideals is stretched to absurd lengths to expose the hypocrisy.

Throughout *Weekend* Godard shocks and surprises. The revolutionary camp is out in the woods. The serenity of the natural environment is shattered by guns and gunfire, by the bloody, wide, and long sword of the butcher/cook, and by one of the radical army members playing a loud rock beat on a full drum kit in the middle of a field.

There are so many cultural, artistic, and political references in *Weekend*, the film could come with end notes to inform the viewer. There are several nods to **film noir** and American crime films, many cued by the music and the plot strand concerning the murder of Corrine's father. Names of prominent fashion designers are used to satirize the bourgeoisie fixation with style. A boy with an Indian headdress and his shotgun-toting father comment on the American tendency toward violence and the sad plight of the Native American. A prominent Shell Oil sign refers to the power of the industrial complex. There are references to the Luis Buñuel film *The Exterminating Angel*, surrealist founder André Breton, *The Count of Monte Cristo*'s Alexandre Dumas, *Alice in Wonderland*'s Lewis Carroll, and the symbol of Middle America's literary tastes, *Reader's Digest*. The numerous title cards become part of the film's structure, and the messages are sources of reference, allusion, and critical comment. Godard's politics are blatantly apparent in a scene in which a red car (a nod to Mao Tse-Tung's little red book) stops for the couple who is asked "Johnson or Mao?"[3] The reply is "Johnson." The car speeds off as one of them screams out "Fascist!" to Roland and Corrine. There are many cinematic references. The question is asked if Roland and Corrine are in a film or reality. Walkie-talkie communications are coded with film titles: "*Battleship Potemkin* calling *The Searchers*."

Godard makes strong pronouncements about art in *Weekend*. As the camera travels 360 degrees and then back in the direction where it started, a man plays a baby grand piano in the middle of a very small town. There is a tractor and middle-class workers listening to the man play Mozart, signifying it is music for the masses. He announces that they should not listen to modern music. At one point he criticizes his own playing and at another celebrates the genius of the composer with the logic of a Zen koan.

In its time, *Weekend* was a radical film. The content champions Communism and violence for political purpose and is a scathing indictment of materialism. The automobile, so prominent in the film, represents everything that is wrong with the capitalist system. Radical political text is not enough. Words alone would be rhetorical and turn everything into propaganda, not art. Godard is a radical filmmaker who applies a non-traditional aesthetic to his ideas. They cannot be separated. The artistic rigor employed by the camera, sound, movement, and composition are the prism through which the text—the essay—is filtered.

Weekend is a film that was made to please no one. Its rad politics were too extreme for the mainstream, the cinematic approach too "difficult" and code-ridden to satisfy the politicos. *Weekend* was not the end of Godard or the end of cinema, but for the director it marked the end of the narrative and cinematic conventions that Godard, the maverick of all mavericks, hated and loved. It was his pure romance with the medium that would drive him forward.

Notes

1. Bertold Brecht (1898–1956) was a poet and playwright whose stage work includes *Mother Courage and Her Children, Galileo, The Good Woman of Szechwan* and *The Caucasian Chalk Circle*. Brecht was opposed to the idea of Aristotelian drama in which the audience identified with the characters. He wanted the audience to think, not to feel. He created an epic theater designed with an "alienation effect"—techniques that encouraged audiences to remain in control of their critical faculties. Brecht achieved this sense of detachment in his theatrical work by applying techniques such as having the characters directly address the audience, a device widely applied in *Weekend*.

2. The Theater of the Absurd is a tendency developed in Paris, France, in the late 1940s through the early 1950s with the work of playwrights Samuel Beckett, Jean Genet, Eugene Ionesco, and Fernando Arrabal. The term is traced to existentialists Albert Camus and Jean Paul Sartre, who both believed that the only rational explanation of the universe was beyond humanity and must be viewed as absurd. The plays project bewilderment, anxiety, and wonder toward the world. Poetic metaphors represent the inner state of the mind. Fantasy, dreams, and nightmares are applied to the playwright's perception of reality.

The Theater of Revolt is a critical classification created by Robert Brustein in his book *The Theatre of Revolt: An Approach to Modern Drama*, which studies the work of playwrights Henrik Ibsen, August Strindberg, Anton Chekov, George Bernard Shaw, Bertolt Brecht, Luigi Pirandello, Eugene O'Neill, and Jean Genet. Brustein's thesis concerned the shift of Western drama from "theater of communion," which reinforces society's belief system, to a "theatre of revolt," in which social and political norms were critiqued and protested through drama.

3. Mao Tse-tung led China's communist revolution and served as chairman of the People's Republic of China from 1949–1959. His book *Quotations from Chairman Mao Tse-tung* expressed his Marxist–Leninist political beliefs. The little book with the red cover was widely read by campus and political radicals of the 1960s

and was often displayed or referred to either directly or symbolically in Godard's films of this period.

Of Further Interest

Screen

The Director and His Actor Look at Footage Showing Preparations for an Unmade Film
Fast, Cheap & Out of Control
A Personal Journey with Martin Scorsese through American Movies
Sans Soleil
Thirty Two Short Films about Glenn Gould

Read

Godard: A Portrait of the Artist at Seventy by Colin MacCabe
Godard on Godard, translation and commentary by Tom Milne
Godard by Richard Roud
Speaking about Godard by Kaja Silverman and Harun Farocki
The Films of Jean-Luc Godard: Seeing The Invisible by David Sterritt

49

Screen Violence as Metaphor

□ ◆ □ ◆ □ ◆ □

The Wild Bunch

The Wild Bunch was released in July of 1969 when the Vietnam War was raging. America was swept up in a social and political upheaval, and "sex, drugs, and rock & roll" was the mantra for the under-thirty generation. The American Western movie had ceased to dominate the country's imagination. Director Sam Peckinpah (1925–1984) was about to change the way we looked at movies.

The Wild Bunch challenged America's values and the very veracity of our history. This was accomplished by a film that was reviled for its content and action by the tastemakers of the time who placed a stigma on it and the director. A decade after Peckinpah's death, the times finally caught up with this brilliant maverick and *The Wild Bunch* was anointed a certified classic of U.S. cinema. It took revisionist film historians to look back and acknowledge a masterpiece of Western genre revisionism not fully appreciated in its time.

The narrative of *The Wild Bunch* is familiar. It is the story of a gang of desperados who rob a bank and are hunted down by a posse. On the run, they pull off one last score that leads to their total destruction in a climactic shoot-out. On the surface this seems a prototypical American Western, but Peckinpah turned the tables on all the conventions. A white or black hat or horse does not identify the morality of a character. The composition of the posse includes a former member of the Bunch and two vile, amoral men, and they are paid by a ruthless corporate agent. The majority of the Bunch are loyal men of honor who view society as cor-

Robert Ryan (left) as Deke Thornton, a former Bunch member now part of a posse, looks on after a massacre between the Bunch and the army of a Mexican general at the dead bodies of Pike Bishop (William Holden, with his hand on the machine gun) and Dutch Engstrom (Ernest Borgnine) at the conclusion of Sam Peckinpah's *The Wild Bunch*. For the maverick director the excessive screen violence was both a cathartic experience for the audience as well as an in-your-face reminder of man's violent nature. Courtesy *Photofest*.

rupt. The law serves the interests of the rich and powerful. The outlaws respect the unwritten code of the land and live off the wealth of the greedy. There are no clear-cut good guys or bad guys, so justice is not served at the conclusion. Peckinpah is a romantic but not in the manner demonstrated by the purveyors of the genre during the studio era. Behavior and values are not romanticized, but male bonding is, along with nostalgia for the unruly past.

Stylistic and aesthetic conventions are radically altered in *The Wild Bunch*. The opening and closing gunfights erupt suddenly on bright sunny days of pictorial beauty rather than in the murky clouded and stormy conditions of an artificial dramatic atmosphere. The generalized pristine architecture and costumes common to the genre are replaced with authentic, aged buildings. The materials are textured and weather-beaten. Clothes are dusty and torn, not tailored to fit. Peckinpah breaks axis (see

breaking axis in glossary) crossing the 180-degree line relied on to protect and distance the viewer from screen action. By shooting around and in the middle of a violent event, Peckinpah places viewers inside the action so they have a visceral experience and do not sit safely on the sidelines. During the gunfights, Peckinpah plays several lines of action at the same time. The result is choreographed chaos, not an organized sequence of events that follows a predictable pattern. Cameras shooting at various slow-motion frame rates were utilized to produce material that would continually alter time and space and emphasize the kinetic energy of violent action. Peckinpah did not sit on a noncommittal perspective. He constantly shifted the point of view from character to character to reveal individual sensibilities and allow the viewer to see through many eyes and emotional states. For Peckinpah, action, reaction and behavior, not windy exposition, were story. Dialogue is spare but full of insight into personality. A look or a pause is an intense emotional communication.

The use of explicit violence in *The Wild Bunch* was received with such revulsion that the film was initially given an X rating. Members of a preview audience in Kansas City ran out to the street retching. Hollywood had produced decades of bloodless Westerns, but Peckinpah showed the pain and destruction of absolute mayhem. The impact of a bullet in *The Wild Bunch* rips into the flesh and causes a body to spasm and contort as blood spurts from an often fatal wound. With anger and justification Peckinpah stated that he wanted to rub the noses of the public in the bloodshed of his film. He believed society was obliged to accept its nature and be accountable for all the savagery it committed out of avarice, domination, predilection, and human desires. Although there are no direct references to America's long and bloody involvement in Vietnam, *The Wild Bunch* was a metaphor in the forefront of Sam Peckinpah's intent, a fact he repeatedly stated in interviews. Peckinpah acknowledged and accepted the violence within him and believed the dramatic presentation of reprehensible events acted as a catharsis to cleanse the soul of its sins. Through staging and structure, carnage in *The Wild Bunch* is orchestrated as a ballet of death. We are horrified at the sight of the slaughter on the screen because we are forced to witness our human condition and face the realization that in destruction there is a fatal beauty.

The authority of the editing is the force that drives *The Wild Bunch.* Peckinpah was an American director influenced by the **montage** practices of Russian filmmakers Sergei Eisenstein (*Strike, The Battleship Potemkin* [see chapter 5], *Alexander Nevsky*), Vsevold Pudovkin (*Mother, Storm over Asia, Deserter*), and Alexander Dovzhenko (*Arsenal, Earth, Frontier*). Peckinpah visualized his scenes in units of action and content and shot them with as many as eight cameras running concurrently to cover the sweep and detail of his intent. Film editor Lou Lombardo (*McCabe and Mrs. Miller, The Long Goodbye, Moonstruck*), working on a Moviola without the corrective bubble that converted the squeezed widescreen image on the film to its proper shape (because it got in his way), cut a final total of 3,642 edits (a record number at the time) into the fabric of *The Wild Bunch.* Although the montage style developed by Peckinpah and Lombardo for *The Wild Bunch* was a radical departure for American film at the time, it became a major force in contemporary filmmaking and can be seen in the work of Martin Scorsese, John Woo, Oliver Stone, Walter Hill, and Quentin Tarantino and in action movies and music video inspired features such as *Flashdance* and *Top Gun*—they all owe a debt to Peckinpah and Lombardo.

The editing of *The Wild Bunch* accomplishes many significant objectives. In action sequences, it integrates slow motion, extensive **coverage**, and **points of view** into the presentation of several events happening simultaneously through intricate **crosscutting** techniques. Rather than compressing time and action, Peckinpah and Lombardo more often extend it. This technique emphasizes the massive damage done during human destruction as well as triggering a range of emotions and reactions in the viewer. By connecting the Bunch's verbal and nonverbal interactions, the editing probes their relationships to each other and to their ever-changing universe. **Intercutting** the posse's pursuit of the Bunch creates a sense of inevitability; the desperados are playing out their string to the very end. The corporate culture that takes over the country at the beginning of the American century will put an end to the individual's ability to roam free.

Men dominate the world of *The Wild Bunch.* Women are tormented and murdered by machismo aggression. They are representatives of a civilized minority or exist for man's carnal cravings. In this film the Mexican women betray the honor of men. True, complete, and faithful love is only shared and experienced by males—not a romantic love but an unequivocal bond. Pike Bishop (William Holden), the leader of the Bunch, shares this with two men. Dutch Engstrom (Ernest Borgnine) is a longtime member who is loyal to the end. He respects, understands, supports, and counsels Pike, who knows he can count on him even when he shouts, "C'mon you lazy bastards." A more complex relationship connects Pike and Deke Thornton (Robert Ryan), who is pressured to hunt down and capture the Bunch to escape a prison sentence. Pike and Deke once ran together. Although they are now apart and on what society defines as different sides of the law, they accept each other for who they are and have been in the past. Each knows how the other man thinks and what he will and will not do. They both mourn a time when they were allowed to be free without federal rule.

Loss of independence and an elegy for the past is a recurring theme of *The Wild Bunch*. The Bunch represents a fading America of open spaces without boundaries, where a man could live by an unspoken law. Political, military, and corporate power embodied in Generalissmo Mapache (Emilio Fernandez) and Harrigan (Albert Dekker) threatens this way of life and signifies a future of repression and classism. The Bunch expresses longing in word and deed, and in the toll the present has taken on the body and mind. Flashbacks show past events and the memory sense that never leaves the men. These recollections are triggered during action or dialogue that reminds them of the way their lives once were. These scenes serve as backstory. They occur while we hear the voices and sounds of the present and are visually transitioned by long overlapping **dissolves** that for a time superimpose (see **superimposition** in glossary) the two time frames; they serve to reflect held memories. Some of these moments are wistful while others are full of regret.

The men ride horses and wear cowboy attire but are surrounded by symbols of an industrialized nation. The car threatens man's relationship to the horse and to the open plains. Mapache uses his ornate red automobile, a sign of affluence, to drag and torture Angel (Jamie Sanchez), a Mexican member of the Bunch. The train is a vehicle to transport goods, but it also is defended by the military and owned by the corporate enemy of the drifters. World War I is referenced, as is the existence of the airplane. The machine gun represents a mechanization that makes widespread warfare possible. The power of this weapon is linked to an unleashed expression of manhood and is ultimately responsible for the demise of the Bunch.

Mexico is a microcosm of the evolving landscape and culture of America. The traditional life is preserved but under constant threat. Life is leisurely, full of laughter and physical pleasures. The society is at war with itself. The power of the people is being taken away by regimes crazed by self-interest. To the Bunch, Mexico is the last outpost where men can live and die by their own hand. Now national, international, and internal powers vie for jurisdiction and rule.

The most forceful argument supporting Peckinpah's argument that man is born with violent attributes is illustrated in the way children are portrayed in *The Wild Bunch*. The gun battle that introduces the film is bookended by a group of young boys and girls at the edge of town who watch and play with glee as a deadly scorpion is devoured by hundreds of ants. They torture and destroy the insects with sticks and fire as a forceful metaphor that we are all born with the capacity to harm. Children in the midst of disorder are ambivalent about the shooting all around them. Children follow Angel as he is dragged through the street by Mapache's car as if they are chasing an ice cream wagon. For all of its polemic and didactic purpose, *The Wild Bunch* manages to entertain by presenting colorful characters, dramatic tension and release, as well as several breathtaking action set pieces. There is a classic train robbery pushed to extremes by involving the Bunch, the posse, and the military in a humorous and thrilling chase. Later the dynamiting of a bridge is a spectacle that sends the posse on their horses into a treacherous river below.

The end of *The Wild Bunch* comes full circle. Although the gang's nucleus is dead, Thornton sits outside as the bodies are carried off by the posse. Freddie Sykes (Edmond O'Brien), an old mule-skinner who helped the Bunch with their business, rides in with some members of Angel's village. They go off and form a new Bunch. The faces of the departed Bunch laugh with them in spirit, dissolving in and out while the reorganized gang vows to continue as long as they can in their vanishing universe. Their image freezes then and recedes into the background until it transforms into the words "The End." The background is a soft-focus leafy cosmos where the Wild Bunch can take their place.

Peckinpah drew inspiration from the bible, Shakespeare, and John Ford to create *The Wild Bunch*. He took the sanitized histories of Western film and replaced them with life as he understood it, both in the past and present. They say all art is autobiographical and film directors identify with their characters. The truth of this statement is revealed in the opening credits when Pike, who is the director's on-screen persona, says, "If they move . . . kill 'em!" The color image turns to black and white and freezes as it heralds, "Directed by Sam Peckinpah."

Of Further Interest

Screen

A Clockwork Orange
Natural Born Killers
Pat Garrett and Billy the Kid
Salo
Straw Dogs

Read

Bloody Sam: The Life and Films of Sam Peckinpah by Marshall Fine
Violent Screen: A Critic's 13 Years on the Frontlines of Movie Mayhem by Stephen Hunter
Sam Peckinpah's The Wild Bunch, edited by Stephen Prince
Peckinpah: A Portrait in Montage by Garner Simmons
"If They Move . . . Kill 'Em!": The Life and Times of Sam Peckinpah by David Weddle

Independent Filmmaking

□ ◆ □ ◆ □ ◆ □

A Woman Under the Influence

John Cassavetes (1929–1989) was a filmmaker so ahead of his time when he created his first groundbreaking film *Shadows* in 1958 that audiences and critics did not understand he was forging a new independent American cinema. Independent filmmaking in its most pristine definition is a cinema separate from Hollywood commercialism and factory-made movies. The budgets are low; the content explores narrative roads less traveled; the director or filmmaker is in total control, and the film represents his or her vision. After *sex, lies, and videotape* became a global phenomenon in 1989, the nature of the independent film movement evolved. Although many filmmakers considered to be indies were independent in spirit and method, the independent film eventually became more of a genre, extolling elements of the pure form but applying the old-money underwriting and marketing methods.

John Cassavetes created films that were independent of the methods, content, conventions, and aesthetics of the classical Hollywood studio system. He took the well-made studio film and tore its form apart bit by bit. Starting from zero, influenced by documentaries and the New York school of filmmaking, John Cassavetes created a new aesthetic that he applied to an honest and direct look at life as he saw it really was. Cassavetes considered all his films as embracing one theme: love. They are not romantic films but in-depth investigations of how humans seek, find, lose, destroy, and enjoy love in all its messy facets.

A Woman Under the Influence (1974) is one of Cassevetes's finest achieve-

Gena Rowlands and Peter Falk as Mabel and Nick Longhetti in the John Cassavetes film *A Woman Under the Influence*. Cassavetes, considered to be the father of the independent film movement, had one narrative theme—love. His cinematic approach was to defy and destroy all the conventions of traditional Hollywood moviemaking. Courtesy *Photofest*.

ments. Nick (Peter Falk) and Mabel (Gena Rowlands) Longhetti have three children and live in a California suburb. Nick is a laborer in public works construction; Mabel, a stay-at-home mom. When a city emergency keeps Nick from a promise of a night alone with his wife, Mabel begins to unravel emotionally. With the children at her mother's and anxieties over her roles as wife and mother whelming within her, Mabel heads out to a bar, gets drunk, and wakes up the next day in her bed with a strange man in the house. Mabel's behavior continues to spiral out of control. She is disoriented, acts inappropriately when Nick and his crew arrive for a spaghetti breakfast, and loses control over a child's birthday party during which the kids run around the house in various states of undress. Nick, pressured by his demanding mother, decides to institutionalize his wife when his limited understanding of how to communicate with her leaves him frustrated, angry, and without choice.

Is Mabel Longhetti mentally ill or, as her family and friends put it, crazy or cuckoo? Her behavior, which began well before the inciting incident, seems unstable by most standards, but clearly she has the director's full support. It is when Mabel is forced into constricting gender and adult roles or is bombarded with extreme angry emotions from her husband and mother-in-law that she begins to decompensate. The people around her are loud, crude, and programmed into society's notion of proper behavior. Mabel's way of coping in this environment is to sing, dance, have fun, and to try to make a party out of every situation. Nick loves her. When he finally comes to terms with who Mabel really is, there is peace within the Longhetti household. Nick also has difficulty with the macho gender role and the restrictions of adult behavior legislated by society. His emotional range is limited and erratic but acceptable to those around him. His anger toward Mabel, and at times directed toward his family and friends, is fueled by frustration and embarrassment but remains within the acceptable definition of the adult male role. Mabel's childish exhibitions are unacceptable to all the adults. They all love her but can not tolerate her nonconformity.

In *A Woman Under the Influence*, the actions and behaviors of the characters are not dramatized by a traditional screenplay. There is little narrative sense of a plot and the events are not structured, so each element has a purpose and stays on screen just long enough for the audience to comprehend it. The method by which Cassavetes created a screenplay and then directed his actors in front of the camera has largely been misunderstood. *A Woman Under the Influence* and most of Cassavetes's later films were not wholly improvised while the camera rolled as is generally believed. A script was written with dialogue and action containing the basic story situation. This script went through an intensive rehearsal process during which the actors were encouraged to improvise dialogue, behavior, and action. This improvisation was recorded on audiotape. The tape was then transcribed word for word and fashioned into the shooting script used during production. The actors adhered to that written word. This is not improvisation but a work process in which discovery and experimentation became part of the final text used to create a film.

The acting method and style is also responsible for the emotionally honest results. The cast did not act in the manner of Hollywood studio films. There was no emphasis on proper elocution, "correct" line readings, and theatrical blocking. The actors, some professional, others not, were directed to be—to live in the situations in which their characters find themselves.

The script and acting procedures created a real life drama closer to cinéma vérité than a fictional film built out of traditional dramaturgy. The results are long, emotionally messy scenes played in what appears to be real time. The events are painful and exhausting to watch. The viewer, who has been acculturated by hundreds of movies to arguments, joy, crisis, and the natural course of feelings in a homogenized story and plot, can find *A Woman Under the Influence* tough going. Cassavetes puts viewers into the film emotionally so that they can experience the lives of the characters as if they were there. The audience is unprotected by editing, composition, art direction, or the craft tools normally used to project and interpret drama rather than to create a documentary-like confrontational experience.

Cassavetes's philosophy goes beyond story and acting. His earlier films, particularly *Shadows* and *Faces*, were shot in a handheld **cinéma vérité** camera style. The constant shake of the camera as well as countless moments in which the lens searches for its subject, shifting in and out of focus, was a radical departure for a fiction film. During the making of *A Woman Under the Influence*, Cassavetes was affiliated with the American Film Institute. Two of the conservatory's fellows, Caleb Deschanel (*The Black Stallion, The Natural, The Right Stuff*) and Fred Elmes (*Blue Velvet, Night on Earth, The Ice Storm*) were members of Cassavetes's cinematography team and later became A-list directors of photography. The compositions, camera positions, lens sizes, and lighting are applied in a straightforward manner devoid of Hollywood conventions such as angles that imply a dramatic suggestion, backlight that romanticizes an image, or **high-key** or **low-key lighting** to insinuate an atmosphere or mood onto the scene. The camera is often locked off. **Handheld camera** shots are reasonably steady and bring immediacy without a self-conscious wobble. The lighting reads as if it were natural light. The hard California light in exteriors or when it floods into the house is slightly overexposed and blown out, simulating the natural tendency of light in this region.

Cassavetes planned his **coverage** carefully. Many of his films, especially *Faces* and *Husbands*, have an overabundance of close-ups to get the viewer to look into the soul of his characters without possibility of escape. *A Woman Under the Influence* is a film in which the main character is judged on her interaction with the environment, so there are fewer close-ups and more medium and wide shots to capture the tension between Mabel and her world and the family and friends with whom she relates. Cassavetes also employed the strategy of having Mabel in a single shot and others who are judgmental or worried about her behavior in a separate shot. When intercut (see **intercutting** in glossary), Mabel's isolation and the family's anxieties toward her actions are contrasted in a manner that creates a palpable stress.

The editing by Tom Cornwell (*Husbands, The Killing of a Chinese Bookie, Opening Night*) preserves the real-time feeling and the extended time agony of this family dilemma. The sequence in which the family doctor arrives to assist Nick and his mother in committing Mabel to a mental institution by eventually giving her a sedative after all methods to "calm" her fail is one of the most agonizing and emotionally fatiguing in American film. Relationships and character development are allowed to progress with a minimum of editorial intervention. Often a shot plays on well past the time it seems needed to achieve its purpose until a gesture, expression, dialogue, or action brings a revelation that would have been disturbed by editorial compression or montage. Many times a character will just appear or turn away from the camera. Again, Cassavetes defies conventions and uses the power of body language or physical presence to resonate.

John Cassavetes did not believe in the artifice of production design. The Longhetti home is the Cassavetes household where the director and his muse, Gena Rowlands, lived and raised their children. The physicality and character of this real space is the reality Cassavetes and Rowlands lived in. The double doors that divide the space are used by the characters to hide, contain, shelter, and expose. The home looks like a working-class family residence. Hollywood décor was usually upscaled to glamorize the film, but it was a false notion. A family such as the Longhetti's would not have had an interior decorator. These are simple hard-working people who have created a family environment, a functional place to live and raise a family. The landscape where Nick and his crew are involved in heavy construction utilizing earthmovers in dangerous physical conditions was shot on location. The men and the action are naturalistic and not embellished for purposes of exploiting action for its own sake. When one of the workers takes a serious fall during an argument with Nick over Mabel's sanity, the scene is staged, photographed, and edited for its relevance to the emotional life and relationships of the characters. Nick feels enormous guilt that he caused serious injury to one of his workers, and the worker feels guilty that he involved himself in another man's personal business and is conflicted toward Mabel and her state of mind. Action is the result of emotional confrontation, not as an impetus to dramatize or to artificially move the story forward.

The formal qualities of *A Woman Under the Influence* reject the gloss and movie trickery in the films John Cassavetes grew up with and worked on as an actor as he was learning his craft and later earning money to support his independent filmmaking. *A Woman Under the Influence* has more in common with the qualities of the home movie. The natural color, grain pattern, exposure, and simple, artless approach to the frame trigger memory responses in the viewer's mind. We are watching life unfold, not a movie that manipulates reactions through overt cinematic means. This Kodachrome reality made it difficult at best for many to enter the world of a John Cassavetes film. With few exceptions, critics derided Cassavetes as an amateur, undisciplined, excessive, and pointless. Audiences had their problems with this unruly artist, but the truth in the content, performances, and aesthetic presentation moved many and influenced a generation of filmmakers who followed the Cassavetes credo of a cinema that embraced the entanglements of life.

The music by Bo Harwood (*Minnie and Moskowitz, Happy Birthday to Me, Love Streams*) utilizes Italian opera and songs sung on camera and as score. There is an extensive piano score performed and played on an upright piano that sounds like a nonprofessional musician playing from his heart. Often there is wordless singing. This approach contributes to ethnic and personal qualities of the characters and story while serving as an alternate means for providing movie music.

Gena Rowlands gives one of the most electrifying female performances in American film. Rowlands is emotionally raw, playing every thought and feeling with abandon and honesty. Her physical beauty, earthiness, vulnerability, childlike nature, and explosive anxieties are riveting to observe. Using gestures and body choreography to communicate when a flood of emotion blocks her speech, Rowlands projects a woman under the influence of a life that disallows the freedom to express herself.

Peter Falk gives his finest performance as a man who loves his wife but can not reject the rules imposed on him. Through his confusion and rage, he learns that the unconditional love he feels for his wife is pure and finds happiness by rejecting the judgmental forces pressuring him. Falk captures the sincerity of a decent man in conflict with his mother and concerned over what others think, but who ultimately trusts his own feelings. Peter Falk is forceful and tender and expresses the process of being lost and then found through Nick's chaotic life experience.

A Woman Under the Influence is not an entertainment film. Cassavetes's brave work is a venue to observe and learn about life one-on-one with the film in front of you. The old Hollywood dream factory packed up and left town. *A Woman Under the Influence* is a roadway where filmmakers and audiences travel not to escape but to seek. That process is not always pretty but is always worth the struggle.

Of Further Interest

Screen

Jazz on a Summer's Day
Little Fugitive
The Return of the Secaucus Seven
The Savage Eye
sex, lies, and videotape
Shadows

Read

American Dreaming: The Films of John Cassavetes and the American Experience by Raymond Carney
Cassavetes on Cassavetes, edited by Ray Carney
The Films of John Cassavetes: Pragmatism, Modernism, and the Movies by Ray Carney
John Cassavetes: Lifeworks by Tom Charity
Cinema of Outsiders: The Rise of American Independent Film by Emanuel Levy

GLOSSARY

anamorphic wide-screen format: Camera lens that squeezes the horizontal plane of an image to approximately half size so it can fit into the width of 35mm film. A deanamorphizing projection lens restores the image to full size on the screen.

anthropological film: Nonfiction form that joins anthropologists and filmmakers who utilize film and video to record the environmental, cultural, racial, and social aspects of human beings.

antihero: A sympathetic character who presents a social, moral, or political point of view indifferent to the world he or she inhabits. James Dean in *Rebel without a Cause,* Paul Newman in *Hud,* and Jack Nicholson in *Five Easy Pieces* all portray characters with the qualities associated with the antihero.

aspect ratio: A measurement of the camera film frame or the projected image, stated as ratio of horizontal to vertical. The most common ratios are 1.85:1 (normal wide-screen) and 2.35:1 (anamorphic).

aural perspective: The volume and tonal qualities of a sound in relation to its distance from the camera.

auteur theory: Theoretical concept formulated in the pages of *Cahier du Cinema* in the 1950s by French New Wave filmmakers and critics and later in the United States by Andrew Sarris in the magazine *Film Culture* and the *Village Voice.* The theory states that the film director is the author of a film.

avant-garde film: Early term used to describe the movement of filmmakers who rebelled against the Hollywood product in content, theme, style, and approach by creating films whose prime goal is art and not commercial narrative storytelling.

background plate: Film, video, digital or photographic slide with a still or moving image of a setting to be used as a background for rear- or front-screen projection.

backstory: Previous events that have occurred in the past of a character prior to the start of a film narrative.

blue-screen shot: Process whereby actors are photographed in front of a blue or green background so that a second image with a background and possibly other actors or created characters can be composited together in a laboratory or through digital means.

breaking axis: Any shot taken from the opposite side of the imaginary line running horizontally through a screen. Also called crossing the line, the 180-degree rule, or direct reverse.

canted angle: An unusual composition that expresses a unique point of view and personal interpretation. Also known as a **dutch angle.**

cinéma vérité: A documentary film form developed in France during the 1950s and 1960s that attempts to film life as it really is without cinematic manipulation or interference.

color palette: A series of related colors used by the production designer to create the mood and atmosphere of a film.

composite shot: When more than one visual element is combined to create an image at the laboratory stage or through manipulation by digital software.

compression: An editing technique that compresses an event into a shorter space of time than it would take in real time. Although the basis of most editing is to compress time, the editor can drastically alter real time when it is dramatically necessary for a scene.

coverage: Footage that duplicates or complements the master shot from a different angle or size, thus allowing the editor to make a match or move the film forward editorially.

crane: Device used to raise the camera and operator high above a scene while shooting. The movement of a camera crane is similar to a cherry picker. Many current cranes are operated remotely from a video console.

crosscutting: Editing technique whereby shots or scenes are cut together in alternate sequence to create a dramatic relationship. Also called ***intercutting.***

deep-focus photography: Style of cinematography that utilizes a depth of field so the fore, middle, and background are all in sharp focus.

desaturation: Process employed either before, during, or after shooting that drains color out of the image to a desired degree.

diegetic sound: Sounds that occur within the screen space.

digital postproduction: Process that includes editing picture and sound and visual effects utilizing computer software such as Photoshop, Maya, and After Effects and nonlinear platforms such as Avid, Final Cut Pro, and ProTools.

direct cinema: The American interpretation of ***cinéma vérité***, in which the camera is nonobjective and as invisible as possible in the manner of the French school but in which films are tightly structured during the editing process.

direct cut: An end-to-end cut without any optical or digital transitions.

dissolve: Optical process whereby one shot fades out as the next shot fades in.

docudrama: A staged recreation of a real event.

documentary: A nonfiction film dealing with facts that attempts to present reality as it is.

dramedy: A film narrative that employs elements of both comedy and drama.

dutch angle: An unusual composition that expresses a unique point of view and personal interpretation. Also known as a **canted angle**.

ethnographic film: The study and systematic recording of human cultures on film.

experimental film: Nonnarrative filmmaking created in opposition to the commercial nature of the Hollywood studio film. A term used in the 1960s and 1970s to identify individual, nontraditional filmmakers with artistic intentions often employing abstract concepts and techniques.

exposition: Establishing the principal story action and the general circumstances of the characters.

eye-line match: When the direction and angle of a character's gaze is staged and photographed by the camera so it will connect with same of another character in the previous or following shot.

fade in: Optical effect or digital transition in which an image appears from black or a solid color field.

fade out: Optical effect or digital transition in which an image disappears into black or a solid color field. Also known as a *fade to black*.

film noir: A Hollywood film style in the post-World War II era of the 1940s and early 1950s identified by French film critics. These black-and-white films took place in the criminal underworld. The characters were cynical and disillusioned. Most scenes took place at night and the atmosphere was doom-laden. The visual style of film noir, which translates literally to "black film," featured squalid settings and deep shadows.

filtration: The use of transparent colored glass or gelatin positioned in front of the lens or lighting instruments to reduce and control light.

flashback: A scene that takes place earlier in time than the one that precedes it.

flashforward: A scene that jumps ahead out of relation to the time frame that has been established.

focal length: Distance from the optical center of a lens to where it brings an object at an infinite distance into critical focus.

forced perspective: Technique used to create depth by foreshortening the background.

freeze frame: A single frame of a motion picture image repeated for a desired length of time.

genre: The organization of films according to type. The musical, crime, Western, action, film noir, and science fiction film are all examples of genres.

glass shot: Special effects technique in which photographs or a painted scene are on a sheet of glass. When the camera shoots through the glass, the images are added to the action in the background.

guerrilla filmmaking: Low-budget, independent films made quickly without permits for locations, a union crew, or elaborate equipment. Filmmaking on the fly, on the cheap, a bare-bones production.

handheld camera: Technique in which the camera is held and operated by the operator without a tripod or dolly.

high-key lighting: An even application of bright light with little or no shadows.

insert: A short shot, usually filmed separately and cut into a scene. An insert can be a shot of a clock, a newspaper headline, or a detail that helps to explain the action or meaning of a scene.

intercutting: Editing technique whereby shots or scenes are cut together in alternate sequence to create a dramatic relationship. Also called ***crosscutting***.

interscene editing: The cuts or edits taking place within a scene.

inter-titles: Text inserted into the body of a film. Utilized in silent films to present dialogue and background information and to establish time and place. In sound films inter-titles provide information or comment on the content of the film.

iris shot: A shot associated with silent filmmaking that is masked, most often in a circular shape, to open or close a scene by expanding or decreasing the image shape to or from full screen, to bring attention to a character or object, or to contrast the context between the isolated image and the full-screen space.

Italian neorealism: A post-War World II film movement active in Italy from 1944 through 1953 with a moral and stylistic commitment to realism.

jump cut: A jump in action caused by removing part of a continuous shot or by joining two shots that do not match in continuity.

light source: Origin of light. A natural light source is the sun; practical light sources are provided by on-screen lamps or bulbs. The moon is a natural light source at night, and a streetlamp is a practical source. Film lighting is based on the nature and direction of the sources. Lighting instruments are positioned to justify and create the proper mood based on the source of light.

linear storytelling: A narrative that utilizes a consecutive time line without flashbacks or flashforwards.

locked-off camera: A camera that is secured in position and composition after a shot is completed. Cameras are often locked off so that another shot with different action can be photographed and later edited together with the former shot to give the illusion of a continuous take. Any shot without camera or lens movement can also be referred to as being locked off.

low-key lighting: Film lighting that achieves a dark scale with a low level of illumination, where shadows are prevalent and pools of bright light emphasize the contrast with the overall darkness.

master shot: Continuous shot that includes the entire action of a scene.

match-back: Process in which a final version of a motion picture photographed on film and edited on a nonlinear computer system is matched to the original film negative to produce a release print.

match cut: Two shots that link or match a related action.

material: Term that refers to the film or videotape available in a raw unedited state for postproduction of a motion picture.

matte painting: A background image painted on glass or on a board or made into a photographic slide, combined with a foreground shot to create a composite image.

miniature: An identical but small-scale model of a set, object, or location.

mise-en-scène: French theater term applied to a film director's use of composition, staging, movement, design, costumes, and lighting as an expressive narrative and stylistic tool.

montage: The French word for editing. The early Russian cinema style in which a collision effect was achieved between shots designed for their graphic, narrative, social, and political purpose. In the classical Hollywood studio model, a series of shots that established the passage of time or compressed an action or event. A contemporary filmmaking style that employs a multitude of individual shot details as the main communication source of storytelling.

morphing: Digital technique in which two or more images are blended together to create a new or interpolated result over a period of screen time.

multiple exposure: When the same section of a film negative is exposed more than twice to superimpose a series of images into one shot.

mythopoetic film: A critical classification termed by avant-garde film historian P. Adams Sitney for films that present the ventures of gods, heroes, organic elements, and animals as they impact the order of the universe through a visual language that governs the filmmaker's expression of thematic content.

narration: Words spoken by an off-screen voice, either an unidentified speaker or one of the characters in a film. Theorists have classified the text of a narrator as being reliable or unreliable as part of a narrative strategy.

narrative conventions: A device, principle, procedure, or form generally accepted between the filmmaker and the viewer. The happy ending, killing off an evil character, and the guy-gets-the-girl were all part of the classical Hollywood studio system mode of storytelling.

negative: Photographic element exposed during the shooting of a motion picture and used to make dupe negatives and positive film prints.

neonoir: A **film noir** created after the classic post-World War II period, often in color and often set in a unidentified contemporary time and place.

nondiegetic sound: Sounds that do not originate or occur within the screen space.

nonfiction film: A film that presents actual, not fictional, situations and people.

nonlinear storytelling: A narrative that does not follow a consecutive time line and moves forward and back in time, place, action, and events.

nonnarrative film: Term used to describe an experimental film that has no discernible story or plot, often employing abstract or nonfigurative images.

off-screen: Action that takes place outside the camera frame.

optical: Any editorial device such as a dissolve, wipe, or fade, or a visual effect achieved on film through the use of a photographic optical printer. When produced digitally, these cinematic elements are termed transitions.

optical printer: A system in which images are projected onto raw stock so that each frame can be rephotographed to produce editing transitions or visual effects.

overlap: The sound of an outgoing shot extended into the incoming shot.

over-the-shoulder shot: A shot in which the camera shoots past the back of the head and shoulder of a character on the left or right side of the frame to the person the character is seeing.

parallel storytelling: When two or more story lines occurring at the same time are presented alternately to show simultaneous and related actions.

persistence of vision: The ability of the human eye to retain an image on the retina for a brief moment after it disappears, which fills in the gap caused by the projection of successive images. The result is a continuity of the visual experience of motion pictures.

plan sequence: A sequence choreographed, staged, photographed, and presented in a long single take without interscene editing.

point of view: Also known as *POV*. When the camera visually presents what a character is seeing through his or her eyes and perspective.

practical lamps: Any on-screen lighting instrument such as a lamp or ceiling fixture that actually operates.

pretitle sequence: A sequence that occurs before the main titles appear. A pretitle sequence may begin the narrative, present the past or future, or serve the purpose of engaging the viewer's attention with a segment unrelated to the principal story.

process shot: A shot in which a foreground action is played live in front of a background image that is rear-screen projected. Also known as **rear-screen projection**.

production sound: The sound track recorded by the production sound mixer during the shooting of the film.

propaganda film: A film that proselytizes a political, personal, or social point of view with the sole intent of convincing the audience of its thesis.

rack focus: When the point of the camera's focus is deliberately shifted from one person or object to another. Used as a storytelling device to direct the viewer's attention.

ramping: Digitally increasing or decreasing the speed of a shot by utilizing a nonlinear computer editing platform such as Avid or Final Cut Pro.

rear-screen projection: A process that allows a background to be projected from behind a screen so that the actors can be photographed in front of it, placing them in the setting. Also known as a **process shot**.

retrofit: Technical addition to an existing structure.

reverse angle: A shot in a dialogue scene that is taken from the direct opposite angle of the previous one.

road movie: A genre that takes place during an automotive trip, which becomes a metaphor for the search to find soul and purpose, often ending in self-discovery, disappointment, and despair. Road moves embrace the mythic quest, the eternal search for identity and home that traces back to Homer's *The Odyssey* and Jack Kerouac's *On the Road.*

roadshow: A release strategy popular during the 1950s through the 1960s when a film was placed in select theaters in major cities at a higher ticket price and reserved seating.

scene in one: A scene presented in one shot without interscene editing.

score: Nondiegetic music created by a film composer that forms an aural, emotional atmosphere in the film by presenting thematic, dramatic, or expressive musical accompaniment.

shot–reverse shot: Technique utilized during a dialogue sequence in which the image of one character is countered with the image of the other character presented from the direct opposite angle. The result links the two shots together and allows the viewer to forget the presence of the camera.

single: A shot that contains one character.

source lighting: When all the lighting in a shot can be traced to a natural source, such as the sun or a lamp.

source music: Music that comes from a direct established source, such as a radio, musicians in the shot, or an on-screen sound system.

split screen: When the screen is divided into two or more separate fields that each present their own image.

stock footage: Pre-existing film, purchased from a stock footage library or archive. Also known as archival footage.

stop-motion photography: An animation technique by which images are exposed a frame at a time to create the illusion of movement by puppets, models, and inanimate objects.

storyboard: Drawings that depict the action of a scene, used to plan the shooting.

superimposition: When one or more images are layered on top of each other in a transparent fashion.

swish pan: A rapid panning of the camera that produces a quick, often blurred action, then settles on its point of destination.

sync-sound: When sound and picture run side by side in direct relationship to each other.

third-person angle: Objective camera position that represents the audience's point of view, not one of the characters in the film.

third-person narration: Objective narrative voice that does not represent the point of view of any of the characters in the film.

time cut: A cut between two shots, which represents a compression of the narrative timeline.

top shot: A camera angle from high above a scene, looking directly down. Also known as God's POV or bird's-eye view.

tracking shot: When the camera is mounted on tracks laid down on the set or location so that it can be moved forward, backward, right to left, or left to right.

visualist: A director or filmmaker who presents a cinematic narrative in expressive or interpretive visual terms by using the camera and design elements.

voice-over: A spoken voice that is not directly connected to any characters on screen. Narration can also be considered voice-over.

walla: A sound effect for the murmur of a crowd in the background.

wipe: An optical effect or digital transition in which one image wipes another image off the screen. Wipes can be made in almost any shape or direction.

zoom lens: A lens that produces a range of focal lengths, giving the ability to move from far to close or close to far within a shot, or to offer an array of frame sizes without moving the camera. Sometimes called a varifocal lens.

BIBLIOGRAPHY

Aberdeen, J. A. *Hollywood Renegades: The Society of Independent Motion Picture Producers*. Los Angeles: Cobblestone Entertainment, 2000.

Affron, Charles, and Mirella Jona Affron. *Sets in Motion: Art Direction and Film Narrative*. New Brunswick, NJ: Rutgers University Press, 1995.

Agel, Jerome, ed. *The Making of Kubrick's 2001*. New York: New American Library, 1970.

Albers, Josef. *The Elements of Color*. New Haven: Yale University Press, 1971.

Albrecht, Donald. *Designing Dreams: Modern Architecture in the Movies*. New York: Harper & Row in collaboration with the Museum of Modern Art, 1986.

Alexander, George. *Why We Make Movies: Black Filmmakers Talk about the Magic of Cinema*. New York: Harlem Moon Broadway Books, 2003.

Allon, Yoram, Del Cullen, and Hannah Patterson, eds. *The Wallflower Critical Guide to Contemporary North American Directors*. London: Wallflower, 2000.

Almendros, Nestor. *A Man with a Camera*. New York: Farrar, Straus & Giroux, 1984.

Altman, Rick, ed. *Sound Theory, Sound Practice*. New York: Routledge, 1992.

Alton, John. *Painting with Light*. Berkeley: University of California Press, 1995.

Amburn, Ellis. *The Sexiest Man Alive: A Biography of Warren Beatty*. New York: HarperCollins, 2002.

Anderson, Lindsay. *About John Ford*. New York: McGraw-Hill, 1983.

Antonioni, Michelangelo. *The Architecture of Vision: Writings and Interviews on Cinema*. Edited by Carlo di Carlo and Giogio Tinazzi. American edition edited by Marga Conttino-Jones. New York: Marsilio Publishers, 1996.

———. *That Bowling Alley on the Tiber: Tales of a Director*. New York: Oxford University Press, 1986.

Aranda, Francisco. *Luis Buñuel: A Critical Biography*. New York: Da Capo Press, 1976.

Armes, Roy. *Third World Film Making and the West*. Berkeley: University of California Press, 1987.

Arrowsmith, William. *Antonioni: The Poet of Image*. Edited with an introduction and notes by Ted Perry. New York: Oxford University Press, 1995.

Atkinson, Michael. *Blue Velvet*. London: BFI Publishing, 1997.

Auiler, Dan. *Hitchcock's Notebooks: An Authorized and Illustrated Look Inside the Creative Mind of Alfred Hitchcock*. New York: Avon, 1999.

Aumont, Jacques. *Montage Eisenstein*. Bloomington: Indiana University Press, 1987.

Baer, William, ed. *Elia Kazan: Interviews*. Jackson: University Press of Mississippi, 2000.

Balio, Tino. *Grand Design: Hollywood as a Modern Business Enterprise, 1930–1939*. Volume 5 of *History of the American Cinema*. Berkeley: University of California Press, 1996.

———. *United Artists: The Company That Changed the Film Industry*. Madison: University of Wisconsin Press, 1987.

Ball, Philip. *Bright Earth: Art and the Invention of Color*. Chicago: University of Chicago Press, 2003.

Barnouw, Erik. *Documentary: A History of the Non-Fiction Film*. New York: Oxford University Press. Second revised edition, 1993.

Barsam, Richard. *Looking at Movies: An Introduction to Film*. New York: W. W. Norton & Company, 2004.

———, ed. *Nonfiction Film: Theory and Criticism*. New York: Dutton, 1976.

Barson, Michael. *The Illustrated Who's Who of Hollywood Directors: The Studio System in the Sound Era*. New York: Noonday Press, 1995.

Batcher, Lutz. *Max Ophuls in the Hollywood Studios*. New Brunswick, NJ: Rutgers University Press, 1996.

Battcock, Gregory, ed. *The New American Cinema: A Critical Anthology*. New York: E. P. Dutton, 1967.

Bazelon, Irwin. *Knowing the Score: Notes on Film Music*. New York: Arco, 1975.

Bazin, André. *Jean Renoir*. New York: Dell, 1974.

Bazin, André, and Hugh Gray, eds. *What Is Cinema?* Vol. I. Berkeley: University of California Press, 1967.

———. *What Is Cinema?* Vol. II. Berkeley: University of California Press, 1971.

Beaver, Frank. *Dictionary of Film Terms: The Aesthetic Companion to Film Analysis*. Rev. and exp. ed. New York: Twayne Publishers, 1994.

Beckerman, Howard. *Animation: The Whole Story*. New York: Allworth Press, 2003.

Begleiter, Marcie. *From Word to Image: Storyboarding and the Filmmaking Process*. Studio City, CA: Michael Wiese Productions, 2001.

Behlmer, Rudy, ed. *Inside Warner Bros. (1935–1951)*. New York: Simon & Schuster, 1985.

———. *Memo from David O. Selznick*. New York: Viking Press, 1972.

Belton, John. *Widescreen Cinema*. Cambridge, MA: Harvard University Press, 1992.

Berg, Chuck, and Tom Erskine. *The Encyclopedia of Orson Welles*. With John C. Tibbetts and James M. Welsh, series eds. New York: Checkmark Books, 2003.

Bergan, Ronald. *Sergei Eisenstein: A Life in Conflict*. Woodstock, NY: Overlook Press, 1999.

Bergman, Ingmar. *Images: My Life in Film*. New York: Arcade Publishing, 1990.

———. *The Magic Lantern: An Autobiography by Ingmar Bergman*. London: Penguin Books, 1988.

Billups, Scott. *Digital Filmmaking*. Studio City, CA: Michael Wiese Productions, 2000.

Biskind, Peter. *Easy Riders, Raging Bulls: How the Sex-Drugs-and-Rock-'n'-Roll Generation Saved Hollywood*. New York: Simon & Schuster, 1998.

———. *Seeing Is Believing: How Hollywood Taught Us to Stop Worrying and Love the Fifties*. New York: Pantheon Books, 1983.

Bitzer, Billy. *Billy Bitzer; His Story*. New York: Farrar, Straus & Giroux, 1973.

Bizony, Piers. *2001: Filming the Future*. London: Aurum Press, 1994.

Björkman, Stig, Torsten Manns, and Jonas Sima. *Bergman on Bergman*. New York: Da Capo Press, 1993.

Blacker, Irwin R. *The Elements of Screenwriting: A Guide for Film and Television Writing*. New York: MacMillan, 1986.

Blesh, Rudi. *Keaton*. New York: Macmillan, 1966.

Block, Bruce. *The Visual Story: Seeing the Structure of Film, TV, and New Media*. Woburn, MA: Focal Press, 2001.

Bluestone, George. *Novels into Film: The Metamorphosis of Fiction into Cinema*. Berkeley: University of California Press, 1957.

Bogdanovich, Peter. *Who the Devil Made It*. New York: Knopf, 1997.

Bondanella, Peter. *Italian Cinema: From Neorealism to the Present*. New York: Frederick Ungar, 1984.

Boorman, John, and Walter Donohue. *Projections 4½ in Association with Positif: Film-makers on Film-making*. London: Faber and Faber, 1995.

———. *Projections 5: Film-makers on Film-making*. London: Faber and Faber, 1996.

———. *Projections 6: Film-makers on Film-making*. London: Faber and Faber, 1996.

———. *Projections 7 in Association with Cahiers du Cinema: Film-makers on Film-making*. London: Faber and Faber, 1997.

———. *Projections 8: Film-makers on Film-making*. London: Faber and Faber, 1998.

———. *Projections 9: French Film-makers on Film-making*. London: Faber and Faber, 1999.

Boorman, John, and Walter Donohue, eds. *Projections: A Forum for Film Makers*. London: Faber and Faber, 1992.

———. *Projections 2: A Forum for Film Makers*. London: Faber and Faber, 1993.

———. *Projections 3: Film-makers on Film-making*. London: Faber and Faber, 1994.

Boorman, John, Walter Donohue, and Fraser MacDonald, eds. *Projections 12: New York Film-makers on Film Schools*. London: Faber and Faber, 2002.

Boorman, John, Walter Donohue, and Mike Figgs, eds. *Projections 10: Hollywood Film-makers on Film-making*. London: Faber and Faber, 2000.

Boorman, John, Walter Donohue, and Tod Lippy, eds. *Projections 11: New York Film-makers on New York Film-making*. London: Faber and Faber, 2000.

Boorman, John, Walter Donohue, Tom Luddy, and David Thomson, eds. *Projections 4: Film-makers on Film-making*. London: Faber and Faber, 1995.

Boorstin, Jon. *The Hollywood Eye: What Makes Movies Work*. New York: Cornelia & Michael Bessie Books, 1990.

Bordwell, David. *The Films of Carl Theodor Dreyer*. Berkeley: University of California Press, 1981.

Bordwell, David, Janet Staiger, and Kristin Thompson. *The Classical Hollywood Cinema: Film Style & Mode of Production to 1960*. New York: Columbia University Press, 1985.

Bourzereau, Laurent. *The Cutting Room Floor: Movie Scenes Which Never Made it to the Screen*. New York: Carol Publishing Group, 1994.

Bowser, Eileen. *The Transformation of Cinema 1907–1915*. Volume 2 of *History of the American Film*. Berkeley: University of California Press, 1990.

Brady, Frank. *Citizen Welles: A Biography of Orson Welles*. New York: Charles Scribner's Sons, 1989.

Bragg, Melvyn. *The Seventh Seal*. London: BFI Publishing, 1993.

Brakhage, Stan. *The Brakhage Lectures: Georges Méliès, David Wark Griffith, Carl Theodore Dreyer, Sergei Eisenstein*. Chicago: GoodLion, 1972.

———. *Brakhage Scrapbook: Collected Writings 1964–1980*. New York: Documentext, 1982.

———. *Essential Brakhage: Selected Writings on Filmmaking*. Kingston, NY: Documentext, 2001.

———. *Film at Wit's End: Eight Avant-Garde Filmmakers*. Kingston, NY: Documentext, 1989.

———. "Metaphors on Vision." *Film Culture*, no. 30 (Fall 1963).

———. *A Moving Picture Giving and Taking Book*. West Newbury, MA: Frontier Press, 1971.

Brenton, André. *What is Surrealism?* New York: Pathfinder, 1978.

Breskin, David. *Inner Views: Filmmakers in Conversation*. Boston: Faber and Faber, 1992.

Brooks, Peter. *Reading for the Plot: Design and Intention in Narrative*. New York: Vintage Books, 1984.

Brosnan, John. *Movie Magic; the Story of Special Effects in the Cinema*. New York: St. Martin's Press, 1974.

Broughton, James. *Making Light of It*. 2nd ed. San Francisco: City Lights Books, 1992.

Brouwer, Alexandra, and Thomas Lee Wright. *Working in Hollywood: 64 Film Professionals Talk about Moviemaking*. New York: Crown, 1990.

Brown, Royal S. *Overtones and Undertones: Reading Film Music*. Berkeley: University of California Press, 1994.

Brownlow, Kevin. *David Lean: A Biography*. New York: St. Martin's Press, 1996.

———. *The Parade's Gone By . . . .* New York: Knopf, 1968.

Brunette, Peter, ed. *Martin Scorsese: Interviews*. Jackson: University Press of Mississippi, 1999.

Bukatman, Scott. *Blade Runner*. London: BFI Publishing, 1997.

Buñuel, Luis. *My Last Sigh: The Autobiography of Luis Buñuel*. New York: Knopf, 1983.

———. *An Unspeakable Betrayal: Selected Writings of Luis Buñuel*. Berkeley: University of California Press, 2000.

Burke, Frank. *Fellini's Films*. New York: Twayne, 1996.

Buscombe, Edward. *The Searchers*. London: BFI Publishing, 2000.

Canton, Steven C. *Lawrence of Arabia: A Film's Anthropology*. Berkeley: University of California Press, 1999.

Card, James. *Seductive Cinema: The Art of Silent Film*. New York: Knopf, 1994.

Cardiff, Jack. *Magic Hour: The Life of a Cameraman*. London: Faber and Faber, 1996.

Cardullo, Bert. *Vittorio De Sica: Director, Actor, Screenwriter*. Jefferson, NC: McFarland, 2002.

Carney, Raymond. *American Dreaming: The Films of John Cassavetes and the American Experience*. Berkeley: University of California Press, 1985.

———. *Cassavetes on Cassavetes*. London: Faber and Faber, 2001.

———. *The Films of John Cassavetes: Pragmatism, Modernism, and the Movies*. Cambridge: Cambridge University Press, 1994.

———. *Speaking the Language of Desire: The Films of Carl Dreyer*. Cambridge: Cambridge University Press, 1989.

Carr, Jay, ed. *The A List: The National Society of Film Critics' 100 Essential Films*. New York: Da Capo Press, 2002.

Carringer, Robert L. *The Making of Citizen Kane*. Berkeley: University of California Press, 1985.

Champlin, Charles. *John Frankenheimer: A Conversation with Charles Champlin*. Burbank, CA: Riverwood Press, 1995.

Chandler, Charlotte. *I, Fellini*. New York: Random House, 1995.

Charity, Tom. *John Cassavetes: Lifeworks*. London: Omnibus Press, 2001.

Chatman, Seymour. *Antonioni or, the Surface of the World*. Berkeley: University of California Press, 1985.

———. *Story and Discourse: Narrative Structure in Fiction and Film*. Ithaca, NY: Cornell University Press, 1978.

Chell, David. *Moviemakers at Work*. Redmond, WA: Microsoft Press, 1997.

Chierchetti, David. *Edith Head: The Life and Times of Hollywood's Celebrated Costume Designer*. New York: HarperCollins, 2003.

Chion, Michel. *Audio-Vision: Sound on Screen*. New York: Columbia University Press, 1994.

———. *David Lynch*. London: BFI Publishers, 1995.

———. *Kubrick's Cinema Odyssey*. London: BFI Publishing, 2001.

Christopher, Nicholas. *Somewhere in the Night: Film Noir and the American City*. New York: Henry Holt, 1997.

Ciment, Michel. *Kazan on Kazan*. New York: Viking Press, 1974.

———. *Kubrick: The Definitive Edition*. New York: Faber and Faber, 1999.
Clagett, Thomas D. *William Friedkin: Films of Aberration, Obsession, and Reality*. Los Angeles: Silman-James Press, 2003, expanded and updated second edition.
Clarens, Carlos. *An Illustrated History of the Horror Film*. New York: Capricorn Books, 1967.
Clarke, James. *Ridley Scott*. London: Virgin Books Ltd., 2002.
Clooney, Nick. *The Movies That Changed Us: Reflections on the Screen*. New York: Atria Books, 2002.
Cohan, Steven, ed. *Hollywood Musicals: The Film Reader*. New York: Routledge, 2002.
Cole, Janis, and Holly Dale. *Calling the Shots: Profiles of Women Filmmakers*. Kingston, Ontario: Quarry Press, 1993.
Cook, David A. *Lost Illusions: American Cinema in the Shadow of Watergate and Vietnam, 1970–1979*. Volume 9 of *History of the American Cinema*. Berkeley: University of California Press, 2000.
Coppola, Eleanor. *Notes*. New York: Simon and Schuster, 1979.
Corman, Roger. *How I Made a Hundred Movies in Hollywood and Never Lost a Dime*. With Jim Jerome. New York: Random House, 1990.
Cowie, Peter. *Annie Hall*. London: BFI Publishing, 1996.
———. *The Apocalypse Now Book*. New York: Da Capo Press, 2001.
Crafton, Donald. *The Talkies: American Cinema's Transition to Sound, 1926–1931*. Volume 4 of *History of the American Cinema*. Berkeley: University of California Press, 1999.
Culhane, Shamus. *Animation: From Script to Screen*. New York: St. Martin's Press, 1988.
Curtis, David. *Experimental Cinema: A Fifty-Year Evolution*. New York: Universe Books, 1971.
Dabashi, Hamid. *Close Up: Iranian Cinema Past, Present, and Future*. London: Verso, 2001.
Dardis, Tom. *Keaton: The Man Who Wouldn't Lie Down*. New York: Penguin Books, 1980.
Davis, Brian. *The Thriller: The Suspense Film from 1946*. London: Studio Vista, 1973.
De Baecque, Antoine, and Serge Toubiana. *Truffant: A Biography*. New York: Knopf, 1999.
de Navacelle, Thierry. *Woody Allen on Location*. New York: William Morrow, 1987.
De Sica, Vittorio. *Miracle in Milan*. Screenplay by Cesare Zavattini and Vitorrio De Sica. New York: Orion Press, 1969.
Dean, Michael W. *$30 Film School*. Boston: Premier Press, 2003.
Derry, Charles. *The Suspense Thriller: Films in the Shadow of Alfred Hitchcock*. Jefferson, NC: McFarland, 1988.
Dick, Phillip, K. *Do Androids Dream of Electric Sheep?* London: Granada Publishing, 1972.
Dixon, Wheeler Winston. *The Exploding Eye: A Re-Visionary History of the 1960s*

American Experimental Cinema. New York: State University of New York Press, 1997.

Dmytryk, Edward. *On Film Editing: An Introduction to the Art of Film Construction*. Boston: Focal Press, 1984.

Doherty, Thomas. *Teenagers and Teenpics: The Juvenilization of American Movies in the 1950s*. Philadelphia: Temple University Press, 2002.

Dougan, Andy. *Untouchable: A Biography of Robert De Niro*. New York: Thunder's Mouth Press. Second edition, 2002.

Dowd, Nancy, and David Shepard. *King Vidor: A Director's Guild of America Oral History*. Metuchen, NJ: Directors Guild of America and Scarecrow Press, 1988.

Drazin, Charles. *Blue Velvet: Bloomsbury Movie Guide No. 3*. New York: Bloomsbury Publishing, 1999.

Drew, William M. *D. W. Griffith's Intolerance: Its Genesis and its Vision*. Jefferson, NC: McFarland, 1986.

Drum, Jean and Dale D. Drum. *My Only Great Passion: The Life and Films of Carl Th. Dreyer*. Lanham, MD: Scarecrow Press, 2000.

Dube, Wolf Dieter. *Expressionism*. New York: Praeger Publishers, 1973.

Dunne, John Gregory. *The Studio*. New York: Farrar, Straus & Giroux, 1969.

Durgnat, Raymond. *A Long Hard Look at Psycho*. London: British Film Institute, 2002.

Durgnat, Raymond, and Scott Simmon. *King Vidor, American*. Berkeley: University of California Press, 1988.

Dyer, Richard. *Seven*. London: BFI, 1999.

Easty, Robert. *On Method Acting*. New York: Allograph Press, 1966.

Ebert, Roger. *The Great Movies*. New York: Broadway Books, 2002.

Ebert, Roger, and Gene Siskel. *The Future of Movies: Interviews with Martin Scorsese, Steven Spielberg, and George Lucas*. Kansas City, MO: Andrews and McMeel, 1991.

Egri, Lajos. *The Art of Creative Writing*. Secaucus, NJ: Citadel Press, 1965.

———. *The Art of Dramatic Writing*. New York: Simon and Schuster, 1946.

Ehrenstein, David. *Film: The Front Line: 1984*. Denver, CO: Arden Press, 1984.

———. *The Scorsese Picture: The Art and Life of Martin Scorsese*. New York: Birch Lane Press, 1992.

Eisenschitz, Bernard. *Nicholas Ray: An American Journey*. London: Faber and Faber, 1993.

Eisenstein, Sergei. *Film Essays and a Lecture*. Edited and translated by Jay Leyda. Princeton, NJ: Princeton University Press, 1982.

———. *Film Form: Essays in Film Theory*. Edited and translated by Jay Leyda. New York: Harcourt, Brace and World, 1949.

———. *The Film Sense*. Edited and translated by Jay Leyda. San Diego, CA: Harcourt Brace Jovanovich Publishers, 1947.

———. *Nonindifferent Nature: Film and the Structure of Things*. Translated by Herbert Marshall. Cambridge: Cambridge University Press, 1987.

Eisner, Lotte. *Fritz Lang*. New York: Da Capo, 1976.
———. *The Haunted Screen: Expressionism in the German Cinema*. Berkeley: University of California Press, 1969.
Elder, R. Bruce. *The Films of Stan Brakhage in the American Tradition of Erza Pound, Gertrude Stein, and Charles Olson*. Waterloo, Ontario, Canada: Wilfrid Laurier University Press, 1998.
Emery, Robert J. *The Directors: Take Two*. New York: Allworth Press, 2002.
———. *The Directors: Take Three*. New York: Allworth Press, 2003.
———. *The Directors: Take Four*. New York: Allworth Press, 2003.
Estrin, Mark W., ed. *Orson Welles: Interviews*. Jackson: University Press of Mississippi, 2002.
Ettedgui, Peter. *Screencraft: Production Design & Art Direction*. Woburn, MA: Focal Press, 1999.
Evans, Mark. *Soundtrack: The Music of the Movies*. New York: Da Capo Press, 1979.
Eyman, Scott. *Five American Cinematographers: Interviews with Karl Struss, Joseph Ruttenberg, James Wong How, Linwood Dunn, and William H. Clothier*. Metuchen, NJ: Scarecrow Press, 1987.
———. *Print the Legend: The Life and Times of John Ford*. New York: Simon and Schuster, 1999.
Falsetto, Mario. *Personal Visions: Conversations with Contemporary Film Directors*. Los Angeles: Silman-James, 2000.
Fell, John L. *Film and the Narrative Tradition*. Berkeley: University of California Press, 1974.
Fellini, Federico. *Fellini on Fellini*. Edited by Anna Kell and Christian Strich. New York: Delacorte Press, 1976.
Field, Syd. *Screenplay: The Foundations of Screenwriting*. New York: Dell, 1984.
———. *The Screenwriter's Workbook*. New York: Dell, 1985.
Fielding, Raymond. *A Technological History of Motion Pictures and Television*. Berkeley: University of California Press, 1983.
Fine, Marshall. *Bloody Sam: The Life and Films of Sam Peckinpah*. New York: Donald I. Fine Inc., 1991.
Frampton, Hollis. *Circles of Confusion: Film, Photography, Video, Texts, 1968–1980*. Rochester, NY: Visual Studies Workshop Press, 1983.
Fraser-Cavassoni, Natasha. *Sam Spiegel*. New York: Simon and Schuster, 2003.
French, Karl. *Apocalypse Now: Pocket Movie Guide 1*. London: Bloomsbury, 1998.
Freud, Sigmund. *The Interpretation of Dreams*. New York: Macmilian, 1937.
Friedman, Lester D. *Bonnie and Clyde*. London: BFI Publishing, 2000.
Froug, William. *Zen and the Art of Screenwriting: Insights and Interviews*. Los Angeles: Silman-James, 1996.
Fuchs, Cynthia, ed. *Spike Lee: Interviews*. Jackson: University Press of Mississippi, 2002.
Fuller, Samuel. *A Third Face: My Tale of Writing, Fighting, and Filmmaking*. With Christa Lang Fuller and Jerome Henry Rudes. New York: Knopf, 2002.

Gabler, Neal. *An Empire of Their Own: How the Jews Invented Hollywood*. New York: Crown Publishers, 1988.
Gado, Frank. *The Passion of Ingmar Bergman*. Durham: Duke University Press, 1986.
Galbraith, Stuart, IV. *The Emperor and the Wolf: The Lives and Films of Akira Kurosawa and Toshiro Mifune*. New York: Faber and Faber, 2001.
Gallagher, John Andrew. *Film Directors on Directors*. New York: Praeger, 1989.
Gallagher, Tag. *John Ford: The Man and his Films*. Berkeley: University of California Press, 1986.
Gelmis, Joseph. *The Film Director as Superstar*. Garden City, NY: Doubleday, 1970.
Georgakas, Dan, and Lenny Rubenstein, eds. *The Cineaste Interviews: On the Art and Politics of the Cinema*. Chicago: Lake View Press, 1983.
Gibbs, John. *Mise-en-Scène: Film Style and Interpretation*. London: Wallflower, 2002.
Ginsberg, Milton Moses. *Coming Apart*. New York: Lancer Books, 1969.
Goodwin, James. *Akira Kurosawa and Intertextural Cinema*. Baltimore, MD: Johns Hopkins University Press, 1994.
Gorbman, Claudia. *Unheard Melodies: Narrative Film Music*. Bloomington: Indiana University Press, 1987.
Gottesman, Ronald, ed. *Focus on Citizen Kane*. Englewood Cliffs, NJ: Prentice-Hall, 1971.
Gottlieb, Sidney, ed. *Hitchcock on Hitchcock: Selected Writings and Interviews*. Berkeley: University of California Press, 1995.
Goulekas, Karen E. *Visual Effects in a Digital World: A Comprehensive Glossary of over 7,000 Visual Effects Terms*. San Diego: Morgan Kaufmann, 2001.
Grant, Barry Keith, ed. *Film Genre Reader*. Austin: University of Texas Press, 1986.
Gray, Beverly. *Roger Corman: An Unauthorized Biography of the Godfather of Indie Filmmaking*. Los Angeles: Renaissance Books, 2000.
Green, Shelly. *Radical Juxtaposition: The Films of Yvonne Rainer*. Metuchen, NJ: Scarecrow Press, 1994.
Griffith, Richard. *The World of Robert Flaherty*. New York: Da Capo Press, 1972.
Guerrero, Ed. *Do the Right Thing*. London: BFI Publishing, 2001.
Haller, Robert A., ed. *Jim Davis: The Flow of Energy*. New York: Anthology Film Archives, 1992.
Hardy, Phil. *Sam Fuller*. New York: Praeger, 1970.
Harmetz, Aljean. *The Making of Casablanca: Bogart, Bergman, and World War II*. New York: Hyperion, 1992.
Hart, John. *The Art of the Storyboard: Storyboarding for Film, TV, and Animation*. Boston: Focal Press, 1999.
Harvey, James. *Movie Love in the Fifties*. New York: Knopf, 2001.
Hay, James. *Popular Film Culture in Fascist Italy: The Passing of the Hex*. Bloomington: Indiana University Press, 1987.
Heisner, Beverly. *Hollywood Art: Art Direction in the Days of the Great Studios*. Jefferson, NC: McFarland, 1990.
Hickenlooper, George. *Reel Conversations: Candid Interviews with Film's Foremost Directors and Critics*. New York: Citadel Press, 1991.

Higham, Charles. *Hollywood Cameramen*. Bloomington: Indiana University Press, 1970.

Higham, Charles, and Joel Greenberg. *The Celluloid Muse: Director's Speak*. Chicago: Henry Regnery, 1969.

Hirsch, Foster. *Film Noir: The Dark Side of the Screen*. New York: Da Capo Press, 1981.

———. *The Hollywood Epic*. South Brunswick, NJ: Barnes, 1978.

———. *A Method to Their Madness: The History of the Actors' Studio*. New York: W. W. Norton, 1984.

Hischak, Thomas S. *The American Musical Theatre Song Encyclopedia*. Westport, CT: Greenwood Press, 1995.

Hoberman, J. *42nd Street*. London: BFI Publishing, 1993.

———. *Vulgar Modernism: Writing on Movies and Other Media*. Philadelphia, PA: Temple University Press, 1991.

Hoberman, J., and Edward Leffingwell, eds. *Wait for Me at the Bottom of the Pool: The Writings of Jack Smith*. New York: High Risk Books, 1997.

Hooks, Bell. *Reel to Real: Race, Sex, and Class at the Movies*. New York: Routledge, 1996.

Horak, Jan Christopher. *Lovers of Cinema: The First American Film Avant-Garde 1919–1945*. Madison: University of Wisconsin Press, 1995.

Horton, Andrew. *Henry Bumstead and the World of Hollywood Art Direction*. Austin: University of Texas Press, 2003.

Hughes, David, Jim Smith, and James Clarke. *The Complete Lynch*. London: Virgin Books Ltd., 2002.

Hunter, Stephen. *Violent Screen: A Critic's 13 Years on the Front Lines of Movie Mayhem*. Baltimore, MD: Bancroft Press, 1995.

Hutchison, David. *Film Magic: The Art and Science of Special Effects*. New York: Prentice-Hall, 1987.

IMAGO, the Federation of European Cinematographers. *Making Pictures: A Century of European Cinematography*. New York: Abrams, 2003.

Insdorf, Annette. *Double Lives, Second Chances: The Cinema of Krzysztof Kieślowski*. New York: Hyperion, 1999.

Itten, Johannes. *The Elements of Color*. New York: Van Nostrand Reinhold Co., 1970.

Jacob, Gilles, and Claude de Givrary, eds. *François Truffaut: Correspondence 1945–1984*. New York: Farrar, Straus & Giroux, 1990.

James, David E. *Allegories of Cinema: American Film in the Sixties*. Princeton, NJ: Princeton University Press, 1989.

———, ed. *To Free the Cinema: Jonas Mekas & the New York Underground*. Princeton, New Jersey: Princeton University Press, 1992.

Jensen, Paul M. *The Men Who Made the Monsters*. New York: Twayne, 1996.

Jessionowski, Joyce E. *Thinking in Pictures: Dramatic Structure in D. W. Griffith's Biograph Films*. Berkeley: University of California Press, 1987.

Jones, Chuck. *Chuck Amuck: The Life and Times of an Animated Cartoonist*. New York: Farrar, Straus & Giroux, 1989.

Jones, John Bush. *Our Musicals, Ourselves: A Social History of the American Musical Theater*. Hanover: Brandeis University Press, 2003.
Jung, Carl Gustav. *Memories, Dreams, Reflections*. New York: Vintage Books, 1989.
Jung, Uli and Walter Schatzberg. *Beyond Caligari: The Films of Robert Wiene*. New York: Berghahn Books, 1999.
Kael, Pauline. *The Citizen Kane Book: Raising Kane*. Boston: Little, Brown, 1971.
Katz, Steven D. *Film Directing Shot by Shot: Visualizing from Concept to Screen*. Studio City, CA: Michael Wiese Productions, 1991.
Kaufman, Lloyd, and James Gunn. *All I Need to Know about Filmmaking I Learned from The Toxic Avenger*. New York: Berkley Boulevard Books, 1998.
Kazan, Elia. *A Life*. New York: Knopf, 1988.
Keaton, Buster with Charles Samuels. *My Wonderful World of Slapstick*. London: Allen Unwin, 1968.
Keaton, Eleanor, and Jeffrey Vance. *Buster Keaton Remembered*. New York: Harry N. Abrams, 2001.
Kelly, Mary Pat. *Martin Scorsese: The First Decade*. Pleasantville, NY: Redgrave Publishing Company, 1980.
Kelly, Richard. *The Name of this Book is Dogme95*. London: Faber and Faber, 2000.
Kieślowski, Krzysztof and Krzysztof Piesiewicz. *Decalogue: The Ten Commandments*. London: Faber and Faber, 1991.
King, Stephen. *On Writing: A Memoir of the Craft*. New York: Pocket Books, 2000.
Kline, Sally, ed. *George Lucas: Interviews*. Jackson: University Press of Mississippi, 1999.
Kline, T. Jefferson. *Screening the Text: Intertexuality in New Wave French Cinema*. Baltimore: Johns Hopkins University Press, 1992.
Knight, Arthur. *The Liveliest Art: A Panoramic History of the Movies*. New York: MacMillan, 1957.
Konigsberg, Ira. *The Complete Film Dictionary*. 2nd ed. New York: Penguin, 1997.
Koszarski, Richard. *An Evening's Entertainment: The Age of the Silent Feature Picture, 1915–1928*. Volume 3 of *History of the American Cinema*. Berkeley: University of California Press, 1994.
Kozloff, Sarah. *Invisible Storytellers: Voice-Over Narration in American Fiction Film*. Berkeley: University of California Press, 1998.
Kracauer, Siegfried. *From Caligari to Hitler: A Psychological History of the German Film*. Princeton, NJ: Princeton University Press, 1947.
———. *Theory of Film: The Redemption of Physical Reality*. London: Oxford University Press, 1960.
Kreimeier, Klaus. *The UFA Story: A History of Germany's Greatest Film Company, 1918–1945*. New York: Hill and Wang, 1996.
Krohn, Bill. *Hitchcock at Work*. London: Phaidon, 2000.
Kuenzli, Rudolf E. *Dada and Surrealist Film*. Cambridge, MA: The MIT Press, 1996.
Kurosawa, Akira. *Something Like an Autobiography*. New York: Vintage Books, 1983.
La Motta, Jake, with Joseph Carter and Peter Savage. *Raging Bull: My Story*. Englewood Cliffs, NJ: Prentice Hall, 1970.

Landis, Deborah Hadoolman. *Screencraft: Costume Design*. Burlington, MA: Focal Press, 2003.

Landy, Marcia. *Italian Film*. Cambridge: Cambridge University Press, 2000.

Lassally, Walter. *Itinerant Cameraman*. London: John Murray, 1987.

Lax, Eric. *Woody Allen: A Biography*. New York: Knopf, 1991.

Laybourne, Kit. *The Animation Book: A Complete Guide to Animated Filmmaking, from Flip-Books to Sand Cartoons*. New York: Three Rivers Press, 1998.

Lebo, Harlan. *Citizen Kane: The Fiftieth Anniversary Album*. New York: Doubleday, 1990.

Leaming, Barbara. *Orson Welles: A Biography*. New York: Viking, 1985.

Lee, Spike. *Do the Right Thing*. With Lisa Jones. New York: Fireside, 1989.

Leemann, Sergio. *Robert Wise on His Films: From Editing Room to Director's Chair*. Los Angeles: Silman-James, 1995.

Leese, Elizabeth. *Costume Design in the Movies: An Illustrated Guide to the Work of 157 Great Designers*. New York: Dover Publications, 1991.

Leigh, Janet, with Christopher Nickens. *Psycho: Behind the Scenes of the Classic Thriller*. New York: Harmony Books, 1995.

Leitch, Thomas, John C. Tibbets, and James M. Welshm, series Eds. *The Encyclopedia of Alfred Hitchcock*. New York: Checkmark Books, 2002.

Levin, G. Roy. *Documentary Explorations; 15 Interviews with Film-Makers*. New York: Anchor Press, 1971.

Levy, Emanuel. *Cinema of Outsiders: The Rise of American Independent Film*. New York: New York University Press, 1999.

Lewis, Jerry. *The Total Film-Maker*. New York: Warner Books, 1973.

Lewis, Jon. *Whom God Wishes to Destroy . . . : Francis Coppola and the New Hollywood*. Durham, NC: Duke University Press, 1995.

Leyda, Jay. *Kino: A History of the Russian and Soviet Film*. 3rd ed. Princeton, NJ: Princeton University Press, 1983.

Leyda, Jay, and Zina Voynow. *Eisenstein at Work*. New York: Pantheon Books and the Museum of Modern Art, 1982.

Liehm, Mira. *Passion and Defiance: Film in Italy from 1942 to the Present*. Berkeley: University of California Press, 1984.

Lindgren, Ernest. *The Art of the Film*. New York: Macmillan, 1963.

Lindsay, Vachel. *The Art of the Moving Picture*. New York: Modern Library, 2000.

LoBrutto, Vincent. *By Design: Interviews with Film Production Designers*. Westport, CT: Praeger, 1992.

———. *The Encyclopedia of American Independent Filmmaking*. Westport, CT: Greenwood Press, 2002.

———. *The Filmmaker's Guide to Production Design*. New York: Allworth Press, 2002.

———. *Principal Photography: Interviews with Feature Film Cinematographers*. Westport, CT: Praeger, 1999.

———. *Selected Takes: Film Editors On Editing*. New York: Praeger, 1991.

———. *Sound-On-Film: Interviews with Creators of Film Sound*. Westport, CT: Praeger, 1994.
———. *Stanley Kubrick: A Biography*. New York: Donald I. Fine, 1997.
Lopate, Phillip. *Totally, Tenderly, Tragically: Essays and Criticism from a Lifelong Love Affair with the Movies*. New York: Anchor Books, 1998.
Lourie, Eugene. *My Work in Films*. San Diego, CA: Harcourt Brace Jovanovich, 1985.
Lowenstein, Stephen, ed. *My First Movie: Twenty Celebrated Directors Talk about Their First Film*. New York: Pantheon, 2000.
Lumet, Sidney. *Making Movies*. New York: Knopf, 1995.
Lyons, Donald. *Independent Visions: A Critical Introduction to Recent Independent American Film*. New York: Ballantine Books, 1994.
MacCabe, Colin. *Godard: A Portrait of the Artist at Seventy*. New York: Farrar, Straus and Giroux, 2003.
MacCann, Richard Dyer, ed. *Film: A Montage of Theories*. New York: E. P. Dutton, 1966.
MacDonald, Scott. *Avant-Garde Film: Motion Studies*. Cambridge: Cambridge University Press, 1993.
———. *Cinema 16: Documents Toward a History of the Film Society*. Philadelphia, PA: Temple University Press, 2001.
———. *A Critical Cinema: Interviews with Independent Filmmakers*. Berkeley: University of California Press, 1988.
———. *A Critical Cinema 2: Interviews with Independent Filmmakers*. Berkeley: University of California Press, 1992.
———. *A Critical Cinema 3: Interviews with Independent Filmmakers*. Berkeley: University of California Press, 1998.
———. *The Garden in the Machine: A Field Guide to Independent Films about Place*. Berkeley: University of California Press, 2001.
MacGowan, Kenneth. *Behind the Screen: The History and Techniques of the Motion Picture*. New York: Delta Books, 1965.
Madsen, Roy Paul. *Working Cinema: Learning from the Masters*. Belmont, CA: Wadsworth, 1990.
Maltin, Leonard. *Behind the Camera: The Cinematographer's Art*. New York: New American Press, 1971.
Manovich, Lev. *The Language of New Media*. Cambridge, MA: The MIT Press, 2001.
Marcus, Greil. *The Manchurian Candidate*. London: BFI Publishing, 2002.
Marie, Michel. *The French New Wave: An Artistic School*. Malden, MA: Blackwell Publishing, 2003.
Mascelli, Joseph V. *The Five C's of Cinematography: Motion Picture Filming Techniques*. Los Angeles: Silman-James, 1965.
Mast, Gerald. *Can't Help Singin': The American Musical on Stage and Screen*. Woodstock, NY: Overlook Press, 1987.
McBride, Joseph. *Searching for John Ford: A Life*. New York: St. Martin's Press, 1999.
McCarthy, Todd, and Charles Flynn, eds. *Kings of the Bs: Working within the Holly-*

wood System: An Anthology of Film History and Criticism. New York: E. P. Dutton, 1975.
McDonough, Tom. *Light Years: Confessions of a Cinematographer*. New York: Grove Press, 1987.
McGee, Mark Thomas, and R. J. Robertson. *The J. D. Films: Juvenile Delinquency in the Movies*. Jefferson, NC: McFarland, 1982.
McGilligan, Patrick. *Alfred Hitchcock: A Life in Darkness and Light*. New York: Regan Books, 2003.
———. *Backstory: Interviews with Screenwriters of Hollywood's Golden Age*. Berkeley: University of California Press, 1986.
———. *Backstory 2: Interviews with Screenwriters of the 1940s and 1950s*. Berkeley: University of California Press, 1991.
———. *Backstory 3: Interviews with Screenwriters of the 1960s*. Berkeley: University of California Press, 1991.
———. *Backstory 4: Interviews with Screenwriters of the 1970s and 1980s*. Berkeley: University of California Press, 2004.
———. *Fritz Lang: The Nature of the Beast*. New York: St. Martin's Press, 1997.
———. *Robert Altman: Jumping Off the Cliff: A Biography of the Great American Director*. New York: St. Martin's Press, 1989.
McGrath, Declan. *Screencraft: Editing & Post-Production*. Boston: Focal Press, 2001.
McKee, Robert. *Story: Substance, Structure, Style, and the Principles of Screenwriting*. New York: HarperCollins, 1997.
Meade, Marion. *Buster Keaton: Cut to the Chase*. New York: Da Capo Press, 1997.
———. *The Unruly Life of Woody Allen: A Biography*. New York: Scribner, 2000.
Mekas, Jonas. *Movie Journal: The Rise of a New American Cinema, 1959–1971*. New York: Collier Books, 1971.
Merritt, Greg. *Celluloid Mavericks: A History of American Independent Film*. New York: Thunder's Mouth Press, 2000.
Michelson, Annette, ed. *Kino-Eye: The Writings of Dziga Vertov*. Berkeley: University of California Press, 1984.
Miller, Don. *B Movies*. New York: Ballantine Books, 1987.
Milne, Tom, translation and commentary. *Godard on Godard*. New York: The Viking Press, 1972.
Monoco, James. *The New Wave: Truffaut, Godard, Chabrol, Rohmer, Rivette*. New York: Oxford University Press, 1976.
Monaco, Paul. *The Sixties: 1960–1969*. Volume 8 of *History of the American Cinema*. Berkeley: University of California Press, 2003.
Mordden, Ethan. *Medium Cool: The Movies of the 1960s*. New York: Knopf, 1990.
Morris, L. Robert, and Lawrence Raskin. *Lawrence of Arabia: The 30th Anniversary Pictorial History*. New York: Anchor Books, 1992.
Muller, Eddie. *Dark City: The Lost World of Film Noir*. New York: St. Martin's Griffin, 1998.
Murch, Walter. *In the Blink of an Eye: A Perspective on Film Editing*. 2nd ed. Los Angeles, Silman-James, 2001.

Musser, Charles. *The Emergence of Cinema: The American Screen to 1907.* Volume 1 of *History of the American Cinema.* Berkeley: University of California Press, 1990.

Narboni, Jean, and Tom Milne, eds. *Godard on Godard.* New York: Viking Press, 1972.

Naremore, James. *More Than Night: Film Noir in its Contexts.* Berkeley: University of California Press, 1998.

Nelson, Al P., and Mel R. Jones. *A Silent Siren Song: The Aitken Brothers' Hollywood Odyssey, 1905–1926.* New York: Cooper Square Press, 2000.

Netzley, Patricia D. *Encyclopedia of Movie Special Effects.* Phoenix, AZ: Oryx Press, 2000.

Neumann, Dietrich, ed. *Film Architecture: Set Designs from Metropolis to Blade Runner.* Munich, Germany: Prestel, 1999.

Neupert, Richard. *A History of the French New Wave Cinema.* Madison: University of Wisconsin Press, 2002.

Newton, Dale, and John Gaspard. *Digital Filmmaking 101: An Essential Guide to Producing Low Budget Movies.* Studio City, CA: Michael Wiese Productions, 2001.

Nichols, Bill, ed. *Maya Deren and the American Avant-Garde.* Berkeley: University of California Press, 2001.

Nochimson, Martha. *The Passion of David Lynch: Wild at Heart in Hollywood.* Austin: University of Texas Press, 1997.

O'Connell, P. J. *Robert Drew and the Development of Cinéma Vérité in America.* Carbondale: Southern Illinois University Press, 1992.

Ondaatje, Michael. *The Conversations: Walter Murch and the Art of Editing Film.* New York: Knopf, 2002.

Osborne. Richard E. *The Casablanca Companion: The Movie Classic and its Place in History.* Indianapolis, IN: Riebel-Roque, 1997.

O'Steen, Sam. *Cut to the Chase: Forty-Five Years of Editing American's Favorite Movies.* As told to Bobbie O'Steen. Studio City, CA: Michael Wiese Productions, 2001.

Oumano, Ellen. *Film Forum: Thirty-Five Top Filmmakers Discuss Their Craft.* New York: St. Martin's Press, 1985.

Peary, Gerald, ed. *John Ford: Interviews.* Jackson: University Press of Mississippi, 2001.

Pecktal, Lynn. *Costume Design: Techniques of Modern Masters.* New York: Back Stage Books, 1993.

Penz, Francois, Maureen Thomas, eds. *Cinema & Architecture: Méliès, Mallet-Stevens Multimedia.* London: British Film Institute, 1997.

Phillips, Gene D., ed. *Stanley Kubrick: Interviews.* Jackson: University Press of Mississippi, 2001.

Phillips, Gene D., and Rodney Hill. *The Encyclopedia of Stanley Kubrick.* With John C. Tibbets, James M. Welsh, series eds. New York: Checkmark Books, 2002.

Pierson, John. *Spike, Mike, Slackers, & Dykes: A Guided Tour across a Decade of American Independent Cinema.* New York: Miramax Books, 1995.

Polanski, Roman. *Roman*. New York: William Morrow, 1984.

Polti, Georges. *The Thirty-Six Dramatic Situations*. Boston: The Writer Inc., 1983.

Pratley, Gerald. *The Cinema of John Frankenheimer*. New York: A. S. Barnes & Co., 1969.

Pratley, Gerald, and John Frankenheimer. *The Films of Frankenheimer*. Bethlehem, PA: Lehigh University Press, 1998.

Prendergast, Roy M. *Film Music: A Neglected Art*. 2nd ed. New York: W. W. Norton, 1992.

Preston, Ward. *What an Art Director Does: An Introduction to Motion Picture Production Design*. Los Angeles: Silman-James, 1994.

Prince, Stephen. *A New Pot of Gold: Hollywood under the Electronic Rainbow, 1980–1989*. Volume 10 of *History of the American Cinema*. Berkeley: University of California Press, 2000.

Pye, Michael, and Lynda Myles. *The Movie Brats: How the Film Generation Took over Hollywood*. New York: Holt, Rinehart and Winston, 1979.

Rabiger, Michael. *Directing the Documentary*. Boston: Focal Press, 1987.

———. *Directing: Film Techniques and Aesthetics*. Boston: Focal Press, 1989.

Rabinovitz, Lauren. *Points of Resistance: Women, Power & Politics in the New York Avant-Garde Cinema, 1943–71*. Urbana: University of Illinois Press, 1991.

Rabourdin, Dominique, ed. *Truffaut by Truffaut*. New York: Abrams, 1987.

Rainsberger, Todd. *James Wong Howe: Cinematographer*. San Diego, CA: A. S. Barnes, 1981.

Rawlence, Christopher. *The Missing Reel: The Untold Story of the Lost Inventor of Moving Pictures*. New York: Atheneum, 1990.

Ray, Nicholas, and Susan Ray, eds. *I Was Interrupted: Nicholas Ray on Making Movies*. Berkeley: University of California Press, 1993.

Rebello, Stephen. *Alfred Hitchcock and the Making of Psycho*. New York: Dembner, 1990.

Rees, A. L. *A History of Experimental Film and Video*. London: BFI Publishing, 1999.

Renoir, Jean. *Renoir, My Father*. Boston: Little Brown, 1962.

———. *My Life and My Films*. New York: Atheneum, 1974.

———. *Renoir on Renoir: Interviews, Essays and Remarks*. New York: Cambridge University Press, 1990.

Richter, Dan. *Moonwatcher's Memoir: A Diary of 2001: A Space Odyssey*. New York: Carroll & Graf, 2002.

Rickitt, Richard. *Special Effects: The History and Technique*. New York: Billboard Books, 2000.

Ritchie, Donald. *The Films of Akira Kurosawa*. Berkeley: University of California Press, revised edition, 1984.

———, ed. *Rashomon (Rutgers Films in Print. Vol. 6)* by Akira Kurosawa. Piscataway, NJ: Rutgers University Press, 1987.

Roberts, Graham. *The Man with the Movie Camera (The Film Companion)*. New York: St. Martin's Press, 2000.

Robertson, James C. *The Casablanca Man: The Cinema of Michael Curtiz*. London: Routledge, 1993.

Robertson, Patrick. *Film Facts.* New York: Billboard Books, 2001.

Robinson, David. *From Peep Show to Palace: The Birth of American Film.* New York: Columbia University Press, 1996.

Rodley, Chris, ed. *Lynch on Lynch.* London: Faber and Faber, 1997.

Rodriguez, Robert. *Rebel without a Crew: Or How a 23-Year-Old Filmmaker with $7,000 Became a Hollywood Player.* New York: Dutton, 1995.

Rogers, Pauline B. *Art of Visual Effects: Interviews on the Tools of the Trade.* Boston: Focal Press, 1999.

Rosen, David. *Off-Hollywood: The Making and Marketing of Independent Films.* With Peter Hamilton in association with the Sundance Institute and the Independent Feature Project. New York: Grove Weidenfeld, 1990.

Rosenbaum, Jonathan. *Film: The Front Line: 1983.* Denver, CO: Arden Press, 1983.

———. *Movies as Politics.* Berkeley: University of California Press, 1997.

———. *Placing Movies: The Practice of Film Criticism.* Berkeley: University of California Press, 1995.

Rosenblum, Ralph, and Robert Karen. *When the Shooting Stops . . . the Cutting Begins: A Film Editor's Story.* New York: Viking Press, 1979.

Rosenthal, Alan. *The Documentary Conscience: A Casebook in Film Making.* Berkeley, University of California Press, 1980.

Rosenthal, Alan, ed. *New Challenges for Documentary.* Berkeley: University of California Press, 1988.

Rotha, Paul. *Robert J. Flaherty: A Biography.* Edited by Jay Ruby. Philadelphia: University of Pennsylvania Press, 1983.

Rotha, Paul, and Richard Griffith. *The Film Till Now: A Survey of World Cinema.* Great Britain: Spring Books, 1967.

Rotha, Paul, with Sinclair Road, and Richard Griffith. *Documentary Film: The Use of the Film Medium to Interpret Creatively and in Social Terms the Life of the People as it Exists in Reality.* New York: Hastings House, third edition, 1963.

Roud, Richard. *Godard.* Bloomington: Indiana University Press, revised edition 1970.

———, ed. *Cinema: A Critical Dictionary: The Major Film-makers Volume One: Aldrich to King.* Great Britain: Nationwide Book Services, 1980.

———, ed. *Cinema: A Critical Dictionary: The Major Film-makers. Volume Two: Kinugasa to Zanussi.* Great Britain: Nationwide Book Services, 1980.

Russell, Catherine. *Experimental Ethnography.* Durham, NC: Duke University Press, 1999.

Russo, John. *Making Movies: The Inside Guide to Independent Movie Production.* New York: Dell, 1989.

Sammon, Paul M. *Future Noir: The Making of Blade Runner.* New York: HarperPrism, 1996.

Samuels, Charles Thomas. *Encountering Directors.* New York: Capricorn Books, 1972.

Sanders, James. *Celluloid Skyline: New York and the Movies.* New York: Knopf, 2001.

Sangster, Jim. *Virgin Film: Scorsese.* London: Virgin, 2002.

Sargeant, Jack, ed. *The Naked Lens: An Illustrated History of Beat Cinema*. London: Creation Books, 1997.

Sarris, Andrew. *The American Cinema: Directors and Directions 1929–1968*. New York: Da Capo Press, 1996.

———, ed. *Interviews with Film Directors*. New York: Avon Books, 1967.

———, ed. *The St. James Film Directors Encyclopedia*. Detroit, MI: Visible Ink, 1998.

Savini, Tom. *Bizarro*. New York: Harmony Books, 1983.

Schaefer, Dennis, and Larry Salvato. *Masters of Light: Conversations with Contemporary Cinematographers*. Berkeley: University of California Press, 1984.

Schaefer, Eric. *Bold! Daring! Shocking! True!: A History of Exploitation Films, 1919–1959*. Durham, NC: Duke University Press, 1999.

Schatz, Thomas. *Boom and Bust: American Cinema in the 1940s*. Volume 6 of *History of the American Cinema*. Berkeley: University of California Press, 1999.

———. *The Genius of the System: Hollywood Filmmaking in the Studio Era*. New York: Pantheon Books, 1988.

Schickel, Richard. *D. W. Griffith: An American Life*. New York: Limelight Editions, 1996.

———. *Woody Allen: A Life in Film*. Chicago: Ivan R. Dee, 2003.

Schrader, Paul. *Transcendental Style in Film: Ozu, Bresson, Dreyer*. New York: Da Capo Press, 1972.

Schulberg, Budd. *On the Waterfront: The Final Shooting Script*. Hollywood: Samuel French, 1988.

Schwam, Stephanie, ed. *The Making of 2001: A Space Odyssey*. With Martin Scorsese, series ed. New York: Modern Library, 2000.

Scorsese, Martin, ed. *The Making of 2001: A Space Odyssey*. Selected by Stephanie Schwam. New York: The Modern Library, 2000.

Scorsese, Martin, and Michael Henry Wilson. *A Personal Journey with Martin Scorsese through American Movies*. New York: Miramax Books, 1997.

Segaloff, Nat. *Hurricane Billy: The Stormy Life and Films of William Friedkin*. New York: William Morrow and Company, Inc., 1990.

Seger, Linda. *Making a Good Script Great*. New York: Dodd, Mead & Company, 1987.

Self, Robert T. *Robert Altman's Subliminal Reality*. Minneapolis: University of Minnesota Press, 2002.

Sennett, Robert S. *Setting the Scene: The Great Hollywood Art Directors*. New York: Abrams, 1994.

Server, Lee. *Sam Fuller: Film is a Battleground: A Critical Study with Interviews, a Filmography and a Bibliography*. Jefferson, NC: McFarland, 1994.

Shepard, Rowena. *1000 Symbols: What Shapes Mean in Art and Myth*. London: Thames & Hudson, 2002.

Sherman, Eric. *Directing the Film: Film Directors on Their Art*. Los Angeles: Acrobat Books, 1976.

Shipman, David. *The Story of Cinema: A Complete Narrative History from the Beginnings to the Present*. New York: St. Martin's Press, 1982.

Shorris, Sylvia, and Marion Abbott Bundy. *Talking Pictures with the People Who Made Them*. New York: New Press, 1994.

Silver, Alain, and Elizabeth Ward. *Film Noir: An Encyclopedic Reference to the American Style*. 3rd ed. Woodstock, NY: Overlook Press, 1992.

Silverman, Kaja and Harun Farocki. *Speaking about Godard*. New York: New York University Press, 1998.

Simmons, Garner. *Peckinpah: A Portrait in Montage*. Austin: University of Texas Press, Austin, 1976.

Simon, Mark. *Storyboards: Motion in Art*. 2nd ed. Boston: Focal Press, 2000.

Singleton, Ralph S., James A. Conrad, and Janna Wong Healy, eds. *Filmmaker's Dictionary*. 2nd ed. Hollywood, CA: Lone Eagle, 2000.

Sitney, P. Adams. *Visionary Film: The American Avant-Garde, 1943–2000*. 3rd ed. Oxford: Oxford University Press, 2001.

———, ed. *Film Culture Reader*. New York: Cooper Square Press, 2000.

Skoller, Donald, ed. *Dreyer in Double Reflection: Translation of Carl Th. Dreyer's Writings about the Film*. New York: E. P. Dutton, 1973.

Smith, Geoffrey Nowell. *L'Avventura*. London: BFI Publishing, 1997.

Smith, Harry. *Think of the Self Speaking: Harry Smith—Selected Interviews*. Seattle, WA: Elbow/Cityful Press, 1999.

Smith, Steven C. *At Heart at Fire's Center: The Life and Music of Bernard Herrmann*. Berkeley: University of California Press, 1991.

Solnit, Rebecca. *River of Shadows: Eadweard Muybridge and the Technological Wild West*. New York: Viking, 2003.

Spoto, Donald. *The Dark Side of Genius: The Life of Alfred Hitchcock*. New York: Ballantine Books, 1983.

Stanislavsky, Konstantin. *An Actor Prepares*. New York: Theatre Arts, Inc., 1936.

Stempel, Tom. *FrameWork: A History of Screenwriting in the American Film*. New York: Continuum, 1988.

Sterling, Anna Kate. *Cinematographers on the Art and Craft of Cinematography*. Metuchen, NJ: Scarecrow Press, 1987.

Sterritt, David. *The Films of Jean-Luc Godard: Seeing the Invisible*. New York: Cambridge University Press, 1999.

Sterrit, David, ed. *Robert Altman: Interviews*. Jackson: University Press of Mississippi, 2000.

Stok, Danusia, ed. *Kieślowski on Kieślowski*. London: Faber and Faber, 1993.

Stone, Judy. *Eye on the World: Conversations with International Filmmakers*. Los Angeles: Silman-James, 1997.

Stuart, Jan. *The Nashville Chronicles: The Making of Robert Altman's Masterpiece*. New York: Simon and Schuster, 2000.

Stubbs, Liz. *Documentary Filmmakers Speak*. New York: Allworth Press, 2002.

Sutin, Lawrence. *Divine Invasions: A Life of Philip K. Dick*. New York: Harmony Books, 1989.

Swallow, James. *Dark Eye: The Films of David Fincher*. London: Reynolds & Hearn Ltd., 2003.

Tashiro, C. S. *Pretty Pictures: Production Design and the History Film*. Austin: University of Texas Press, 1998.

Thomas, Bob. *King Cohn: The Life and Times of Harry Cohn*. New York: G. P. Putnam's Sons, 1967.

Thomas, Tony. *Film Score: The Art & Craft of Movie Music*. Burbank, CA: Riverwood Press, 1991.

Thompson, David, and Ian Christie, eds. *Scorsese on Scorsese*. London: Faber and Faber, 1989.

Thompson, Kristin, and David Bordwell. *Film History: An Introduction*. New York: McGraw-Hill, 1994.

Tirard, Laurent. *Moviemakers' Master Class: Private Lessons from the World's Foremost Directors*. New York: Faber and Faber, 2002.

Tobias, Michael, ed. *The Search for Reality: The Art of Documentary Filmmaking*. Studio City, CA: Michael Wiese Productions, 1997.

Treherne, John E. *The Strange History of Bonnie and Clyde*. New York: Cooper Square Press, 2000.

Truffaut, François. *Hitchcock*. New York: Touchstone, 1985. First published in 1966 by Simon and Schuster.

Turim, Maureen. *Flashbacks in Film: Memory & History*. New York: Rouledge, 1989.

Tyler, Parker. *Underground Film: A Critical History*. New York: Grove Press, 1969.

Unterburger, Amy L., ed. *The St. James Women Filmmakers Encyclopedia: Women on the Other Side of the Camera*. Detroit, MI: Visible Ink, 1999.

Usai, Paolo Cherchi. *Silent Cinema: An Introduction*. London: BFI Publishing, 2000.

Vachon, Christine. *Shooting to Kill: How an Independent Producer Blasts through the Barriers to Make Movies That Matter*. With David Edelstein. New York: Avon Books, 1998.

Vaughan, Dai. *For Documentary: Twelve Essays*. Berkeley: University of California Press, 1999.

———. *Portrait of an Invisible Man: The Working Life of Steward McAllister, Film Editor*. London: BFI Publishing, 1983.

Vaz, Mark Cotta, and Patricia Rose Duignan. *Industrial Light + Magic: Into the Digital Realm*. New York: Ballantine Books, 1996.

Vidor, King. *On Film Making*. New York: David McKay, 1972.

———. *A Tree is a Tree: An Autobiography*. Hollywood: Samuel French, 1981.

Wake, Sandra, and Nicola Hayden, eds. *The Bonnie and Clyde Book*. New York: Simon and Schuster, 1972.

Walker, Alexander. *Hollywood, England: The British Film Industry in the Sixties*. London: Harrap, 1986.

———. *National Heroes: British Cinema in the Seventies and Eighties*. London: Harrap, 1985.

———. *The Shattered Silents: How the Talkies Came to Stay*. New York: William Morrow, 1979.

Walker, Joseph, and Juanita Walker. *The Light on Her Face*. Hollywood, CA: ASC Press, 1984.

Wayne, Mike. *Political Film: The Dialectics of Third Cinema*. London: Pluto Press, 2001.
Weddle, David. *"If They Move . . . Kill 'Em!": The Life and Times of Sam Peckinpah*. New York: Grove Press, 1994.
Wees, William C. *Light Moving in Time: Studies in the Visual Aesthetics of Avant-Garde Film*. Berkeley: University of California Press, 1992.
Weinberg, Herman G. *Saint Cinema: Writings on Film, 1929–1970*. Rev. ed. New York: Dover, 1970.
Weis, Elisabeth, and John Belton, eds. *Film Sound: Theory and Practice*. New York: Columbia University Press, 1985.
Wells, Lynn. *Allegories of Telling: Self-Referential Narrative in Contemporary British Fiction*. Amsterdam; New York: Rodopi, 2003.
Wiegand, Christopher. *Federico Fellini*. Los Angeles: TACHEN America, 2003.
Williams, Alan Larson. *Max Ophuls and the Cinema of Desire: Style and Spectacle in Four Films 1948–1955*. New York: Arno Press, 1980.
Williams, Richard. *The Animator's Survival Kit*. London: Faber and Faber, 2001.
Winters, Ralph E. *Some Cutting Remarks: Seventy Years a Film Editor*. Lanham, MD: Scarecrow Press, 2001.
Wood, Robin. *Arthur Penn*. London: Studio Vista, 1969.
Yacowar, Maurice. *Method in Madness: The Art of Mel Brooks*. New York: St. Martins Press, 1981.
Young, Freddie. *Seventy Light Years: A Life in the Movies*. London: Faber and Faber, 1999.
Youngblood, Gene. *Expanded Cinema*. New York: E. P. Dutton, 1970.
Zavattini, Ceasare. *Sequences from a Cinematic Life*. Englewood Cliffs, NJ: Prentice-Hall, 1970.
Zaza, Tony. *Audio Design: Sound Recording Techniques for Film and Video*. Englewood Cliffs, NJ: Prentice-Hall, 1991.
———. *Mechanics of Sound Recording*. Englewood Cliffs, NJ: Prentice-Hall, 1991.
Zizek, Slavoj. *The Fright of Real Tears: Krzysztof Kieślowski Between Theory and Post-Theory*. London: BFI Publishing, 2001.
Zucker, Carole. *Figures of Light: Actors and Directors Illuminate the Art of Film Acting*. New York: Plenum Press, 1995.

INDEX

About the Author

VINCENT LoBRUTTO is an instructor of editing, production design, and cinema studies for the Department of Film, Video, and Animation at the School of Visual Arts, where he is a thesis advisor and member of the Thesis Committee. He is the author of *Selected Takes: Film Editors on Editing* (Praeger, 1991), *By Design: Interviews with Film Production Designers* (Praeger, 1992), *Sound-On-Film: Interviews with Creators of Film Sound* (Praeger, 1994), *Stanley Kubrick: A Biography* (1997), *Principal Photography: Interviews with Feature Film Cinematographers* (Praeger, 1999), *The Filmmaker's Guide to Production Design* (2002), and *The Encyclopedia of American Independent Filmmaking* (Greenwood, 2002). A member of the American Cinema Editors (ACE), LoBrutto is the associate editor of *CinemaEditor* and is a contributing author to *American Cinematographer* and *Films In Review*. His frequent media appearances include *Entertainment Tonight*, National Public Radio's *All Things Considered,* and CNN.